CADOGAN
city guides

FLOR
SIENA

Cadogan Books plc
London House, Parkgate Road, London SW11 4NQ

Distributed in the USA by
The Globe Pequot Press
6 Business Park Road, PO Box 833, Old Saybrook,
Connecticut 06475–0833

Copyright © Dana Facaros and Michael Pauls 1994
Illustrations © Horatio Monteverde 1994;
Pauline Pears 1989 (pp.98, 172, 266, 300)
Book and cover design by Animage
Cover illustrations by Animage
Maps © Cadogan Guides, drawn by Thames Cartographic Ltd

Series Editors: Rachel Fielding and Vicki Ingle
Editing: Vicki Ingle and Louisa McDonnell
Editorial Assistant: Emma Johnson
Additional Research: Sam Cole
Proofreading: Annabel Frary
Indexing: Dorothy Frame
Production: Rupert Wheeler Book Production Services

ISBN 0–947754–95–4
A catalogue record for this book is available from the British Library
US Library of Congress Cataloging-in-Publication-Data available

The author and publishers have made every effort to ensure the accuracy of the information in this book at
the time of going to press. However, they cannot accept any responsibility for any loss, injury or inconvenience resulting from the use of information contained in this guide.

Printed and bound in Great Britain by The Lavenham Press Ltd, Suffolk on Challenger Offset supplied by
McNaughton Publishing Papers Ltd.

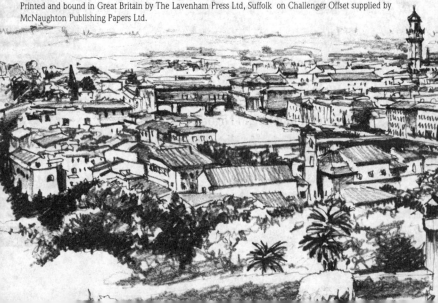

About the Authors

This guide is Dana and Michael's 20th for Cadogan, and their 12th on Italy. For three years they and their children lived in a tiny Umbrian hilltop village. Now they have moved to a remote French village in the Lot. From here, the Cadogan France series is evolving—interspersed with work on new Cadogan guides and revisions. (For 1995: *Northern Spain*, *Crete*, *Turkey* and *The Greek Islands*.)

Acknowledgements

In Italy, special thanks to Sam Cole for his invaluable revisions and additions to the practical information sections. In the UK, we are particularly grateful to Gio from the Italian Tourist Office; to Horatio for the drawings; to Kicca for the picture research; and to Louisa and Emma for their editing and organisational skills.

Please help us to keep this guide up to date

We have done our best to ensure that the information in this guide is correct at the time of going to press. However, places and facilities are constantly changing, standards and prices in hotels and restaurants fluctuate. We would be delighted to receive any comments concerning existing entries or omissions, as well as suggestions for new features. Significant contributions will be acknowledged in the next edition, and authors of the best letters will receive a copy of the Cadogan Guide of their choice.

Contents

Sant'Apollonia–Chiostro dello Scalzo–Galleria dell'Accademia–
Opificio delle Pietre Dure

Piazza Santissima Annunziata–Spedale degli Innocenti–Santissima
Annunziata–Museo Archeologico–Santa Maria Maddalena dei
Pazzi–Synagogue and Sant'Ambrogio–Flea Market–Casa Buonarroti

Santa Croce–Giotto's Chapels–Pazzi Chapel–Museo dell'Opera
di Santa Croce–Around Santa Croce: the Horne Museum

Santa Felicitá–Pitti Palace–Galleria Palatina–State Apartments–
Galleria d'Arte Moderna–Museo degli Argenti–More Pitti
Museums–Boboli Gardens–Casa Guidi–La Specola: Stuffed Animals
and Wax Cadavers–Santo Spirito–Santa Maria del Carmine–San
Frediano in Cestello–Museo Bardini/Galleria Corsi– San Niccolò
sopr'Arno

Peripheral Attractions

Day Trips   205–214

Introduction

Once there were four cities,
bearing names as rich and resonant as rare
flowers. Although close to one another in many
ways, each blossomed in different forms and hues, and
in the very springtime of modern western civilization,
they astounded the world.

And so these hothouse blooms of Tuscany slip easily into
the realm of fairytale or myth. Pictures crowd the imagination: bold Pisa, the first city off the mark, a maritime republic that sent its entire fleet off to the First Crusade with banners flapping and its bishop at the prow, sailing back with holds full of Arabic mathematics and sciences, and enough plunder to erect a Field of Miracles; lovely Siena, starry queen of all hilltowns, city of bankers and elegant storybook art, where the inhabitants annually gathered in their sublime conch shell of a piazza to punch each other in the nose; gentle, urbane Lucca, the medieval city of silk and candy-striped churches, enclosed in green garden walls. Then there's that most precocious Renaissance genius, Florence, first and foremost in a hundred fields, yet full of contradictions: where Dante's house was set ablaze by political rivals and a friend had to brave the flames to rescue the manuscript of the *Inferno*, where Brunelleschi could weave a dome of perfect beauty, only to have to enter a contest to be able to design its lantern.

The stories of Florence, Siena, Pisa and Lucca are especially alive because the sets are still there, nearly intact. It's as if at the height of their respective golden ages these four cities decided they themselves were works of art, *città dell'arte* according to the wonderful Italian expression, and coated themselves with a varnish. Sprawl, suburbia and progress have been kept at the gate and within these inner sanctums nothing has been allowed to change, at least on the surface.

Linger over a glass of Chianti in a quiet little out-of-the-way piazza in any of these cities, watching another day of sun soak into bricks and stones that have soaked in seven or eight centuries of suns and witnessed all that transcendent brilliance, beauty and creativity, and all the violence, too: when the juices were flowing in these cities they were not unlike Chicago in the Roaring Twenties. Fat cat merchants and bankers wrote their own laws. Political factions and gangsters made the streets so dangerous that the big bosses lived high up in Manhattanish skyscrapers. Rather than work together as neighbours, Florence, Siena, Pisa and Lucca constantly clobbered one another and did all they could to drag all the great powers of Europe into the fray. Betrayals, conspiracies, intrigues and vendettas were the order of the day, and if you had any scruples you could read Machiavelli to put your mind at ease. A Medici could order a work from Botticelli one minute, and have a political nuisance rubbed out the next. The juices were flowing, and it doesn't seem quite fair that we have a lot of the same troubles today, but no Fra Angelicos or Donatellos to compensate.

But these varnished, pickled and potted Tuscan cities compensate for a lot in themselves. 'I went to sleep at dawn in Tuscany,' wrote Hilaire Belloc in a poem that ends:

> *This sleep I swear shall last the length of day;*
> *Not noise, not chance, shall drive this dream away;*
> *Not time, not treachery, not good fortune—no,*
> *Not all the weight of all the wears of the world.*

Travel

By Air

From London Heathrow there are daily Alitalia and British Airways flights to the international airport at **Pisa**. You can also fly directly to **Florence** from Stansted with Air UK or from Gatwick with Meridiana (twice daily Mon–Fri, once a day Sat and Sun). Florence has flight **connections** to Milan, Naples, Lugano, Rome, Munich, Paris and Nice. The real challenge is finding a bargain, especially in the high season (mid-May–mid-September); start hunting around a few months in advance, or, if you're a gambler, at the last minute. Most of the cheap flights from London are on cryptic Third World airlines with a stopover in Rome.

There are advantages in paying an airline's **standard** fare, mainly that the ticket does not impose any restrictions on when you go or return; most are valid for a year. To sweeten the deal, Alitalia in particular often has promotional perks like rental cars (Jetdrive), or discounts on domestic flights within Italy, on hotels, or on tours. British Airways do a fly-drive package to Pisa and Florence. Ask your travel agent.

The carriers listed below have a variety of **discounts** for those who book in advance or are able to decide their departure and return dates in advance. If you're travelling from Europe, you can save quite a tidy sum by paying for your ticket when you make your reservations (Eurobudget); an extra advantage is that the return date is left open. PEX (or APEX) fares have fixed arrival and departure dates, and the stay in Italy must include at least one Saturday night. Children under the age of two usually travel free and both British Airways and Alitalia offer cheaper tickets on some flights for students and those under 26.

main carriers

Air UK: flights from Stansted, ℭ 680146.

Alitalia: 205 Holland Park Avenue, London W11 4XB, ℭ (081) 745 8200.

British Airways: information and reservations if calling from within London, ℭ (081)897 4000; from outside London, ℭ (0345) 222111.

Meridiana: 15 Charles II Street, London SW1Y 4QU, ℭ (071) 839 2222, fax (071) 839 3700.

charter flights

These aren't as much of a bargain to Italy as they are to other Mediterranean destinations, though they're certainly worth looking into—check the advertisements in the travel section of your newspaper (*The Sunday Times* and *Time Out* are especially good), and ask your travel agent. From London, TransEuropean, 227 Shepherds Bush Rd, London W6 7AS, ℂ (081) 748 1333, has regularly scheduled charters to Milan; other charter flights are usually booked by the big holiday companies. To find out about extra seats on these and on commercial flights, visit your local bucket shop. Pickings are fairly easy in the off-season, and tight in the summer months, but not impossible. You take your chances, but you can save some of your hard-earned dough. The cheapest fare from London to Rome at the time of writing is £109.

The problems with charters are they are delayed more often than not, you have to accept the given dates, and if you miss your flight (bus and train strikes in Italy do make this a distinct possibility) there's no refund. Most travel agencies, however, offer traveller's insurance that includes at least a partial refund of your charter fare if strikes and illness keep you from the airport.

Other advantages of taking a regular flight over a charter are an increase in reliability in dates and in punctuality, and you're not out of a wad of cash if you miss your flight.

Student Travel

Campus Travel, 52 Grosvenor Gardens, SW1, ℂ (071) 730 3402.
CTS Travel, 44 Goodge Street, London W1, ℂ (071) 637 5601.
STA Travel,117 Euston Road, NW1 or 86 Old Brompton Rd, SW7.
Ring ℂ (071) 937 9921 for enquiries on European destinations.

By Rail

From London's Victoria Station it's roughly a 24-hour journey to Florence, and will set you back around £177 second class return, £249 first class. The fare to Pisa is £171 second class, £239 first class. Tickets are valid for two months. These trains require reservations and a *couchette*, and on the whole are a fairly painless way of getting there.

discounts

Discounts are available for families travelling together and for children—free for those under four and there's a 40% discount for children between four and eight. Under 26-ers, students or not, can purchase the **BIJ** ticket offering discounts on tickets from London to any Italian city. They are valid for two months and you can make as many stopovers as you wish. BIJ tickets are available from **Eurotrain**, 52 Grosvenor Gardens, London SW1, ℂ (071) 730 8518, and throughout Europe at student offices (CTS in Italy) in main railway stations. Rail travel to Italy becomes an even more attractive option if you intend to purchase an **Inter-Rail** pass (in Europe). These passes are a good deal if you plan to do lots and lots of rail travel and can't be bothered to buy tickets, so they are probably only worth using if you are visiting the Tuscan cities as part of a rail tour around Europe. They seem a rather less rosy option if your travelling is limited to Italy, where domestic rail tickets are one of the few bargains available. Within Italy itself there are several discount tickets available (*see* 'Getting Around', p.11), which you can obtain at any branch of Thomas Cook Ltd or from CIT (Italian State Railways) offices before you leave home:

CIT Offices

CIT, Marco Polo House, 3–5 Landsdowne Rd, Croydon, Surrey, ℂ (081) 686 5533, fax (081) 686 0328.

Wasteels Travel, Adjacent to Platform 2, Victoria Station, London SW1V 1JT, ℂ (071) 834 7066, fax (071) 630 7628.

By Coach

Visually more expensive than a charter, the coach is the last refuge of airplane-phobic bargain-hunters. The journey time from London to Florence is 26–7 hours; the return full fare is £136. For Siena, change at Florence and take a blue bus from the other side of Florence station (1hr). Change at Florence for Lucca and Pisa onto a Eurolines coach, although it is quicker to take the train. There are, again, discounts for students, senior citizens and children and off-peak travel. Contact **National Express** at Victoria Coach Station, London SW1, ℂ (071) 730 0202, for times and bookings.

By Car

Driving to Italy from the UK is a rather lengthy and expensive proposition, and if you're only staying for a short period, figure your costs against Alitalia's or other airlines' fly-drive scheme. No matter how you cross the Channel, it is a good two-day drive—about 1300km from Calais to Florence. Ferry information is available at any travel agent or direct from the ferry companies. You can cut many of the costly motorway tolls by going from Dover to Calais, through France, to Basle, Switzerland, and then through the Gotthard Tunnel over the Alps; in the summer you can save the steep tunnel tolls by taking one of the passes. You can avoid some of the driving by putting your car on the train (although, again, you should balance the sizeable expense against the price of hiring a car for the period of your stay). Express sleeper cars run to Milan from Paris or Boulogne, and to Bologna from Boulogne. Services are drastically cut outside the summer months, however. For more information, contact the CIT offices listed above.

To bring your car into Italy, you need your **car registration** (log book), valid **driving licence** and valid **insurance** (a Green Card is not necessary, but you'll need one if you go through Switzerland). Make sure everything is in excellent working order or your slightly bald tyre may enrich the coffers of the Swiss or Italian police—it's not uncommon to be stopped for no reason and have your car searched until the police find something on which to stick a fine. Also, be aware that spare parts for some non-Italian cars are difficult to come by, almost impossible for pre-1988 Japanese models. If you're coming to live in Italy, remember that cars with foreign plates are obliged to leave the country every six months for a hazily defined period of time.

Until December 1995 and maybe after, any foreign-plated car is entitled to free breakdown service by the **Italian Auto Club** (ACI) (for local offices, *see* p.15). Phone ACI on ✆ (06) 44 77 to find out the current rates. At the time of writing the motorway tunnel tolls are:

Mont Blanc Tunnel, from Chamonix (France) to Courmayeur. Small car or motorcycle L22,000 single, L27,000 return. Medium-sized car (axle distance 2.31–2.63m) L36,000 single, L39,000 return. Large cars (axle distance 2.64–3.30m) or cars with caravans L48,000 single or L51,000 return.

Fréjus Tunnel, from Modane (France) to Bardonècchia. Prices range from L23,000–L47,000.

Gran San Bernardo, from Bourg St Pierre (Switzerland) to Aosta. Small car or motorcycle L22,000 single, L25,000 return. Medium car L46,000 single, L52,000 return. Large car or car with caravan L74,000 single, L90,000 return.

Getting There from Mainland Europe

Pisa is easily reached **by air** from other European cities: there are direct daily flights on Air France from Paris and also from Frankfurt on Lufthansa. You can also fly daily with Olympic Airlines from Athens to Pisa, changing at Milan, Naples or Rome; on Iberia from Madrid connecting with Alitalia flights at Nice or Milan; on Scandinavian Airlines from Oslo via Rome or Milan. Lufthansa also fly daily from Munich to Florence.

Rail links are excellent: Florence is on the main Rome–Bologna line and accessible to the main European destinations via Milan or Munich.

Travelling **by coach** is the most arduous but cheapest way to get around Europe. Eurolines coaches operate throughout Europe from all the principal cities. Contact them in Florence, ℂ (55) 215 155; Paris, ℂ (331) 4972 5151; Munich, ℂ (49) 8977 8068; Madrid, ℂ (341) 408 5398.

Getting There from North America

By Air

From North America the major carriers are TWA and Air Canada, with flights to Rome or Milan, though British Airways has just begun a new New York–London–Pisa service called the Manhattan Express that departs at 9pm and has you in Florence by 4pm the next day. Fares from Canada are often much higher than they are from the States.

It's worth checking budget fares to London, Brussels, Paris, Frankfurt or Amsterdam; these routes are more competitive than the Italian ones, and you may save money by either flying or riding the rails to Italy from there.

There are SUPERPEX discounts available for booking in advance (14–21 days) providing you obey certain conditions: at least a week's stay but not more than 90 days, and there are penalty fees if you change your flight dates.

If you live in the US boondocks, **Alitalia** has a toll-free number, ℂ 800 223 5730.

charter flights

Try the listings in The Sunday New York Times, and talk to your travel agent. Delta Airlines has regular charters from New York, Chicago and Los Angeles to Rome and Milan, ℂ 800 241 4141. Other charter flights are usually booked by the big holiday companies. To find out about extra seats on these and on commercial flights, contact one of the numerous last-minute, discount services (in the USA, call Access, ℂ 800 333 7280, or Air Hitch, ℂ (212) 864 2000 or Uni-Travel ℂ (800) 325 2222 for similar services—check the listings in The Sunday New York Times). The cheapest fare from New York to Rome at the time of writing is $768.

flights for students

From the USA, a good place to start looking is STA Travel, 48 East 11th St, New York NY 10003, ℂ (212) 477 7166 and also 166 Geary Street, Suite 702, San Francisco, CA 94108, ℂ (415) 391 8407.

From Canada, contact Travel Cuts (Canadian Universities Travel Services), 187 College St, Toronto, Ontario M5T 1P7, ℂ (416) 979 2406.

The North American **Eurail Pass**, which must be purchased before you leave the States, is a good deal only if you plan to use the trains every day in Italy or elsewhere—though it's not valid in the UK, Morocco or countries outside the European Union. In the USA, contact **CIT Tours Corporation**, 342 Madison Avenue, Suite 207, New York, NY 10173, ✆ (212) 697 2100, fax (212) 697 1394. There's also an 800 number that you can call from anywhere: ✆ (800) 248 8687. In Canada CIT tours are based at: 1450 City Counsellors, Suite 750, Montreal, Quebec H3A 2E6, ✆ (514) 845 9101.

Passports and Customs Formalities

To get into Italy you need a valid **passport** or a **British Visitor's Card**. EC citizens do not need visas to get into Italy. US, Canadian and Australian nationals do not need visas for stays of up to three months. (However, if you're not an EC national and mean to reach Italy through France, see if you need to pick up a **French transit visa**). If you mean to stay longer than three months in Italy you will have to get a *permesso di soggiorno*. For this you will need to state your reason for staying, be able to prove a source of income and have medical insurance. After a couple of exasperating days filling out forms at some provincial *questura* office, you should walk out with your permit.

According to Italian law, you must **register with the police** within eight days of arriving. If you check into a hotel this is done automatically. If you come to grief in the mesh of rules and forms, you can at least get someone to explain it to you in English by calling the Rome Police Office for Visitors, ✆ (06) 4686 ext. 2987.

EC nationals over the age of 17 can now import a limitless amount of goods for their personal use. Non-EC nationals have to pass through the **Italian Customs** which are usually benign. Nevertheless, how the frontier police manage to recruit such ugly, mean-looking characters to hold the submachine guns and drug-sniffing dogs from such a good-looking population is a mystery, but they'll let you alone if you don't look suspicious and haven't brought along more than 150 cigarettes or 75 cigars, a litre of hard drink or three bottles of wine, a couple of cameras, a movie camera, 10 rolls of film for each, a tape recorder, radio, record-player, one canoe less than 5.5m, sports equipment for personal use, and one TV (though you'll have to pay for a licence for it at Customs). Pets must be accompanied by a bilingual **Certificate of Health** from your local veterinary inspector. You can take the same items listed above home with you without hassle—except of course your British pet. US citizens may return with $400 worth of merchandise—keep your receipts.

There are no limits to how much money you bring into Italy: legally you may not export more than L400,000 in Italian banknotes, though they rarely check.

Courses for Foreigners and Special-interest Holidays

The **Italian Institute**, 39 Belgrave Square, London SW1X 8NX, ℂ (071) 235 1461, or 686 Park Avenue, New York, NY 10021, ℂ (212) 397 9300, is the main source of information on courses for foreigners in Italy. Graduate students should also contact their nearest Italian consulate to find out about scholarships—apparently many go unused each year because no one knows about them.

One obvious course to take, especially in this linguistically pure land of Dante, is **Italian language and culture**: there are special summer classes offered by the Scuola Lingua e Cultura per Stranieri of the University of Siena, with special classes in August for teachers of Italian. Similar courses are held in Florence—sometimes there seem to be more American students than Florentines in the city. The following have courses all year round:

British Institute, Palazzo Lanfredini, Lungarno Giucciardini 9, ℂ (055) 284 033, fax (055) 287 056, runs courses on Florentine art and history. The school is at Via Tornabuoni 2, ℂ 284 033.

Centro di Cultura per Stranieri, Via di Santo Spirito, ℂ 287 148, offers history, literature and art at both basic and advanced levels.

Scuola Lorenzo de' Medici, Via dell'Alloro, ℂ 289 514, has classes in language and art.

Centro Linguistico Italiano Dante Alighieri, Via de' Bardi 12, ℂ 234 2984, specializes in language courses.

Music courses complement the regions' numerous music festivals: in the summer Florence's Villa Schifanoia holds master classes for instrumentalists and singers; and Siena's Accademia Musicale Chigiana, Via di Città, offers master classes for instrumentalists and conductors.

Art-lovers can take a course on medieval art at Florence's Università Internazionale dell'Arte, in the Villa Tornabuoni, Via Incontri 3; courses are offered from October to April in history of art, restoration and design, while the Istituto per l'Arte e il Restauro, in Palazzo Spinelli, Borgo Santa Croce 10, holds workshops in art restoration.

Specialist Tour Operators in the UK

Alternative Travel (walking, cycling and wine tours that include Siena and Pisa), 69–71 Banbury Road, Oxford OX2 6PE, ℂ (0865) 310399, fax (0865) 310299.

Citalia (tailor-made tours for individuals and groups), Marco Polo House, 3–5 Lansdowne Rd, Croydon, Surrey, ✆ (081) 686 5533.

CV Travel (villa holidays in Florence), 43 Cadogan Street, London SW3 2PR, ✆ (071) 581 0851, fax (071) 584 5229.

Italiatour (city breaks to Florence and Siena), 205 Holland Park Ave, London W11 4 XV, ✆ (071) 371 1114.

James Keogh Tours (upmarket package holidays, everything from art and archi-tecture to history, religion and archaeology), 138 Hanworth Road, Hounslow, Middx TW3 1UG, ✆ (081) 570 4228.

Kirker Europe (weekend breaks to Florence and Siena with bus tours to Pisa), 3 New Concordia Wharf, Mill Street, London SE1 2BB, ✆ (071) 231 3333, fax (071) 231 4771.

Magic of Italy (honeymoon holidays), 227 Shepherds Bush Rd, London W6 7AS, ✆ (081) 748 7575.

Magnum (senior citizens in Florence and Siena), 7 Westleigh Park, Blaby, Leicester, ✆ (0533) 777 123.

Martin Randall Travel (art, architecture, history and wine tours; also visits to Florence, Siena and Lucca according to season),10 Barley Mow Passage, Chiswick, London W4 4PH, ✆ (081) 742 3355, fax (081) 742 1066.

Nadfas (National Association of Decorative and Fine Arts Societies; art tours of Florence and Siena), Hermes House, 80–89 Beckenham Rd, Beckenham, Kent, ✆ (081) 658 2308, fax (081) 658 4478, for members only.

Prospect Art Tours (art tours in Florence), 454–458 Chiswick High Rd, London W4 5TT, ✆ 081 995 2151.

Ramblers (walking tours in Siena), Box 43, Welwyn Garden City, Herts AL8 6PQ, ✆ (0707) 331 133, fax (0707) 333276.

SJA (educational art tours to Pisa and Florence), 48 Cavendish Rd, London SW12 0DG, ✆ (081) 673 4849.

Specialtours (cultural tours of Florence), 81 Elizabeth St, London SW1W 9PG, ✆ (071) 730 2297.

Swan Hellenic (only Siena as part of hill towns art and architecture tours), 77 New Oxford Street, London WC1A 1PP, ✆ (071) 831 1616.

Tour de Force Travel (first-class all-inclusive study tours in destinations which range from Sicily to the Italian hill towns), 31 Crawford Place, London W1H 1HY, ✆ (081) 983 1487.

Specialist Tour Operators in the USA

The Bombard Society (organizes balloon flights that take in Florence and Siena, 6727 Curran St, McLean, VA 22101, ✆ (703) 448 9407.

Esplanade Tours (art and architecture tours Florence, Siena and Pisa), 581 Boylston Street, Boston, MA 02116, ✆ (617) 266 7465.

NRCSA (arranges language courses in Florence and Siena), 823 North 2nd St, Milwaukee, WI 53203, ✆ (414) 278 0631.

University Vacations (offers a cultural programme for adult Americans in Cambridge and Florence), 10461 NW 26th St, Miami, FL 33172, ✆ (305) 591 1736.

Getting Around

Tuscany has an excellent network of railways and highways and byways, and you'll find getting between Florence, Siena, Pisa and Lucca fairly easy—unless one union or another takes it into its head to go on strike (to be fair, this rarely happens during the main holiday season). There's plenty of talk about passing a law to regulate strikes, but don't count on it happening soon. Instead learn how to recognize the word in Italian: *sciopero* (SHO-PER-O) and be prepared to do as the Romans do when you hear it—quiver with resignation. There's always a day or two's notice in advance, and usually strikes last only 12 or 24 hours—but long enough to throw a spanner in the works. Keep your ears open.

Transport to and from the Airports

Pisa's international airport, Galileo Galilei, ✆ 44 325, 3km to the south, is linked to the city by train, or city bus no. 5 which arrives at Piazza Stazione in front of the main station on the south side of the Arno. A special train service runs from Pisa airport to the central Santa Maria Novella Station in Florence (1hr, daily every 1–2hrs); you can call the air terminal in the station for flight information, ✆ 216 073. **Florence**'s dinky civil airport, Amerigo Vespucci, soon to be enlarged to take in international traffic is 6km outside the city at Peretola, ✆ 373 498, flight information ✆ 27 88. It is connected to the city by a regular bus service to Santa Maria Novella Station (15mins). There is also a plentiful supply of taxis at both airports.

Alitalia: Lungarno Acciaioli 10/12r, © 27 881; Piazza dell'Oro 1, © 27 881, fax 27 88 400.

British Airways: Via Vigna Nuova 36r, © 218 655.

Meridiana (for London, Gatwick), Lungarno Vespucci 28/R, © 230 2334/5, fax 230 2046/2314.

TWA: Via dei Vecchietti 4, © 239 6856, fax 214 634.

airlines in Pisa

Alitalia: Via Puccini 21, © 48 025/6/7, fax 48 028.

British Airways: Società Aeroporto Toscana, Galileo Galilei Airport, © 501 838.

By Train

Florence, Siena, Pisa and Lucca are linked by regular trains, so in theory it is possible to do a whistle-stop rail tour of all four cities in one day, but that would not leave a great deal of time for the sights!

Florence is the central transport node for Tuscany and harder to avoid than to reach. The central station is **Santa Maria Novella**, © 288 785; there is another, **Campo di Marte**, located at the east end of town, mainly used for local lines and some trains to Rome. Bus 19 connects the two stations.

There are trains roughly every hour between Florence and Siena (97km, 1½hrs)—the journey takes a little longer if you have to change at Empoli. Pisa, 81km from Florence, is on the main Florence–Livorno line with one or two trains every hour (55mins). Lucca can be reached from Florence hourly via the Florence–Pistoia–Viareggio line (78km, 80mins). The journey from Pisa to Lucca (24km) takes only 25 minutes. To travel from Siena to Lucca, you could go via either Florence or Pisa (125km, 2hrs).

Italy's national railway, the FS (*Ferrovie dello Stato*) is well run, cheap (by British standards) and often a pleasure to ride. Possible FS unpleasantnesses you may encounter, besides a strike, are delays, crowding (especially at weekends and in the summer). Reserve a seat in advance (*fare una prenotazione*). The fee is small and on the Intercity trains it is free and can save you hours standing. On the upper echelon trains, reservations are mandatory. Do check when you purchase your ticket in advance that the date is correct; tickets are only valid the day they're purchased unless you specify otherwise.

Tickets may be purchased not only in the stations, but at many travel agents. Be sure you ask which platform (*binario*) your train arrives at; the big permanent boards posted in the stations are not always correct. If you get on a train without a ticket you can buy one from the conductor, with an added 20 per cent penalty. You can also pay a conductor to move up to first class if there are places available.

There is a fairly straightforward hierarchy of trains. At the bottom of the pyramid is the humble *Locale* (euphemistically known sometimes as an *Accelerato*), which often stops even where there's no station in sight; it can be excruciatingly slow. A *Diretto* stops far less, an *Espresso* just at the main towns. *Intercity* trains whoosh between the major cities and rarely deign to stop and the *Eurocity* trains link Italian cities with major European ones. Both of these services require a supplement—some 30 per cent more than a regular fare and on some there are only first-class coaches. Reservations are free but must be made at least five hours before the trip. Trains serving the most important routes have names such as the *Vesuvio* (Milan, Bologna, Florence, Rome, Naples), the *Colosseo/Ambrosiano* (Milan, Bologna, Florence, Rome) and the *Napoli Express* (Paris, Genoa, Pisa, Rome, Naples). The real lords of the rails are the *ETR 450 Pendolino* trains, kilometre-eaters that will speed you to your destination as fast as trains can go. For these there is a more costly supplement and on some only first-class luxury cars.

The FS offers several passes. A flexible option is the 'Flexi Card' which allows unlimited travel for either four days within a nine-day period (second class £66, first class £98), 8 days within 12 (second class £94, first class around £140), 12 days within 30 (second class £120, first class £190) and you don't have to pay any supplements. Another ticket, the *Kilometrico* gives you 3000 kilometres of travel, made on a maximum of 20 journeys and is valid for two months; one advantage is that it can be used by up to five people at the same time. However, supplements are payable on Intercity trains. Second-class tickets are currently £90, first-class £152. Other discounts, available only once you're in Italy, are 15 per cent on same-day return tickets and three-day returns (depending on the distance involved), and discounts for families of at least four travelling together. Senior citizens (men 65 and over, women 60) can also get a *Carta d'Argento* ('silver card') for L40,000 entitling them to a 20 per cent reduction in fares. A *Carta Verde* bestows a 20 per cent discount on people under 26 and costs L40,000.

Refreshments on routes of any great distance are provided by bar cars or trolleys; you can usually get sandwiches and coffee from vendors along the tracks at intermediary stops. Station bars often have a good variety of take-away travellers' fare; consider at least investing in a plastic bottle of mineral water, since there's no drinking water on the trains.

Besides trains and bars, Italy's stations offer other facilities. All have a *Deposito*, where you can leave your bags for hours or days for a small fee. The larger ones have porters (who charge L1000–1500 per piece) and some even have luggage trolleys; major stations have an *Albergo Diurno* ('Day Hotel', where you can take a shower, get a shave and haircut, etc.), information offices, currency exchanges open at weekends (not at the most advantageous rates, however), hotel-finding and reservation services, kiosks with foreign papers, restaurants, etc. You can also arrange to have a rental car awaiting you at your destination—Avis, Hertz, Eurotrans and Maggiore are the firms that provide this service.

By Bus

The four cities are also well served by bus. From Florence SITA buses go to Siena, LAZZI to Lucca and Pisa and CLAP to Lucca; SITA buses run between Siena and Pisa; TRA-IN buses operate from Siena covering Siena province.

It's possible to reach nearly every city, town and village in Tuscany from Florence, which is wonderfully convenient—once you know which of several bus companies to patronize. The tourist office has a complete list of destinations, but here are some of the most popular.

SITA (near the station, Via S. Caterina da Siena 15, © 214 721 Mon–Fri, 211 487 weekends): towns in the Val d'Elsa, Chianti, Val di Pesa, Mugello and Casentino; Arezzo, Bibbiena, Castelfiorentino, Certaldo, Consuma, Figline Valdarno, Firenzuola, Marina di Grosseto, Montevarchi, Poggibonsi (for San Gimignano and Volterra), Pontassieve, Poppi, Pratovecchio, Scarperia, **Siena**, Stia, Vallombrosa.

LAZZI (Piazza Stazione 4, © 239 8840): along the Arno to the coast, including Calenzano, Cerreto Guidi, Empoli, Forte dei Marmi, Livorno, **Lucca**, Marina di Carrara, Marina di Massa, Montecatini Terme, Montelupo, Montevarchi, Pescia, **Pisa**, Pistoia, Pontedera, Prato, Signa, Tirrenia, Torre del Lago, and Viareggio.

CAT (Via Fiume 2r, © 283 400): Anghiari, Arezzo, Caprese, Città di Castello, Incisa Valdarno, Sansepolcro.

CLAP (Piazza Stazione 15r, © 283 734): **Lucca**.

CAP (Via Nazionale 13, © 214 637): Borgo S. Lorenzo, Impruneta, Incisa Valdarno, Montepiano, Prato.

COPIT (Piazza S. Maria Novella, © 215 451): Abetone, Cerreto Guidi, Pistoia, Poggio a Caiano, Vinci.

RAMA (Lazzi Station, © 239 8840): Grosseto.

Within the cities buses are the traveller's friend. Most cities label routes well; all charge flat fees for rides within the city limits and immediate suburbs, at the time of writing around L1200. Bus tickets must always be purchased before you get on, either at a tobacconist's, a newspaper kiosk, in many bars, or from ticket machines near the main stops. Once you get on, you must 'obliterate' your ticket in the machines in the front or back of the bus; controllers stage random checks to make sure you've punched your ticket. Fines for cheaters are about L50,000, and the odds are about 12 to 1 against a check, so you may take your chances against how lucky you feel. If you're good-hearted, you'll buy a ticket and help some overburdened municipal transit line meet its annual deficit.

By Taxi

Taxi rides are about the same price as in London. The average meter starts at L6400, and adds L300 per kilometre. There's an extra charge for luggage and for trips to the airport; and rates go up after 10pm and on Sundays and holidays.

Guided Coach Tours

SITA run morning and afternoon tours of Florence. Transport, museum admission and guide are included in the price of L45,000 (daily 9.30–12.30, 2.30–5.30). They also run excursions to Pisa (2.30–7 Tues, Thurs, Sat, Sun); and Siena with San Gimignano (9–6.30 Mon, Wed, Fri, Sat).

By Car

For this tour of the art cities, you're probably better off not driving at all: parking is impossible, traffic impossible, deciphering one-way streets, signals and signs impossible. However, given these difficulties, a car does give you the freedom and possibility of making your way through Tuscany's lovely countryside.

The distances between the cities are short: from Florence to Siena is 68km, to Pisa 91km and to Lucca 73km; from Siena to Pisa is 109km and to Lucca is 102km; from Pisa to Lucca is 22km. The roads are good: the A1 Milan–Naples motorway (Autostrada del Sole) skirts Florence and is linked to the A11 which runs west in the direction of Lucca and Pisa; the unnumbered Superstrada del Palio runs south from the A1 to Siena. Although it may be easy to reach the cities, in the case of Florence and Siena, which both have traffic-free central zones, you will have to leave your car in a car park on the outskirts. It is possible to take a car into the centre of Pisa and Lucca apart from a few restricted areas.

Be prepared to encounter some of the highest fuel costs in Europe (when everyone else lowered theirs with slumping international prices, Italy raised them. The Italians themselves behind the wheel, many of whom, from 21-year-old madcaps to elderly nuns, drive like idiots, taking particular delight in overtaking at blind curves on mountainous roads. No matter how fast you're going on the *autostrade* (Italy's toll motorways, official speed limit **130km** per hour) someone will pass you going twice as fast. Americans in particular should be wary about driving in Italy. If you're accustomed to the generally civilized rules of motoring that North Americans adhere to, Italy will be a big surprise. Italians do not seem to care if someone kills them or not. Especially in the cities, rules do not seem to exist, and if you expect them to stop riding your tail you'll have a long time to wait. Even the most cultured Italians become aggressive, murderous humanoids behind the wheel, and if you value your peace of mind you should stick with public transport.

If you aren't intimidated, buy a good road map of Italy or a more detailed one of Tuscany (the Italian Touring Club produces excellent ones). Many petrol stations close for lunch in the afternoon, and few stay open late at night, though you may find a 'self-service' where you feed a machine nice smooth L10,000 notes. Autostrada tolls are high—for example, to drive on the A1 from Milan to Rome will cost you around L60,000 at the time of writing. The rest stops and petrol stations along the motorways are open 24 hours. Other roads—*superstrade* on down through the Italian grading system—are free of charge. The Italians are very good about signposting, and roads are almost all excellently maintained—some highways seem to be built of sheer bravura, suspended on cliffs, crossing valleys on enormous piers—feats of engineering that will remind you, more than almost anything else, that this is the land of the ancient Romans. Beware that you may be fined on the spot for speeding, a burnt-out headlamp, etc; if you're especially unlucky you may be slapped with a *super multa*, a superfine, of L150,000 or more. You may even be fined for not having a portable triangle danger signal (pick one up at the frontier or from an ACI office for L2500).

The **Automobile Club of Italy** (ACI) is a good friend to the foreign motorist. Besides having bushels of useful information and tips, they offer a free breakdown service, and can be reached from anywhere by dialling 116—also use this number if you have an accident, need an ambulance, or simply have to find the nearest service station. If you need major repairs, the ACI can make sure the prices charged are according to their guidelines.

Automobile Club of Italy (ACI)

Florence	Viale Amendola 36, ✆ (055) 24 861.
Lucca	Via Catalani 59, ✆ (0583) 582 627.
Pisa	Via San Martino 1, ✆ (050) 47 333.
Siena	Viale Vittorio Veneto 47, ✆ (0577) 49 001.

Hiring a car is fairly simple if not particularly cheap. Italian car rental firms are called *Autonoleggi*. There are both large international firms through which you can reserve a car in advance, and local agencies, which often have lower prices. Air or train travellers should check out possible discount packages.

Most companies will require a deposit amounting to the estimated cost of the hire, and there is 19 per cent VAT added to the final cost. At the time of writing, a 5-seat Fiat Panda costs around L70,000 a day. Petrol is 50 per cent more expensive than in the UK. Rates become more advantageous if you take the car for a week with unlimited mileage. If you need a car for more than three weeks, leasing is a more economic alternative. The National Tourist Office has a list of firms in Italy that hire caravans (trailers) and campers.

Car Hire at Pisa Airport

Hertz, ℭ 491 87	**Budget**, ℭ 45 490
Avis, ℭ 42 028	**Program**, ℭ 500 296
Maggiore, ℭ 42 574	

By Carriage

The **carozze** of Florence are now used only by tourists. Negotiate times and dates before you begin: prices can be as high as L150,000 per hour.

By Motorbike or Bicycle

The means of transport of choice for many Italians; motorbikes, mopeds and Vespas can be a delightful way to get between the cities and see the countryside. You should only consider it, however, if you've ridden them before—Italy's hills and aggravating traffic make it no place to learn. Helmets are compulsory. Hirecosts for a *motorino* (moped) range from about L20,000–35,000 per day; Vespas (scooters) somewhat more (up to L50,000).

Italians are keen cyclists as well, racing drivers up the steepest hills; if you're not training for the Tour de France, consider the region's hills well before planning a bicycling tour—especially in the hot summer months. Bikes can be transported by train in Italy, either with you or within a couple of days—apply at the baggage office (*ufficio bagagli*). Hire prices range from about L10,000–20,000 per day, which may make buying one interesting if you are planning to spend much time in the saddle, L190,000–L300,000, either in a bike shop or through the classified ad papers which are put out in nearly every city and region. Alternatively, if you bring your own bike, do check the airlines to see what their policies are on transporting them.

Practical A–Z

Climate and When to Go

Winter can be an agreeable time to visit the indoor attractions of the cities and avoid crowds, particularly in Florence, where it seldom snows but may rain for several days at a time.

Average Temperatures in °C (°F)

	January	April	July	October
Florence	6 (42)	13 (55)	25 (77)	16 (60)
Siena	5 (40)	12 (54)	25 (77)	15 (59)

Average Monthly Rainfall in mm (in)

	January	April	July	October
Florence	61 (3)	74 (3)	23 (1)	96 (4)
Siena	70 (3)	61 (3)	21 (1)	112 (4)

Disabled Travellers

Facilities aren't great for the disabled anywhere in Tuscany. Churches are a special problem: long flights of steps in front designed to impress on the would-be worshipper the feeling of going upwards to God create another raw deal for those with limited mobility. The best thing you can do once you're in Italy is contact the local tourist offices; they're generally very helpful, and have even been known to find pushers on the spot.

Some Specialist Organizations in Italy

CO.IN (Consorzio Cooperative Integrate), Via Enrico Giglioli 54a, 00169 Rome, © (6) 232 67504, fax (6) 232 67505. Their tourist information centre (open 9–5 Mon–Fri) offers advice and information on accessibility.

Centro Studi Consulenza Invalidi, Via Gozzadini 7, 20148 Milan. Publishes an annual guide, *Vacanze per Disabili*, with details of suitable accommodation in Italy.

Some Specialist Organizations in the UK

Holiday Care Service, 2 Old Bank Chambers, Station Road, Horley, Surrey RH6 9HW, © (0293) 774535, for travel information and details of accessible accommodation and care holidays.

RADAR (Royal Association for Disability and Rehabilitation), 12 City Forum, 250 City Road, London EC1V 8AF, ✆ (071) 250 3222. They publish *Holidays and Travel Abroad: a Guide for Disabled People* (£3.50) listing hotels with facilities, specialist tour operators, self-catering apartments and more.

Royal National Institute for the Blind, 224 Great Portland Street, London W15 5TB, ✆ (071) 388 1266. Its mobility unit offers a 'Plane Easy' audio-cassette with advice for blind people travelling by plane. It will also advise on finding accommodation.

Tripscope, The Courtyard, Evelyn Road, London W4 5JL, ✆ (081) 994 9294 (also minicom), offers practical advice and information on every aspect of travel and transport for elderly and disabled travellers. On request, information can be provided by letter or tape.

Some Specialist Organizations in the USA

American Foundation for the Blind, 15 West 16th Street, New York, NY 10011, ✆ (212) 620 2000; toll free, ✆ 800 2323 5463. The best source of information in the USA for visually impaired travellers.

Mobility International USA, PO Box 10767, Eugene, OR 97440, ✆ (503) 343 1284, fax (503) 343 6812. Practical advice and information.

SATD (Society for the Advancement of Travel for the Disabled), 347 5th Ave, Suite 610, NY 10016, ✆ (212) 447 7284, offers advice on all aspects of travel for the disabled, on an ad hoc basis for a $3 charge, or unlimited to members ($45, concessions $25).

Travel Information Service, MossRehab Hospital, 1200 West Tabor Road, Philadelphia, PA 19141, ✆ (215) 456 99 00. Telephone information service supplying travel advice to people with disabilities.

Embassies and Consulates

British: Lungarno Corsini 2, Florence ✆ (055) 284 133.
Irish: Largo Nazareno 3, Rome, ✆ (06) 678 2541.
US: Lungarno Amerigo Vespucci 38, Florence ✆ (055) 239 8276.
Canadian: Via Zara 30, Rome ✆ (06) 445 891.

Festivals

Although festivals in Florence, Siena, Pisa and Lucca are often more show than spirit (though there are several exceptions to the rule), they can add a note of pageantry or culture to your holiday. Some are great costume affairs, with roots dating back to the Middle Ages, and there are quite a few music festivals, antique fairs and, most of all, festivals devoted to food and drink.

Traditional festivals in **Florence** date back centuries. Easter Sunday's *Scoppio del Carro*, or 'Explosion of the Cart', commemorates Florentine participation in the First Crusade in 1096. The Florentines were led by Pazzino de' Pazzi, who upon returning home, received the special custody of the flame of Holy Saturday, with which the Florentines traditionally relit their family hearths. To make the event more colourful, the Pazzi constructed a decorated wooden ox cart to carry the flame. They lost the job after the Pazzi conspiracy in 1478, and since then the city has taken over the responsibility. In the morning, a firework-filled wooden float is pulled by white oxen from the Porta a Prato to the cathedral, where, at noon, during the singing of the Gloria, it is ignited by a model dove that descends on a wire from the high altar.

On Ascension Day (in May), there's the *Festa del Grillo* (cricket festival) in the Cascine; Michelangelo was thinking of its little wooden cricket cages when he mocked Ammanati's gallery on the cathedral dome. June is the time of the three matches of *Calcio Storico in Costume* (historical football in 16th-century costume) in the Piazza Santa Croce, played by 27-man teams from Florence's four quarters, in memory of a defiant football match played in Piazza Santa Croce in 1530, during the siege by Charles V. Flag-throwing and a parade in historical costume are part of the pre-game ceremonies. The *Festa delle Rificolone* on 7 September is one of Florence's livelier festivals, with a parade of floats followed by a party in the streets. The best fireworks are reserved for the day of Florence's patron, St John (24 June).

Florentines adore cultural events. The big summer festival is the *Estate Fiesolana*: from late June–August the old Roman theatre is the site of concerts, ballet, theatre and films, for reasonable prices. The *Maggio Musicale Fiorentino*, the city's big music festival, spans from late April to the beginning of July and brings in big-name concert stars. Events take place in the Teatro Comunale, Corso Italia 12 (just off Lungarno Vespucci, © 277 91 or 277 9236 for ticket information). There's usually some kind of music in the Piazza della Signoria on Thursday nights during the summer, and the **summer season** of the Teatro Comunale (opera, concerts and ballet) which take place in the Boboli Gardens, the Teatro Comunale and the Teatro della Pergola (Via della Pergola 18, © 247 9651). From April to June you can see the offerings of independent film makers at the Florence Festival in the Palazzo dei Congressi, © 238 2241. In May, don't miss the Iris Festival up at Piazzale Michelangelo.

In July and August Italy's best-known festival is held in **Siena**—the *Palio*, the famous horse race run in the Campo when ten of the local neighbourhoods (or *contrade*) compete furiously against each other (*see* p.225). **Pisa** holds the *Gioco del Ponte* and historic procession in June (*see* p.268) as well as the historic regatta and lights festival of San Ranieri, when the banks of the Arno glimmer with tens of thousands of bulbs. Folklore displays are in order for San Sisto (6 August). Every four years in June Pisa is the site of the Old Maritime Republics' boat race (next 1995), a race between old sea rivals Pisa, Venice, Genoa and Amalfi. The Feast of San Paolino, **Lucca**'s patron saint, is celebrated on 12 July with the offering of a votive candle and the blessing of the *palio* or banner followed by a crossbow contest between the city's three districts in the evening.

major events

March

19	San Giuseppe, **Siena** (with rice fritters) and **Torrita di Siena**, with a donkey race and tournament.

April

Good Friday	Way of the Cross candlelight procession, **Gràssina**, near Florence.

May

All month	Iris Festivals, **Florence**.
Ascension Day	Cricket Festival, with floats, and crickets sold in little cages, **Florence.**
May and June	Maggio Musicale Fiorentino, **Florence**.

June

Mid-June–August	*Estate Fiesolana*—music, cinema, ballet and theatre, in **Florence**.
16–17	*Festa di San Ranieri*—lights festival and historic regatta, **Pisa**.
3 weekends	*Calcio in Costume*, Renaissance football game, **Florence**.
24	St John the Baptist's Day, with fireworks, **Florence**.
25	*Gioco del Ponte*, a traditional bridge tug-of-war game with a cart in the middle, **Pisa**.
Last Sunday	**San Donato in Poggio** (Florence province), *La Bruscellata*, a week of dancing and old love songs around a flowering tree.

July

2	*Palio*, since1147, **Siena**.
12	Feast of San Paolino, **Lucca**.

August

First weekend	Traditional thanksgiving festival in honour of San Sisto, **Pisa**.
16	*Palio*, **Siena**.

September

First Sunday	Processions; lantern festival, **Florence**.
13–14	Feast of Santa Croce, **Lucca**; candlelit procession in honour of the *Volto Santo* (11th-century crucifix) followed by a fair the next day in Piazza San Michele.

November

22	Santa Cecilia, patroness of music, celebrated with concerts in **Siena**.

December

13	Santa Lucia, celebrated with a pottery fair in **Siena**.

Insurance and Health

Emergencies, © 113

You can insure yourself against almost any mishap—cancelled flight, stolen or lost baggage, health. While national health services in the UK and Canada take care of their citizens while travelling, the USA doesn't. Check your current policies to see if they cover you while abroad, and under what circumstances, and judge whether you need a special traveller's insurance policy. Travel agencies sell policies, as well as insurance companies, but they are not cheap.

Minor illnesses and problems that crop up in Italy can usually be handled free of charge in a public hospital clinic or *ambulatorio*. If you need minor aid, Italian pharmacists are highly trained and can probably diagnose your problem; look for a *Farmacia* (they all have a list in the window with details of which ones are open during the night and on holidays). Extreme cases should head for the *Pronto Soccorso* (First Aid Service). Few Italian doctors speak even rudimentary English; contact your embassy or consulate for a list of English-speaking doctors.

Florence: for an ambulance or first aid, Misericordia, Piazza del Duomo 20, © 21 2222. Doctor's night service, © 477 891. The general hospital Santa Maria Nuova, in Piazza S. M. Nuova, © 27 581, is the most convenient. Tourist Medical Service, 24 hours a day, is staffed by English- and French-speaking physicians at Via Lorenzo il Magnifico 59, ring first on © 475 411. There is a pharmacy open 24 hours every day in S. Maria Novella Station, also Molteni, Via Calzaiuoli 7r and Taverna, Piazza S. Giovanni 20r, by the Baptistry.

Siena: ambulance, © 290 807; hospital © 290 111; doctor's night service © 299 466; Farmacia Centrale, Via Banchi di Sotto 2, © 286 109

Pisa: Farmacia dell'Ospedale, Via Roma ©592 111.

Lavatories

Frequent travellers have noted a steady improvement over the years in the cleanliness of Italy's public conveniences, although as ever you will only find them in places like train and bus stations and bars. Ask for the *bagno, toilette,* or *gabinetto*; in stations and the smarter bars and cafés, there are washroom attendants who expect a few hundred lire for keeping the place decent. You'll probably have to ask them for paper (*carta*). Don't confuse the Italian plurals: *signori* (gents), *signore* (ladies).

Libraries

Florence: British Institute Library, Lungarno Guicciardini 9, © 284 031, open 9.45–1 and 3.15–6.30, closed Sat and Sun. American Library, Via S. Gallo 10, open 9–12.30, closed Sat and Sun. There are so many other libraries in Florence that one, the Biblioteca del Servizio Beni Librari, Via G. Modena 13, © 438 2266 does nothing but dispense information on all the others.

Pisa: Biblioteca Provinciale, Via Betti, © 929 111.

Lucca: Biblioteca Statale, 12 Via Santa Maria Orlandini, © 412 71.

Lost Property

In Italian lost property is *oggetti smarriti* or *oggetti ritrovati*. The main office in Florence is at Via Circondaria 19, © 36 79 43. The pound for **towed-away cars** in Florence is at Via Circondaria 16, © 35 15 62. Open 9–12, closed Thurs and Sun. In Siena the lost propery office is at Casato di Sotto 23 (open 9–12.30 Mon–Sat).

Maps

For a wide range of maps, try **Stanford**'s, 12–14 Long Acre, London WC2 9LP, © (071) 836 1321; in the US try **The Complete Traveller**, 199 Madison Ave, NY 10016, © (0212) 685 9007. The best maps are *Firenze Piantà* (Touring Club Italiano, 1:12500) and *Firenze* (Litografia Artistica, 1:9000); *Siena City Plan* (Freytag and Berndt, 1:5000); *Pisa City Plan* (Freytag and Berndt, 1:8000); *Lucca Città Piantà* (Studio F.M.B., 1:6000).

Money

It's a good idea to bring some Italian lire with you; unforeseen delays and unexpected public holidays may foul up your plans to find a bank open when you arrive. **Traveller's cheques** or Eurocheques remain the most secure way of financing your holiday in Italy; they are easy to change and an insurance against unpleasant surprises. **Credit cards** (American Express, Diner's Club, Mastercard, Access, Eurocard, Barclaycard, Visa) are accepted in most hotels, restaurants and shops (but rarely at any petrol stations). If you have a PIN number you can use the many **cashpoint machines**. Do not be surprised if you are asked to show identification when paying with a credit card.

There's been a lot of loose talk about knocking three noughts off the Italian lira, but it never seems to happen; as it is, everybody can be a 'millionaire'. It is also confusing to the visitor unaccustomed to dealing with rows of zeros, and more than once you'll think you're getting a great deal until you recount the zeros on the price tag. Some unscrupulous operators may try to take advantage of the confusion when you're changing money, so do be careful.

Notes come in denominations of L100,000, L50,000, L10,000, L5,000, L2000 and L1000; coins are in L500, L200, L100, L50, all the way down to the, now rare, ridiculous and practically worthless aluminium coinage of L20 and L10. **Telephone tokens** (*gettoni*) may be used as coins as well and are worth L200.

The easiest way to **receive money** sent to you in Italy is for someone from home to get a bank to telex the amount to an Italian bank, and for you to go and pick it up. Technically, it shouldn't take more than a couple of days to arrive, but make sure the telex includes the number of your passport, ID card, or driver's licence, or the Italians may not give you your money. Save all the receipts from your currency exchanges. Money can also be sent through Thomas Cook travel agents, Western Union and American Express.

Banks are usually open 8.30am–1.20pm, and for one hour in the afternoon (3–4 or 4–5pm). They are closed on Saturdays, Sundays and national holidays. Some are worth visiting for their space-capsule doors alone.

American Express in Florence: Via Dante Alighieri 22R, © 509 81, just off Piazza della Repubblica and Via Guicciardini 49R, PO Box 617, © 288 751.

Official Holidays

The Italians have cut down somewhat on their official national holidays, but note that every town has one or two holidays of its own—usually the feast day of its patron saint. Official holidays, shown on transport timetables and museum opening hours etcetera, are treated the same as Sundays.

1 January	New Year's Day—*Capodanno*.
6 January	Epiphany, better known to Italians as the day of *La Befana*—a kindly witch who brings the *bambini* the toys Santa Claus or *Babbo Natale* somehow forgot.
Easter Monday	Usually pretty dull.
25 April	Liberation Day—even duller.
1 May	Labour Day—lots of parades, speeches, picnics, music and drinking.
15 August	Assumption, or *Ferragosto*—the biggest of them all. Woe to the innocent traveller on the road or train!
1 November	All Saints, or *Ognissanti*—liveliest at the cemeteries.
8 December	Immaculate Conception of the Virgin Mary—another dull one.
25 December	Christmas Day.
Boxing Day	*Santo Stefano*.

Opening Hours and Museums

Most of Tuscany closes down at 1pm until 3 or 4pm, to eat and properly digest the main meal of the day, although things are now beginning to change in the cities. Afternoon working hours are from 4 to 7, often from 5 to 8 in the hot summer months.

Food shops shut on Thursday afternoons in the winter and Saturday afternoons in the summer. Other shops often shut on Monday mornings or all day Saturday, and on a Sunday you'll be lucky to find anything open. Bars are often the only places open during the early afternoon and sometimes on a Sunday. (For **bank** opening hours, *see* p.25).

Churches have always been a prime target for art thieves and as a consequence are usually locked when there isn't a sacristan or caretaker to keep an eye on things. All churches, except for the really important cathedrals and basilicas, close in the afternoon at the same hours as the shops, and the little ones tend to stay closed. Always have a pocketful of L100, L200 and L500 coins to batten the light machines in churches, or what you came to see is bound to be hidden in ecclesiastical shadows. Some churches now have light machines that accept only L1000 notes, but the light-up time rarely lasts more than a minute. Don't do your visiting during services, and don't come to see paintings and statues in churches the week preceding Easter—you will probably find them covered with mourning shrouds.

Most **museums** are now open all day from 9am to 7pm and tend to close on a Monday. Many are magnificent, many are run with shameful neglect, and many have been closed for years for 'restoration' with slim prospects of reopening in the near future. With an estimated one work of great art per inhabitant, Italy has a hard time financing the preservation of its national heritage; you would do well to enquire at the tourist office to find out exactly what is open and what is 'temporarily' closed before setting out on a wild goose chase across town.

We have listed the hours of the **important sights** and museums within the main text. In general, Monday and Sunday afternoons are dead periods for the sightseer—you may want to make these your travelling days. Places without hours usually open on request—but it is best to go before 1pm. We have also specified which attractions charge admission; unless sights are labelled *adm exp*, you'll have to pay between L500 and L5000 to get in. Expensive ones are more—up to L10,000 for the Uffizi and other purveyors of big-league culture. Citizens of EU countries who are under 18 or over 60 get in free.

Packing

You simply cannot overdress in Italy. Now, whether or not you want to try to keep up with the natives is your own affair and your own heavy suitcase—you may do well to compromise and just bring a couple of smart outfits for big nights out. It's not that the Italians are very formal; they simply like to dress up with a gorgeousness that adorns their cities just as much as those old Renaissance churches and palaces. The few places with dress codes are the major churches and basilicas (no shorts or sleeveless shirts), and the smarter restaurants.

After agonizing over fashion, remember to pack small and light: transatlantic airlines limit baggage by size (two pieces are free, up to 1.5m, in height and width; in second class you're allowed one of 1.5m and another up to 110cm). Within Europe limits are by weight: 20 kilos (44lbs) in second class, 30 kilos (66lbs) in first. You may well be penalized for anything bigger. If you're travelling mainly by train, you'll especially want to keep bags to a minimum: jamming big suitcases in overhead racks isn't much fun. Never take more than you can carry, but do bring the following: any prescription medicine you need, an extra pair of glasses or contact lenses, a pocket knife and corkscrew (for picnics), a torch (for dark frescoed churches and hotel corridors), a travel alarm (for those early trains) and a pocket Italian-English dictionary (for flirting and other emergencies). You may want to invest in earplugs. Your electric appliances will work in Italy; just change your plug to the two-prong variety or buy a travel plug. Of course, what you bring depends on when and where you go (see 'Climate' p.18).

Photography

Film and developing are much more expensive than they are in the USA or UK. You are not allowed to take pictures in most museums and in some churches. Most cities now offer one-hour processing if you need your pics in a hurry.

Police Business

Police/Emergency, © 113

There is a fair amount of petty crime in the cities—purse snatchings, pickpocketing, minor thievery of the white-collar kind (always check your change) and car break-ins and theft—but violent crime is rare. Nearly all mishaps can be avoided with adequate precautions. Scooter-borne purse-snatchers can be foiled if you stay on the inside of the pavement and keep a firm hold on your property; pickpockets most often strike in crowded buses and gatherings; don't carry too much cash or keep some of it in another place. Be extra careful in train stations, don't leave valuables in hotel rooms, and always park your car in garages, guarded car parks, or on well-lit streets, with temptations like radios, cassettes, etc., out of sight. Purchasing small quantities of reefers, hashish, cocaine and LSD is legal although what a small quantity might be exactly is unspecified, so if the police don't like you to begin with, it will probably be enough to get you into big trouble.

Once the scourge of Italy, political terrorism has declined drastically in recent years, mainly thanks to special squads of the *Carabinieri*, the black-uniformed national police, technically part of the Italian army. Local matters are usually in the hands of the *Polizia Urbana*; the nattily dressed *Vigili Urbani* concern them-selves with directing traffic and handing out parking fines. You probably will not have anything to do with the *Guardia di Finanza*, the financial police, who spend their time chasing corrupt politicians and their friends. If you need to summon any of them, dial © 113.

Florence: the *Ufficio Stranieri*, in the *questura*, Via Zara 2, © 49 771, handles most foreigners' problems, and usually has someone around who speaks English. Go here for residents' permits, etc.

Siena: the *Ufficio Stranieri* is in Jacopo della Quercia (open 10–12 Mon–Sat).

Post Offices

The postal service in Italy is both the least efficient and the most expensive in Europe, and disgracefully slow; if you're sending postcards back home you often arrive there before they do. If it's important that it arrive in less than a week send your letter *Espresso* (Swift Air Mail) or *Raccomandata* (registered delivery), for a L2000 supplement fee. Stamps (*francobolli*) may also be purchased at tobac-conists (look for a big black T on the sign), but you're bound to get differing opinions on your exact postage. Mail to the UK goes at the same rate as domestic Italian mail, but it's still twice as much to send a letter from Italy to Britain as vice versa. Airmail letters to and from North America can quite often take up to two weeks. This can be a nightmare if you're making hotel reservations and are sending a deposit—telex or telephoning ahead is far more secure if time is short. Most hotels now have a fax machine.

Ask for mail to be sent to you in Italy either care of your hotel or addressed *Fermo Posta* (poste restante: general delivery) to a post office, or, if you're a card-holder, to an American Express Office. When you pick up your mail at the *Fermo Posta* window, bring your passport for identification. Make sure that your mail is sent to the proper post office; the **Posta Centrale** is often the easiest option.

The Italian postal code is most inscrutable in dealing with packages sent overseas. Packages have to be of a certain size, under a certain weight to be sent in certain ways, and must have a flap open for inspection or be sealed with string and lead. You're best off taking it to a stationer's shop (*cartoleria*) and paying L800 for them to wrap it—they usually know what the postal people are going to require.

Telegrams (sent from post offices) are expensive but they are the surest way to get your message out of Italy. You can save money by sending it as a night letter (22 words or less).

Florence: Via Pellicceria, near Piazza della Repubblica, open 8–7, Sat 8.15–12.30, © 21 41 45; telegram and telephone office open 8–11.30pm, or © 184.

Siena: Piazza Matteotti 37, © 284 105.

Pisa: Piazza Vittorio Emanuele II, © 261 48.

Lucca: 2 Via Vallisneri, © 475 43.

Telephones

Direct-dial Codes

USA and Canada, © 001.

UK, © 0044 (omitting the first 0 of the British area code).

To call Italy from abroad, dial © 39 followed by the area prefix—omitting the first 0.

Like many things in Italy, telephoning can be unduly complicated and usually costs over the odds to boot. Only a few places still have the old token (*gettoni*) telephones, in which you must insert a token (or better yet, several) before dialling. *Gettoni* cost L200 and are often available in machines next to the telephones, or from bars, news-stands, or *tabacchi*. Other public phones will accept regular coinage, as well as *gettoni* and telephone cards. A digital display will indicate the money you have put in or how much credit is left on your card. When you hear the beep it is usually too late to put any more money in, so keep an eye on the display. If your credit on the phone card runs out, insert another one when you hear a beep. The cards are the best option for long-distance phoning and are available from tobacconist shops for L5,000 and L10,000.

Alternatively, head either for a telephone office with booths, operated by either SIP or ASST, or a bar with a telephone meter. If you want to reverse charges (call collect) you can call from a phone box; dial © 172 followed by the country code and you will be connected to an international operator.

Rates are lower if you call on Sunday or after 10pm until 8am—unfortunately just when many provincial telephone offices are closed. Phoning long-distance from your hotel can mean big surcharges.

public telephones

Florence: open 24 hours in the Central Post Office, and in Via della Pelliceria.

Siena: Via dei Termini 40 (closed Sun and public holidays).

Tourist Offices

UK

1 Princes Street, London W1R 8AY, © (071) 408 1254; telex 22402.

Eire

47 Merrion Square, Dublin 2, Eire, © (001) 766397; telex 31682.

USA

630 Fifth Avenue, Suite 1565, New York, NY 10111, © (212) 245 4822; telex 236024.

500 N. Michigan Avenue, Chicago, Ill. 60611, © (312) 644 0990/1; telex 0255160.

360 Post Street, Suite 801, San Francisco, California 94108, © (415) 392 6206; telex 67623.

Canada

Store 56, Plaza 3, Place Ville Marie, Montreal, Quebec, © (514) 866 7667; telex 525607.

You can pick up more detailed information by writing directly to any of the city tourist offices. These are usually very helpful in sending out lists of flats or villas to hire, or lists of agents who handle the properties.

Women Travellers

Italian men, with the heritage of Casanova, Don Giovanni and Rudolph Valentino as their birthright, are very confident in their role as great Latin lovers, and local swains will invariably pick on any female under a certain age, Italian or foreign. Most of these are unlikely to give any trouble but obviously you should avoid lonely streets and train stations after dark. Travelling with a male companion practically cancels out any problems—you're instantly a man's property and as such inviolable—an aspect of Italian culture most women find extremely galling.

History and Art

At times, the history of Tuscany has been a small part of a bigger story—Rome's, or modern Italy's. However, in the crucial eras of the Middle Ages and the Renaissance each of the city states had a complex history of its own; these are covered in detail under each city.

City Origins

Florence, Siena and Pisa all originated with the first baby steps, or rather stomps, of the Roman empire. As with southern Etruria, the old Etruscan heartland, shrivelled and died under Roman misrule in the 4th and 3rd centuries BC, northern Etruria, colonyed by Romans, became more prosperous, and important new cities appeared: Lucca, Pisa, Florence, and to a lesser extent, Siena. After the fall of Rome, these cities limped through the various wars and barbarian invasions; only Lucca, the late Roman and Gothic capital of Etruria, managed to keep out the nastiest brutes of all, the bloodthirsty Lombards (AD 568). By this time, low-lying Florence had practically disappeared, while the remnants of the other towns survived under the control of local barons, or occasionally under their bishops. Feudal warfare and marauding became endemic.

By the 9th century, things were looking up. Florence had re-established itself, and built its famous baptistry. The old counts of Lucca extended their power to become counts of Tuscany, under the Attoni family, lords of Canossa. As the leading power in the region, they made themselves a force in European affairs. In 1077, the great Countess Matilda, allied with the Pope, humbled Emperor Henry IV at Canossa—the famous 'penance in the snow' during the struggles over investiture. Perhaps most important of all was the growth of the maritime city of Pisa, which had cleverly allied itself with the Normans as they devoured all of south Italy and Sicily, at the expense of the Byzantines and Muslims. Pisa's bold conquests over Muslim fleets in Palermo and North Africa made her the mistress of the western Mediterranean by the 1080s, giving Tuscany a new window on the world, building wealth through trade and inviting new cultural influences from France, Byzantium and the Muslim world.

Medieval *Comuni*

By 1000, with the new millennium, all of northern Italy was poised to rebuild the civilization that had been lost centuries before. In Tuscany, as elsewhere, increasing trade had created a rebirth of towns, each doing its best to establish its independence from local nobles or bishops, and to increase its influence at the expense of its neighbours. Thus a thousand minor squabbles were played out

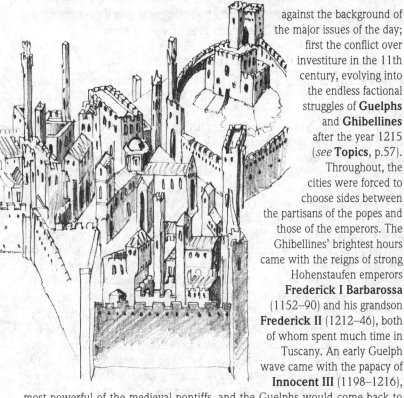

against the background of the major issues of the day; first the conflict over investiture in the 11th century, evolving into the endless factional struggles of **Guelphs** and **Ghibellines** after the year 1215 (*see* **Topics**, p.57). Throughout, the cities were forced to choose sides between the partisans of the popes and those of the emperors. The Ghibellines' brightest hours came with the reigns of strong Hohenstaufen emperors **Frederick I Barbarossa** (1152–90) and his grandson **Frederick II** (1212–46), both of whom spent much time in Tuscany. An early Guelph wave came with the papacy of **Innocent III** (1198–1216), most powerful of the medieval pontiffs, and the Guelphs would come back to dominate Tuscany after the invasion of Charles of Anjou in 1261. Florence and Lucca were mainstays of the Guelphs, while Pisa and Siena usually supported the Ghibellines.

In truth, it was every city for itself. By 1200, most towns had become free *comuni*; their imposing public buildings can be seen to this day. All the trouble they caused fighting each other (at first with citizen militias, later increasingly with the use of hired *condottieri*) never troubled the booming economy. Florence and Siena became bankers to all Europe, beginning their fierce rivalry—Florentine bankers collaborated to finance kings and other great men with Europe's first gold coin, the florin (1252); Sienese bankers raked in huge profits by holding the leases and collecting the debts for the popes and the Curia. Great building programmes went up, beginning with the Pisa cathedral complex in the 1100s, while the now tamed and urbanized nobles built fantastical skyscraper skylines of tower-fortresses in the cities. Above all, it was a great age for culture, the age of Dante

(b. 1265) and Giotto (b. 1266). Another feature of the time was the 13th-century religious revival, dominated by the figure of **St Francis of Assisi**.

The Background of the Renaissance

Florence, biggest and richest of the Tuscan cities, increased its influence all through the late 1200s and 1300s, in spite of the humiliating defeat at the hands of Siena in 1260 at the battle of Monteaperti (all of the Sienese captains were for razing arrogant Florence, once and for all, but their commander, a turn-coat Florentine gangster named Farinata degli Uberti, surprised all by standing up and announcing that, even if he had to stand alone, he would defend Florence for as long as he lived. The Sienese were so surprised they let Farinata have his way and lost their chance of ever becoming *numero uno* in Tuscany). The Sienese had cause to regret their clemency nine years later, when Florence soundly defeating them at the battle of Colle Val d'Elsa; in 1298, they even took most of Siena's business away when the city's leading bank, the Tavola dei Bonsignori, collapsed. Left the undisputed financial centre of Europe, Florence gobbled up Prato and Pistoia, and finally won a seaport with the capture of declining Pisa in 1406. This set the stage for the relative political equilibrium of Tuscany during the early Renaissance, the height of the region's wealth and artistic achievement.

The **Wars of Italy**, beginning in 1494, put an end to Renaissance tranquillity. Florence was once more lost in its internal convolutions, twice expelling the **Medici**, while French and Spanish Imperial armies marched over Tuscany. When the dust had cleared, the Republic of Siena, which had dared to side with the French, had been extinguished, and with the rest of Tuscany came under the rule of the Grand Duke **Cosimo I** (1537–74), the Medici propped on a newly-made throne by Emperor Charles V. Only the tiny duchy of Lucca kept its independence.

The Modern Era

Though maintaining a relative independence, Tuscany had little to say in Italian affairs. Cosimo I proved a vigorous ruler, though his successors gradually declined in ability. By 1600 it didn't matter. The total exhaustion of the Florentine economy kept pace with that of the Florentine imagination. By 1737, when the Medici dynasty became extinct, Tuscany was one of the torpid backwaters of Europe. It had no chance to decide its own destiny; the European powers agreed to bestow Tuscany on the House of Lorraine, cousins to the Austrian Habsburgs. Surprisingly enough, the Lorraines proved able and popular rulers, especially during the rule of the enlightened, progressive Peter Leopold (1765–90).

The languor of Lorraine was interrupted by Napoleon, who invaded central Italy twice and established a Kingdom of Etruria from 1801 to 1807. Austrian rule then returned after 1815, continuing the series of well-meaning, intelligent Grand Dukes. By now, however, the Tuscans and the rest of the Italians wanted something better. In the tumults of the Risorgimento, one of the greatest and kindest of the Lorraines, Leopold II, saw the writing on the wall and allowed himself to be overthrown in 1859. Tuscany was almost immediately annexed to the new Italian kingdom. Since then, the region has followed the history of modern Italy. The head start that Tuscany gained under the Lorraine dukes allowed it to keep up economically with northern Italy. Florence had a brief moment of glory (1865–70) as capital of Italy, awaiting the capture of Rome. Since then, the biggest affair was World War II; the Germans based their Gothic Line on the Arno, blowing up all but one of Florence's bridges, and all of Pisa's.

Stendhal once wrote: 'Ask the Florentines what they are, and they will respond by telling you what they were.' Tuscany's separate sense of identity has spared it most of the convulsions that have shaken Italy in recent years—the corruption and bribe scandals have mostly happened elsewhere, in Sicily, Rome and Milan. The Tuscany of the 1990s has concentrated on safeguarding its tremendous patrimony of art and architecture while trying to create new jobs and investments to re-ignite the spark that made the region the wealthiest and most innovative in Europe 800 years ago.

Art and Architecture

Etruscans, Romans and Dark Ages

Although we have no way of knowing what life was like for the average Etruscan, their tomb sculptures and paintings convince us that they were a talented, likeable people. Almost all their art derives from the Greek; the Etruscans built classical temples (unfortunately of wood, with terracotta embellishments, so little survives), carved themselves sarcophagi decorated with scenes from Homer, and painted their pottery in red and black after the latest styles from Athens or Corinth. They excelled at portrait sculpture, and had a remarkable gift for capturing personality, sometimes seriously, though never heroically, often with an entirely intentional humour, and usually the serene smiles of people who truly enjoyed life.

Etruscan art, as in Florence's archaeology museum, is often maddening; some of the works are among the finest productions of antiquity, while others—from the same time and place—are more awkward and childish. Their talent for portraiture, among much else, was carried on by the Romans, and they bequeathed their love of fresco painting to the artists of the Middle Ages and Renaissance, who of course weren't even aware of the debt. After introducing yourself to the art of the

Etruscans, it will be interesting to reconsider all that came later—in Tuscany especially, you will find subtle reminders of this enigmatic people.

After destroying the Etruscan nation, the Romans also began the extinction of its artistic tradition; by the Empire, there was almost nothing left that could be called distinctively Etruscan. Artistically, neither Florence, Siena, Pisa nor Lucca contributed much under the Empire. In the chaos that followed, there was little room for art. What painting survived followed styles current in Byzantium, a stylization that lingered into the 13th century in Tuscan panel painting.

The Middle Ages

In both architecture and sculpture, the first influence came from the north. Lombard masons filled Tuscany with simple Romanesque churches, although it wasn't long before two distinctive Tuscan forms emerged: the Pisan style, characterized by blind rows of colonnades, black and white zebra stripes, and lozeng shaped designs; and the 'Tuscan Romanesque' which developed around Florence, notable for its use of dark and light marble patterns and simple geometric patterns, often with intricate mosaic floors to match (the Baptistry and San Miniato in Florence are the chief examples). In the cities in between, such as Lucca, there are interesting variations on the two different styles, often carrying an element like stripes or arcades to remarkable extremes. Siena was perhaps the most receptive to Gothic styles from the north, but adapted to an Italian sensibility that produced not only churches but unique public buildings such as the Palazzo Comunale, all of good siena-coloured brick.

From the large pool of talent working on Pisa's great cathedral complex in the 13th century emerged Italy's first great sculptor, **Nicola Pisano**, whose Baptistry pulpit, with its naturalistic figures, derived from ancient reliefs, and finally broke away from the stiff hieratic figures of Byzantium. His even more remarkable son, **Giovanni Pisano**, prefigures Donatello in the expressiveness of his statues and the vigour of his pulpits; his façade of Siena cathedral, though altered, is a unique work of art. **Arnolfo di Cambio**, a student of Nicola Pisano, became chief sculptor-architect of Florence during its building boom in the 1290s, designing its cathedral and Palazzo Vecchio with a hitherto unheard-of scale and grandeur.

Painting at first lagged behind the new realism and more complex composition of sculpture. The first to depart from Byzantine stylization, at least according to the account in Vasari's *Lives of the Artists* (*see* **Topics**, p.55), was **Cimabue**, in the late 1200s, who forsook Greek forms for a more 'Latin' or 'natural' way of painting. Cimabue found his greatest pupil, **Giotto**, as a young shepherd, chalk-sketching sheep on a piece of slate. Brought to Florence, Giotto soon eclipsed his master's fame (artistic celebrity being a recent Florentine invention) and achieved the greatest advances on the road to the new painting with a plain, rather severe approach that shunned Gothic prettiness while exploring new ideas in composition and expressing psychological depth in his subjects. Even more importantly, Giotto through his intuitive grasp of perspective was able to go further than any previous artist in representing his subjects as actual figures in space. In a sense Giotto actually invented space; it was this, despite his often awkward and graceless draughtsmanship, that so astounded his contemporaries. His followers, **Taddeo** and **Agnolo Gaddi** (father and son), **Giovanni da Milano**, and **Maso di Banco** filled Florence's churches with their own interpretations of the master's style. In the latter half of the 1300s, however, there also appeared the key figure of **Andrea Orcagna**, the most important Florentine sculptor, painter and architect of his day. Inspired by the more elegant style of **Andrea Pisano**'s Baptistry doors, Orcagna broke away from the simple Giottesque forms for a more elaborate, detailed style in his sculpture, while the fragments of his frescoes that survive have a vivid dramatic power which undoubtedly owes something to the time of the Black Death and social upheavals in which they were painted.

Siena never produced a Vasari to chronicle its accomplishments, though they were considerable; in the 13th and 14th centuries, Siena's Golden Age, the city's artists, like its soldiers, rivalled and often surpassed those of Florence. For whatever reason, it seemed purposefully to seek inspiration in different directions from Florence; at first from central Italian styles around Spoleto, then, with prosperity and the advent of **Guido da Siena** in the early 1200s, to the more elegant line and colour of Byzantium. Guido's work paved the way for the pivotal figure of **Duccio di Buoninsegna**, the catalyst who founded the essentials of Sienese art by uniting the beauty of Byzantine line and colour with the sweet finesse and new human warmth of western Gothic art. With Duccio's great followers **Pietro** and **Ambrogio Lorenzetti** and **Simone Martini**, the Sienese produced an increasingly elegant and rarefied art, almost oriental in its refined stylization. They were less innovative than the Florentines, though they brought the 'International Gothic' style—flowery and ornate, with all the bright tones of May—to its highest form in Italy. Simone Martini introduced the Sienese manner to Florence in the early 1400s, where it influenced most notably the work of **Lorenzo Monaco**, **Masolino**, and the young goldsmith and sculptor, **Ghiberti**.

The Renaissance

Under the assaults of historians and critics over the last two centuries, the term 'Renaissance' has become a vague and controversial word. Nevertheless, however you choose to interpret this rebirth of the arts, and whatever dates you assign to it, Florence inescapably takes the credit for it. This is no small claim. Combining art, science and humanist scholarship into a visual revolution that often seemed pure sorcery to their contemporaries, a handful of Florentine geniuses taught the Western eye a new way of seeing. Perspective seems a simple enough trick to us now, but its discovery determined everything that followed, not only in art, but in science and philosophy as well.

Leading what scholars used self-assuredly to call the 'Early Renaissance' is a triumvirate of three geniuses: **Brunelleschi**, **Donatello** and **Masaccio**. Brunelleschi, neglecting his considerable talents in sculpture for architecture and science, not only built the majestic dome of Florence cathedral, but threw the Pandora's box of perspective wide open by mathematically codifying the principles of foreshortening. His good friend Donatello, the greatest sculptor since the ancient Greeks, inspired a new generation of both sculptors and painters to explore new horizons in portraiture and three-dimensional representation. The first painter to incorporate Brunelleschi and Donatello's lessons of spatiality, perspective and expressiveness was the young prodigy Masaccio, who along with his master Masolino painted the famous Brancacci Chapel in the Carmine, studied by nearly every Florentine artist down to Michelangelo.

The new science of architecture, sculpture and painting introduced by this triumvirate ignited an explosion of talent unequalled before or since—a score of masters, most of them Tuscan, each following the dictates of his own genius to create a remarkable range of themes and styles. To mention only the most prominent: **Lorenzo Ghiberti**, who followed Donatello's advice on his second set of Baptistry doors to cause a Renaissance revolution; **Leon Battista Alberti**, who took Brunelleschi's ideas to their most classical extreme in architecture, creating new forms in the process; **Paolo Uccello**, one of the most provocative of artists, who according to Vasari drove himself bats with the study of perspective and the possibilities of illusionism; **Piero della Francesca**, who explored the limits of perspective and geometrical forms to create the most compelling, haunting images of the quattrocento; **Fra Angelico**, who combined Masaccio's innovations and International Gothic colours and his own deep faith to create the most purely spiritual art of his time; **Andrea del Castagno**, who made use of perspective to create monumental, if often restless figures.

And still more: **Benozzo Gozzoli**, whose enchanting springtime colours and delight in detail are a throwback to the International Gothic; **Antonio** and **Piero Pollaiuolo**, sons of a poultryman, whose new, dramatic use of line and form, often violent and writhing, would be echoed in Florentine Mannerism; **Fra Filippo Lippi**, a monk like Fra Angelico but far more earthly, the master of lovely Madonnas, teacher of his talented son **Filippino Lippi**; **Domenico Ghirlandaio**, whose gift of easy charm and flawless technique made him society's fresco painter; **Andrea del Verrocchio**, who could cast in bronze, paint, or carve with perfect detail; **Perugino** (Pietro Vannucci) of Umbria, who painted the stillness of his native region into his landscapes and taught the young Raphael; and finally **Sandro Botticelli**, whose highly intellectual, but lovely and melancholy, mythological paintings are in a class of their own.

Some of Donatello's gifted followers were **Agostino di Duccio**, **Benedetto da Maiano**, **Desiderio da Settignano**, **Antonio** and **Bernardo Rossellino**, **Mino da Fiesole** and perhaps most famously, **Luca della Robbia**, who invented the coloured terracottas his family spread throughout Tuscany. The leading sculptor in Siena, **Jacopo della Quercia**, also left a number of works elsewhere, especially the lovely tomb of Ilaria del Carretto in Lucca (1408). A few decades later Lucca produced its own great sculptor, **Matteo Civitali**.

The 'Early Renaissance' came to a close near the end of the 1400s with the advent of **Leonardo da Vinci**, whose unique talent in painting, only one of his hundred interests, challenged the certainty of naturalism with a subtlety and chiaroscuro that approaches magic. One passion, however, obsessed the other great figure of the 'High Renaissance', **Michelangelo Buonarroti**: his consummate interest was the human body, at first graceful and serene as in most of his Florentine works, and later, contorted and anguished after he left for Rome.

Mannerism

Michelangelo left in Florence the seeds for the bold, neurotic avant-garde art that has come to be known as Mannerism. The first conscious 'movement' in Western art can be seen as a last fling amid the growing intellectual and spiritual exhaustion of 1530s Florence, conquered once and for all by the Medici. The Mannerists' calculated exoticism and exaggerated, tortured poses, together with the brooding self-absorption of Michelangelo, are a prelude to Florentine art's remarkably abrupt turn into decadence and prophesy its final extinction. Foremost among the Mannerist painters are two surpassingly strange characters, **Jacopo Pontormo** and **Rosso Fiorentino**, who were not in such great demand as the coldly classical **Andrea del Sarto** and **Bronzino** who were consummate perfectionists of the brush, both much less intense and demanding. There were also charming reactionaries working at the same time, especially **Il Sodoma** and **Pinturicchio**, both of whom left their best works in Siena. In sculpture **Giambologna** and to a lesser extent **Bartolommeo Ammannati** specialized in virtuoso *contrapposto* figures, each one more impossible than the last. In sculpture, too, Siena shied away from Florentine exaggeration, as in the work of Jacopo della Quercia's chief disciple, **Vecchietta**.

With the advent of Giambologna and Ammannati's contemporary, **Giorgio Vasari**, Florentine art lost almost all imaginative and intellectual content, and became a virtuoso style of interior decoration perfectly adaptable to saccharine holy pictures, portraits of newly enthroned dukes, or absurd mythological fountains and ballroom ceilings. In the cinquecento, with plenty of money to spend and a long Medici tradition of patronage to uphold, this tendency soon got out of hand. Under the reign of Cosimo I, indefatigable collector of *pietra dura* tables, silver and gold gimcracks, and exotic stuffed animals, Florence gave birth to yet another artistic phenomenon—one that modern critics call kitsch.

The Rest Compressed

In the long, dark night of later Tuscan art a few artists stand out—the often whimsical architect and engineer, **Buontalenti**; **Pietro Tacca**, Giambologna's pupil with a taste for the grotesque; the charming Baroque fresco master **Pietro da Cortona**. Most of Tuscany, and particularly Florence, chose to sit out the Baroque—almost by choice, it seems, and we can race up to the 19th century for the often delightful 'Tuscan Impressionists' or *Macchiaioli* ('Splatterers'; the best collection is in the Modern Art section of the Pitti Palace); and in the 20th century **Ottone Rosai**, the master of the quiet Florentine countryside.

Artists' Directory

This includes the principal architects, painters and sculptors whose works you'll see in Florence, Siena, Pisa and Lucca. The works listed are far from exhaustive, bound to exasperate partisans of some artists and do scant justice to the rest, but we have tried to include only the best and most representative works.

Agostino di Duccio (Florence, 1418–81). A precocious and talented sculptor, his best work is in the Malatesta Temple at Rimini. Sometimes seems a precursor of Art Deco (**Florence**, Bargello).

Alberti, Leon Battista (1404–72). Architect, theorist, and writer. His greatest contribution was recycling the classical orders and the principles of Vitruvius into Renaissance architecture. (**Florence**, Palazzo Rucellai, façade of S. Maria Novella, SS. Annunziata).

Allori, Alessandro (1535–1607). Florentine Mannerist painter, prolific follower of Michelangelo and Bronzino (**Florence**, SS. Annunziata, S. Spirito, Spedale degli Innocenti).

Ammannati, Bartolommeo (1511–92). Florentine architect and sculptor. Restrained, elegant in building (**Florence**, S. Trínita bridge, courtyard of Pitti Palace); neurotic, twisted Mannerist sculpture (**Florence**, Fountain of Neptune, Villa di Castello).

Andrea del Castagno (*c.* 1423–57). Precise, dry Florentine painter, one of the first and greatest slaves of perspective (**Florence**, Uffizi, S. Apollonia, SS. Annunziata).

Angelico, Fra (or Beato) (Giovanni da Fiesole, *c.* 1387–1455). Monk first and painter second, but still one of the great visionary artists of the Renaissance (**Florence**, S. Marco—spectacular Annunciation and many more; Fiesole, S. Domenico).

Arnolfo di Cambio (born in Colle di Val d'Elsa; *c.* 1245–1302). Architect and sculptor, pupil of Nicola Pisano and a key figure in his own right. Much of his best sculpture is in Rome, but he changed the face of Florence as main architect to the city's greatest building programme of the 1290s (**Florence**, cathedral and Palazzo Vecchio).

Baldovinetti, Alesso (Florence, 1425–99). A delightful student of Fra Angelico who left few tracks; most famous for fresco work in **Florence** (SS. Annunziata, Uffizi, S. Niccolò sopr'Arno, S. Miniato).

Bandinelli, Baccio (1488–1559). Florence's comic relief of the late Renaissance; a supremely serious man, vain, and so awful it hurts—of course he was court sculptor to Cosimo I (**Florence**, Piazza della Signoria and SS. Annunziata).

Beccafumi, Domenico (*c.* 1486–1551). Sienese painter; odd mixture of Sienese conservatism and Florentine Mannerism (**Siena**, Pinacoteca).

Benedetto da Maiano (**Florence**, 1442–97). Sculptor, specialist in narrative reliefs (**Florence**, S. Croce, Strozzi Palace, Bargello).

Bigarelli, Guido (13th century). Talented, travelling sculptor from Como, who excelled in elaborate and sometimes bizarre pulpits (**Pisa**, Baptistry).

Botticelli, Sandro (Florence, 1445–1510). Though technically excellent in every respect, and a master of both line and colour, there is more to Botticelli than this. Above every other quattrocento artist, his works reveal the imaginative soul of the Florentine Renaissance, particularly the great series of mythological paintings (**Florence**, Uffizi). Later, a little deranged and under the spell of Savonarola, he reverted to intense, though conventional religious paintings. Almost forgotten in the philistine 1500s and not rediscovered until the 19th century, many of his best works are probably lost (**Florence**, Accademia).

Bronzino, Agnolo (1503–72). Virtuoso Florentine Mannerist with a cool, glossy hyper-elegant style, at his best in portraiture; a close friend of Pontormo (**Florence**, Palazzo Vecchio, Uffizi, S. Lorenzo, SS. Annunziata).

Brunelleschi, Filippo (1377–1446). Florentine architect of genius, credited in his own time with restoring the ancient Roman manner of building—but really deserves more credit for developing a brilliant new approach of his own (**Florence**, Duomo cupola, Spedale degli Innocenti, S. Spirito, S. Croce's Pazzi Chapel, S. Lorenzo). He was also one of the first theorists on perspective.

Buontalenti, Bernardo (1536–1608). Late Florentine Mannerist architect and planner, better known for his Medici villas (**Artimino**, also the fascinating grotto in **Florence's** Boboli Gardens, the Belvedere Fort and Uffizi Tribuna).

Cellini, Benvenuto (1500–71). Goldsmith and sculptor. Though he was a native of the city of Florence, Cellini spent much of his time in Rome. In 1545 he came to work for Cosimo I and to torment Bandinelli (*Perseus*, Loggia dei Lanzi; also works in the Bargello). As famed for his catty *Autobiography* as for his sculpture.

Cimabue (*c.* 1240–1302). Florentine painter credited by Vasari with initiating the 'rebirth of the arts'; one of the first painters to depart from the stylization of the Byzantine style (**Florence**, mosaics in Baptistry, *Crucifix* in Santa Croce; **Pisa**, cathedral mosaic).

Civitali, Matteo (Lucca, *c.* 1435–1501). Sweet yet imaginative, apparently self-taught. He would be much better known if all of his works weren't in Lucca (**Lucca**, cathedral, Guinigi Museum).

Coppo di Marcovaldo (Florence, active *c.* 1261–75). Another very early painter, as good as Cimabue if not as famous (**Siena**, S. Maria dei Servi).

Daddi, Bernardo (active 1290–*c.* 1349). Master of delicate altarpieces (**Florence**, Orsanmichele, S. Maria Novella's Spanish chapel).

Desiderio da Settignano (Florence, 1428/31–61). Sculptor, follower of Donatello (**Florence**, S. Croce, Bargello, S. Lorenzo).

Dolci, Carlo (1616–86). Unsurpassed Baroque master of the 'whites of their eyes' school of religious art (**Florence**, Palazzo Corsini).

Domenico di Bartolo (*c.* 1400–46). An interesting painter, well out of the Sienese mainstream; the unique naturalism of his art is a Florentine influence. His best work are the frescoes of 15th-century hospital life in the Spedale di Santa Maria della Scala in **Siena**.

Domenico Veneziano (Florence 1404–61). Painter, taught Piero della Francesca; master of perspective with few surviving works (**Florence**, Uffizi).

Donatello (Florence, 1386–1466). The greatest Renaissance sculptor appeared as suddenly as a comet at the beginning of Florence's quattrocento. Never equalled in technical ability, expressiveness, or imaginative content, his works influenced Renaissance painters as much as sculptors. A prolific worker, and a quiet fellow who lived with his mum, Donatello was the perfect model of the early Renaissance artist—passionate about art, self-effacing, and a little eccentric (**Florence**, Bargello—the greatest works including the original *St George* from Orsanmichele, *David* and *Cupid-Atys*, also at San Lorenzo, Palazzo Vecchio, and the Cathedral Museum; **Siena**, cathedral).

Duccio di Buoninsegna (d. 1319). One of the first and greatest Sienese painters, Duccio was to Sienese art what Giotto was to Florence; ignored by Vasari, though his contributions to the new visual language of the Renaissance are comparable to Giotto's (**Siena**, parts of the great *Maestà* in the Cathedral Museum, also Pinacoteca; **Florence**, altarpiece in the Uffizi).

Francesco di Giorgio Martini (Siena, 1439–1502). Architect—mostly of fortresses—sculptor and painter, his works are scattered all over Italy. (**Siena**, Pinacoteca Nazionale and bronze angels in the cathedral).

Franciabigio (1482–1525). Most temperamental of Andrea del Sarto's pupils but only mildly Mannerist (**Florence**, Poggio a Caiano and SS. Annunziata).

Gaddi, Taddeo (*c.* 1300–*c.* 1366). Florentine; most important of the followers of Giotto. He and his son **Agnolo** (d. 1396) contributed some of the finest trecento fresco cycles (notably at S. Croce and S. Ambrogio, **Florence**).

Gentile da Fabriano, Francesco di (*c.*1360–1427). Master nonpareil of the International Gothic style. Best works in the Uffizi, **Florence**.

Gentileschi, Artemisia (1593–1652). Precocious talented daughter of Orazio and likewise a Caravaggist, although unlike her father she concentrated on powerful, more natural images as well as *chiaroscuro* light effects. One of the very few women artists of the period to have a successful, independent career (Uffizi and Pitti gallery, **Florence**).

Gentileschi, Orazio (1563–1639). Sometimes (and more correctly) known as Orazio Lomi, a native of Pisa who went from Mannerism to become a friend and close follower of Caravaggio, although Gentileschi is too much of a refined Tuscan to copy his master's powerful naturalism. In 1626 he settled in England as court painter to Charles I (San Frediano, Santo Stefano, **Pisa**).

Ghiberti, Lorenzo (1378–1455). The first artist to write an autobiography was naturally a Florentine. He would probably be better known had he not spent most of his career working on the two sets of doors for the Florence Baptistry after winning the famous competition of 1401 (also **Florence**, statues at Orsanmichele).

Ghirlandaio, Domenico (Florence, *c.* 1448–94). The painter of the quattrocento establishment, master of elegant fresco cycles in which he painted all the Medici and Florence's banking elite. A great portraitist with a distinctive, dry, restrained style (**Florence**, Ognissanti, S. Maria Novella, S. Trínita, Spedale degli Innocenti).

Giambologna (1529–1608). A Fleming, born Jean Boulogne; court sculptor to the Medici after 1567 and one of the masters of Mannerist virtuosity— also a man with a taste for the outlandish (**Florence**, Loggia dei Lanzi, Bargello, Villa della Petraia; **Pratolino**, the *Appennino*).

Giotto (*c.* 1266–1337). Shepherd boy of the Mugello, discovered by Cimabue, who became the first great Florentine painter—and recognized as such in his own time. Invented an essential and direct approach to portraying narrative fresco cycles, but is even more important for his revolutionary treatment of space and of the human figure (**Florence**, S. Croce, cathedral campanile, Horne Museum, S. Maria Novella).

Giovanni da Milano (14th century). An innovative Lombard inspired by Giotto (**Florence**, S. Croce).

Giovanni di Paolo (d. 1483). One of the best of the quattrocento Sienese painters; like most of them, a colourful reactionary who continued the traditions of the Sienese trecento (**Siena**, Pinacoteca).

Giovanni di San Giovanni (1592–1633). One of Tuscany's more prolific, but winning Baroque fresco painters (**Florence**, Pitti Palace, Villa della Petraia).

Giuliano da Rimini (active 1350s). Recent studies attribute to this obscure figure the striking blue-green frescoes in the Basilica of San Nicola **Tolentino**.

Gozzoli, **Benozzo** (Florence, d. 1497). Learned his trade from Fra Angelico, but few artists could have less in common. The most light-hearted and colourful of quattrocento artists, Gozzoli created enchanting frescoes at **Florence**, Medici chapel; **Pisa**, Camposanto and Museo di San Matteo.

Guido da Siena (active *c.* 1345–70). Interesting Sienese trecento painter; little is known about his life (**Siena**, Pinacoteca Nazionale and Palazzo Pubblico).

Leonardo da Vinci (1452–1519). We could grieve that Florence's 'universal genius' spent so much time on his scientific interests and building fortifications, and that his meagre artistic output was left unfinished or lost. All that is left in Tuscany is the *Annunciation* and the unfinished *Adoration of the Magi* (**Florence**, Uffizi). As the pinnacle of the Renaissance marriage of science and art, Leonardo requires endless volumes of interpretation. As for his personal life, Vasari records him buying up caged birds in the market-place just to set them free.

Lippi, **Filippino** (Florence, 1457–1504). Son and artistic heir of Fra Filippo. Often seems a neurotic Gozzoli, or at least one of the most thoughtful and serious artists of the quattrocento (**Florence**, S. Maria Novella, S. Maria del Carmine, Badia, Uffizi).

Lippi, **Fra Filippo** (Florence, d. 1469). Never should have been a monk in the first place. A painter of exquisite, ethereal Madonnas, one of whom he ran off with (the model, at least, a brown-eyed nun named Lucrezia). The pope forgave them both. Lippi was a key figure in the increasingly complex, detailed painting of the middle 1400s (**Florence**, Uffizi).

Lorenzetti, Ambrogio (Siena, d. 1348). He could crank out golden Madonnas as well as any Sienese painter, but Lorenzetti was also a great innovator in subject matter and the treatment of landscapes. Created the first and greatest of secular frescoes, the *Allegories of Good and Bad Government* in **Siena's** Palazzo Pubblico, while his last known work, the 1344 *Annunciation* in Siena's Pinacoteca is one of the 14th century's most revolutionary treatments of perspective.

Lorenzetti, Pietro (Siena, d. 1348). Ambrogio's big brother, and also an innovator, standing square between Duccio di Buoninsegna and Giotto; one of the precursors of the Renaissance's new treatment of space (**Siena**, S. Spirito and Pinacoteca Nazionale). Both Lorenzettis seem to have died in Siena during the Black Death.

Lorenzo di Credi (1439–1537). One of the most important followers of Leonardo da Vinci, was always technically perfect if occasionally vacuous (**Florence**, Uffizi).

Lorenzo Monaco (Siena, 1370–1425). A monk at S. Maria degli Angeli in Florence and a brilliant colourist, Lorenzo forms an uncommon connection between the Gothic style of Sienese painting and the new developments in early Renaissance Florence (**Florence**, Uffizi, S. Trínita).

Manetti, Rutilio (1571–1639). Quirky but likeable Baroque painter, the last artist of any standing produced by Siena (**Siena**, San Pietro alle Scale).

Martini, Simone (Siena, d. 1344). Possibly a pupil of Giotto, Martini took the Sienese version of International Gothic to an almost metaphysical perfection, creating luminous, lyrical, and exquisitely drawn altarpieces and frescoes perhaps unsurpassed in the trecento (**Siena**, Palazzo Pubblico; **Pisa**, Museo S. Matteo).

Masaccio (Florence, 1401–c. 1428). Though he died young and left few works behind, this precocious 'shabby Tom' gets credit for inaugurating the Renaissance in painting by translating Donatello and Brunelleschi's perspective onto a flat surface. Also revolutionary in his use of light and shadow, and in expressing emotion in his subjects' faces (**Florence**, S. Maria del Carmine, S. Maria Novella; **Pisa**, Museo S. Matteo).

Maso di Banco (Florence, active 1340s). One of the more colourful and original followers of Giotto (**Florence**, S. Croce).

Masolino (Florence, d. 1447). Perhaps 'little Tom' also deserves much of the credit, along with Masaccio, for the new advances in art at the Carmine in **Florence**; art historians dispute endlessly how to attribute the frescoes. It's hard to tell, for this brilliant painter left little other work behind to prove his case.

Matteo di Giovanni (Siena, 1435–95). One Sienese quattrocento painter who could keep up with the Florentines; a contemporary described him as 'Simone Martini come to life again' (**Siena**, Pinacoteca, S. Agostino, S. Maria delle Neve).

Memmi, Lippo (Siena, 1317–47). Brother-in-law and assistant of Simone Martini (**Siena**, S. Spirito).

Michelangelo Buonarroti (Florence, 1475–1564).
Born in Caprese (now Caprese Michelangelo) into a Florentine family of the minor nobility come down in the world, Michelangelo's early years and training are obscure; he was apprenticed to Ghirlandaio, but showing a preference for sculpture was sent to the court of Lorenzo de' Medici. Nicknamed Il Divino in his lifetime, he was a complex, difficult character, who seldom got along with mere mortals, popes, or patrons. What he couldn't express by means of the male nude in paint or marble, he did in his beautiful but difficult sonnets. In many ways he was the first modern artist, unsurpassed in technique but also the first genius to go over the top (**Florence**, Medici tombs and library in San Lorenzo, three works in the Bargello, the *Pietà* in the Museo del Duomo, *David* in the Accademia, Casa Buonarroti, and his only oil painting, in the Uffizi).

Michelozzo di Bartolomeo (Florence, 1396–1472). Sculptor who worked with Donatello (the tomb in **Florence's** Baptistry), he is better known as the classicizing architect favoured by the elder Cosimo de' Medici (**Florence**, Medici Palace, Chiostro of SS. Annunziata, convent of San Marco).

Mino da Fiesole (Florence, 1429–84). Sculptor of portrait busts and tombs; like the della Robbias a representative of the Florentine 'sweet style' (**Fiesole**, cathedral; **Florence**, Badia, Sant'Ambrogio).

Nanni di Banco (Florence, 1384–1421). Florentine sculptor influenced by the Gothic style (**Florence**, Orsanmichele, Porta della Mandorla).

Orcagna, Andrea (Florence, d. 1368). Sculptor, painter and architect who dominated the middle 1300s in Florence, though greatly disparaged by Vasari, who destroyed much of his work. Many believe he is the mysterious 'Master of the Triumph of Death' of Pisa's Camposanto (**Florence**, Orsanmichele, S. Croce, S. Maria Novella, *Crucifixion* in refectory of S. Spirito, also often given credit for the Loggia dei Lanzi).

Perugino (Pietro Vannucci, Perugia, d. 1523). Perhaps the most distinctive of the Umbrian painters; created some works of genius, along with countless idyllic nativity scenes, each with its impeccably sweet Madonna and characteristic blue-green tinted background (**Florence**, Uffizi, S. Maddalena dei Pazzi, Cenacolo di Foligno).

Piero della Francesca (d. 1492). Painter, born at Sansepolcro, and one of the really unique quattrocento artists. Piero wrote two of the most important theoretical works on perspective, then illustrated them with a lifetime's work reducing painting to the bare essentials: geometry, light and colour. In his best work his reduction creates nothing dry or academic, but magic and almost eerie scenes similar to those of Uccello. And like Uccello or Botticelli, his subjects are often archetypes of immense psychological depth, not to be fully explained now or ever (**Florence**, Uffizi).

Piero di Cosimo (Florence, 1462–1521). Painter better known for his personal eccentricities than his art, which in itself is pretty odd (**Florence**, Uffizi; **Fiesole**, S. Francesco).

Pietro da Cortona (1596–1699). Perhaps the most charming of Tuscan Baroque painters; his best is in Rome, but there are some florid ceilings in the Pitti Palace, **Florence**.

Pinturicchio (Perugia, 1454–1513). This painter got his name for his use of gold and rich colours. Never an innovator, but as an absolute virtuoso in colour, style and grace no one could beat him. Another establishment artist, especially favoured by the popes, and like Perugino he was slandered most vilely by Vasari (**Siena**, Piccolomini Library).

Pisano, Andrea (Pisa, d. 1348). Artistic heir of Giovanni and Nicola Pisano and teacher of Orcagna; probably a key figure in introducing new artistic ideas to **Florence** (Baptistry, south doors).

Pisano, Nicola (Pisa, active *c.* 1258–78). The first great medieval Tuscan sculptor created a little Renaissance all his own, when he adapted the figures and composition of ancient reliefs to make his wonderful pulpit reliefs in **Siena** and **Pisa Baptistry**. His son **Giovanni Pisano** (active *c.* 1265–1314) carried on the tradition, notably in the façade sculptures at **Siena** cathedral (also great relief pulpits in **Pisa** cathedral).

Pollaiuolo, Antonio (Florence, d. 1498). A sculptor, painter and goldsmith whose fame rests on his brilliant, unmistakable line; he occasionally worked with his less gifted brother **Piero** (**Florence**, Uffizi and Bargello).

Pontormo, Jacopo (Florence, 1494–1556). You haven't seen pink and orange until you've seen the work of this determined Mannerist eccentric. After the initial shock, though, you'll meet an artist of real genius, one whose use of the human body as sole means for communicating ideas is equal to Michelangelo's (**Florence**, S. Felicità—his *Deposition*—and Uffizi; **Poggio a Caiano**; **Carmignano**).

Quercia, Jacopo della (Siena, 1374–1438). Sculptor who learned his style from Pisano's cathedral pulpit; one of the unsuccessful contestants for the Florence baptistry doors. Maybe Siena's greatest sculptor, though his most celebrated work, that city's Fonte Gaia, is now ruined (**Lucca**, cathedral, *tomb of Ilaria del Carretto*; **Siena**, Baptistry).

Raphael (1483–1520). Born in Urbino in the Marches, Raphael spent time in Città di Castello, Perugia, and Florence before establishing himself in Rome. Only a few of the best works of this High Renaissance master remain in **Florence** in the Pitti Palace and Uffizi.

Robbia, Luca della (Florence, 1400–82). Greatest of the famous family of sculptors; he invented the coloured glaze for terracottas that we associate with the della Robbias, but was also a first-rate relief sculptor (the *cantorie* in **Florence's** cathedral museum). His nephew **Andrea** (1435–1525; best work **Lucca**, San Frediano) and Andrea's son **Giovanni** (1469–1529; best work **Florence**, Certosa del Galluzzo) carried on the blue and white terracotta sweet style in innumerable buildings across Tuscany.

Rosselli, Cosimo (1434–1507). Competent middle of the road Renaissance painter who occasionally excelled (**Florence**, S. Ambrogio).

Rossellino, Bernardo (1409–64). Florentine architect best known as the architect-planner of the new town of Pienza. Also a sculptor (**Florence**, S. Croce, S. Miniato; **Siena**, Palazzo Piccolomini). His brother **Antonio Rossellino** (1427–79) was also a talented sculptor (**Florence**, S. Croce).

Rossi, Vicenzo de' (1525–87). Florentine Mannerist sculptor of chunky male nudes (**Florence**, Palazzo Vecchio).

Rosso Fiorentino (Giovanni Battista di Jacopo, 1494–1540). Florentine Mannerist painter, perhaps very much underrated. He makes a fitting complement to Pontormo, both for his tortured soul and for the exaggerations of form and colour he used to create gripping, dramatic effects. Fled Italy after the Sack of Rome and worked for Francis I at Fontainebleau. (**Florence**, Uffizi, S. Lorenzo and SS. Annunziata).

Salviati, Francesco (Florence, 1510–63). Friend of Vasari and a similar sort of painter—though much more talented. Odd perspectives and decoration, often bizarre imagery (**Florence**, Palazzo Vecchio and Uffizi).

Sangallo, Giuliano da (Florence, 1443–1516). Architect of humble origins who became the favourite of Lorenzo de' Medici. Had an obsession, inherited from Alberti, with making architecture conform to philosophical principles (**Poggio a Caiano**; **Florence**, S. Maddalena dei Pazzi).

Il Sassetta (Stefano di Giovanni; active *c.* 1390–1450). One of the great Sienese quattrocento painters, though still working in a style the Florentines would have found hopelessly reactionary; an artist who studied Masaccio but preferred the Gothic elegance of Masolino. His masterpiece, the Borgo Sansepolcro polyptych, is dispersed through half the museums of Europe.

Signorelli, Luca (Cortona, d. 1523). A rarefied Umbrian painter and an important influence on Michelangelo. Imaginative, forceful compositions, combining geometrical rigour with a touch of unreality, much like his master Piero della Francesca (**Florence**, Uffizi and Horne Museum).

Il Sodoma (Giovanni Antonio Bazzi, 1477–1549). Born in Piedmont, but a Sienese by choice, he was probably not the libertine his nickname, and Vasari's biography, suggest. An endearing, serene artist, who usually eschewed Mannerist distortion, he became rich through his work, then blew it all feeding his exotic menagerie and died in the poorhouse (**Siena**, Pinacoteca and S. Domenico).

Spinello Aretino (late 14th century–1410). A link between Giotto and the International Gothic style; imaginative and colourful in his compositions (**Florence**, S. Miniato; **Siena**, Palazzo Pubblico).

Tacca, Pietro (1580–1640). Born in Carrara, pupil of Giambologna and one of the best early Baroque sculptors (**Florence**, Piazza SS. Annunziata fountain).

Taddeo di Bartolo (1363–1422). The greatest Sienese painter of the late 1300s—also the least conventional; never a consummate stylist, he often shows a remarkable imagination in composition and treatment of subject matter (**Siena**, Palazzo Pubblico, Pinacoteca Nazionale, S. Spirito).

Talenti, **Francesco** (early 14th century). Chief architect of **Florence** cathedral and campanile after Arnolfo di Cambio and Giotto; his son **Simone** made the beautiful windows in **Orsanmichele** (and perhaps the Loggia dei Lanzi) in **Florence**.

Torrigiano, **Pietro** (1472–1528). Florentine portrait sculptor, famous for his work in Westminster Abbey in London and for breaking Michelangelo's nose (**Siena**, cathedral).

Uccello, **Paolo** (1397–1475). No artist has ever been more obsessed with the possibilities of artificial perspective. Like Piero della Francesca, he used the new technique to create a magic world of his own; contemplation of it made him increasingly eccentric in his later years. Uccello's provocative, visionary subjects (*Noah* fresco in S. Maria Novella, and *Battle of San Romano* in the Uffizi, **Florence**) put him up with Piero della Francesca and Botticelli as the most intellectually stimulating of quattrocento artists.

Vasari, **Giorgio** (Arezzo, 1511–74). Florentine sycophant, writer and artist; *see* p.55. Also a fair architect (**Florence**, Uffizi, Corridoio, and Fish Loggia).

Il Vecchietta (Lorenzo di Pietro, 1412–80). Sienese painter and sculptor, dry and linear, part Sienese Pollaiuolo and part Donatello; his larger works have a monumentality rare in Sienese art (**Siena**, Loggia della Mercanzia, Baptistry, Ospedale di Santa Maria della Scala).

Verrocchio, **Andrea del** (1435–88). Florentine sculptor who worked in bronze; spent his life trying to outdo Donatello. Mystic alchemist in his spare time, and interestingly enough the master of both Botticelli and Leonardo (Uffizi, S. Lorenzo, Orsanmichele, Palazzo Vecchio, and Bargello, **Florence**).

Masters and Students: the Progress of the Renaissance

The purpose of this chart is to show who learned from whom, an insight into some 300 years of artistic continuity.

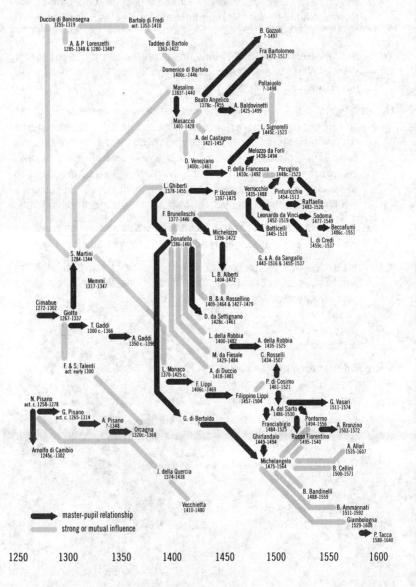

Duccio di Boninsegna 1255-1319
Bartolo di Fredi act. 1353-1410
A. & P. Lorenzetti 1285-1348 & 1280-1348?
Taddeo di Bartolo 1363-1422
B. Gozzoli ?-1497
Domenico di Bartolo 1400c.-1446
Fra Bartolomeo 1472-1517
Masolino 1383?-1440
Beato Angelico 1378c.-1455
Pollaiuolo ?-1498
A. Baldovinetti 1425-1499
Masaccio 1401-1428
A. del Castagno 1421-1457
L. Signorelli 1445c.-1523
D. Veneziano 1400c.-1461
Melozzo da Forlì 1438-1494
P. della Francesca 1410c.-1492
Perugino 1448c.-1523
L. Ghiberti 1378-1455
P. Uccello 1397-1475
Verrocchio 1435-1488
Pinturicchio 1454-1513
Raffaello 1483-1520
F. Brunelleschi 1377-1446
Leonardo da Vinci 1452-1519
Sodoma 1477-1549
Botticelli 1445-1510
Beccafumi 1486c.-1551
Michelozzo 1396-1472
L. di Credi 1459c.-1537
S. Martini 1284-1344
Donatello 1386-1466
G. & A. da Sangallo 1443-1516 & 1455-1537
Memmi 1317-1347
L. B. Alberti 1404-1472
B. & A. Rossellino 1409-1464 & 1427-1479
Cimabue 1272-1302
Giotto 1267-1337
D. da Settignano 1428c.-1461
T. Gaddi 1300 c.-1366
A. Gaddi 1350 c.-1396
L. della Robbia 1400-1482
A. della Robbia 1435-1525
M. da Fiesole 1429-1484
C. Rosselli 1434-1507
F. & S. Talenti act. early 1300
L. Monaco 1370-1425 c.
A. di Duccio 1418-1481
P. di Cosimo 1461-1521
F. Lippi 1406c.-1469
Filippino Lippi 1457-1504
G. Vasari 1511-1574
N. Pisano act. c. 1258-1278
A. del Sarto 1486-1530
G. Pisano act. c. 1265-1314
A. Pisano ?-1348
G. di Bertoldo ?
Franciabigio 1484-1525
Pontormo 1494-1556
A. Bronzino 1503-1572
Orcagna 1320c.-1368
Ghirlandaio 1449-1494
Rosso Fiorentino 1495-1540
A. Allori 1535-1607
Arnolfo di Cambio 1245c.-1302
Michelangelo 1475-1564
B. Cellini 1500-1571
J. della Quercia 1374-1438
B. Bandinelli 1488-1559
B. Ammannati 1511-1592
Vecchietta 1410-1480
Giambologna 1529-1608
P. Tacca 1580-1640

➤ master-pupil relationship
➤ strong or mutual influence

1250   1300   1350   1400   1450   1500   1550   1600

Topics

Galileo Galilei

Death was on everyone's mind when the Great Plague rolled through Italy in 1348. In art, the most striking memories of those harrowing days are the powerful frescoes by the Master of the Triumph of Death in Pisa's Campo Santo; in literature, no account surpasses Boccaccio's introduction to his masterpiece, the *Decameron*, the 'Human Comedy' that complements the *Divine Comedy* of his fellow Florentine.

Boccaccio, the son of a prosperous banker, was the first great writer from the urban middle class. Born either in Florence or in the Florentine town of Certaldo in 1313, he spent much of his youth in the literate, art-loving court of Robert of Anjou in Naples. He returned to Florence shortly before 1348, when the sight of the bodies of plague victims piled in the street sent deep cracks into his belief about the divinely ordered medieval cosmos that he had been reared on and loved in the *Divine Comedy*. Boccaccio's great feat would be to disenchant Dante's world in the most entertaining way possible.

He takes a detached view of the great theatre of life from the very beginning of *The Decameron*. Despite the Church's claims that the plague was 'a punishment signifying God's righteous anger at our iniquitous way of life', Boccaccio notes that in fact it was a highly contagious disease that had come out of the East, and that fate and chance alone seemed to spare some Florentines while others were struck down whether they responded to the plague by praying for deliverance, hiding out, or living riotously as if there would be no tomorrow.

His ten young storytellers gather in Santa Maria Novella and escape the plague for a country villa, where they pass the days by telling tales. These stories sparkle with a secular, spunky vitality and sense of humour that is fresh and new; sex, for the first time in literature, becomes a pleasurable end in itself. Fate and chance, however, decide most of the plots and outcomes of the hundred tales they tell; with few exceptions, the belief in the just outcome of human endeavour is an illusion.

In his old age Boccaccio wrote exclusively in Latin and earned himself a reputation as one of the great humanists of the 14th century, regretting the frivolity of the *Decameron* in his old age. As Giuliano Procacci wrote, 'He put himself in the position of a calmly objective recorder of life's dramas and chances; it was a difficult and exhausting mental standpoint, and a new one, demanding nervous energy and courage. Is it any wonder that Boccaccio too, in his premature old age, should have sought comfort and refuge in study and piety?'

For a century after Boccaccio Florence led the world in humanistic thought. The horrors of the plague were forgotten as victories in diplomacy and the battlefield, a hitherto unknown prosperity, and tremendous strides in architecture, art and science made the city radiate confidence. The fatalism of the *Decameron* seemed unduly pessimistic by the end of the 15th century. The humanists were keenly aware of Florence's special destiny, as described by Leonardo Bruni in his proud, patriotic *Laudatio Florentinae Urbis* or in Coloccio Salutati's 'What city, not merely in Italy but in the whole world, is stronger within the circle of its walls, prouder in palaces, richer in temples, more lovely in buildings...Where is trade richer in its variety, abler in subtle understandings? Where are there more famous men?' Brave new words before the mass neurotic religious revival orchestrated by Savonarola and the return of the wrath of God as the prime mover. Even Pico della Mirandola the most optimistic of humanists, himself fell under the fanatic's spell.

Florence was never the same, and the repercussions were dire: for a city that practically invented humanism to toss its books and art in the proto-Ayatollah's bonfire of the vanities cast long shadows into everyone's future. Don't forget that only in the 20th century has the *Decameron* been translated complete with all the naughty bits.

The First Professional Philistine

Many who have seen Vasari's work in Florence will be wondering how such a mediocre painter should rate so much attention. Ingratiating companion of the rich and famous, workmanlike over-achiever and tireless self-promoter, Vasari was the perfect man for his time. Born in Arezzo, in 1511, a fortunate introduction to Cardinal Silvio Passerini gave him the chance of an education in Florence with the young Medici heirs, Ippolito and Alessandro. In his early years, he became a fast and reliable frescoist gaining a reputation for customer satisfaction—a real innovation in an age when artists were increasingly becoming eccentric prima donnas. In the 1530s, after travelling around Italy on various commissions, he returned to Florence just when Cosimo I was beginning his plans to remake the city in the image of the Medici. It was a marriage made in heaven. Vasari became Cosimo's court painter and architect, with a limitless budget and a large group of assistants, the most prolific fresco machine ever seen in Italy— painting over countless good frescoes of the 1300s along the way.

But more than for his paintings, Vasari lives on through his book, the *Lives of the Artists*, a series of exhaustive biographies of artists. Beginning with Cimabue, Vasari traces the rise of art out of Byzantine and Gothic barbarism, through Giotto and his followers, towards an ever-improving naturalism, finally culminating in the great age of Leonardo, Raphael, and the divine Michelangelo, who not only mastered nature but outdid her. Leon Battista Alberti gets the credit for drafting the first principles of artistic criticism, but it was Vasari who first applied such ideas on a grand scale. His book, being the first of its kind, and containing a mine of valuable information on dozens of Renaissance artists, naturally has had a tremendous influence on all subsequent criticism. Art critics have never really been able to break out of the Vasarian straitjacket.

Much of Vasari's world seems quaint to us now: the idea of the artist as a kind of knight of the brush, striving for Virtue and Glory, the slavish worship of anything that survived from ancient Rome, artistic 'progress' and the conviction that art's purpose was to imitate nature.

But many of Vasari's opinions have had a long and mischievous career in the world of ideas. His blind disparagement of everything medieval—really the prejudice of his entire generation—lived on until the 1800s. His dismissal of Sienese, Umbrian and northern artists—of anyone who was not a Florentine—has not been entirely corrected even today. Vasari was the sort who founded academies, a cheerful conformist who believed in a nice, tidy art that went by the book. With his interior decorator's concept of Beauty, he created a style of criticism in which virtuosity, not imagination, became the standard by which art was to be judged; history offers few more instructive examples of the stamina and resilience of dubious ideas.

A Florentine Puzzle

In a city as visually dry and restrained as Florence, every detail of decoration stands out. In the Middle Ages and Renaissance, Florentine builders combined their passion for geometry with their love of making a little go a long way; they evolved a habit of embellishing buildings with simple geometrical designs. Though nothing special in themselves—most are easily drawn with a compass and straight edge—in the context of Florence they stand out like mystic hieroglyphs, symbols upon which to meditate while contemplating old Florence's remarkable journey through the Western mind.

The city is full of them, incorporated into façades and mosaics, windows and decorative friezes. Here are eight of them, a little exercise for the eye while tramping the hard pavements of Florence. Your job is to find them. Some are really obvious, others obscure. For no. 6 you should be able to find at least three examples (two across the street from each other) and if you're clever you'll find not only no. 5, a rather late addition to the cityscape, but also the medieval work that inspired it. Don't worry too much about the last one. But if you're an art historian or a Florentinophile, it's only fair that you seek out this hard one too. Answers can be found on the last page of the index.

Guelphs and Ghibellines

One medieval Italian writer claimed that the great age of factional strife began with two brothers of Pistoia, named Guelf and Gibel. Like Cain and Abel, or Romulus and Remus, one murdered the other, starting the seemingly endless troubles that to many seemed a God-sent plague, meant to punish the proud and wealthy Italians for their sins. Medieval Italy may in fact have been guilty of every sort of jealousy, greed and wrath, but most historians trace the beginnings of this party conflict to two great German houses, Welf and Waiblingen.

To the Italians, what those barbarians did across the Alps meant little; the chroniclers pinpoint the outbreak of the troubles to the year 1215, when a politically prominent Florentine noble named Buondelmonte dei Buondelmonti was assassinated by his enemies while crossing the Ponte Vecchio. It was the tinder that ignited a smouldering quarrel all over Italy, particularly in Tuscany. The atmosphere of contentious city-states, each with its own internal struggles between nobles, the rich merchant class and the commons, crystallized rapidly into parties. In the beginning, at least, they stood for something. The Guelphs, largely a creation of the newly-wealthy bourgeois, were all for free trade and the rights of the free cities; the Ghibellines from the start were the party of the German emperors, nominal overlords of Italy who had been trying to assert their control ever since the days of Charlemagne. Naturally, the Guelphs found their protector in the emperors' bitter temporal rivals, the popes. This brought a religious angle into the story, especially with the advent of the heretical Emperor Frederick II.

Everything about this convoluted history confirms the worst suspicions of modern behaviourist scientists. Before long, the labels Guelph and Ghibelline ceased to have any meaning. In the 13th and 14th centuries, the emperors and their Ghibelline allies helped the church root out heretical movements like the Patarenes, while the popes schemed to destroy the liberty of good Guelph cities, and incorporate them into the Papal State. In cities, like Florence, where the

Guelphs won a final victory, they themselves split into parties, battling with the same barbaric gusto. Black was the Ghibelline colour, white the Guelph, and cities arranged themselves like squares on a chessboard. When one suffered a revolution and changed from Guelph to Ghibelline, or vice-versa, of course its nearest enemies would soon change the other way. Often the public buildings give us a clue as to the loyalties of a city in any given time. Simple, squared crenellations are Guelph (as in Florence's Palazzo Vecchio, or in a score of other town halls); ornate 'swallow-tail' crenellations are the mark of the Ghibelline. Siena was a generally Ghibelline city, but its great Palazzo Pubblico was built with square crenellations during a Guelph interlude under the rule of the Council of the Nine.

The English, like many uninvolved European nations, looked on all this with bewilderment. Edmund Spenser, in glosses to his *Shepheards' Calendar* (1579), wrote this fanciful etymology: 'when all Italy was distraicte into the Factions of the Guelfes and the Gibelins, being two famous houses in Florence, the name began through their great mischiefes and many outrages, to be so odious or rather dreadfull in the peoples eares, that if theyr children at any time were frowarde and wanton, they would say to them the Guelfe or the Gibeline came. Which words nowe from them (as may thinge els) be come into our vsage, and for Guelfes and Gibelines, we say *Elfes* and *Goblins*.'

The Heresy of Science

The starry Galileo, with his woes

Childe Harold's Pilgrimage, Byron

Frankly, Galileo deserves better in his home town of Pisa than the dusty bits and bobs displayed at his old address, now loftily known as the Domus Galileana. Born in 1564, son of a blue-blooded Pisan mother and Vincenzo Galilei, a brilliant musical theorist whose ideas gave rise to the invention of opera, the young Galileo was nurtured in the lofty intellectual environment of Late Renaissance Tuscany. His father introduced him early to the Medici academies, where he was drawn irresistibly to mathematics from an early age—one thing he did was calculate the precise dimensions of the circles of hell, according to the information provided in the *Inferno*. His real mission, however, as it developed over the years, was far more serious: to overthrow Aristotelian science.

Before Galileo was appointed professor of mathematics at Pisa (1589) and Padua (1592), all scientific learning came from books arguing for or against Aristotle's writings. Galileo taught that you could learn much more by studying nature, and in the process became the founding father of experimental physics—he showed that air had weight by weighing a pig's bladder full of air, then puncturing it to show the difference; he defied the Aristotelian concept of opposites in nature by inventing the principle of the thermometer, demonstrating that hot and cold were merely relative aspects of the same phenonemon, which he called temperature; he debunked Aristotle's precept that heavy bodies had a tendency to fall and light ones rise with his famous experiment at the Leaning Tower, when he dropped variously sized balls and bullets and weights simultaneously and they all hit the ground at once. His celebrated experiment with the inclined plane established the first principles of dynamics.

In 1609, news reached Galileo of a Dutch spectacle-maker who had made a pipe with lenses that enabled one to see ships far out to sea. Galileo quickly put together one of his own with a convex lens in front, and a concave lens behind, that he soon improved to make the first telescope—with a magnification power of 30. Even so, when Galileo pointed his instrument at the heavens, it was an incredible revelation: he was the first man ever to see the surface of the moon, the moons of Jupiter, what appeared to be ears on Saturn (his telescope was too weak to discern the rings), the phases of Venus, the uncountable stars in the Milky Way, and sunspots, although the last discovery permanently affected his eyesight. In 1610 he published all his discoveries in a little book called *Sidereus Nuncius*, 'The Starry Messenger'. He became an instant celebrity. Cosimo de' Medici made him Grand Ducal mathematician and philosopher with a salary of a thousand florins a year. The Jesuit astronomers in Rome received him as a hero; a certain Cardinal Barberini looked through Galileo's magic tube and wrote him a fulsome eulogy called, prophetically, 'Dangerous Flattery'.

Galileo (along with many Jesuits) had long believed in Copernicus's *De revolutionibus Orbium Coelestium* (1543) and its theory that the earth revolved around the sun, a belief confirmed in Galileo's mind by his discoveries through the telescope. However, by 1615, so many theologians thought that the theory was inconsistent with Biblical teachings that, in spite all of Galileo's energetic efforts in Rome, *De revolutionibus* was placed on the Index of prohibited books until it could be amended with a statement that it was an unproved hypothesis. The Holy Office then forbade Galileo from teaching it.

When the same Cardinal Barberini who wrote the eulogy to Galileo became Pope Urban VIII in 1624, the 60-year-old scientist thought the chance had come to break the silence that was killing him. He went to Rome and asked to discuss Copernicanism in a new book, emphasizing to the Pope that it was to the glory of the Catholic Church to promote learning. Urban permitted Galileo to write, as long as he fairly stated the case for the Ptolemaic system as well, because, the Pope added, as God was not constrained by human logic, any arguments based on what appeared to be physical evidence to the human mind were fallible.

Galileo spent the next five years writing (in Italian, instead of the usual Latin) the first ever book of popular science, a witty and lively masterpiece called the *Dialogue on the Two Chief Systems of the World*, in which three characters (a Copernican, an Aristotelian and an amateur) discuss the two systems, with the Copernican clearly winning the argument. At the end of the book the trapped Aristotelian falls back on the Pope's argument, to which all the characters submit. Although at first greeted with enthusiasm, the *Dialogue* was soon withdrawn by the Pope, who believed he had been duped. A special commission he set up agreed with him: that although Galileo followed the Pope's conditions to the letter, he was advocating an unproved hypothesis as the truth and disobeying the order from the Holy Office of 17 years ago not to teach Copernicanism. In the famous Inquisition trial he was accused of relapsing—a much worse crime than heresy—and made to recant his belief that the earth moved, although, legend has it, with the famous aside:'*eppur si muove*!', 'But it does move!'

The Inquisition was lenient with the old man, first placing him under house arrest in Siena, and then in his villa at Arcetri, just outside Florence. There he wrote (or rather dictated, as he was going blind) his even more influential *The Two New Sciences* (1638), on the mathematical study of motion and the strength of materials, a work that became the basis for the study of physics as a science. He died in 1642, if not a martyr, at least a hero to science.

Yet as much as Galileo accomplished, his conviction that mechanistic explanations were exclusively true created a whole new set of idols, holy scriptures and diehard Inquisitors in the name of a new god called Science. It is no small irony that, 350 years after Galileo's death, most physicists today would admit that actually the Pope had been right all along; the more they find out, the more the universe shows itself unconstrained by human logic, stranger not only than anyone ever thought, but stranger than anyone could even imagine.

Hermes Trismegistus

As you pass through the main portal of Siena cathedral, the figure before you on the famous marble pavement comes as a surprise—Hermes Trismegistus, someone rarely seen in art, though a mysterious protagonist in a great undercurrent of Renaissance thought. 'Thrice-great Hermes', mythical author of a series of mystic philosophical dialogues from the 2nd century AD, had a profound influence on Greek and Arabic thought, gradually becoming associated (correctly or not) with the Egyptian god Thoth, inventor of writing and father of a deep mystical tradition that continues to this day. In the 1400s, the Hermetic writings were introduced in the West, largely the work of Greek scholars fleeing the Ottoman conquest of Constantinople and Trebizond. They made quite a splash. Marsilio Ficino, the Florentine humanist and friend of Cosimo de' Medici, completed the first Latin translation of the Hermetic books in 1471—Cosimo specifically asked him to put off his translations of Plato to get this more important work finished!

To the men of the Renaissance, Hermes was a real person, an Egyptian prophet, who lived in the time of Moses and was perhaps his teacher. They saw, revealed in the Hermetic books, an ancient, natural religion, prefiguring Christianity and complementary to it—and in fact much more fun than Christianity, for the magical elements in it were entirely to the taste of neo-Platonists like Ficino. From a contemporary point of view, the recovery of Hermes Trismegistus was one of the main intellectual events of the century, a century that witnessed a tremendous revival of natural magic, alchemy and astrology.

The memorable Hermes in Siena is surrounded by a bevy of ten sybils: those of Cumae and Tivoli (the Italians), Delphi, Libya, the Hellespont, Phrygia and the rest. These ladies, part of a pan-Mediterranean religious tradition even older than Hermes Trismegistus, are far more common in Tuscan religious iconography (as in the Baptistry and Santa Trínita in Florence, or most famously on Michelangelo's Sistine Chapel ceiling), for the belief that they all foretold the birth of Christ.

Leaning Towers

This isn't a subject the Italians like to discuss. They will be happy to sell you all the little plastic souvenirs you want of the most celebrated of the species—the one in Pisa—but a mention of the other dozens of listing landmarks scattered around Bologna, Venice, Ravenna, Rovigo and Rome makes them uneasy. Italians, of course, rightfully think of themselves as the most skilled engineers on this planet. They built the Roman roads and aqueducts, the Pantheon, the domes of Florence cathedral and St Peter's, the biggest in the world. They invented concrete. Today their *autostrade* zoom through mile-long tunnels and skim over deep valleys on stilts, remarkable *tours de force* of engineering that would make the Romans proud. They have built more railway tunnels, perhaps, than the rest of Europe put together. Why can't they keep their towers from drooping?

The key to the answer is in Pisa, where the campanile stands 54.5m high and is 4.5m out of true. The greatest lean is in the first three storeys of the tower; above, there is an attempt to curve the tower back towards perpendicular by slightly changing the pitch of the columns and raising the galleries on the lower side. From the beginning, nearly everyone swallowed Vasari's explanation for this: that the architects, Guglielmo and Bonanno, noticed the subsidence in the foundations once the third storey had been completed, and endeavoured to right the tilt.

Yet for centuries there has been a dark undercurrent of thought that claims Pisa's tower was intentionally built to lean. Goethe thought so, and architects who have carefully measured the foundation stones came to the same conclusion. There is damning technical evidence in the change in the lengths of the colonnades, most noticeable at the top storey, that would have only been necessary to a tower meant to tilt, not one that was being corrected after accidental subsidence; the line of the soffit of the staircase has been measured to show a deliberate slope meant to throw the weight of the campanile off the overhanging side.

A certain Professor Goodyear, who wrote over a hundred years ago, exposed the whole business as what he called 'symmetrophobia'—not really a fear of the symmetrical, but more a disdain for it. Italy's medieval master builders, not yet squeezed into the Renaissance straitjacket of monumental symmetry, could still be playful now and then, and had the subtle skill to build a token in stone to remind all who saw it that life itself is full of growth and curves and spirals and energy and that nothing alive comes in those uniform straight lines, squares and true circles that were all too soon to dominate architecture in the West.

The Italians of today do not like this explanation any better; they brusquely reject any suggestion that their ancestors could have been tempted away from the perpendicular on a whim. You can judge for yourself at Pisa—that campanile simply would not look right without its tilt.

Trends in Taste

> *I took a quick walk through the city to see the Duomo and the Battistero. Once more, a completely new world opened up before me, but I did not wish to stay long. The location of the Boboli Gardens is marvellous. I hurried out of the city as quickly as I entered it.*

Goethe, on Florence in *Italian Journey*

Goethe, the father of the Italian Grand Tour, on his way from Venice to Rome, did not have much time for the city that likes to call itself 'The Capital of Culture'. Like nearly every traveller in the 18th and early 19th centuries, he knew nothing of Giotto, Masaccio, Botticelli, or Piero della Francesca; it was Roman statues that wowed him, the very same ones that the modern visitor passes in the corridors of the Uffizi without a second glance. Shelley managed to write pages on his visits to the museum without mentioning a single painting.

Some Tuscan attractions never change—the Leaning Tower, Michelangelo's *David*, the villas, the gardens and the cheap wine. Others have gone through an amazing rise or fall in popularity, thanks in part to John Ruskin, whose *Mornings in Florence* introduced the charms of the Romanesque architecture, Giotto, and the masters of the trecento; for him Orcagna was the master of them all (but in the 18th century, the Giottos in Santa Croce were whitewashed over, while many works of Orcagna had been destroyed earlier, by Vasari). Botticelli went from total obscurity in the 18th century to become the darling of the Victorians. Livorno and Viareggio on the coast, and Bagni di Lucca near the Garfagnana, used to have thriving English colonies—no more. But Tuscany itself used to be a very different place, where they used to play a betting game called *pallone*, somewhere between lawn tennis and jai alai; where in 1900 a herd of 150 camels, introduced by Grand Duke Ferdinand II in 1622, roamed the Pisan Park of San Rossore; where, as Robert and Elizabeth Browning found, the rent for a palazzo used to be laughably cheap.

But the story of the Venus de' Medici is perhaps the most instructive. The statue is a pleasant, if unremarkable Greek work of the 2nd century BC, but for two centuries it was Florence's chief attraction; the minute visitors arrived in Florence they would rush off to gaze upon her; those prone to write gushed rapturously of her perfect beauty. Napoleon kidnapped her for France, asking the great neoclassical sculptor Canova to sculpt a replacement; afterwards the Venus was one of the things Florence managed to get back, though her reign was soon to be undermined—Ruskin called her an 'uninteresting little person'. Since then she has stood forlornly in the Tribunale of the Uffizi, unnoticed and unloved.

Some things don't change. Over a hundred years after Goethe's blitz tour of Florence, Aldous Huxley had no time for the city, either: 'We came back through Florence and the spectacle of that second-rate provincial town with its repulsive Gothic architecture and its acres of Christmas card primitives made me almost sick. The only points about Florence are the country outside it, the Michelangelo tombs, Brunelleschi's dome, and a few rare pictures. The rest is simply dung when compared to Rome.'

Tuscany on Wheels

Tuscans have always loved a parade, and to the casual reader of Renaissance history, it seems they're forever proceeding somewhere or another, even to their own detriment—during outbreaks of plague, holy companies would parade through an afflicted area, invoking divine mercy, while in effect aiding the spread of the pestilence. They also had a great weakness for allegorical parade floats. During the centuries of endless war each Tuscan city rolled out its war chariot or battle wagon, called the *Carroccio*, invented by a Milanese bishop in the 11th century. A *Carroccio*, drawn by six white oxen, was a kind of holy ship of state in a hay cart; a mast held up a crucifix while a battle standard flew from the yard-arm, there was an altar for priests to say mass during the battle and a large bell to send signals over the din to the armies. The worst possible outcome of a battle was to lose one's *Carroccio* to the enemy, as Fiesole did to Florence. One is still in operation, in Siena, rumbling out twice a year for the Palio.

Medieval clerical processions, by the time of Dante, became melded with the idea of the Roman 'triumph' (*trionfo*); in Purgatory, the poet finds Beatrice triumphing with a cast of characters from the Apocalypse. Savonarola wrote of a *Triumph of the Cross*; Petrarch and Boccaccio wrote allegorical triumphs of virtues, love and death. More interesting, however, are the secular Roman-style Triumphs which were staged by the Medici, especially at Carnival (the name of which, according to Burckhardt, comes from a cart, the pagan *carrus navalis*, the ship of Isis, launched every 5 March to symbolize the reopening of navigation). You can get a hint of their splendour from the frescoes at Poggio a Caiano; the best artists of the day would be commissioned to design the decorations—two particularly famous *trionfi* in Florence celebrated the election of the Medici Pope Leo X.

Two lovely memories of Florence's processions remain. One is Gozzoli's fairy-tale frescoes in the chapel of the Medici palace, of the annual procession staged by the Compagnia de' Re Magi, the most splendid and aristocratic of pageants. The other comes from the Florentine Carnival, famous for its enormous floats, in which scenes from mythology were portrayed to songs and music. One year, for the masque of Bacchus and Ariadne, Lorenzo de' Medici composed the loveliest Italian poem to come out of the Renaissance, with the melancholy refrain:

Quanto è bella giovinezza,	*How fair is youth,*
Che si fugge tuttavia!	*How fast it flies away!*
Chi vuol esser lieto, sia:	*Let him who will, be merry:*
Di doman non c'è certezza.	*Of tomorrow nothing is certain.*

Florence

Fine balm let Arno be;
The walls of Florence all of silver rear'd,
And crystal pavements in the public way ...

14th-century madrigal by Lapo Gianni

'*Magari!*'—If only!—the modern Florentine would add to this
vision, to this city of art and birthplace of the Renaissance, built by
bankers and merchants whose sole preoccupation was making
more florins. The precocious capital of Tuscany began to slip into
legend back in the 14th century, during the lifetime of Dante; it
was noted as different even before the Renaissance, before
Boccaccio, Masaccio, Brunelleschi, Donatello, Leonardo da Vinci,
Botticelli, Michelangelo, Machiavelli, the Medici...

> *This city of Florence is well populated, its good air a*
> *healthy tonic; its citizens are well dressed, and its women*
> *lovely and fashionable, its buildings are very beautiful, and*
> *every sort of useful craft is carried on in them, more so*
> *than any other Italian city. For this many come from dis-*
> *tant lands to see her, not out of necessity, but for the*
> *quality of its manufactures and arts, and for the beauty*
> *and ornament of the city.*

Dino Compagni in his *Chronicle* of 1312

According to the tourist office, in 1993, 681 years after Dino, a
grand total of over 2,300,000 Americans, Germans, French,
Britons (the top four groups) as well as Spanish, Brazilians,
Egyptians, and some 800,000 Italians spent at least one night in a
Florentine hotel. Some, perhaps, had orthodontist appointments.
A large percentage of the others came to inhale the rarefied air of
the cradle of Western civilization, to gaze at some of the loveliest
things made by mortal hands and minds, to walk the streets of new
Athens, the great humanist 'city built to the measure of man'.
Calling Florence's visitors 'tourists', however, doesn't seem quite
right; 'tourism' implies pleasure, a principle alien to this dour,
intellectual, measured town; 'pilgrims' is perhaps the better word,
cultural pilgrims who throng the Uffizi, the Accademia, the
Bargello to gaze upon the holy mysteries of our secular society,
to buy postcards and replicas, the holy cards of our day.

Someone wrote a warning on a wall near Brunelleschi's Santo Spirito, in the Oltrarno: 'Turista con mappa/alla caccia del tesoro/ per finire davanti a un piatto/di spaghetti al pomodoro' (Tourist with a map, on a treasure hunt, only to end up in front of a plate of spaghetti with tomato sauce). Unless you bring the right attitude, Florence can be as disenchanting as cold spaghetti. It only blossoms if you apply mind as well as vision, if you go slowly and do not let the art bedazzle until your eyes glaze over in dizzy excess (a common complaint, known in medical circles as the Stendhal syndrome). Realize that loving and hating Florence at the same time may be the only rational response. It is the capital of contradiction; you begin to like it because it goes out of its way to annoy.

Florentine Schizophrenia

Dante's *Vita Nuova*, the autobiography of his young soul, was only the beginning of Florentine analysis; Petrarch who was the introspective 'first modern man', was a Florentine born in exile; Ghiberti was the first artist to write an autobiography, Cellini wrote one of the most readable; Alberti invented art criticism; Vasari invented art history; Michelangelo's personality, in his letters and sonnets, looms as large as his art. In many ways Florence broke away from the medieval idea of community and invented the modern concept of the individual, most famously expressed by Lorenzo de' Medici's friend, Pico della Mirandola, whose *Oration on the Dignity of Man* tells us what the God on the Sistine Chapel ceiling was saying when he created Adam: '...And I have created you neither celestial nor terrestrial, neither mortal nor immortal, so that, like a free and able sculptor and painter of yourself, you may mould yourself entirely in the form of your choice.'

To attempt to understand Florence, remember one historical constant: no matter what the issue, the city always takes both sides, vehemently and often violently, especially in the Punch and Judy days of Guelphs and Ghibellines. In the 1300s this was explained by the fact that the city was founded under the sign of Mars, the war god; but in medieval astronomy Mars is also connected with Aries, another Florentine symbol and the time of

Dante

spring blossoms. (The Annunciation, at the beginning of spring, was Florence's most important festival.) One of the city's oldest symbols is the lily (or iris), flying on its oldest gonfalons. Perhaps even older is its *marzocco*, originally an equestrian statue of Mars on the Ponte Vecchio, later replaced by Donatello's grim lion.

Whatever dispute rocked the streets, Great Aunt Florence often expressed her schizophrenia in art, floral Florence versus stone Florence, epitomized by the irreconcilable differences between the two most famous works of art in the city: Botticelli's graceful, enigmatic *Primavera* and Michelangelo's cold perfect *David*. The 'city of flowers' seems a joke; it has nary a real flower, nor even a tree, in its stone streets; indeed, all effort has gone into keeping nature at bay, surpassing it with geometry and art. And yet the Florentines were perhaps the first since the Romans to discover the joys of the countryside. The rough, rusticated stone palaces, like fortresses or prisons, hide charms as delightful as Gozzoli's frescoes in the Palazzo Medici. Luca della Robbia's dancing children and floral wreaths are contemporary with the naked, violent warriors of the Pollaiuolo brothers; the writhing, quarrelsome statuary in the Piazza della Signoria is sheltered by the most delicate and beautiful loggia imaginable.

After 1500, all of the good, bad and ugly symptoms of the Renaissance peaked in the mass fever of Mannerism. Then, drifting into a debilitating twilight of *pietra dura* tables, gold gimcracks, and interior decoration, Florence gave birth to the artistic phenomenon known as kitsch—the Medici Princes' chapel is an early kitsch classic, still one of the heaviest baubles in the solar system. Since then, worn out perhaps, or embarrassed, this city built by merchants has kept its own counsel, expressing its argumentative soul in overblown controversies about traffic, art restoration, and the undesirability of fast-food counters and cheap pensions. We who find her fascinating hope she some day comes to remember her proper role, bearing the torch of culture instead of merely collecting tickets for the culture torture.

History

The identity of Florence's first inhabitants is a matter of dispute. There seems to have been some kind of settlement along the Arno long before the Roman era, perhaps as early as 1000 BC; the original founders may have been either native Italics or Etruscans. Throughout the period of Etruscan dominance, the village on the river lived in the shadow of *Faesulae*—Florence's present-day suburb of Fiesole was then an important city, the northernmost member of the Etruscan Dodecapolis. The Arno river cuts across central Italy like a wall. This narrow stretch of it, close to the mountain pass over to Emilia, was always the most logical place for a bridge.

Roman Florence can claim no less a figure than **Julius Caesar** for its founder. Like so many other Italian cities, the city began as a planned urban enterprise in an underdeveloped province; Caesar started it as a colony for his army veterans in 59 BC. The origin of the name—so suggestive of springtime and flowers—is another mystery. First it was *Florentia*, then *Fiorenza* in the Middle Ages, and finally *Firenze*. One guess is that its foundation took place in April, when the Romans were celebrating the games of the Floralia.

The original street plan of *Florentia* can be seen today in the neat rectangle of blocks between Via Tornabuoni and Via del Proconsolo, between the Duomo and Piazza della Signoria. Its Forum occupied roughly the site of the modern Piazza della Repubblica, and the outline of its amphitheatre can be traced in the oval of streets just west of Piazza Santa Croce. Roman *Florentia* never really imposed itself on the historian. One writer mentions it as a *municipia splendidissima*, a major town and river crossing along the Via Cassia, connected to Rome and the thriving new cities of northern Italy, such as Bononia and Mediolanum (Bologna and Milan). At the height of Empire, the municipal boundaries had expanded out to Via de' Fossi, Via S. Egidio, and Via de' Benci. Nevertheless, Florentia did not play a significant role either in the Empire's heyday or in its decline.

After the fall of Rome, Florence weathered its troubles comparatively well. We hear of it withstanding sieges by the Goths around the year 400, when it was defended by the famous imperial general Stilicho, and again in 541, during the campaigns of Totila and Belisarius; all through the Greek–Gothic wars Florence seems to have taken the side of Constantinople. The Lombards arrived around 570; under their rule Florence was the seat of a duchy subject to the then Tuscan capital of Lucca. The next mention in the chronicles refers to Charlemagne spending Christmas with the Florentines in the year 786. Like the rest of Italy, Florence had undoubtedly declined; a new set of walls went up under Carolingian rule, about 800, enclosing an area scarcely larger than the original Roman settlement of 59 BC. In such times Florence was lucky to be around at all; most likely throughout the Dark Ages the city was gradually increasing its relative importance and strength at the expense of its neighbours. The famous Baptistry, erected some time between the 6th and 9th centuries, is the only important building from that troubled age in all Tuscany.

By the 1100s, Florence was the leading city of the County of Tuscany. **Countess Matilda**, ally of Pope Gregory VII against the emperors, oversaw the construction of a new set of walls in 1078, this time coinciding with the widest Roman-era boundaries. Already the city had recovered all the ground lost during the Dark Ages, and the momentum of growth did not abate. New walls were needed again in the 1170s, to enclose what was becoming one of the largest cities in Europe. In this period, Florence owed its growth and prosperity largely to the textile industry—weaving and 'finishing' cloth not only from Tuscany but wool shipped from as far afield as Spain and England. The capital gain from this trade, managed by the *Calimala* and the *Arte della Lana*, Florence's richest guilds, led naturally to an even more profitable business—banking and finance.

The Florentine Republic Battles with the Barons

In 1125, Florence once and for all conquered its ancient rival Fiesole. Wealth and influence brought with them increasing political responsibilities. Externally the city often found itself at war with one or other of its neighbours. Since Countess Matilda's death in 1115, Florence had become a self-governing *comune*, largely independent of the emperor and local barons. The new city republic's hardest problems, however, were closer to home. The nobles of the county, encouraged in their anachronistic feudal behaviour by representatives of the imperial government, proved irreconcilable enemies to the new merchant republic, and Florence spent most of the 12th century trying to keep them in line. Often the city actually declared war on a noble clan, as with the Alberti, or the Counts of Guidi, and razed their castles whenever they captured one. To complicate the situation, nobles attracted by the stimulation of urban life—not to mention the opportunities for making money there—often moved their entire families into Florence itself. They brought their country habits with them, a boyish eagerness to brawl with their neighbours on the slightest pretext, and a complete disregard for the laws of the *comune*. Naturally, they couldn't feel secure without a little urban castle of their own, and before long Florence, like any prosperous Italian city of the Middle Ages, featured a remarkable skyline of hundreds of tower-fortresses, built as much for status as for defence. Many were over 60m in height. It wasn't uncommon for the honest citizen to come home from a hard day's work at the bank, hoping for a little peace and quiet, only to find siege engines parked in front of the house and a company of bowmen commandeering the children's bedroom.

But just as Florence was able to break the power of the rural nobles, those in the town also eventually had to succumb. The last tower-fortresses were chopped down to size in the early 1300s. But even without the nobles, the Florentines found new ways to keep the pot boiling. The rich merchants who dominated the government, familiarly known as the *popolari grossi*, resorted to every sort of murder and mayhem to beat down the demands of the lesser guilds, the *popolari minuti*, for a fair share of the wealth; the two only managed to settle their differences when confronted by murmurs of discontent from what was then one of Europe's largest urban proletariats. But even beyond simple class issues, the city born under the sign of Mars always found a way to make trouble for itself. Not only did Florentines pursue the Guelph–Ghibelline conflict with greater zest than almost any Tuscan city; according to the chronicles of the time, they actually started it. In 1215, men of the Amidei family murdered a prominent citizen named Buondelmonte de' Buondelmonti over a broken engagement, the spark that touched off the factionalist struggles first in Florence, then quickly throughout Italy.

Guelphs and Ghibellines

In the 13th-century, there was never a dull moment in Florence. Guelphs and Ghibellines, often more involved with some feud between noble families than with real political issues, cast each other into exile and confiscated each other's property with every change of the wind. Religious strife occasionally pushed politics off the front page. In the 1240s, a curious foreshadowing of the Reformation saw Florence wrapped up in the **Patarene heresy**. This sect, closely related to the Albigensians of southern France, was as obsessed with the presence of Evil in the world as John Calvin—or Florence's own future fire-and-brimstone preacher, Savonarola. Exploiting a streak of religious eccentricity that has always seemed to be present in the Florentine psyche, the Patarenes thrived in the city, even electing their own bishop. The established Church was up to the challenge; St Peter Martyr, a bloodthirsty Dominican, led his armies of axe-wielding monks to the assault in 1244, exterminating almost the entire Patarene community.

In 1248, with help from Emperor Frederick II, Florence's Ghibellines booted out the Guelphs—once and for all, they thought, but two years later the Guelphs were back, and it was the Ghibellines' turn to pack their grips. The new Guelph regime, called the *primo popolo*, was for the first time completely in the control of the bankers and merchants. It passed the first measures to control the privileges of the turbulent, largely Ghibelline nobles, and forced them all to chop the tops off their tower-fortresses. The next decades witnessed a series of wars with the Ghibelline cities of Tuscany—Siena, Pisa and Pistoia, not just by coincidence Florence's habitual enemies. Usually the Florentines were the aggressors, and more often than not fortune favoured them. In 1260, however, the Sienese, reinforced by Ghibelline exiles from Florence and a few imperial cavalry, destroyed an invading Florentine army at the **Battle of Monteaperti**. Florence was temporarily at the Ghibellines' mercy. Only the refusal of Farinata degli Uberti, the leader of the exiles, to allow the city's destruction kept the Sienese from putting it to the torch—a famous episode recounted by Dante in the *Inferno*. (In a typical Florentine gesture of gratitude, Dante found a home for Uberti in one of the lower circles of hell.)

In Florence, a Ghibelline regime under Count Guido Novello made life rough for the wealthy Guelph bourgeoisie. As luck would have it, though, only a few years later the Guelphs were back in power, and Florence was winning on the battle-field again. The new Guelph government, the *secondo popolo*, earned a brief respite from factional strife. In 1289, Florence won a great victory over another old rival, Arezzo. This was the **Battle of Campaldino**, where the Florentine citizen army included young Dante Alighieri. In 1282, and again in 1293, Florence tried to clean up an increasingly corrupt government with a series of reforms. The 1293 *Ordinamenti della Giustizia* once and for all excluded the nobles from the important political offices. By now, however, the real threat to the Guelph merchants' rule did no come so much from the nobility, which had been steadily falling behind in wealth and power over a period of two centuries, but from the lesser guilds, which had been completely excluded from a share of the power, and also from the growing working class who were employed in the textile mills and the foundries.

Despite all the troubles, the city's wealth and population grew tremendously throughout the 1200s. Its trade contacts spread across Europe, and crowned heads from London to Constantinople found Florentine bankers ready to float them a loan. About 1235 Florence minted modern Europe's first gold coin, the *florin*, which soon became a standard currency across the continent. By 1300 Florence counted over 100,000 souls—a little cramped, even inside the vast new circuit of walls built by the *comune* in the 1280s. It was not only one of the largest cities in Europe, but certainly one of the richest. Besides banking, the wool trade was also booming: by 1300 the wool guild, the *Arte della Lana*, had over 200 large workshops in the city alone.

Naturally, this new opulence created new possibilities for culture and art. Florence's golden age began perhaps in the 1290s, when the *comune* started its tremendous programme of public buildings—including the Palazzo della Signoria and the cathedral; important religious structures, such as Santa Croce, were under way at the same time. Cimabue was the artist of the day; Giotto was just beginning, and his friend Dante was hard at work on the *Commedia*.

As in so many other Italian cities, Florence had been developing its republican institutions slowly and painfully. At the beginning of the *comune* in 1115, the leaders were a class called the *boni homines*, made up mostly of nobles. Only a few decades later, these were calling themselves *consules*, evoking a memory of the ancient Roman republic. When the Ghibellines took over, the leading official was a *podestà* appointed by the Emperor. Later, under the Guelphs, the *podestà* and a new officer called the *capitano del popolo* were both elected by the citizens. With the reforms of the 1290s Florence's republican constitution was perfected—if that is the proper word for an arrangement that satisfied few citizens and guaranteed lots of trouble for the future. Under the new dispensation, power was invested in the council of the richer guilds, the *Signoria*; the new Palazzo della Signoria was designed expressly as a symbol of their authority, replacing the old Bargello, which had been the seat of the *podestà*. The most novel feature of the government, designed to overcome Florence's past incapacity to avoid violent factionalism, was the selection of officials by lot from among the guild members. In effect, politics was to be abolished.

Business as Usual: Riot, War, Plagues and Revolution

Despite the reforms of the *Ordinamenti*, Florence found little peace in the new century. As if following some strange and immutable law of city-state behaviour, no sooner had the Guelphs established total control than they themselves split into new factions. The radically anti-imperial **Blacks** and the more conciliatory **Whites** fought each other through the early 1300s with the same fervour they both had once exercised against the Ghibellines. The Whites, who included Dante among their partisans, came out losers when the Blacks conspired with the pope to bring Charles of Valois' French army into Florence; almost all the losing faction were forced into exile in 1302. Some of them must have sneaked back, for the chronicles of 1304 record the Blacks trying to burn them out of their houses with incendiary bombs, resulting in a fire that consumed a quarter of the city.

Beginning in 1313, Florence was involved in a constant series of inconclusive wars with Pisa, Lucca and Arezzo, among others. In 1325, the city was defeated and nearly destroyed by the great Lucchese general **Castruccio Castracani** (*see* **Lucca**). Castruccio died of a common cold while the siege was already under way, another example of Florence's famous good luck, but unfortunately one of the last.

The factions may have been suppressed, but fate had found some more novel disasters for the city. One far-off monarch did more damage to Florence than its Italian enemies had ever managed—King Edward III of England, who in 1339 found it expedient to repudiate his foreign debts. Florence's two biggest banks, the Bardi and the Peruzzi, immediately went bust, and the city's standing as the centre of international finance was gravely damaged.

If anything was constant throughout the history of the republic, it was the oppression of the poor. The ruling bankers and merchants exploited their labour and gave them only the bare minimum in return. In the 14th century, overcrowding, undernourishment and plenty of rats made Florence's poorer neighbourhoods a perfect breeding ground for epidemics. Famine, plagues and riots became common in the 1340s, causing a severe political crisis. At one point, in 1342, the Florentines gave over their government to a foreign dictator, Walter de Brienne, the French–Greek 'Duke of Athens'. He lasted only for a year before a popular revolt ended the experiment. The **Black Death** of 1348, which was the background for Boccaccio's *Decameron*, carried off perhaps one half of the population. Coming on the heels of a serious depression, it was a blow from which Florence would never really recover.

In the next two centuries, when the city was to be the great innovator in Western culture, it was already in relative decline, a politically decadent republic with a stagnant economy, barely holding its own among the turbulent changes in trade and diplomacy. For the time being, however, things didn't look too bad. Florence found enough ready cash to buy control of Prato, in 1350, and was successful in a defensive war against expansionist Milan in 1351. Warfare was almost continuous for the last half of the century, a strain on the exchequer but not usually a threat to the city's survival; this was the heyday of the mercenary companies, led by *condottieri* like **Sir John Hawkwood** (Giovanni Acuto), immortalized by the equestrian 'statue' in Florence's cathedral. Before the Florentines made him a better offer, Hawkwood was often in the employ of their enemies.

Throughout the century, the Guelph party had been steadily tightening its grip over the republic's affairs. Despite the selection of officials by lot, by the 1370s the party organization bore an uncanny resemblance to some of the big-city political machines common not so long ago in America. The merchants and the bankers who ran the party used it to turn the Florentine Republic into a profit-making business. With the increasingly limited opportunities for making money in trade and finance, the Guelph ruling class tried to make up the difference by soaking the poor. Wars and taxes stretched Florentine tolerance to breaking point, and finally, in 1378, came revolution. The **Ciompi Revolt** (*ciompi*—wage labourers in the textile industries) began in July, when a mob of workers seized the Bargello. Under the leadership of a wool-carder named Michele di Lando, they executed a few of the Guelph bosses and announced a new, reformed constitution. They were also foolish enough to believe the Guelph magnates when they promised to abide by the new arrangement if only the *ciompi* would go home. Before long di Lando was in exile, and the ruling class firmly back in the seat of power, more than ever determined to eliminate the last vestiges of democracy from the republic.

The Rise of the Medici

In 1393, Florentines celebrated the 100th anniversary of the great reform of the *Ordinamenti*, while watching their republic descend irresistibly into oligarchy. In that year **Maso degli Albizzi** became *gonfaloniere* (the head of the *Signoria*) and served as virtual dictator for many

Medici - coat of arms

years afterwards. The ruling class of merchants, more than a bit paranoid after the Ciompi revolt, were generally relieved to see power concentrated in strong hands; the ascendancy of the Albizzi family was to set the pattern for the rest of the republic's existence. In a poisoned atmosphere of repression and conspiracy, the spies of the Signoria's new secret police hunted down malcontents while whole legions of Florentine exiles plotted against the republic in foreign courts. Florence was almost constantly at war. In 1398 she defeated an attempt at conquest by Giangaleazzo Visconti of Milan. The imperialist policy of the Albizzi and their allies resulted in important territorial gains, including the conquest of Pisa in 1406, and the purchase of Livorno from the Genoese in 1421. Unsuccessful wars against Lucca finally disenchanted the Florentines with Albizzi rule. An emergency *parlamento* (the infrequent popular assembly usually called when a coming change of rulers was obvious) in 1434 decreed the recall from exile of the head of the popular opposition, **Cosimo de' Medici**.

Perhaps it was something that could only have happened in Florence—the darling of the plebeians, the great hope for reform, happened to be the head of Florence's biggest bank. The Medici family had their roots in the Mugello region north of Florence. Their name seems to suggest that they once were pharmacists (later enemies would jibe at the balls on the family arms as 'the pills'). For two centuries they had been active in Florentine politics; many had acquired reputations as troublemakers; their names turned up often in the lists of exiles and records of lawsuits. None of the Medici had ever been particularly rich until **Giovanni di Bicci de' Medici** (1360–1429) parlayed his wife's dowry into the founding of a bank. Good fortune—and a temporary monopoly on the handling of the pope's finances—made the Medici Bank Florence's biggest.

Giovanni had been content to stay on the fringe of politics; his son, **Cosimo** (known in Florentine history as '**il Vecchio**', the 'old man') took good care of the bank's affairs but aimed his sights much higher. His strategy was as old as Julius Caesar—the patrician reformer, cultivating the best men, winning the favour of the poor with largesse and gradually, carefully forming a party under a system specifically designed to prevent such things. In 1433 Rinaldo degli Albizzi had him exiled, but too late; continuing discontent forced his return only a year later, and for the next 35 years Cosimo would be the unchallenged ruler of Florence. Throughout this period, Cosimo occasionally held public office—this was done by lottery, with the electoral lists manipulated to ensure a majority of Medici supporters at all times. Nevertheless, he received ambassadors at the new family palace (built in 1444), entertained visiting popes and emperors, and made all the important decisions. A canny political godfather and usually a gentleman, Cosimo also proved a useful patron to the great figures of the early Renaissance—

including Donatello and Brunelleschi. His father had served as one of the judges in the famous competition for the Baptistry doors, and Cosimo was a member of the commission that picked Brunelleschi to design the cathedral dome.

Cosimo did oversee some genuine reforms; under his leadership Florence began Europe's first progressive income tax, and a few years later the state invented the modern concept of the national debt—endlessly rolling over bonds to keep the republic afloat and the creditors happy. The poor, with fewer taxes to pay, were also happy, and the ruling classes, after some initial distaste, were positively delighted; never in Florence's history had any government so successfully muted class conflict and the desire for a genuine democracy. Wars were few, and the internal friction negligible. Cosimo died in August 1464; his tomb in San Lorenzo bears the inscription *Pater patriae,* and no dissent was registered when his 40-year-old son **Piero** took up the boss's role.

Lorenzo the Magnificent

Piero didn't quite have the touch of his masterful father, but he survived a stiff political crisis in 1466, outmanoeuvring a new faction led by wealthy banker Luca Pitti. In 1469 he succumbed to the Medici family disease, the gout, and his 20-year-old son **Lorenzo** succeeded him in an equally smooth transition. He was to last for 23 years. Not necessarily more 'magnificent' than other contemporary princes, or other Medici, Lorenzo's honorific reveals something of the myth that was to grow up around him in later centuries. His long reign corresponded to the height of the Florentine Renaissance. It was a relatively peaceful time, and in the light of the disasters that were to follow, Florentines could not help looking back on it as a golden age.

As a ruler, Lorenzo showed many virtues. Still keeping up the pretence of living as a private citizen, he lived relatively simply, always accessible to the voices and concerns of his fellow citizens, who would often see him walking the city streets. In the field of foreign policy he was indispensable to Florence and indeed all Italy; he did more than anyone to keep the precarious peninsular balance of power from

Lorenzo de' Medici
(dalla Primavera di Botticelli)

disintegrating. The most dramatic affair of his reign was the **Pazzi conspiracy**, an attempt to assassinate Lorenzo plotted by Pope Sixtus IV and the wealthy Pazzi family, the pope's bankers and ancient rivals of the Medici. In 1478, two of the younger Pazzi attacked Lorenzo and his brother Giuliano during mass at the cathedral. Giuliano was killed, but Lorenzo managed to escape into the sacristy. The botched murder aborted the planned revolt; Florentines showed little interest in the Pazzis' call to arms, and before nightfall most of the conspirators were dangling from the cornice of the Palazzo Vecchio.

Apparently, Lorenzo had angered the pope by starting a syndicate to mine for alum in Volterra, threatening the papal monopoly. Since Sixtus failed to murder Lorenzo, he had to settle for excommunicating him, and declaring war in alliance with King Ferrante of Naples. The war went badly for Florence and, in the most memorable act of his career, Lorenzo walked into the lion's cage, travelling to negotiate with the terrible Neapolitan, who had already murdered more than one important guest. As it turned out, Ferrante was only too happy to dump his papal entanglements; Florence found itself at peace once more, and Lorenzo returned home to a hero's welcome.

In other affairs, both foreign and domestic, Lorenzo was more a lucky ruler than a skilled one. Florence's economy was entering a long, slow decline, but for the moment the banks and mills were churning out just enough profit to keep up the accustomed level of opulence. The Medici Bank, unfortunately, was on the ropes. Partly because of Lorenzo's neglect, the bank came close to collapsing on several occasions—it seems Lorenzo made up the losses with public funds. Culturally, he was fortunate to be nabob of Florence at its most artistically creative period; future historians and Medici propagandists gave him a reputation as an art patron that is entirely undeserved. His own tastes tended towards bric-à-brac, jewellery, antique statues and vases; there is little evidence that he really understood or could appreciate the scores of great artists around him. Perhaps because he was too nearsighted to see anything very clearly, he did not ever commission an important canvas or fresco in Florence (except for Luca Signorelli's mysterious *Pan*, lost in Berlin during the last war). His favourite architect was the hack Giuliano da Sangallo.

The Medici had taken great care with Lorenzo's education; he was brought up with some of the leading humanist scholars of Tuscany for tutors and his real interests were literary. His well-formed lyrics and winsome pastorals have earned him a place among Italy's greatest 15th-century poets; they neatly reflect the private side of Lorenzo, the retiring, scholarly family man who enjoyed life better on one of the many rural Medici estates than in the busy city. In this, he was perfectly in tune with his class and his age. Plenty of Florentine bankers were learning the joys of country life, reading Horace or Catullus in their geometrical gardens and pestering their tenant farmers with well-meant advice.

Back in town, they had thick new walls of rusticated sandstone between them and the bustle of the streets. The late 15th century was the great age of palace building in Florence. Following the example of Cosimo de' Medici, the bankers and merchants erected dozens of palaces (some of the best can be seen around Via Tornabuoni). Each one turns blank walls and iron-barred windows to the street. Historians always note one very pronounced phenomenon of this period— a turning inward, a 'privatization' of Florentine life. In a city that had become a republic only in name, civic interest and public life ceased to matter so much. The very rich began to assume the airs of an aristocracy, and did everything they could to distance themselves from their fellow citizens. Ironically, just at the time when Florence's artists were creating their greatest achievements, the republican ethos, the civic soul that had made Florence great, began to disintegrate.

Savonarola

Lorenzo's death, in 1492, was followed by another apparently smooth transition of power to his son **Piero**. But after 58 years of Medicean quiet and stability, the city was ready for a change. The opportunity for the malcontents came soon enough, when the timid and inept Piero allowed the invading King of France, **Charles VIII**, to occupy Pisa and the Tuscan coast. A spontaneous revolt chased Piero and the rest of the Medici into exile, while a mob sacked the family's palace. A new regime, hastily put together under **Piero Capponi**, dealt more sternly with the French (*see* p.113) and tried to pump some new life into the long-dormant republican constitution.

The Florence that threw out the Medici was a city in the mood for some radical reform. Already, the dominating figure on the political stage was an intense Dominican friar from Ferrara named **Girolamo Savonarola**. Perhaps not surprisingly, this oversophisticated and overstimulated city was also in the mood to be told how wicked and decadent it was, and Savonarola was happy to oblige. A spellbinding revival preacher with a touch of erudition, Savonarola packed as many as 10,000 into the Duomo to hear his weekly sermons, which were laced with political sarcasm and social criticism. Though an insufferable prig, he was also a sincere democrat. There is a story that the dying Lorenzo called Savonarola to his bedside for the last rites, and that the friar refused him absolution unless he 'restored the liberty of the Florentines', a proposal that only made the dying despot sneer with contempt.

Savonarola also talked Charles VIII into leaving Florence in peace. Pisa, however, took advantage of the confusion to revolt, and the restored republic's attempts to recapture it were in vain. Things were going badly. Piero Capponi's death in 1496 left Florence without a really able leader, and Savonarolan extremists became ever more influential. The French invasion and the incessant wars that followed cost the city dearly in trade, while the Medici, now in Rome, intrigued endlessly to destroy the republic. Worst of all, Savonarola's attacks on clerical corruption made him another bitter enemy in Rome—none other than **Pope Alexander VI** himself, the most corrupt cleric who ever lived. The Borgia pope scraped together a league of allies to make war on Florence in 1497.

This war proceeded without serious reverses for either side, but Savonarola was able to exploit it brilliantly, convincing the Florentines that they were on a moral crusade against the hated and dissolute Borgias, Medici, French, Venetians and Milanese. 1497 was undoubtedly the high point of Savonarola's career. The good friar's spies—mostly children—kept a close eye on any Florentines who were suspected of enjoying themselves, and collected books, fancy clothes and works of art for the famous **Bonfire of Vanities**. It was a climactic moment in the history of Florence's delicate psyche. Somehow the spell had been broken; like the deranged old Michelangelo, taking a hammer to his own work, the Florentines gathered the objects that had once been their greatest pride and put them to the torch. The bonfire was held in the centre of the Piazza della Signoria; a visiting Venetian offered to buy the whole lot, but the Florentines had someone hastily sketch his portrait and threw that on the flames, too.

One vanity the Florentines could not quite bring themselves to part with was their violent factionalism. On one side were the *Piagnoni* ('weepers') of Savonarola's party, on the other the party of the *Arrabbiati* ('the angry'), including the gangs of young delinquents who would demonstrate their opposition to piety and holiness by sneaking into the cathedral and filling Savonarola's pulpit with cow dung. A Medicean party was also gathering strength, a sort of fifth column sowing discontent within the city and undermining the war effort. Three times, unsuccessfully, the exiled Medici attempted to seize the city with bands of mercenaries. The Pisan revolt continued, and Pope Alexander had excommunicated Savonarola and was threatening to place all Florence under an interdict. In the long hangover after the Bonfire of Vanities, the Florentines were growing weary of their preacher. When the *Arrabbiati* won the elections of 1498, his doom was sealed. A kangaroo court found the new scapegoat guilty of heresy and treason. After some gratuitous torture and public mockery, the very spot where the Bonfire of Vanities had been held now witnessed a bonfire of Savonarola.

Pope Alexander still wasn't happy. He sent an army under his son, Cesare Borgia, to menace the city. Florence weathered this threat, and the relatively democratic 'Savonarolan' constitution of 1494 seemed to be working out well. Under an innovative idea, borrowed from Venice and designed to circumvent party strife, a public-spirited gentleman named **Piero Soderini** was elected *gonfaloniere* for life in 1502. With the help of his friend and adviser, **Niccolò Machiavelli**, Soderini kept the ship of state on an even keel. Pisa finally surrendered in 1509. Serious trouble returned in 1512, and once more the popes were behind it. As France's only ally in Italy, Florence ran foul of Julius II. Papal and Spanish armies invaded Florentine territory, and after their gruesome sack of Prato, designed specifically to overawe Florence, the frightened and politically apathetic city was ready to submit to the pope's conditions—the expulsion of Soderini, a change of alliance, and the return of the Medici.

The End of the Republic

At first, the understanding was that the Medici would live in Florence strictly as private citizens. But **Giuliano de' Medici**, son of Lorenzo and current leader, soon united the upper classes for a rolling back of Savonarolan democracy. With plenty of hired soldiers to intimidate the populace, a rigged *parlamento* in September 1512 restored Medici control. The democratic Grand Council was abolished; its new meeting hall in the Palazzo Vecchio (where Leonardo and Michelangelo were to have their 'Battle of the Frescoes') was broken up into apartments for soldiers. Soldiers were everywhere, and the Medicean restoration took on the aspect of a police state. Hundreds of political prisoners spent time undergoing torture in the Palazzo Vecchio's dungeons, among them Machiavelli.

Giuliano died in 1516, succeeded by his nephew **Lorenzo, Duke of Urbino**, a snotty young sport with a tyrant's bad manners. Nobody mourned much when syphilis carried him off in 1519, but the family paid Michelangelo to give both Lorenzo and Giuliano fancy tombs. Ever since Giuliano's death, however, the real Medici boss had been not Lorenzo, but his uncle Giovanni, who in that year became **Pope Leo X**. The Medici, original masters of nepotism, had been planning this for years. Back in the 1470s, Lorenzo il Magnifico realized that the surest way of maintaining the family fortunes would be to get a Medici on the papal throne. He had little Giovanni ordained at the age of eight, purchased him a cardinal's hat at 13, and used bribery and diplomacy to help him accumulate dozens of benefices all over France and Italy.

For his easy-going civility (as exemplified in his famous quote: 'God has given us the papacy so let us enjoy it'), and his patronage of scholars and artists, Leo became one of the best-remembered Renaissance popes. On the other side of the coin was his criminal mismanagement of the Church; having learned the advantages of parasitism, the Medici were eager to pass it on to their friends. Upper-class Florentines descended on Rome like a plague of locusts, occupying all

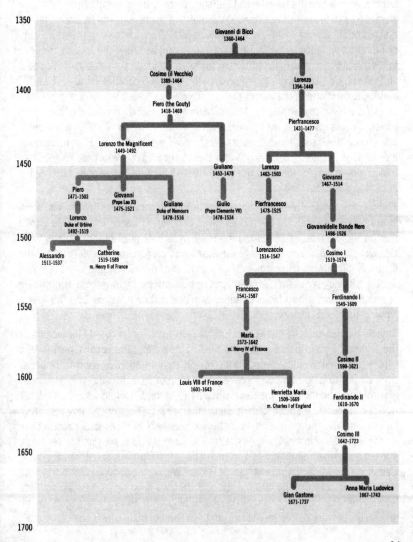

1350	
1400	
1450	
1500	
1550	
1600	
1650	
1700	

Giovanni di Bicci
1360-1464

Cosimo (il Vecchio)
1389-1464

Lorenzo
1394-1440

Piero (the Gouty)
1418-1469

Pierfrancesco
1431-1477

Lorenzo the Magnificent
1449-1492

Giuliano
1453-1478

Lorenzo
1463-1503

Giovanni
1467-1514

Piero
1471-1503

Giovanni
(Pope Leo XI)
1475-1521

Giuliano
Duke of Nemours
1478-1516

Giulio
(Pope Clemente VII)
1478-1534

Pierfrancesco
1478-1525

Lorenzo
Duke of Urbino
1492-1519

Giovannidelle Bande Nere
1498-1526

Alessandro
1511-1537

Catherine
1519-1589
m. Henry II of France

Lorenzaccio
1514-1547

Cosimo I
1519-1574

Francesco
1541-1587

Ferdinando I
1549-1609

Maria
1573-1642
m. Henry IV of France

Cosimo II
1590-1621

Louis VIII of France
1601-1643

Henrietta Maria
1509-1669
m. Charles I of England

Ferdinando II
1610-1670

Cosimo III
1642-1723

Gian Gastone
1671-1737

Anna Maria Ludovica
1667-1743

the important sinecures and rapidly emptying the papal treasury. Their rapacity, plus the tremendous expenses involved in building the new St Peter's, caused Leo to step up the sale of indulgences all over Europe—disgusting reformers like Luther and greatly hastening the onset of the Reformation.

Back in Florence, Lorenzo Duke of Urbino and his successor Giulio, bastard son of Lorenzo's brother the murdered Giuliano, were little more than puppets; Leo always found enough time between banquets to manage the city's affairs. Giulio himself became pope in 1523, as **Clement VII**, thanks largely to the new finan-cial interdependence between Florence and Rome, and now the Medici presence in their home city was reduced to two more unattractive young bastards, Ippolito and Alessandro, under the guardianship of Cardinal Silvio Passerini. As Leo had done, Clement attempted to run the city from Rome, but high taxes and the lack of a strong hand made the new Medici regime increasingly precarious; its end fol-lowed almost immediately upon the sack of Rome in 1527. With Clement a prisoner in the Vatican and unable to intervene, a delegation of Florentine nota-bles discreetly informed Passerini and the Medicis that it was time to go. They took the hint, and for the third time in less than a century Florence had succeeded in getting rid of the Medici.

The new republic, though initiated by the disillusioned wealthy classes, soon found radical Savonarolan democrats gaining the upper hand. The Grand Council met once more, and extended the franchise to include most of the citizens. Vani-ties were cursed again, books were banned and carnival parades forbidden; the Council officially pronounced Jesus Christ 'King of the Florentines', just as it had done in the heyday of the Savonarolan camp meetings. In an intense atmosphere of republican virtue and pious crusade, Florence rushed headlong into the apoca-lyptic climax of its history.

This time it did not take the Medici long to recover. In order to get Florence back, the witless Clement became allied to his former enemy, **Emperor Charles V**, a sordid deal that would eventually betray all Italy to Spanish control. Imperial troops were to help subdue Florence, and Clement's illegitimate son Alessandro was to wed Charles' illegitimate daughter. The bastards were closing in. Charles' troops put Florence under siege in December 1529. The city had few resources for the struggle, and no friends, but a heroic resistance kept the imperialists at bay all through the winter and spring. Citizens gave up their gold and silver to be minted into the republic's last coins. The councillors debated seizing little Catherine de' Medici, future Queen of France, but then a prisoner of the republic, and dangling her from the walls to give the enemy a good target. Few artists were left in Florence, but Michelangelo stayed to help with his city's fortifications (by night he was working on the Medici tombs in San Lorenzo, surely one of the most astounding feats of fence-straddling in history, both sides gave him safe passage when he wanted to leave Florence, and again when he decided to return.

In August of 1530, the Florentines' skilful commander, Francesco Ferruccio, was killed in a skirmish near Pistoia; at about the same time the republic realized that its mercenary captain within the walls, Malatesta Baglioni, had sold them out to the pope and emperor. When they tried to arrest him, Baglioni only laughed, and directed his men to turn their artillery on the city. The inevitable capitulation came on 12 August; after almost 400 years, the Florentine republic had breathed its last.

At first, this third Medici return seemed to be just another dreary round of history repeating itself. Again, a packed *parlamento* gutted the constitution and legitimized the Medici takeover. Again the family and its minions combed the city, confiscating back every penny's worth of property that had been confiscated from them. This time, however, was to be different. Florence had gone from being a large fish in a small Italian pond to a minuscule but hindersome nuisance in the pan-European world of papal and imperial politics. Charles V didn't much like republics, or disorderly politicking, or indeed anyone who might conceivably say no to him. The orders came down from the emperor in Brussels; it was to be Medici for ever.

Cosimo I: the Medici as Grand Dukes

At first little was changed; the shell of the republican constitution was maintained, but with the 20-year-old illegitimate **Alessandro** as 'Duke of the Florentine Republic'; the harsh reality was under construction on the height above the city's west end—the Fortezza da Basso, with its Spanish garrison, demanded by Charles V as insurance that Florence would never again be able to assert its independence. If any further symbolism was necessary, Alessandro ordered the great bell to be removed from the tower of the Palazzo Vecchio, the bell that had always summoned the citizens to political assemblies and the mustering of the army.

In 1537, Alessandro was treacherously murdered by his jealous cousin Lorenzino de' Medici. With no legitimate heirs in the direct line Florence was in danger of falling under direct imperial rule, as had happened to Milan two years earlier, upon the extinction of the Sforza dukes. The assassination was kept secret while the Medici and the diplomats angled for a solution. The only reasonable choice turned out to be 18-year-old **Cosimo de' Medici**, heir of the family's cadet branch. This son of a famous mercenary commander, Giovanni of the Black Bands, had grown up on a farm and had never been involved with Florentine affairs; both the elder statesmen of the family and the imperial representatives thought they would easily be able to manipulate him.

It soon became clear that they had picked the wrong boy. Right from the start, young Cosimo had a surprisingly complete idea of how he meant to rule Florence, and also the will and strength of personality to see his commands carried out. No one ever admitted liking him; his puritanical court dismayed even the old partisans of Savonarola, and Florentines always enjoyed grumbling over his high taxes, going to support 'colonels, spies, Spaniards, and women to serve Madame' (his Spanish consort Eleanor of Toledo).

More surprising still, in this pathetic age when bowing and scraping Italians were everywhere else losing both their liberty and their dignity, Cosimo held his own against both pope and Spaniard. To back up his growing independence, Cosimo put his domains on an almost permanent war footing. New fortresses were built, a big fleet begun, and a paid standing army took the place of mercenaries and citizen levies. The skeleton of the old republic was revamped into a modern, bureaucratic state, governed as scientifically and rationally as any in Europe. The new regime, well prepared as it was, never had a severe test. Early in his reign Cosimo defeated the last-ditch effort of the republican exiles, unreconstructed oligarchs led by the banker Filippo Strozzi, at the **Battle of Montemurlo**, the last threat ever to Medici rule. Cosimo's masterstroke came in 1557, when with the help of an Imperial army he was able to gobble up the entire Republic of Siena. Now the Medici rule extended over roughly the boundaries of modern Tuscany; Cosimo was able to cap off his reign in 1569 by purchasing from the Pope the title of Grand Duke of Tuscany.

Knick-knacks and Tedium: the Later Medici

For all Cosimo's efforts, Florence was a city entering a very evident decline. Banking and trade did well throughout the late 16th century, a prosperous time for almost all of Italy, but there were very few opportunities for growth, and few Florentines interested in looking for it. More than ever, wealth was going into land, palaces and government bonds; the old tradition of mercantile venture among the Florentine élite was rapidly becoming a thing of the past. For culture and art, Cosimo's reign turned out to be a disaster. It wasn't what he intended; indeed the Duke brought to the field his accustomed energy and compulsion to improve and organize. Academies were founded, and research underwritten. Cosimo's big purse and his emphasis on art as political propaganda helped change the Florentine artist from a slightly eccentric guild artisan to a flouncing courtier, ready to roll over at his master's command.

Michelangelo, despite frequent entreaties, always refused to work for Cosimo. Most of the other talented Florentines eventually found one excuse or another to bolt for Rome or even further afield, leaving lapdogs like **Giorgio Vasari** to carry on the grand traditions of Florentine art. Vasari, with help from such artists as Ammannati and Bandinelli, transformed much of the city—especially the interiors of its churches and public buildings. Florence began to fill up with equestrian statues of Medici, pageants and plaster triumphal arches displaying the triumphs of the Medici, sculptural allegories (like Cellini's *Perseus*) reminding us of the inevitability of the Medici and best of all, portraits of semi-divine Medici floating up in the clouds with little Cupids and Virtues.

It was all the same to Cosimo and his successors, whose personal tastes tended more to engraved jewels, exotic taxidermy and sculptures made of seashells. But it helped hasten the extinction of Florentine culture and the quiet transformation of the city into just another Mediterranean backwater. Cosimo himself grew ill in his later years, abdicating most responsibility to his son **Francesco** from 1564 to his death ten years later. Francesco, the genuine oddball among the Medici, was a moody, melancholic sort who cared little for government, preferring to lock himself up in the family palaces to pursue his passion for alchemy, as well as occasional researches into such subjects as perpetual motion and poisons—his agents around the Mediterranean had to ship him crates of scorpions every now and then. Despite his lack of interest, Francesco was a capable ruler, best known for his founding of the port city of Livorno.

Later Medici followed the general course established by other great families, such as the Habsburgs and Bourbons—each one was worse than the last. Francesco's death in 1587 gave the throne to his brother, **Ferdinando I**, founder of the Medici Chapels at San Lorenzo and another indefatigable collector of bric-à-brac. Next came **Cosimo II** (1609–21), a sickly nonentity who eventually succumbed to tuberculosis, and **Ferdinando II** (1621–70), whose long and uneventful reign oversaw the impoverishment of Florence and most of Tuscany. For this the Medici do not deserve much blame. A long string of bad harvests, beginning in the 1590s, plagues that recurred with terrible frequency as late as the 1630s, and general trade patterns that redistributed wealth and power from the Mediterranean to northern Europe, all set the stage for the collapse of the Florentine economy. The fatal blow came in the 1630s, when the long-deteriorating wool trade collapsed with sudden finality. Banking was going too, partly a victim of the age's continuing inflation, partly of high taxes and lack of worthwhile investments. Florence, by mid-century, found itself with no prospects at all, a pensioner city drawing a barely respectable income from its glorious past.

With **Cosimo III** (1670–1723), the line of the Medici crossed over into the realm of the ridiculous. A religious crank and anti-Semite, this Cosimo temporarily wiped out free thought in the universities, allowed Tuscany to fill up with nuns and Jesuits, and decreed fantastical laws like the one that forbade any man to enter a house where an unmarried woman lived. To support his lavish court and pay the big tributes demanded by Spain and Austria (something earlier Medici would have scorned) Cosimo taxed what was left of the Florentine economy into an early grave. His heir was the incredible **Gian Gastone** (1723–37). This last Medici, an obese drunkard, senile and slobbering at the age of fifty, has been immortalized by the equally incredible bust in the Pitti Palace. Gian Gastone had to be carried up and down stairs on the rare occasions when he ever got out of bed (mainly to disprove rumours that he was dead); on the one occasion he appeared in public, the chronicles report him vomiting repeatedly out of the carriage window.

As a footnote on the Medici there is Gian Gastone's perfectly sensible sister, **Anna Maria Ludovica**. As the very last surviving Medici, it fell to her to dispose of the family's vast wealth and hoards of art. When she died, in 1743, her will revealed that the whole bundle was to become the property of the future rulers of Tuscany—whoever they should be—with the provision that not one bit of it should ever, ever be moved outside Florence. Without her, the great collections of the Uffizi and the Bargello might long ago have been packed away to Vienna or to Paris.

Post-Medici Florence

When Gian Gastone died in 1737, Tuscany's fate had already been decided by the great powers of Europe. The Grand Duchy would fall to **Francis Stephen**, Duke of Lorraine and husband-to-be of the Austrian Empress Maria Theresa; the new duke's troops were already installed in the Fortezza da Basso a year before Gian Gastone died. For most of the next century, Florence slumbered peacefully under a benign Austrian rule. Already the first Grand Tourists were arriving on their way to Rome and Naples, sons of the Enlightenment like Goethe, who never imagined anything in Florence could possibly interest him and didn't stop, or relics like the Pretender Charles Edward Stuart, 'Bonnie Prince Charlie', Duke of Albany, who stayed two years. Napoleon's men occupied the city for most of two decades, without making much of an impression.

After the Napoleonic Wars, the Habsburg restoration brought back the Lorraine dynasty. From 1824 to 1859, Florence and Tuscany were ruled by **Leopold II**, that most useful and likeable of all Grand Dukes. This was the age when Florence first became popular among the northern Europeans and the time when the Brownings, Dostoevsky, Leigh Hunt and dozens of other artists and writers took up residence, rediscovering the glories of the city and of the early Renaissance. Grand Duke Leopold was decent enough to let himself be overthrown in 1859, during the tumults of the Risorgimento. In 1865, when only the Papal State remained to be incorporated into the Kingdom of Italy, Florence briefly became the new nation's capital. King Vittorio Emanuele moved into the Pitti Palace, and the Italian Parliament met in the great hall of the Palazzo Vecchio.

It was really not meant to last. When the Italian troops entered Rome in 1870, Florence's brief hour as a major capital was at an end. Not, however, without giving the staid old city a memorable jolt towards the modern world. In an unusual flurry of exertion, Florence finally threw up a façade for its cathedral, and levelled the picturesque though squalid market area and Jewish ghetto to build the dolorous Piazza della Repubblica. Fortunately, the city regained its senses before too much damage was done. Throughout this century, Florence's role as a museum city has been confirmed with each passing year. The hiatus provided by World War II allowed the city to resume briefly its ancient delight in black-and-white political epic. In 1944–5, Florence offered some of the most outrageous spectacles of Fascist fanaticism, and also some of the most courageous stories of the Resistance—including that of the German consul Gerhard Wolf, who used his position to protect Florentines from the Nazi terror, often at great personal risk.

In August 1944, the Allied armies were poised to advance through northern Tuscany. For the Germans, the Arno made a convenient defensive line, requiring that all the bridges of Florence be demolished. All were, except for the Ponte Vecchio, saved in a last-minute deal, though the buildings on either side of it were destroyed to provide piles of rubble around the bridge approaches. After the war, all were repaired; the city had the Ponte della Trinità rebuilt stone by stone exactly as it was. No sooner was the war damage redeemed, however, than an even greater disaster attacked the Florentine past. The flood of 1966, when water reached as high as 6.5m, did more damage than Nazis or Napoleons; an international effort was raised to preserve and restore the city's art and monuments. Since then the Arno's bed has been deepened under the Ponte Vecchio and six-metre earthen walls have been erected around Ponte Amerigo Vespucci; video screens and computers monitor every fluctuation in the water level. If a flood happens again, Florence will have time to protect herself. Far more insoluble is the problem of terrorism, which touched the city, in May 1993, when a bomb attack destroyed the Gregoriophilus library opposite the Uffizi and damaged the Vasari Corridor. Florence, shocked by this intrusion from the outside world into its holy of holies, repaired most of the damage in record time with funds which were raised by a national subscription.

Careful planning has saved the best of Florence's immediate countryside from a different sort of flood—post-war suburbanization—but much of the territory around the city has been coated by an atrocity of suburban sprawl, some of the most degraded landscapes in all Italy. The building of a new airport extension, which the Florentines hope will help make up some of the economic ground they've lost to Milan, may also include the building of a whole new business city, a new Florence, nothing less than 'the greatest urban planning operation of the century' they say, with some of the old audacity of Brunelleschi. There are plans for an underground, and perhaps even a new high-speed train between Milan and Rome that would pass under Florence in a tunnel. Ideas there are, but getting them past the city's innate factionalism and its own mania for perfectionism has proved to be a mountain of a stumbling block.

Meanwhile Florence works hard to preserve what it already has. Although new measures to control the city's bugbear—the traffic problems of a city of 400,000 that receives 7 million visitors a year—have been enacted to protect the historic centre, pollution from nearby industry continues to eat away at monuments—Donatello's statue of St Mark at Orsanmichele, perfectly intact 50 years ago, is now a mutilated leper. Private companies, banks, and even individuals finance 90 per cent of the art restoration in Florence, with techniques invented by the city's innovative Institute of Restoration. Increasingly copies are made to replace original works. Naturally, half the city is for them, and the other half, against.

Getting Around

Florence is now one of the best Italian cities to get around; best, because nearly everything you'll want to see is within easy walking distance and large areas in the centre are pedestrian zones; there are no hills to climb, and it's hard to lose your way for very long.

Just a few years ago the traffic problem in Florence was one of the grimmest and most carcinogenic in Italy; a walk along the Lungarno or the remaining streets where the traffic is now channelled will demonstrate that Dante didn't have to go far to find Purgatorio. But in 1988, with great fanfare and howls of protest, Florence attempted to do something about the cars that were choking it to death by greatly enlarging the limited access zone, the *zona a traffico limitato*, which the Florentines, with clenched teeth, somehow pronounce as ZTL. Within ZTL only buses, taxis, and cars belonging to residents are permitted; otherwise, you may pay to park in one of the city's car parks (the Fortezza da Basso is biggest and perhaps most convenient) or take your chances on a side street. This new regulation was then followed by whole areas especially around Piazza della Signoria and the Duomo becoming totally traffic-free zones. The only danger in these areas is the odd ambulance or police car, the speeding mopeds (all of which you can usually hear) and the deadly silent bicycle.

Just to make life difficult, Florence has two sets of address numbers on every street—red ones for business, blue for residences; your hotel might be either one.

by bus

City buses (ATAF) can whizz or inch you across Florence, and are an excellent means of reaching sights on the periphery. Most lines begin at Santa Maria Novella station, and pass by Piazza del Duomo or Piazza San Marco. There's an information/ticket booth in the station, and at ATAF's central office in Piazza della Stazione, © 580 528. Tickets are good for 90 minutes after validation on the bus; 24-hour passes are available as well. The most useful buses for visitors are listed below.

6: Via Rondinella–Duomo–Piazza San Marco–Piazza Unità–Soffiano

7: Station–Duomo–San Domenico–Fiesole

10: Station–Duomo–S. Marco–Ponte a Mensola–Settignano

11A: Viale Calatafimi–Duomo–Porta Romana–Poggio Imperiale

13: Station–Duomo–Piazzale Michelangelo–Porta Romana

14: Rovezzano–Duomo–Station–Careggi

19: Station–Fortezza da Basso–Piazza della Libertà–Ponte alle Grazie–Piazza Pitti–Piazza S. Spirito–Piazza Mazzini–Proconsolo–Beccaria.

17B: Cascine–Station–Duomo–Via Lamarmora–Salviatino (for the youth hostel)

25A: Station–S. Marco–Piazza Libertà–Via Bologna–Pratolino

28: Station–Via R. Giuliani–Castello–Sesto Fiorentino

37: Station–Ponte alla Carraia–Porta Romana–Certosa del Galluzzo

38: Porta Romana–Pian del Giullari

by taxi

Taxis in Florence don't cruise; you'll find them in ranks at the station and in the major piazze, or else ring for a radio taxi, © 4798 or 4390.

bicycle, scooter and car hire

Hiring a bike can save you tramping time and angst, but watch out for cars and pedestrians. If park your car at the car park at the Fortezza da Basso, you can have two bikes for two hours for free, between the hours of 8am and 8pm, on the presentation of your SCAF parking coupon at the Bici-Città booth, on the north side near the tour bus parking area.

You can also hire a bike at **Ciao & Basta**, © 234 2726, located in Lungarno Pecori Girardi 1, down the steps from the station or at Costa dei Magnoli 24, or in spring and summer in Piazza Libertà. **Vesparent**,Via Pisana, 103r, © 715691, hires out bikes and motorbikes and scooters; motorbikes are also available from **Alinari**, Via Guelfa 85r, © 211 748 and 280 500 or Via dei Bardi 35, © 234 6436; **Motorent**, Via S. Zanobi 9r, © 490 113; mountain bikes only can be hired from **Promoturist**, Via Baccio Bandinelli 43, © 701 863.

When you can't take any more art, hire a car and escape into the ravishing countryside. Most firms are in easy walking distance from the station. **Avis**, Borgo Ognissanti 128r, © 213 629; **Europcar**, Borgo Ognissanti 53r, © 294 130; **Hertz**, Via M. Finiguerra 33, © 239 8205; **Maggiore**, Via M. Finiguerra 11, © 294 578; **Program**, Borgo Ognissanti 135, © 282 916; **Italy by Car**, Borgo Ognissanti 134r, © 293 021.

Tourist Information

The head office is a bit out of the way, near Piazza Beccaria on Via Manzoni 16, © 290 832, open 8.30–1.30 Mon–Sat. There's also a booth outside the station, at the end of the bus ranks, that is open daily until 9pm in summer and very genial (© 212 245). There's an office in Fiesole at Piazza Mino 37, © 598 720, open 9–1 and 3–6.

There are no end of places to help you find a hotel (*see* **Where to Stay**, p.313) but these tourist offices usually cannot help.

Now that the Florentines have dismissed most of the traffic from their historic centre, the city is extremely pleasant to tackle on foot—the only real way to absorb its beauties and contradictions.

Florence Walks

The attractions are so dense that none of the nine walks we've divided it up into should cause any fallen arches, except perhaps Walk IX, a tramp through the Oltrarno, but blame the Medici and their mastodontic Pitti palace for that.

The other eight walks more or less have themes—the Cathedral complex (Walk I); the two great churches of the preaching orders, Franciscan Santa Croce (VIII) and Dominican Santa Maria Novella (V), a walk which also includes the Medici palace and tombs; Piazza della Signoria and Uffizi, the centre of civic life (II); the early medieval core of Florence, where Dante once lived (III); mercantile banking Florence (IV). Walks VI and VII encompass the northeast side with a grab-bag of Florentine essentials: the Accademia, Fra Angelico's San Marco, Brunelleschi's Spedale degli Innocenti, Santissima Annunziata and the Archaeology Museum. At the end comes The Oltrano (IX), literally the area 'beyond the Arno', and a list of peripheral attractions just outside the centre including the most magnificent views over Florence from the surrounding hills.

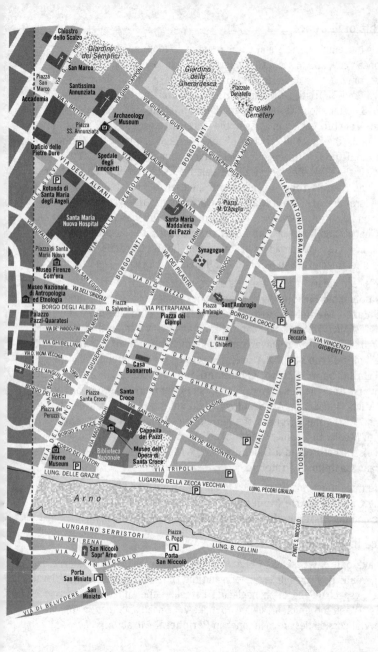

Highlights of Florence

Florence's museums, palaces and churches contain more good art than perhaps any European city, and to see it all comfortably would take at least three weeks. If you have only a few days, the highlights will take up all your time—the **Cathedral** and **Baptistry**, the paintings in the **Uffizi** and the sculptures in the **Bargello**. Stop for a look at the eccentric **Orsanmichele**, and see the Arno from the **Ponte Vecchio**, taking in some of the oldest streets in the city. If your heart leans towards the graceful lyricism of the 1400s, don't miss the **Cathedral Museum** and the Fra Angelicos in **San Marco**; for the lush virtuosity of the 1500s, visit the **Pitti Palace**'s Galleria Palatina. The churches **Santa Maria Novella** and **Santa Croce** are galleries in themselves, containing some of the greatest Florentine art; **Santa Maria del Carmine** has the restored frescoes of Masaccio and company. Devotees of the Michelangelo cult won't want to miss the Medici Chapels and library at **San Lorenzo** or *David* in the **Accademia**. When the stones begin to weary, head for the oasis of the **Boboli Gardens**. Finally, climb up to beautiful, medieval **San Miniato** and the enchanting view over the city.

Florence's 'secondary' sights are just as interesting. You could spend a day walking around old **Fiesole**, or 15 minutes looking at Gozzoli's charming fresco in the **Palazzo Medici-Riccardi**. The **Palazzo Vecchio** has more, but less charming, Medici frescoes. You can see how a wealthy medieval Tuscan merchant lived at the **Palazzo Davanzati**, while the **Museum of the History of Science** will tell you about the scientific side of the Florentine Renaissance; **Santa Trínita**, **Santo Spirito**, **Ognissanti** and the **Annunziata** all contain famous works from the Renaissance. The **Casa Buonarroti** has some early sculptures of Michelangelo; the **Archaeology Museum** has even earlier ones by the Etruscans, Greeks and Egyptians; the Pitti Palace's **Museo degli Argenti** overflows with Medicean jewellery and trinkets. Take a bus or car out to Lorenzo il Magnifico's villa at **Poggio a Caiano**, or to the Medicis' other garden villas: **La Petraia** and **Castello**, or **Pratolino**.

There are three museums nearer the present with 19th- and 20th-century collections: the **Galleria d'Arte Moderna** in the Pitti Palace, the **Collezione della Ragione** and the **Photography Museum** in the Palazzo Rucellai.

Florence in a Weekend

If you have only a weekend in Florence, concentrate on **Walk I** (Piazza del Duomo), **Walk II** (Piazza della Signoria and the Uffizi) and **Walk III** (Medieval Florence), especially the often neglected Bargello—the Uffizi of Renaissance sculpture. When too much art begins to make your head spin, get on top of the city—several possibilities are mentioned in **Peripheral Attractions**.

Start: *Piazza del Duomo*

Finish: *Orsanmichele*

Walking time: *a morning or afternoon*

I: Piazza del Duomo

giotto's campanile

Florence's holy centre is in many way the key to the city, and essential to understanding everything that comes after.

Lunch/Cafés

Perche Nò, Via dei Tavolini 19r. Very good ice cream in 1940s surroundings.

Da Pennello, Via Dante Alighieri 4r, ✆ 29 48 48. Very popular and lively, where you can go for great antipasti and large plates of different types of pasta (closed Mon, around L40,000).

Piazza della Repubblica has three historic and elegant bars, now more popular with tourists than Florentines but all three have an atmosphere of dated elegance:

Gilli del 1733, Piazza della Repubblica 39r, ✆ 213 896. Dates back to 1733, when the Mercato Vecchio still occupied this area; its two panelled back rooms are especially pleasant in winter.

Giubbe Rosse, Piazza della Repubblica 13–14r. Its chandelier-lit interior has changed little since the turn of the century when it was the rendezvous of Florence's *literati*.

Paszkowski, Piazza della Repubblica 6r, ✆ 210 236.

Giovacchino, Via dei Tosinghi 34r. Very conveniently located food bar and *tavola calda*.

Bar Manaresi, Via de Lamberti 16r. Many say that the best coffee in Florence is to be had here.

Tour groups circle around the three great spiritual monuments of medieval Florence like sharks around their prey. Saxophone players by the cathedral croon to a human carnival from a hundred nations that mills about good-naturedly, while ambulances of a medieval first-aid brotherhood stand at the ready in case anyone swoons from ecstasy or art-glut. As bewildering as it often is, however, the Piazza del Duomo and the adjacent Piazza di San Giovanni are the best introduction to this often bewildering city.

*This walk begins with the **Baptistry** in Piazza di San Giovanni at the west end of Piazza del Duomo.*

In order to begin to understand what magic made the Renaissance first bloom by the Arno, look here; this ancient and mysterious building is the egg from which Florence's golden age was hatched. By the quattrocento Florentines firmly

Florence Walk I:
Piazza del Duomo

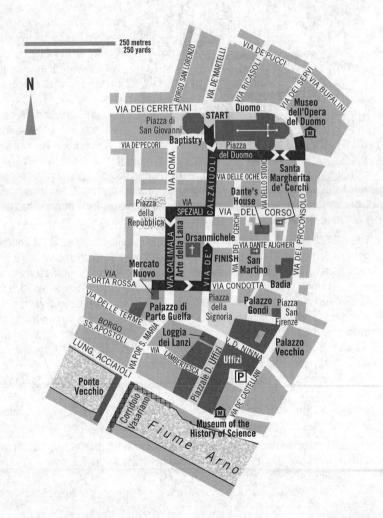

250 metres
250 yards

N

VIA DEI CERRETANI
BORGO SAN LORENZO
VIA DE'MARTELLI
VIA RICASOLI
VIA DE'PUCCI
VIA DEI SERVI
VIA BUFALINI
VIA DEI SERVI

Duomo
START
Piazza di
San Giovanni
Baptistry
VIA DE'PECORI

VIA DE' CALZAIUOLI
VIA DELLE OCHE

**Museo
dell'Opera
del Duomo**
Piazza
del Duomo
VIA DELLO STUDIO

**Santa
Margherita
de' Cerchi**

VIA ROMA

VIA
SPEZIALI

**Dante's
House**
VIA DEL CORSO
VIA DEI CERCHI

Piazza
della
Repubblica

Orsanmichele
VIA DEL PROCONSOLO

VIA CALIMALA
Arte della Lana

VIA DANTE ALIGHIERI
FINISH
**San
Martino**
Badia

**Mercato
Nuovo**
VIA
PORTA ROSSA

VIA CONDOTTA
Piazza
della
Signoria

**Palazzo
Gondi**
Piazza
San
Firenze

VIA DELLE TERME
**Palazzo di
Parte Guelfa**

**Loggia
dei Lanzi**

BORGO
SS.APOSTOLI
VIA POR S. MARIA

V.D. NINNA
**Palazzo
Vecchio**

LUNG. ACCIAIOLI
VIA LAMBERTESCA
Piazzale D. Uffizi
Uffizi
P
VIA DE'CASTELLANI

**Ponte
Vecchio**

Corridoio
Vasariano
**Museum of the
History of Science**

Fiume Arno

97

believed their baptistry was originally a Roman temple to Mars, a touchstone linking them to a legendary past. Scholarship sets its date of construction between the 6th and 9th centuries, in the darkest Dark Ages, which makes it even more remarkable; it may as well have dropped from heaven. Its distinctive dark green and white marble facing, the tidily classical pattern of arches and rectangles that deceived Brunelleschi and Alberti, was probably added around the 11th century. The masters who built it remain unknown, but their strikingly original exercise in geometry provided the model for all of Florence's great church façades. When it was new, there was nothing remotely like it in Europe; to visitors from outside the city it must have seemed almost miraculous.

Every 21 March, New Year's Day on the old Florentine calendar, all the children born over the last 12 months would be brought here for a great communal baptism, a habit that helped make the baptistry not merely a religious monument but a civic symbol, in fact the oldest and dearest symbol of the republic. As such the Florentines never tired of embellishing it. Under the octagonal cupola, the glittering 13th- and 14th-century gold-ground mosaics show a strong Byzantine influence, perhaps laid by mosaicists from Venice. The decoration is divided into concentric strips: over the apse, dominated by a 8.5m figure of Christ, is a *Last Judgement*, while the other bands, from the inside out, portray the *Hierarchy of Heaven*, *Story of Genesis*, *Life of Joseph*, *Life of Christ* and the *Life of St John the Baptist*, the last band believed to be the work of Cimabue. The equally beautiful mosaics over the altar and in the vault are the earliest, signed by a monk named Iacopo in the first decades of the 1200s.

To match the mosaics, there is an intricate tessellated marble floor, decorated with signs of the Zodiac; the blank, octagonal space in the centre was formerly occupied by the huge font. The green and white patterned walls of the interior, even more than the exterior, are remarkable, combining influences from the ancient world and modern inspiration for something entirely new, the perfect source that architects of the Middle Ages and Renaissance would ever strive to match. Much of the best design work is up in the **galleries**, not accessible, but partially visible from the floor.

The baptistry is hardly cluttered; besides a 13th-century Pisan style baptismal font, only the **Tomb of Anti-Pope John XXIII** by Donatello and Michelozzo stands out. This funerary monument, with scenographic marble draperies softening its classical lines, is one of the great prototypes of the early Renaissance. But how did this Anti-Pope John, deposed by the Council of Constance in 1415, earn the unique privilege of a fancy tomb in the baptistry? Why, it was thanks to him that Giovanni di Bicci de' Medici made the family fortune as head banker to the Curia.

The Gates of Paradise

Historians used to pinpoint the beginning of the 'Renaissance' as the year 1401, when the merchants' guild, the Arte di Calimala, sponsored a competition for the baptistry's north doors. The **South Doors** (the main entrance into the baptistry) had already been completed by Andrea Pisano in 1330, and they give an excellent lesson on the style of the day. The doors are divided into 28 panels in quatrefoil frames with scenes from the life of St John the Baptist and the eight Cardinal and Theological Virtues—formal and elegant works in the best Gothic manner.

The celebrated competition of 1401—perhaps the first ever held in the annals of art—pitted the seven greatest sculptors of the day against one another. Judgement was based on trial panels on the subject of the *Sacrifice of Isaac*, and in a dead heat at the end of the day were the two by Brunelleschi and Lorenzo Ghiberti, now displayed in the Bargello. Ghiberti's more classical-style figures were eventually judged the better, and it was a serendipitous choice; he devoted nearly the rest of his life to creating the most beautiful bronze doors in the world while Brunelleschi, disgusted by his defeat, went on to build the most perfect dome. Ghiberti's first efforts, the **North Doors** (1403–24), are contained, like Pisano's, in 28 quatrefoil frames. In their scenes on the Life of Christ, the Evangelists, and the Doctors of the Church, you can trace Ghiberti's progress over the 20 years he worked in the increased depth of his compositions, not only visually but dramatically; classical backgrounds begin to fill up the frames, ready to break out of their Gothic confines. Ghiberti also designed the lovely floral frame of the doors; the three statues, of John the Baptist, the Levite and the Pharisee, by Francesco Rustici, were based on a design by Leonardo da Vinci and added in 1511.

Ghiberti's work pleased the Arte di Calimala, and they set him loose on another pair of portals, the **East Doors** (1425–52), his masterpiece and one of the most awesome achievements of the age. Here Ghiberti (perhaps under the guidance of

Donatello) dispensed with the small Gothic frames and instead cast 10 large panels that depict the Old Testament in Renaissance high gear, reinterpreting the forms of antiquity with a depth and drama that have never been surpassed. Michelangelo declared them 'worthy to be the Gates of Paradise', and indeed it's hard to believe these are people, buildings and trees of bronze and not creatures frozen in time by some celestial alchemy.

Ghiberti wasn't exactly slow to toot his own horn; according to himself, he personally planned and designed the Renaissance on his own. His unabashedly conceited *Commentarii* were the first attempt at art history and autobiography by an artist, and a work as revolutionary as his doors in its presentation of the creative God-like powers of the artist. It is also a typical exhibition of Florentine pride that he should put busts of his friends among the prophets and sibyls that adorn the frames of the East Doors. Near the centre, the balding figure with arched eyebrows and a little smile is Ghiberti himself.

> *For all its importance and prosperity, Florence was one of the last cities to plan a great cathedral or **Duomo**. Work began in the 1290s, with the sculptor Arnolfo di Cambio in charge, and from the beginning the Florentines attempted to make up for their delay with sheer audacity. 'It will be so magnificent in size and beauty', according to a decree of 1296, 'as to surpass anything built by the Greeks and Romans'. In response Arnolfo planned what in its day was the largest church in Catholicism; he confidently laid the foundations for an enormous octagonal crossing 44.5m in diameter. He then died before working out a way to cover it, leaving future architects the job of designing the biggest dome in the world.*

Beyond its presumptuous size, the cathedral of Santa Maria del Fiore shows little interest in contemporary innovations and styles; a visitor from France or England in the 1400s would certainly have found it somewhat drab and architecturally primitive. Visitors today often don't know what to make of it; they circle confusedly around its grimy, ponderous bulk (this is one of the very few cathedrals in Italy that you can walk completely around). Instead of the striped bravura of Siena or the elegant colonnades of Pisa, they behold an astonishingly eccentric green, white and red pattern of marble rectangles and flowers—like Victorian wallpaper, or as one critic better expressed it, 'a cathedral wearing pyjamas'. On a sunny day, the cathedral under its sublime dome seems to sport festively above the dullish dun and ochre sea of Florence; in dismal weather it sprawls morosely across its piazza like a beached whale tarted up with a lace doily front.

The fondly foolish **façade** cannot be blamed on Arnolfo. His original design, only one-quarter completed, was taken down in a late 16th-century Medici rebuilding programme that never got off the ground. The Duomo turned a blank face to the world until the present neogothic extravaganza was added in 1888. Walk around to the north side to see what many consider a more fitting door, the **Porta della Mandorla** crowned with an Assumption of the Virgin in an almond-shaped frame (hence *Mandorla*) made by Nanni di Banco in 1420.

> *Yet if this behemoth of a cathedral, this St Mary of the Floral Wallpaper, was created for no other reason than to serve as a base for its dome, it would be more than enough.* **Brunelleschi's dome**, *more than any landmark, makes Florence Florence.*

Many have noted how the dome repeats the rhythm of the surrounding hills, echoing them with its height and beauty; from those city streets fortunate enough to have a clear view, it rises among the clouds with all the confident mastery, proportions, and perfect form that characterize the highest aspirations of the Renaissance. But if it seems miraculous, it certainly isn't divine; unlike the dome of the Hagia Sophia, suspended from heaven by a golden chain, Florence's was made by man—one man, to be precise.

Losing the competition for the baptistry doors was a bitter disappointment to Filippo Brunelleschi. His reaction was typically Florentine; not content with being the second-best sculptor, he turned his talents to a field where he thought no one could beat him. He launched himself into an intense study of architecture and engineering, visiting Rome and probably Ravenna to snatch secrets from the ancients. When proposals were solicited for the cathedral's dome in 1418, he was ready with a brilliant *tour de force*. Not only would he build the biggest, most beautiful dome of the time, but he would do it without any need for expensive supports while work was in progress, making use of a cantilevered system of bricks that could support itself while it ascended.

Brunelleschi studied, then surpassed the technique of

Brunelleschi's Cupola

the ancients with a system more simple than that of the Pantheon or Hagia Sophia. To the Florentines, a people who could have invented the slogan 'form follows function' for their own tastes in building, it must have come as a revelation; the most logical way of covering the space turned out to be a work of perfect beauty. Brunelleschi, in building this dome, put a crown on the achievements of Florence. After 500 years it is still the city's pride and symbol.

The best way to appreciate Brunelleschi's genius is by touring inside the two concentric shells of the dome (*see p.104*), but before entering, note the eight marble ribs that define its octagonal shape; hidden inside are the three huge stone chains that bind them together. Work on the balcony around the base of the dome, designed by Giuliano da Sangallo, was halted in 1515 after Michelangelo commented that it resembled a cricket's cage. As for the **lantern**, the Florentines were famous for their fondness and admiration for Doubting Thomas, and here they showed why. Even though they marvelled at the dome, they still doubted that Brunelleschi could construct a proper lantern, and forced him to submit to yet another competition. He died before it was begun, and it was completed to his design by Michelozzo.

*After the façade, the austerity of the **Duomo interior** is almost startling.*

There is plenty of room; contemporary writers mention 10,000 souls packed inside to hear the brimstone and hell-fire sermons of Savonarola. Even with that in mind, the duomo hardly seems a religious building—more a Florentine building, with simple arches and counterpoint of grey stone and white plaster, full of old familiar Florentine things. Near the entrance, on the right-hand side, are busts of Brunelleschi and Giotto. On the left wall, posed inconspicuously, are the two most conspicuous monuments to private individuals ever erected by the Florentine Republic. The older one, on the right, is to **Sir John Hawkwood**, the famous English *condottiere* whose name the Italians mangled to Giovanni Acuto, a legendary commander who served Florence for many years and is perhaps best known to English speakers as the hero of *The White Company* by Arthur Conan Doyle. All along, Hawkwood had the promise of the Florentines to build him an equestrian statue after his death; it was a typical Florentine trick to pinch pennies and cheat a dead man—but they hired the greatest master of perspective, Paolo Uccello, to make a fresco that looked like a statue (1436). Twenty years later, they pulled the same trick again, commissioning another great illusionist, Andrea del Castagno, to paint the non-existent equestrian statue of another condottiere, Niccolò da Tolentino. A little further down, Florence commemorates its own secular scripture with Michelino's well-known fresco of Dante, a vision of the poet and his *Paradiso* outside the walls of Florence. Two singular icons of Florence's fascination with science stand at opposite ends of the building: behind the west front, a bizarre clock painted by Uccello, and in the pavement of the left apse, a gnomon fixed by the astronomer Toscanelli in 1475. A beam of sunlight strikes it every year on the day of the summer solstice.

For building the great dome, Brunelleschi was accorded a special honour—he is one of the few Florentines to be buried in the cathedral. His tomb may be seen in the **Excavations of Santa Reparata** (*the stairway descending on the right of the nave; open 10–5, closed Sun; adm*). Arnolfo di Cambio's cathedral was constructed on the ruins of the ancient church of Santa Reparata, which lay forgotten until 1965. Excavations have revealed not only the palaeo-Christian church and its several reconstructions, but also the remains of its Roman predecessor—a rather confusing muddle of walls that have been tidied up in an ambience that resembles an archaeological shopping centre. A coloured model helps explain what is what, and glass cases display items found in the dig, including the spurs of Giovanni de' Medici, who was buried here in 1351. In the ancient crypt of Santa Reparata are 13th-century tomb slabs, and in another section there's a fine pre-Romanesque mosaic pavement.

There is surprisingly little religious art—the Florentines for reasons of their own have carted most of it off into the Cathedral Museum (*see* p.106).The only really conventional religious decorations are the hack but scarcely visible frescoes high in the dome (some 90m up, and at present being restored), mostly the work of Vasari. As you stand there squinting at them, try not to think that the cupola weighs an estimated 25,000 tons. In the middle apse, there is a beautiful bronze urn by Ghiberti containing relics of the Florentine St Zenobius. Under the dome are the entrances to the two sacristies, with terracotta lunettes over the doors by Luca della Robbia; the scene of the *Resurrection* over the north sacristy is one of his earliest and best works. He also did the bronze doors beneath it, with tiny portraits on the handles of Lorenzo il Magnifico and his brother Giuliano de' Medici, targets of the Pazzi conspiracy in 1478.

Murder in the Cathedral

On 28 April 1478, at the moment of the elevation of the Host, Francesco Pazzi, Florentine banker to the Pope, and his bravo Bandini jumped the Medici brothers, leading an attack carefully conceived with Sixtus IV and the King of Naples. Pazzi plunged his dagger 21 times into the handsome Giuliano, while Lorenzo, cape wrapped around one arm as a shield, sword unsheathed, fought off his aggressors, leaping over the then-extant choir screen and taking refuge with his supporters behind the bronze door. He had only a scratch on his neck; his friend Ridolfi sucked it, in case of poison.

At the same time, another intriguer, the archbishop of Pisa, Francesco Salviati, who hated Lorenzo for not making him archbishop of Florence, failed in his attempt to capture and seize power in the Palazzo Vecchio. His body was soon seen dangling from the window, joined shortly after by that of Francesco Pazzi and all their co-conspirators, hanged or defenestrated without trial, to the cheers of the pro-Medici mob. Sandro Botticelli was given the job of painting their likenesses on the walls of the Palazzo Vecchio, so all Florence could witness their infamy.

The cultivated, refined Lorenzo then demonstrated the vindictiveness that was an integral part of the Medici character. The mutilations and executions without trial of over a hundred people suspected to have been involved in the plot continued for days, for months; those who fled abroad were relentlessly tracked down. The body of Jacopo, the chief of the Pazzi clan, was exhumed, dragged mockingly through the streets and thrown into the Arno, then fished out again, and cudgelled until the bones were broken into tiny bits, before being tossed back into the river. When Lorenzo had finished, the entire Pazzi clan had been annihilated, their goods were confiscated, and Lorenzo the Magnificent, conveniently relieved of his popular brother, was the undisputed master of Florence.

*A door on the left aisle near the Dante fresco leads up **into the dome** (open daily 8.30–12.30 and 2.30–5.30, closed Sun; adm).*

The complicated network of stairs and walks between the inner and outer domes (not too difficult, if occasionally claustrophobic and vertiginous) was designed by Brunelleschi for the builders, and offers an insight on how thoroughly the architect thought out the problems of the dome's construction, even inserting hooks to hold up scaffolding for future cleaning or repairs; Brunelleschi installed restaurants to save workers the trouble of descending for meals. There is also no better place to get an idea of the dome's scale; the walls of the inner dome are 4m thick, and those of the outer dome 2m. These give the dome enough strength and support to preclude the need for further buttressing.

From the gallery of the dome you can get a good look at the lovely **stained glass** by Uccello, Donatello, Ghiberti and Castagno, in the seven circular windows, or *occhi*, made during the construction of the dome. Further up, the views through the small windows offer tantalizing hints of the breathtaking panorama of the city from the marble lantern at the top. The bronze ball at the very top was added by Verrocchio, and can hold almost a dozen people when it's open.

There's no doubt about it; the dome steals the show on Piazza del Duomo, putting one of Italy's most beautiful bell towers in the shade *both figuratively and literally. The dome's great size—111.6m to the bronze ball—makes **Giotto's Campanile** look small, though 85.4m is not exactly tiny.*

Giotto was made director of the cathedral works in 1334, and his basic design was completed after his death (1337) by Andrea Pisano and Francesco Talenti. It is difficult to say whether they were entirely faithful to the plan. Giotto was an artist, not an engineer. After he died, his successors realized that the thing, then only 12m high, was about to tumble over, a problem they overcame by doubling the thickness of the walls.

Besides its lovely form, the green, pink and white campanile's major fame rests with Pisano and Talenti's **sculptural reliefs**—a veritable encyclopaedia of the medieval world view with prophets, saints and sibyls, allegories of the planets, virtues and sacraments, the liberal arts and industries (the artist's craft is fittingly symbolized by a winged figure of Daedalus). All of these are copies of the originals now in the Cathedral Museum. If you can take another 400 steps or so, the terrace on top offers a slightly different view of Florence and of the cathedral itself (*open summer, daily 9–7.30, winter 9–5.30; adm*).

*The most striking secular building on the Piazza del Duomo is the **Loggia del Bigallo**, south of the baptistry near the beginning of Via de' Calzaiuoli.*

This 14th-century porch was built for one of Florence's great charitable confraternities, the Misericordia, which still has its headquarters across the street and operates the ambulances parked in front; in the 13th and 14th centuries members courageously nursed and buried victims of the plague. The Loggia itself originally served as a lost and found office, although instead of umbrellas it dealt in children; if unclaimed after three days they were sent to foster homes. In the 15th century the Misericordia merged with a similar charitable confraternity called the Bigallo, and works of art accumulated by both organizations over centuries are displayed in the diminutive but choice **Museo del Bigallo**, located next to the loggia at Piazza San Giovanni 1 (*closed temporarily at the time of writing, © 215 440*). The most famous picture here is the fresco of *Madonna della Misericordia*, featuring the earliest known view of Florence (1342); other 14th-century works (by Bernardo Daddi, Niccolò di Pietro Gerini, and sculptor Alberto Arnoldi) portray the activities of the brotherhood, members of which may still be seen wearing the traditional black hoods that preserve their anonymity.

*East of the Loggia del Bigallo, between Via dello Studio and Via del Proconsolo, is a stone bench labelled 'Sasso di Dante'—**Dante's Seat**—where the poet would sit and take the air, observing his fellow citizens and watching the construction of the cathedral. From here walk* *around the central apse of the cathedral to the **Museo dell'Opera del Duomo** at Piazza del Duomo 9 (open 9–8 summer, 9–6 winter, closed Sun; adm).*

The cathedral museum is one of Florence's finest, and houses both relics from the actual construction of the cathedral and the masterpieces that once adorned it. The first room is devoted to the cathedral's sculptor-architect Arnolfo di Cambio and contains a drawing of his ornate, sculpture-filled façade that was but a quarter completed when the Medici had it removed in 1587. Here, too, are the statues he made to adorn it: the unusual Madonna with the glass eyes, Florence's old patron saints, Reparata and Zenobius, and nasty old Boniface VIII, who sits stiffly on his throne like an Egyptian god. There are the four Evangelists, including a St John by Donatello, and a small collection of ancient works—Roman sarcophagi and an Etruscan cippus carved with dancers.

Two small rooms nearby contain materials from the construction of the dome—wooden models, tools, brick moulds and instruments—as well as Brunelleschi's death mask. Also on the ground floor are several hack Mannerist models (one by dilettante Giovanni de' Medici) proposed in the 1580s for the cathedral, reminders that the façade could have been much, much worse. The Florentines were never enthusiastic about the worship of relics, and long ago they shipped San Girolamo's jaw-bone, John the Baptist's index finger and St Philip's arm across the street to this museum; note the 16th-century *Libretto*, a fold-out display case of saintly odds and ends, all neatly labelled.

On the landing of the stairs stands the Pietà that Michelangelo intended for his own tomb. The artist, increasingly cantankerous and full of terribilità in his old age, became exasperated with this complex work and took a hammer to the arm of the Christ—the first known instance of an artist vandalizing his own creation. His assistant repaired the damage and finished part of the figures of Mary Magdalene and Christ. According to Vasari, the hooded figure of Nicodemus is Michelangelo's self-portrait.

Upstairs, the first room is dominated by the two **Cantorie**, two marble choir balconies with exquisite bas-reliefs, made in the 1430s by Luca della Robbia and Donatello. Both works rank among the Renaissance's greatest productions. Della Robbia's delightful horde of laughing children dancing, singing and playing instruments is a truly angelic choir, Apollonian in its calm and beauty, perhaps the most charming work ever to have been inspired by the forms of antiquity. Donatello's *putti*, by contrast, dance, or rather race, through their quattrocento decorative motifs with Dionysian frenzy. Even less serene is his statue of *Mary Magdalene*, surely one of the most jarring figures ever sculpted, ravaged by her own piety and penance, her sunken eyes fixed on a point beyond this vale of tears. Grey and weathered prophets by Donatello and others stand along the white walls. These originally adorned the façade of the campanile. According to Vasari, while carving the most famous bald one, *Habbakuk* (better known as '*lo zuccone*'), Donatello would mutter 'Speak, damn you. Speak!' The next room contains the original panels on the *Spiritual Progress of Man* from Giotto's campanile which was made by Andrea Pisano.

The last room is dedicated to works removed from the baptistry, especially the lavish silver altar (14th–15th century), made by Florentine goldsmiths, portraying scenes from the life of the Baptist. Antonio Pollaiuolo used the same subject to design the 27 needlework panels that once were part of the priest's vestments. There are two 12th-century Byzantine mosaic miniatures, masterpieces of the intricate, and a *St Sebastian* triptych by Giovanni del Biondo that may well be the record for arrows; the poor saint looks like a hedgehog. Usually this room also contains four panels from Ghiberti's 'Gates of Paradise', which are being restored one by one and make fascinating viewing close up.

> *Of all the streets that radiate from the Piazza del Duomo, most people almost intuitively turn down the straight, pedestrian-only* **Via de' Calzaiuoli***, the Roman street that became the main thoroughfare of medieval Florence, linking the city's religious centre with the Piazza della Signoria. Widening of this 'Street of the Shoemakers' in the 1840s has destroyed much of its medieval character, and the only shoe shops to be seen are designer-label. Its fate seems benign, though, compared with what happened to the Mercato Vecchio, in the fit of post-Risorgimento 'progress' that converted it into the* **Piazza della Repubblica***, a block to the right along Via Speziali.*

On the map, it's easy to pick out the small rectangle of narrow, straight streets around Piazza della Repubblica; these remain unchanged from the little *castrum* of Roman days. At its centre, the old forum deteriorated through the Dark Ages into a shabby market square and the Jewish ghetto, a piquant, densely populated quarter known as the Mercato Vecchio, the epitome of the picturesque for 19th-century tourists but an eyesore for the movers and shakers of the new Italy, who tore down its alleys and miniature *piazze* to create a fit symbol of Florence's reawakening. They erected a triumphal arch to themselves and proudly blazoned it with the inscription: 'THE ANCIENT CITY CENTRE RESTORED TO NEW LIFE FROM THE SQUALOR OF CENTURIES'. The sad result of this well-intentioned urban renewal, the Piazza della Repubblica, is one of the most ghastly squares in Italy, a brash intrusion of ponderous 19th-century buildings and parked cars. Just the same it is popular with locals and tourists alike, full of outdoor cafés, something of an oasis among the narrow, stern streets of medieval Florence.

Mercato Nuovo

*From Piazza della Repubblica the natural flow of street life will sweep you down to the **Mercato Nuovo**, the old Straw Market, bustling under a beautiful loggia built by Grand Duke Cosimo in the 1500s.*

Although you won't see more than a wisp of straw these days, vendors hawk purses, stationery, toys, clothes, umbrellas and knick-knacks. In medieval times this was the merchants' exchange, where any merchant who committed the crime of bankruptcy was publicly spanked before being carted off to prison; in times of peace it sheltered Florence's battle-stained *carroccio*. Florentines often call the market the '*Porcellino*' (piglet) after the large bronze boar erected in 1612, a copy of the ancient statue in the Uffizi. The drool spilling from the side of its mouth reminds us that unlike Rome, Florence is no splashy city of springs and fountains. Rub the piglet's shiny snout, and supposedly destiny will one day bring you back to Florence. The pungent aroma of the tripe sandwiches sold nearby may give you second thoughts.

*From the Mercato Nuovo take Via Condotta back to Via de' Calzaiuoli and turn left. There is a wonderfully eccentric church here that looks like no other church in the world: **Orsanmichele** rises up just on your left in a tall, neat three-storey rectangle.*

It was built on the site of ancient San Michele ad Hortum (popularly reduced to 'Orsanmichele'), a 9th-century church located near a vegetable garden, which the *comune* destroyed in 1240 in order to erect a grain market; after a fire in 1337 the current market building (by Francesco Talenti and others) was erected, with a loggia on the ground floor and emergency storehouses on top where grain was kept against a siege.

The original market had a pilaster with a painting of the Virgin that became increasingly celebrated for performing miracles. The area around the Virgin became known as the Oratory, and when Talenti reconstructed the market, his intention was to combine its secular and religious functions; each pilaster of the loggia was assigned to a guild to adorn with an image of its patron saint. In 1380, when the market was relocated, the entire ground floor was given over to the functions of the church, and Francesco Talenti's talented son Simone was given the task of closing in the arcades with lovely Gothic windows, later bricked in.

The church is most famous as a showcase of 15th-century Florentine sculpture; there is no better place to get an idea of the stylistic innovations that succeeded one another throughout the decades. Each guild sought to outdo the others by commissioning the finest artists of the day to carve their patron saints and create elaborate canopied niches to hold them. The first statue to the left of the door is one of the oldest; Ghiberti's bronze *St John the Baptist*, erected in 1416 for the Arte di Calimala, was the first life-sized Renaissance statue cast in bronze. Continuing to the left on Via de' Lamberti you can compare it with Donatello's *St Mark*, patron of the linen dealers and used-cloth merchants. Finished in 1411, it is considered the first free-standing marble statue of the Renaissance.

The niches continue around Via dell'Arte della Lana, named after the Wool Merchants' Guild, the richest after that of the Bankers. Their headquarters, the **Palazzo dell'Arte della Lana** is linked by an overhead arch with Orsanmichele; built in 1308, it was restored in 1905 in a delightful William Morris style of medieval picturesque. The first statue on this façade of Orsanmichele is *St Eligio*, patron of smiths, by Nanni di Banco (1415), with a niche embellished with the guild's emblem (black pincers) and a bas-relief below showing one of this rather obscure saint's miracles—apparently he shod a horse the hard way, by cutting off its hoof, shoeing it, then sticking it back on the leg. The other two statues on this street are bronzes by Ghiberti, the Wool Guild's *St Stephen* (1426) and the Exchange Guild's *St Matthew* (1422), the latter an especially fine work in a classical niche. On the Via Orsanmichele façade stands a copy of Donatello's famous *St George* (the original now in the Bargello) done in 1417 for the Armourers' Guild, with a dramatic predella of the saint slaying the dragon, also by Donatello, that is one of the first-known works making use of perspective; next are the Stonecutters' and Carpenters' Guild's *Four Crowned Saints* (1415, by Nanni di Banco), inspired by Roman statues. Nanni also contributed the Shoemakers' *St Philip* (1415), while the next figure, *St Peter* is commonly attributed to

Donatello (1413). Around the corner on Via Calzaiuoli stands the bronze *St Luke*, patron of the Judges and Notaries, by Giambologna, a work of 1602 in a 15th-century niche, and the *Doubting of St Thomas* by Andrea del Verrocchio (1484), made not for a guild but the Tribunal of Merchandise, who like St Thomas wanted to be certain before making a judgement. In the rondels above some of the niches are terracottas of the guilds' symbols by Luca della Robbia.

Orsanmichele's dark **interior** *(open 8–12 and 3–6.30)* is ornate and cosy, with more of the air of a guildhall than a church. It makes a picturebook medieval setting for one of the masterpieces of the trecento: Andrea Orcagna's beautiful Gothic **Tabernacle**, a large, exquisite work in marble, bronze and coloured glass framing a contemporary painting of the Madonna (either by Bernardo Daddi or Orcagna himself), replacing the miraculous one, lost in a fire. The Tabernacle was commissioned by survivors of the 1348 Black Death. On the walls and pilasters are faded 14th-century frescoes of saints, placed as if members of the congregation; if you look at the pilasters on the left as you enter and along the right wall you can see the old chutes used to transfer grain.

II: Piazza della Signoria

Start: *Piazza della Signoria*
Finish: *Palazzo Davanzati*
Walking time: *one full day*
                 plus an evening

Palazzo Vecchio

This walk takes in the essentials of Florence's genius—the show-case of her civic virtue, the masterpieces of her greatest painters and marvels of Brunelleschi's heirs in science and engineering.

Lunch/Cafés

Benvenuto, Via Mosca 16r (just behind the Uffizi). Good simple food in a busy atmosphere as tourists mix with office workers on their lunch break (closed Mon, around L20,000).

Buca dell'Orafo, Volta de' Girolami 28r. Homemade pasta in a friendly atmosphere frequented by Florentines and tourists (closed Mon, around L40,000)

Rivoire, Piazza della Signoria 5, © 21 4412. A beautiful old-fashioned bar over-looking the Palazzo Vecchio, very elegant and very expensive.

Antico Fattore, Via Lambertesca 1–3r, © 238 1215. Simple fare at fair prices.

Il Boccale, Borgo SS. Apostoli 33r, © 283 384. A handy pizzeria cum-restaurant (closed Mon, around L15–25000).

Oliviero, Via delle Terme 51/r, © 21 2421. Despite the chi-chi atmosphere with piano bar and red velvet seats, the food is excellent (closed Sun and lunch, around L60,000).

*Italian city builders are renowned for effortlessly creating beautiful squares, but it's an art where the Florentines are generally all thumbs. Only here, in the city's civic stage, the **Piazza della Signoria**, do they achieve a grand, meaningful space, a much needed antidote to the stone gullies of the ancient centre, dominated by the sombre fortress and tower of the **Palazzo Vecchio** and a lively gathering of some of the best and worst of Florentine sculpture.*

Although the Piazza della Signoria currently serves as Great Aunt Florence's drawing-room-cum-tourist-overflow-tank, in the old days it saw the public assemblies of the republic, which in Florence meant that the square often degenerated into a battleground for impossibly inscrutable internecine quarrels. These could be stirred up to mythic levels of violence; in the 14th century a man was eaten by a crowd maddened by a political speech. Such speeches were given from the *arringhiera*, or oration terrace in front of the Palazzo Vecchio, a word which gave us 'harangue'. It was in the Piazza della Signoria that Savonarola ignited his notorious Bonfire of Vanities in 1497, and here, too, the following year, the disillusioned Florentines ignited Savonarola himself. A small plaque in the pavement marks the exact spot, not far from Ammannati's fountain.

Florence Walk II:
Piazza della Signoria

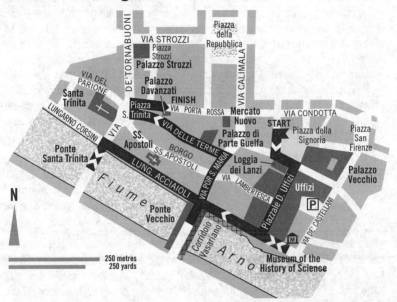

If, on the other hand, trouble came from without, the Florentines would toll the famous bell in the tower of the Palazzo Vecchio, and the square would rapidly fill with the gonfalons of the citizens' militia and the guilds. 'We will sound our trumpets!' threatened the French King Charles VIII, when the Florentines refused to shell out enough florins to make him and his army leave town. 'And we will ring our bell!' countered the courageous republican Piero Capponi—a threat that worked; Charles had to settle for a smaller sum. When Alessandro de' Medici was restored as duke of Tuscany three years later, one of his first acts was to smash the bell as a symbol of Florence's lost liberty.

Having a citizens' militia, as opposed to depending on foreign mercenaries, answered one of Machiavelli's requirements for a well-governed state. Training was taken fairly seriously; to build up their endurance, the republic's citizens played a ball game similar to rugby, believed to be descended from a Roman sport. Known these days as *Calcio in Costume*, it is played every June in Piazza Santa Croce, and it's good fun to watch the usually immaculate Florentines in their Renaissance duds mixing it up in the dirt (fighting is more than permitted, as long as it's one to one).

Since the 1970s and 80s a different kind of battle has been waged in this piazza, spiced with good old-fashioned Florentine factionalism. At stake is the future of the Piazza della Signoria itself. In 1974, while searching for signs of the original paving stones, the Soprintendenza ai Beni Archeologici found, much to their surprise, an underground medieval kasbah of narrow lanes, houses and wells—the ruins of 12th-century Ghibelline Florence, built over the baths and other portions of Roman and Etruscan *Florentia*. The *comune* ordered the excavations filled in; from the city's point of view, the piazza, essential to the essential tourist trade, was untouchable. In the 80s, the communal government fell, and the excavations were reopened on the portion of the piazza near the loggia. There are proposals to excavate the rest of the square, much to the horror of the *comune*, and to create eventually an underground museum similar to the one in Assisi. Until the issue is decided, don't be surprised to find the piazza full of gaping holes.

> *Generally of a lower key than a political harangue was the* parlamento, *a meeting of eligible male citizens to vote on an important issue (usually already decided by the bosses). On these occasions, the Florentines heard speeches from the platform of the graceful three-arched* **Loggia dei Lanzi,** *also known as the Loggia della Signoria or the Loggia dell'Orcagna, after Andrea Orcagna, the probable architect.*

Completed in 1382, when pointed Gothic was still the rage, the loggia with its lofty round arches looks back to classical antiquity and looks forward to the Renaissance; it is the germ of Brunelleschi's revolutionary architecture. If the impenetrable, stone Palazzo Vecchio is a symbol of the republic's strength and authority, the Loggia dei Lanzi is a symbol of its capacity for beauty.

The loggia received its name 'of the lances' after the Swiss lancers, the private bodyguard of Cosimo I, and it was the Grand Duke who, in 1560, commissioned the most famous sculpture sheltered in the arcade, Cellini's bronze *Perseus*, a *tour de force* with its attention to detail and expressive composition, graceful and poised atop the gruesome bleeding trunk, eyes averted from the horrible head capable of turning the onlookers into stone. The subject was a hint to the Florentines, to inspire their gratitude for Grand Ducal rule which spared them from the monstrosity of their own unworkable republic. Nearby Giambologna's *Rape of the Sabines* (1583) is an essay in three-dimensional Mannerism. Its three figures of an old man, a young man and a woman spiral upwards in a fluid *contrapposto* convulsion, one of the first sculptures designed to be seen from all sides. The loggia also shelters Giambologna's less successful *Hercules and Nessus*, a chorus line of six Roman vestal wallflowers, and several other works that contribute to the rather curious effect, especially at night, of people at a wild party frozen into stone by Medusa's magical gaze.

Loggia dei Lanzi

The first two statues placed in the square were carried there by republican enthusiasm. Donatello's *Judith and Holofernes* was hauled from the Medici palace and placed here in 1494 as a symbol of the defeat of tyranny. Michelangelo's *David* was equally seen as the embodiment of republican triumph (when it was finished in 1504, the Medici were in exile), though it is doubtful whether Michelangelo himself had such symbolism in mind, as the statue was intended to stand next to the cathedral, only to be shanghaied to the Piazza della Signoria by eager republican partisans. It was replaced by a copy in 1873 when the original was relocated (with much pomp and on a specially built train) to the Accademia. Later Florentine sculptors attempted to rival the *David*, especially the awful Baccio Bandinelli, who managed to get the commission to create a pendant to the statue and boasted that he could surpass Il Divino himself. The pathetic result, *Hercules and Cacus*, was completed in 1534; as a reward, Bandinelli had to listen to his archenemy Cellini insult the statue in front of their patron, Cosimo I. An 'old sack full of melons' he called it, bestowing the sculpture's alternative title.

Another overgrown victim of the chisel stands at the corner of the Palazzo Vecchio. Ammannati's **Neptune Fountain** (1575) was dubbed *Il Biancone* ('Big Whitey') almost as soon as it was unveiled; Michelangelo felt sorry for the huge block of marble Ammannati 'ruined' to produce Neptune, a lumpy, bloated symbol of Cosimo I's naval victories, who stands arrogantly over a low basin and a few half-hearted spurts of water, pulled along by four struggling sea steeds, mere hobby-horses compared with Big Whitey himself.

The last colossus in Piazza della Signoria is the *Equestrian Monument to Cosimo I* by Giambologna (1595), the only large-scale equestrian bronze of the Late Renaissance. The scheme on the panels below the statue depicts scenes of Cosimo's brutal conquest of Siena, and of the 'Florentine Senate' and the Pope conferring the Grand Dukedom on Cosimo. Directly behind Cosimo stands the **Tribunale di Mercanzia**, built in the 14th century as a commercial court for merchants of the guilds and adorned with heraldic arms. To the left of this (no. 7) is a fine, 16th-century contribution, the **Palazzo Uguccioni**, very much in the spirit of High Renaissance in Rome, and sometimes attributed to a design by Raphael.

> *When Goethe made his blitz-tour of Florence, the **Palazzo Vecchio** (also called the Palazzo della Signoria) helped pull the wool over his eyes. 'Obviously,' thought the great poet, 'the people . . . enjoyed a lucky succession of good governments'—a remark which, as Mary McCarthy wrote, could make the angels in heaven weep.*

But none of Florence's chronic factionalism mars Arnolfo di Cambio's temple of civic aspirations, part council hall and part fortress. In many ways, the Palazzo Vecchio is the ideal of stone Florence: rugged and imposing, with a rusticated façade that was to inspire so many of the city's private palaces, yet designed according to the proportions of the Golden Section of the ancient Greeks. Its dominant feature, the 94-m tower, is a typical piece of Florentine bravado, for long the highest point in the city.

The Palazzo Vecchio occupies the site of the old Roman theatre and the medieval Palazzo dei Priori. In the 13th century this earlier palace was flattened along with the Ghibelline quarter interred under the piazza, and in 1299, the now ascendant Guelphs called upon Arnolfo di Cambio, master builder of the cathedral, to design the most impressive 'Palazzo del Popolo' (as the building was originally called) possible, with an eye to upstaging rival cities. The palace's unusual trapezoidal shape is often, but rather dubiously, explained as Guelph care not to have any of the building touch land once owned by Ghibellines. One doubts that even in the 13th century real estate realities allowed such delicacy of sentiments; nor does the theory explain why the tower has swallowtail Ghibelline crenellations, as opposed to the square Guelph ones on the palace itself. Later additions to the rear of the palace have obscured its shape even more, though the façade is essentially as Arnolfo built it, except for the bet-hedging monogram over the door hailing Christ the King of Florence, put up in the nervous days of 1529, when the imperial army of Charles V was on its way to destroy the last Florentine republic; the inscription replaces an earlier one left by Savonarola. The room at the top of the tower was used as prison for celebrities and dubbed the *alberghetto* ('the little hotel'); inmates included Cosimo il Vecchio before his brief exile, and Savonarola, who spent his last months, between torture sessions, enjoying a superb view of the city before his execution in the piazza below.

> Today the Palazzo Vecchio serves as Florence's city hall, but nearly all of its **historical rooms** are open to the public (open 9–7; holidays 8–1; closed Sat; adm exp).

With few exceptions, the interior decorations date from the time of Cosimo I, when he moved his Grand Ducal self from the Medici palace in 1540. To politically 'correct' its acres of walls and ceilings in the shortest amount of time, he turned to his court artist Giorgio Vasari, famed more for the speed at which he could execute a commission than for its quality. On the ground floor of the palazzo, before you buy your ticket, you can take a gander at some of Vasari's more elaborate handiwork in the **Courtyard**, redone for the occasion of Francesco I's unhappy marriage to the plain and stupid Habsburg Joanna of Austria in 1565.

Vasari's suitably grand staircase ascends to the largest room in the palace, the vast **Salone dei Cinquecento**. The *salone* was added at the insistence of Savonarola for meetings of the 500-strong Consiglio Maggiore, the reformed republic's democratic assembly. Art's two reigning divinities, Leonardo da Vinci and Michelangelo, were commissioned in 1503 to paint the two long walls of the *salone* in a kind of Battle of the Brushes to which the city eagerly looked forward. Sadly, neither of the artists came near to completing the project; Leonardo managed to fresco a section of the wall, using the experimental techniques that were to prove the undoing of his *Last Supper* in Milan, while Michelangelo only completed the cartoons before being summoned to Rome by Julius II, who required the sculptor of the *David* to pander to his own personal megalomania.

In the 1560s Vasari removed what was left of Leonardo's efforts and refrescoed the entire room as a celebration of Cosimo's military triumphs over Pisa and Siena, complete with an apotheosis of the Grand Duke on the ceiling. These wall scenes are inane, big and busy, crowded with men and horses who appear to have all the substance of overcooked pasta. The sculptural groups lining the walls of this almost uncomfortably large room (the Italian parliament sat here from 1865 to 1870 when Florence was the capital) are only slightly more stimulating; even Michelangelo's *Victory*, on the wall opposite the entrance, is more virtuosity than vision: a vacuous young idiot posing with one knee atop a defeated old man still half submerged in stone, said to be a self-portrait of the sculptor, which lends the work a certain bitter poignancy. The neighbouring work which is a muscle-bound *Hercules and Diomedes* by Vicenzo de' Rossi, probably was inevitable in this city obsessed by the possibilities of the male nude.

Beyond the *salone*, behind a modern glass door, is a much smaller and much more intriguing room the size of a closet. This is the **Studiolo of Francesco I**, designed by Vasari in 1572 for Cosimo's melancholic and reclusive son, where he would escape to brood over his real interests in natural curiosities and alchemy. The little study, windowless and more than a little claustrophobic, has been restored to its original appearance, lined with allegorical paintings by Vasari, Bronzino and Allori, and bronze statuettes by Giambologna and Ammannati, their refined, polished, and erotic mythological subjects part of a carefully thought-out 16th-century programme on Man and Nature. The lower row of paintings conceals Francesco's secret cupboards where he kept his most precious belongings, his pearls and crystals and gold.

After the *salone* a certain fuzziness begins to set in. Cosimo I's propaganda machine in league with Vasari's fresco factory produced room after room of self-glorifying Medicean poofery. The first series of rooms, known as the **Quartiere di Leone X**, carry ancestor worship to extremes, each chamber dedicated to a different Medici: in the first Cosimo il Vecchio returns from exile amid tumultuous acclaim; in the second Lorenzo il Magnifico receives the ambassadors in the company of a dignified giraffe; the third and fourth are dedicated to the Medici popes, while the fifth, naturally, is for Cosimo I, who gets the most elaborate treatment of all.

Upstairs the next series of rooms is known as the **Quartiere degli Elementi**, with more works of Vasari and his studio, depicting allegories of the elements. Beyond these are several rooms currently used to display works pilfered by the Nazis during the war and since recovered (*closed at the time of writing*). Many of the paintings were personally selected by Goering and Hitler, who were apparently quite fond of *Leda and the Swan* and other mild mythological erotica. In a small room is the original of Verrocchio's boy with the dolphin, from the courtyard fountain.

A balcony across the Salone dei Cinquecento leads to the **Quartiere di Eleonora di Toledo**, Mrs Cosimo I's private apartments. Of special note here is her chapel, one of the masterpieces of Bronzino, who seemed to relish the opportunity to paint something besides Medici portraits. The next room, the **Sala dell'Udienza**, has a quattrocento coffered ceiling by Benedetto and Giuliano da Maiano, and walls painted with a rather fine romp by Mannerist Francesco Salviati (1550–60).

The last room, the **Sala dei Gigli** ('of the lilies') boasts another fine ceiling by the da Maiano brothers; it contains Donatello's recently restored bronze *Judith and Holofernes*, a late and rather gruesome work of 1455; the warning to tyrants inscribed on its base was added when the statue was abducted from the Medici palace and placed in the Piazza della Signoria. Off the Sala dei Gigli are two small rooms of interest: the **Guardaroba**, or unique 'wardrobe' adorned with 57 maps painted by Fra Egnazio Danti in 1563, depicting all the world known at the time. The **Cancelleria** was Machiavelli's office from 1498–1512, when he served the republic as a secretary and diplomat. He is commemorated with a bust and a portrait. Poor Machiavelli died bitter and unaware of the notoriety that his works would one day bring him, and he would probably be amazed to learn that his very name had become synonymous with cunning, amoral intrigue. After losing his job upon the return of the Medici, and at one point tortured and imprisoned on a false suspicion of conspiracy, Machiavelli was forced into idleness in the country, where he wrote his political works and two fine plays, feverishly trying to return to favour, even dedicating his most famous book, *The Prince*, to the incompetent Lorenzo, Duke of Urbino (further glorified by Michelangelo's Medici tombs); his concern throughout was to advise realistically, without mincing words, the fractious and increasingly weak Italians on how to create a strong state. His evil reputation came from openly stating what rulers do, rather than what they would like other people to think they do.

Two collections long housed in the Palazzo Vecchio, the excellent **Collection of Old Musical Instruments**, and the **Collezione Loeser**, a fine assortment of Renaissance art left to the city in 1928 by Charles Loeser, the Macy's department-store heir, have at the time of writing tumbled into Italian museum limbo. The violins and cellos (several by Cremona greats like Stradivarius and Guarneri) have been earmarked for a new destination; the tourist office can give you a status report.

> After the pomposity of the Palazzo Vecchio and a Campari cure at the Piazza della Signoria's landmark **Café Rivoire**, you may be in the mood to reconsider the 20th century. The best place to do this in Florence is at its only museum of modern art, the **Collezione della Ragione**, located on the Piazza della Signoria, above the Cassa di Risparmio bank (open 9–2 Sat and sometimes during the week, information © 217305).

There are typical still lifes by De Pisis; equally still landscapes by Carlo Carra; mysterious baths by De Chirico; Tuscan landscapes by Mario Mafai, Antonio Donghi and Ottone Rosai; a speedy Futurist horse by Fortunato Depero and a window with doves by Gino Severini; a number of richly coloured canvases by Renato Guttuso and paintings after Tintoretto by Emilio Vedova, and many others, surprises, perhaps, for those unfamiliar with living Italians as opposed to dead ones.

> Just south of the Palazzo Vecchio is the entrance to the **Uffizi**; queues in the summer are very common; try to arrive early (open daily exc Mon 9–7, and 9–1 Sun; adm exp).

Florence has the most fabulous art museum in Italy, and as usual we have the Medici to thank; for the building that holds these treasures, however, credit goes to Grand Duke Cosimo's much maligned court painter. Poor Giorgio Vasari! His roosterish boastfulness and the conviction that his was the best of all possible artistic worlds, set next to his very modest talents, have made him a comic figure in most art criticism. Even the Florentines don't like him. On one of the rare occasions when he tried his hand as an architect, though, he gave Florence something to be proud of. The Uffizi ('offices') were built as Cosimo's secretariat, incorporating the old mint (producer of the first gold florins in 1252), the archives, and the large church of San Pier Scheraggio, with plenty of room for the bureaucrats needed to run Cosimo's efficient, modern state. The matched pair of arcaded buildings have cold elegant façades that conceal Vasari's surprising innovation: iron reinforcements that make the huge amount of window area possible and keep the building stable on the soft sandy ground. It was a trick that would be almost forgotten until the Crystal Palace and the first American skyscrapers.

Almost from the start the Medici began to store some of their huge art collection in parts of the building. There are galleries in the world with more works of art—the Uffizi counts some 1800—but the Uffizi overwhelms by the fact that every one of its paintings is worth looking at.

Near the ticket counter you are able to see what remains of the church of San Pier Scheraggio which is now decorated with Andrea del Castagno's stately **Frescoes of Illustrious Men** (1450), including the Cumaean Sibyl(!) as well as Dante and Boccaccio, both of whom attended political debates in this very church. From here you can take the lift or sweeping grand stair up to the second floor, where the Medici once had a huge theatre, now home to the **Cabinet of Drawings and Prints**. Although the bulk of this extensive and renowned collection is only open to scholars with special permission, a roomful of tempting samples gives a hint at what they have a chance to see.

Nowadays one thinks of the Uffizi as primarily a gallery of paintings, but for some hundred years after its opening, visitors came almost exclusively for the fine collection of Hellenistic and Roman marbles. Most of these were collected in Rome by Medici cardinals, and not a few were sources of Renaissance inspiration. The **Vestibule** at the top of the stair contains some of the best, together with Flemish and Tuscan tapestries made for Cosimo I and his successors. **Room 1**, usually shut, contains excellent early Roman sculpture.

Rooms 2–6: 13th and 14th centuries

The Uffizi's paintings are arranged in chronological order, the better to educate its visitors on trends in Italian art. The roots of the Early Renaissance are strikingly revealed in **Room 2**, dedicated to the three great **Maestà** altarpieces by the masters of the 13th century. All portray the same subject of the Madonna and Child enthroned with angels. The one on the right, by Cimabue, was painted in around the year1285 and represents a breaking away from the flat, stylized Byzantine tradition. To the left is the so-called *Rucellai Madonna*, painted in the same period by the Sienese Duccio di Buoninsegna for Santa Maria Novella. It resembles Cimabue's in many ways, but has a more advanced technique for creating depth, and the bright colouring that characterizes the Sienese school. Giotto's altarpiece, painted some 25 years later, takes a great leap forward, not only in his use of perspective, but in the arrangement of the angels, standing naturally, and in the portrayal of the Virgin, gently smiling, with real fingers and breasts.

To the left, **Room 3** contains representative Sienese works of the 14th century, with a beautiful Gothic *Annunciation* (1333) by Simone Martini and the brothers Pietro and Ambrogio Lorenzetti. **Room 4** is dedicated to 14th-century Florentines: Bernardo Daddi, Nardo di Cione, and the delicately coloured *San Remigio Pietà* by Giottino. **Rooms 5 and 6** portray Italian contributions to the International Gothic school, most dazzlingly Gentile da Fabriano's *Adoration of the Magi* (1423), two good works by Lorenzo Monaco, and the *Thebaid* of Gherardo Starnina, depicting the rather unusual activities of the 4th-century monks of St Pancratius of Thebes, in Egypt; a composition strikingly like Chinese scroll scenes of hermits.

Rooms 7–9: Early Renaissance

In the Uffizi, at least, it's but a few short steps from the superbly decorative International Gothic to the masters of the Early Renaissance. **Room 7** contains minor works by Fra Angelico, Masaccio and Masolino, and three masterpieces: Domenico Veneziano's pastel *Madonna and Child with Saints* (1448), one of the rare pictures by this Venetian master who died a pauper in Florence. It is a new departure not only for its soft colours but for the subject matter, unifying the enthroned Virgin and saints in one panel, in what is known as a *Sacra Conversazione*. Piero della Francesca's famous *Double Portrait of the Duke Federigo da Montefeltro and his Duchess Battista Sforza of Urbino* (1465) depicts one of Italy's noblest Renaissance princes—and surely the one with the most distinctive nose. Piero's ability to create perfectly still, timeless worlds is even more evident in the allegorical 'Triumphs' of the Duke and Duchess painted on the back of their portraits. A similar stillness and fascination floats over into the surreal in Uccello's *Rout of San Romano* (1456), or at least the third of it still present (the other two panels are in the Louvre and London's National Gallery; all three once decorated the bedroom of Lorenzo il Magnifico in the Medici palace). Both Piero and Uccello were deep students of perspective, but Uccello went half-crazy; applying his principles to a violent battle scene has left us one of the most provocative works of all time—a vision of warfare in suspended animation, with pink, white and blue toy horses, robot-like knights, and rabbits bouncing in the background.

Room 8 is devoted to the works of the rascally romantic Fra Filippo Lippi, whose ethereally lovely Madonnas were modelled after his brown-eyed nun. In his *Coronation of the Virgin* (1447) she kneels in the foreground with two children, while the artist, dressed in a brown habit, looks dreamily towards her; in his celebrated *Madonna and Child with Two Angels* (1445) she plays the lead before the kind of mysterious landscape Leonardo would later perfect. Lippi taught the art of enchanting Madonnas to his student Botticelli, who has some lovely works in this room and the next; Alesso Baldovinetti, a pupil of the far more holy Fra Angelico, painted the room's beautiful *Annunciation* (1447). **Room 9** has two small scenes from the *Labours of Hercules* (1470) by Antonio Pollaiuolo, whose interest in anatomy, muscular expressiveness and violence presages a strain in Florentine art that would culminate in the great Mannerists. He worked with his younger brother Piero on the refined, elegant *SS. Vincent, James and Eustace*, transferred here from San Miniato. This room also contains the Uffizi's best-known forgery: *The Young Man in a Red Hat* or self-portrait of Filippino Lippi, believed to have been the work of a clever 18th-century English art dealer who palmed it off on the Grand Dukes.

Botticelli: Rooms 10–14

To accommodate the bewitching art of 'Little Barrels' and his throngs of 20th-century admirers, the Uffizi converted four small rooms into one great Botticellian shrine. Although his masterpieces displayed here have become almost synonymous with the Florentine Renaissance at its most spring-like and charming, they were not publicly displayed until the beginning of the 19th century, nor given much consideration outside Florence until the turn of the century.

Botticelli's best works date from the days when he was a darling of the Medici—family members crop up most noticeably in the *Adoration of the Magi* (1476), where you can pick out Cosimo il Vecchio, Lorenzo il Magnifico and Botticelli himself (in the right foreground, in a yellow robe, gazing at the spectator). His *Annunciation* is a graceful, cosmic dance between the Virgin and the Angel Gabriel. In the *Tondo of the Virgin of the Pomegranate* the lovely melancholy goddess who was to become his Venus makes her first appearance.

Botticelli is best known for his sublime mythological allegories, nearly all painted for the Medici and inspired by the Neoplatonic, humanistic and hermetic currents that pervaded the intelligentsia of the late 15th century. Perhaps no painting has been debated so fervently as *La Primavera* (1478). This hung for years in the Medici Villa at Castello, and it is believed that the subject of the Allegory of Spring was suggested by Marsilio Ficino, one of the great natural magicians of the Renaissance, and that the figures represent the 'beneficial' planets able to dispel sadness. *Pallas and the Centaur* has been called another subtle allegory of Medici triumph—the rings of Athene's gown are supposedly a family symbol. Other interpretations see the taming of the sorrowful centaur as a melancholy comment on reason and civilization. Botticelli's last great mythological painting, *The Birth of Venus*, was commissioned by Lorenzo di Pierfrancesco and inspired by a poem by Poliziano, Lorenzo il Magnifico's Latin and Greek scholar, who described how Zephyr and Chloris blew the newborn goddess to shore on a scallop shell, while Hora hastened to robe her, a scene Botticelli portrays once again with dance-like rhythm and delicacy of line. Yet the goddess of love floats towards the spectator with an expression of wistfulness—perhaps reflecting the artist's own feelings of regret. For artistically, the poetic, decorative style he perfected in this painting would be disdained and forgotten in his own lifetime. Spiritually, Botticelli also turned a corner after creating this haunting, uncanny beauty—his, and Florence's, farewell to a lovely road not taken. Although Vasari's biography of Botticelli portrays a prankster rather than a sensitive soul, the painter absorbed more than any other artist the *fin-de-siècle* neuroticism that beset the city with the rise of Savonarola. So thoroughly did he reject his Neoplatonism that he would only accept commissions of sacred subjects or supposedly edifying allegories like his *Calumny*, a small but disturbing work, and a fitting introduction to the dark side of the quattrocento psyche.

This large room also contains works by Botticelli's contemporaries. Two paintings of the *Adoration of the Magi*, one by Ghirlandaio and one by Filippino Lippi, show the influence of Leonardo's unfinished but radical work in pyramidal composition (in the next room); Leonardo himself got the idea from the large *Portinari Altarpiece* (1471) by Hugo Van der Goes in the middle of the room, a work brought back from Bruges by Medici agent Tommaso Portinari. Behind it hangs Lorenzo di Credi's *Venus*, a charmer inspired by Botticelli.

Rooms 15–24: More Renaissance

Room 15 is dedicated to the Florentine works of Leonardo da Vinci's early career. Here are works by his master Andrea Verrocchio, including the *Baptism of Christ*, in which the young Leonardo painted the angel on the left. Modern art critics believe the large *Annunciation* (1475) is almost entirely by Leonardo's hand—the soft faces, the botanical details, the misty, watery background would become the trademarks of his magical brush. Most influential, however, was his unfinished *Adoration of the Magi* (1481), a highly unconventional composition that Leonardo abandoned when he left Florence for Milan. Although at first glance it's hard to make out much more than a mass of reddish chiaroscuro, the longer you stare, the better you'll see the serene Madonna and Child surrounded by a crowd of anxious, troubled humanity, with an exotic background of ruins, trees and horsemen, all charged with expressive energy. Other artists in Room 15 include Leonardo's peers: Lorenzo di Credi, whose religious works have eerie garden-like backgrounds, and the nutty Piero di Cosimo, whose dreamy *Perseus Liberating Andromeda* includes an endearing mongrel of a dragon that gives even the most reserved Japanese tourist fits of giggles. Tuscan maps adorn **Room 16**, as well as scenes by Hans Memling.

The octagonal **Tribuna** (Room 18) with its mother-of-pearl dome and *pietra dura* floor and table was built by Buontalenti in 1584 for Francesco I, and like the Studiolo in the Palazzo Vecchio, was designed to hold Medici treasures. For centuries the best-known of these was the *Venus de' Medici*, a 2nd-century BC Greek sculpture, farcically claimed as a copy of Praxiteles' celebrated Aphrodite of Cnidos, the most erotic statue in antiquity. In the 18th century, amazingly, this rather ordinary girl was considered the greatest sculpture in Florence; today most visitors walk right by without a second glance. Other antique works include the *Wrestlers* and the *Knife Grinder*, both copies of Pergamese originals, the *Dancing Faun*, the *Young Apollo*, and the *Sleeping Hermaphrodite* in the adjacent room, which sounds fascinating but is usually curtained off.

The real stars of the Tribuna are the Medici court portraits, many by Bronzino, who could not only catch the likeness of Cosimo I, Eleanor of Toledo and their children, but aptly portrayed the spirit of the day—these are people who took themselves very seriously indeed. They have for company Vasari's posthumous portrait of *Lorenzo il Magnifico* and Pontormo's *Cosimo il Vecchio*, Andrea del Sarto's *Girl with a Book by Petrarch*, and Rosso Fiorentino's *Angel Musician*, an enchanting work entirely out of place in this stodgy temple.

Two followers of Piero della Francesca, Perugino and Luca Signorelli, hold pride of place in **Room 19**; Perugino's *Portrait of a Young Man* is believed to be modelled on his pupil Raphael. Signorelli's *Tondo of the Holy Family* was to become the inspiration for Michelangelo's (*see p.125*). The Germans appear in **Room 20**, led by Dürer and his earliest known work, the *Portrait of his Father* (1490), done at age 19, and *The Adoration of the Magi* (1504), painted after his first trip to Italy. Also here are Lucas Cranach's Teutonic *Adam and Eve* and *Portrait of Martin Luther* (1543), not someone you'd expect to see in Florence. **Room 21** is dedicated to the great Venetians, most famously Bellini and his uncanny *Sacred Allegory* (1490s), the meaning of which has never been satisfactorily explained. There are two minor works by the elusive Giorgione, and a typically weird *St Dominic* by Cosmè Tura. Later Flemish and German artists appear in **Room 22**, works by Gerard David and proto-Romantic Albrecht Altdorfer, and a portrait attributed to Hans Holbein of *Sir Thomas More*. **Room 23** is dedicated to non-Tuscans Correggio of Parma and Mantegna of the Veneto, as well as Boltraffio's strange *Narcissus* with an eerie background reminiscent of Leonardo.

Rooms 25–27: Mannerism

The window-filled **South Corridor**, with its views over the city and fine display of antique sculpture, marks only the halfway point in the Uffizi but nearly the end of Florence's contribution. In the first three rooms, however, local talent rallies to produce a brilliantly coloured twilight in Florentine Mannerism. By most accounts, Michelangelo's only completed oil painting, the *Tondo Doni* (1506), was the spark that ignited Mannerism's flaming orange and turquoise hues. Michelangelo was 30 when he painted this unconventional work, in a medium he disliked (sculpture and fresco being the only fit occupations for a man, or so he believed). It is a typical Michelangelo story that when the purchaser complained the artist was asking too much for it, Michelangelo promptly doubled the price. As shocking as the colours are the spiralling poses of the Holy Family, sharply delineated against a background of five nude, slightly out-of-focus young men of uncertain purpose (are they pagans? angels? boyfriends? or just filler?)—an ambiguity that was to become a hallmark of Mannerism. In itself, the *Tondo Doni* is more provocative than immediately appealing; the violent canvas in **Room 27**, Rosso Fiorentino's *Moses Defending the Children of Jethro*, was painted some 20 years later and at least in its intention to shock the viewer puts a cap on what Michelangelo began.

Room 26 is dedicated mainly to Raphael, who was in and out of Florence 1504–8. Never temperamental or eccentric like his contemporaries, Raphael was the sweetheart of the High Renaissance. His Madonnas, like *The Madonna of the Goldfinch*, a luminous work painted in Florence, have a tenderness that was soon to be over-popularized by others and turned into holy cards, a cloying sentimentality added like layers of varnish over the centuries. It's easier, perhaps, to see Raphael's genius in non-sacred subjects, like *Leo X with Two Cardinals*, a perceptive portrait study of the first Medici pope with his nephew Giulio de' Medici, later Clement VII. The same room contains Andrea del Sarto's most original work, the fluorescent *Madonna of the Harpies* (1517), named after the figures on the Virgin's pedestal. Of the works by Pontormo, the best is in **Room 27**,

Supper at Emmaus (1525), a strange canvas with peasant-faced monks emerging out of the darkness, brightly clad diners with dirty feet, and the Masonic symbol of the Eye of God hovering over Christ's head.

Rooms 28–45

Although we now bid a fond farewell to the Florentines, the Uffizi fairly bristles with masterpieces from other parts of Italy and abroad. Titian's delicious nudes, especially the incomparably voluptuous *Venus of Urbino*, raise the temperature in **Room 28**; Parmigianino's hyper-elegant *Madonna with the Long Neck* (1536) in **Room 30** is a fascinating Mannerist evolutionary dead-end, possessing all the weird beauty of a foot-long dragonfly. Sebastiano del Piombo's recently restored *Death of Adonis*, in **Room 32**, is notable for its melancholy, lagoony, autumn atmosphere and the annoyed look on Venus' face. **Room 34** holds Paolo Veronese's *Holy Family with St Barbara*, a late work bathed in a golden Venetian light, with a gorgeously opulent Barbara gazing on. In **Room 35** his contemporary Tintoretto is represented by a shadowy *Leda* languidly pretending to restrain the lusty swan; the Uffizi's El Greco is here as well, reminding us that this most Mannerist of Mannerists learned how to do it in Venice.

Room 41 is Flemish domain, with brand-name art by Rubens and Van Dyck; the former's *Baccanale* may be the most grotesque canvas in Florence. Struggle on gamely to **Room 43** to see three striking Caravaggios. His *Bacchus* and *The Head of Medusa* are believed to be self-portraits; in its day the fleshy and heavy-eyed Bacchus, half portrait and half still life, but lacking the usual mythological appurtenances, was considered highly iconoclastic. Here, too, is one of the best versions of *Judith and Holofernes* by Artemisia Gentileschi; after being allegedly raped by a fellow artist (who was acquitted in court), the subject of a woman slicing off a man's head became her favourite theme. There are three portraits by Rembrandt in **Room 44**, including two of himself, young and old, and landscapes by Ruysdael. **Room 45** is given over to some fine 18th-century works, including two charming portraits of children by Chardin, and others by Goya and Longhi, and Venetian landscapes by Guardi and Canaletto. Even more welcome by this time is the bar at the end of the corridor, with a lovely summer terrace.

Corridoio Vasariano

In 1565, when Francesco I married Joanna of Austria, the Medici commissioned Vasari to link their new digs in the Pitti Palace with the Uffizi and the Palazzo Vecchio in such a manner that the Archdukes could make their rounds without having to rub elbows with their subjects. With a patina of 400 years, it seems that Florence wouldn't look quite right without this covered catwalk, leapfrogging on rounded arches from the back of the Uffizi, over the Ponte Vecchio, daintily skirting a medieval tower, and darting past the façade of Santa Felicità to the Pitti Palace.

The Corridoio not only offers interesting views of Florence, but has been hung with a celebrated collection of artists' self-portraits, beginning with Vasari himself before continuing in chronological order, past the Gaddis and Raphael to Rembrandt, Van Dyck, Velazquez, Hogarth, Reynolds, Delacroix, Corot and scores in between. (*The bomb of May 1993 damaged parts of the Vasari Corridor and it is now closed for restoration. Other parts of the gallery are also temporarily closed to repair bomb damage, but all the major works displayed in these areas have been moved and are visible*).

> For all that Florence and Tuscany contributed to the birth of science, it is only fitting to have the **Museum of the History of Science** in the centre of the city, behind the Uffizi in Piazza Giudici (open 9.30–1 Mon–Sat, 2–5 also Mon, Wed and Fri, closed Sun; adm exp).

Much of the ground floor is devoted to instruments measuring time and distance that are often works of art in themselves: Arabian astrolabes and pocket sundials, Tuscan sundials in the shape of Platonic solids, enormous elaborate armillary spheres and a small reliquary holding the bone of Galileo's finger, erect, like a final gesture to the city that until 1737 denied him a Christian burial. Here, too, are two of his original telescopes and the lens with which he discovered the four moons of Jupiter. Other scientific instruments come from the Accademia del Cimento (of 'trial', or 'experiment'), founded in 1657 by Cardinal Leopoldo de' Medici, the world's first scientific organization, dedicated to Galileo's principle of inquiry and proof by experimentation. 'Try and try again' was its motto.

Upstairs, there's a large room filled with machines used to demonstrate principles of physics, which the ladies who run the museum will operate if you ask. Two unusual ones are the 18th-century automatic writer and the instrument of perpetual motion. The rooms devoted to medicine contain a collection of 18th-century wax anatomical models, designed to teach budding obstetricians about unfortunate foetal positions, as well as a fine display of surgical instruments from the period.

> From the museum, follow the Arno down to the **Ponte Vecchio.**

> > Bent bridges seeming to strain like bows
> > And tremble with arrowy undertide . . .

> > 'Casa Guidi Windows', Elizabeth Barrett Browning

Ponte Vecchio

Often at sunset the Arno becomes a stream of molten gold, confined in its walls of stone and laced into its bed with the curving arches of its spans. That is, during those months when it has a respectable flow of water. But even in the torrid days of August, when the Arno shrivels into muck and spittle, its two famous bridges retain their distinctive beauty. The most famous of these, the Ponte Vecchio, the 'Old Bridge', crosses the Arno at its narrowest point; the present bridge, with its three stone arches, was built in 1345, and replaces a wooden construction from the 970s, the successor to a span that may well have dated back to the Romans.

On this bridge, at the foot of the Marzocco, or statue of Mars, Buondelmonte dei Buondelmonti was murdered in 1215, setting off the wars of the Guelphs and Ghibellines. The original Marzocco was washed away in a 14th-century flood, and Donatello's later version has been carted off to the Bargello.

Like old London Bridge, the Ponte Vecchio is covered with shops and houses. By the 1500s, for hygienic reasons, it had become the street of hog butchers, though after Vasari built Cosimo's secret passage on top, the Grand Duke, for personal hygienic reasons, evicted the butchers and replaced them with goldsmiths. They have been there ever since, and shoppers from around the world descend on it each year to scrutinize the traditional Florentine talent for jewellery—many of the city's great artists began their careers as goldsmiths, from Ghiberti and Donatello, to Cellini, who never gave up the craft, and whose bust adorns the middle of the bridge. In the 1966 flood the shops did not prove as resilient as the Ponte Vecchio itself, and a fortune of gold was washed down the Arno. All is since restored.

In the summer of 1944, the river briefly became a German defensive line during the slow painful retreat across Italy. Before leaving Florence, the

*Nazis blew up every one of the city's bridges, saving only, on Hitler's special orders, the Ponte Vecchio, though they blasted a large number of ancient buildings on each side of the span to create piles of rubble to block the approaches. Florence's most beautiful span, the **Ponte Santa Trìnita** was the most tragic victim.*

Immediately after the war the Florentines set about replacing the bridges exactly as they were: for Santa Trínita, old quarries had to be reopened to duplicate the stone, and old methods revived to cut it (modern power saws would have done it too cleanly). The graceful curve of the three arches was a problem; they could not be constructed geometrically, and considerable speculation went on over how the architect (Ammannati, in 1567) did it. Finally, recalling that Michelangelo had advised Ammannati on the project, someone noticed that the same form of arch could be seen on the decoration of the tombs in Michelangelo's Medici Chapel, constructed most likely by pure artistic imagination. Fortune lent a hand in the reconstruction; of the original statues of the 'Four Seasons', almost all the pieces were fished out of the Arno and rebuilt. Spring's head was eventually found by divers completely by accident in 1961.

*Just west of **Via Por S. Maria**, the main street leading to the Ponte Vecchio, you'll find some of the oldest, best-preserved lanes in Florence. Near the Mercato Nuovo at the top of the street (see p.108) stands the **Palazzo di Parte Guelfa**, the 13th-century headquarters of the Guelph party, and often the real seat of power in the city, paid for by property confiscated from the Ghibellines; in the 15th century Brunelleschi added a hall on the top floor and an extension. Next door is the guildhall of the silk makers, the 14th-century **Palazzo dell'Arte della Seta**, still bearing its bas-relief emblem, or 'stemma', of a closed door, the age-old guild symbol. It's worth continuing around the Guelph Palace to Via Pellicceria to see the fine ensemble of medieval buildings on the tiny square near Via delle Terme, named after the old Roman baths.*

*To get an idea of what life was like inside these sombre palaces some 600 years ago, stroll over to nearby Via Porta Rossa, site of the elegant **Palazzo Davanzati**, now arranged as the **Museo della Casa Fiorentina Antica**, a delightful museum, offering a chance to step back into domestic life of yore (open 9–2, Sun 9–12.45, closed Mon; adm).*

Originally built in the mid-14th century for the Davizzi family, the house was purchased by merchant Bernardo Davanzati in 1578 and stayed in the family until the 1900s. Restored by an antique collector in 1904, it is the best-preserved medieval-Renaissance house in Florence and has been furnished with period trappings and art.

The façade is basically as it was, except for a 16th-century addition of a fifth-floor loggia, replacing the battlements—in the rough-and-tumble urban 14th century, a man's home literally had to be a castle. But it was also a showroom for his prosperity, and by the standards of the day, the dwellers of this huge palace were multi-millionaires. From the grand loggia, used for sumptuous public entertainment, enter the palace by way of a striking vertical **Courtyard**, which was cut off from the street in times of danger, as evidenced by the stout, iron-bolted door. No family would feel safe without a year's store of grain and oil—against famine, siege, plagues or inflation. One storeroom is now used for an audio-visual history of the house. The well in the corner served all the floors of the house, and there is a medieval dumb waiter to transport shopping up to the kitchen on the top floor.

Upstairs, past a 14th-century fresco of St Christopher on the landing, you arrive at the elegant **Sala Grande** used for formal gatherings, and again, for defence, when boiling oil and such could be dropped through the four hatches in the floor. The room contains a beautiful 16th-century table and cupboard, and luxuries such as automatic bellows and flues at the fireplace, glass windows, and a prettily painted ceiling. The bright, cosy dining room, the **Sala dei Pappagalli**, was named after the parrots that adorn the frescoes, cleverly painted with pretend hooks to resemble far more costly tapestries. Off the **Sala Piccola**, a child's bedroom, is one of the palace's bathrooms, which must have seemed almost decadently luxurious in the medieval city, where one of the laws declared that one had to shout three loud warnings before emptying a chamber pot into the street. The last room on the floor is an elegant bedroom called the **Sala dei Pavoni**, with an almost Moorish-style pattern painted on the walls with coats-of-arms, topped by a frieze of peacocks and other exotic birds flitting among the trees. The bedspread is a rare 14th-century example from Sicily, portraying the story of Tristan and King Mark.

The pattern of rooms is repeated on the next floor. The **Salone** is adorned with 15th-century Flemish tapestries and a portrait of Giovanni di Bicci de' Medici. The dining room contains outlandish salt cellars (17–18th centuries) and games chests. The **Sala Piccola** houses a collection of 15th-century *cassoni*, elaborate wedding chests in which a bride stored her dowry of household linen—especially interesting for the secular subjects chosen to adorn them, often depicted in contemporary dress. The bedroom, the **Camera della Castellana di Vergi**, is decorated with a lovely if slightly faded fresco from a medieval French romance. The 14th-century shoes displayed here were discovered in Boccaccio's house.

The **kitchen**, as is usual in a medieval house, is located on the top floor in the hope that in case of fire, only that part would burn. Women would spend most of their day here, supervising the servants, sewing and gossiping; as no servants' quarters existed in the palace, it is believed that the help sacked out on the floor.

Start: *north of Piazza della Signoria*
Finish: *Santa Maria Nuova*
Walking time: *a morning for Dante's Florence,
          an afternoon for Florence as It Was*

III: Medieval Florence

Dante's
house

131

Between the Piazza del Duomo and Piazza della Signoria lies the medieval kernel from which the Florentine Renaissance emerged like a hot-house flower; here too, is the Bargello, home to some of the finest sculpture in the world.

Lunch/Cafés

Osteria del Chiassovia, Via Fiesolana 13r, ✆ 242 241. Has a traditional menu with homemade pastas and hearty Tuscan soups (closed Sun and Mon lunch, around L30,000).

Bar Cucciolo, Via del Corso, ✆ 287 727. A coffee bar with fresh hot pastries which come shooting down a tube into the shop (closed Sun).

Le Mosacce, Via del Proconsolo 55r, ✆ 294 361. Here you can eat one course or all three—good quality regional food, lively atmosphere (closed Sat, Sun, Mon and evenings).

Enoteca Birreria Centrale, Piazza dei Cimatori 1r, ✆ 211 915. Draught beer and an extensive wine and grappa selection are on offer in this smart, stylish bar. Seasonal dishes are prepared and there is a garden with tables outdoors (closed Sun, around L25,000).

Vineria, Via dei Cimatori 18r. A hole-in-the-wall sandwich bar and wine counter.

Da Gianino, Piazza dei Cimatori 4, ✆ 21 41 25. Not bad food and pleasant atmosphere next door to the Birreria Centrale, tables outdoors (closed Sun, around L40,000).

In 1265 Dante Alighieri was born in the quarter just to the north of the Piazza della Signoria; he was nine, attending a May Feast, 'when first the glorious Lady of my mind was made manifest to mine eyes; even she who was called Beatrice by many who know not wherefore'. Beatrice went on to wed another, and died suddenly in 1290; Dante tried to forget his disappointment and grief in battle, fighting in the wars against Arezzo and Pisa, then in writing his 'autopsychology' *La Vita Nuova.* In 1302, as a White Guelph, he was exiled. A friend just managed to rescue the manuscript of the *Inferno* from the crowds who came to sack and pillage his home. Dante died in Ravenna in 1321, and although he was never allowed to return home, the Florentines have belatedly tried to make amends to their poet. Yet the memorials fall curiously flat. His grand tomb in Santa Croce is empty and his huge statue in front of the church a glowering failure.

> *The best place to summon the shade of Italy's greatest poet is in the narrow medieval lanes of Florence, especially in his old haunts just to the north of Piazza della Signoria. Most scholars believe Dante was born*

on what is now **Via Dante Alighieri**. A modern bas-relief on one of the buildings shows the sights that would have been familiar to Dante, one of which would have been the sturdy well-preserved **Torre del Castagno** on Piazza San Martino, used as the residence of the priori before the construction of the Palazzo Vecchio. Here, too, is the tiny **San Martino del Vescovo**, Dante's parish church.

Medieval Florence

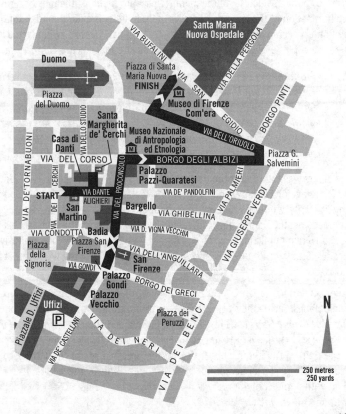

Founded in 986, San Martino was rebuilt in 1479 when it became the headquarters of the charitable Compagnia dei Buonuomini. The Compagnia commissioned a follower of Ghirlandaio to paint a series of colourful frescoes on the Life of St Martin and the Works of Charity, scenes acted out by quattrocento Florentines, in their own fashions on their own streets. The church also has a fine Byzantine Madonna, and one by Perugino (*open 10–12 and 3–5, closed Sun*).

> *Opposite the Piazza San Martino, an alley leads north to the **Casa di Dante**, traditionally considered the poet's birthplace.*

Now a museum dedicated to Dante (*open 9.30–12.30 and 3.30–6.30, Sun 9.30–12.30, closed Wed; donation*), it makes a game attempt to evoke Dante's life and times, in spite of neglect and stingy Florentine low-watt light bulbs. Near the entrance is an edition of *The Divine Comedy*, printed in tiny letters on a poster by a mad Milanese; of the manuscript reproductions, the most interesting is an illumination of the infamous murder of Buondelmonte dei Buondelmonti, with the Ponte Vecchio and a statue of Mars, the original *Marzocco*, in place. Upstairs there are copies of Botticelli's beautiful line illustrations for the *Commedia*.

> *From the house, Via S. Margherita continues to **Santa Margherita de' Cerchi**, where Dante married his second choice, Gemma Donati, whose family arms are among those adorning the 13th-century porch. Dante would also recognize the two great towers in Piazza San Firenze, the looming Bargello and the beautiful Romanesque campanile of the ancient Benedictine abbey, or **Badia**, which he cited in the Paradiso.*

The abbey was founded at the end of the 10th century by the widow of Umberto, the Margrave of Tuscany, and further endowed by their son Ugo, 'the Good Margrave'. Dante would come here to gaze upon Beatrice, and some 50 years after the poet's death, Dante's first biographer, Boccaccio, used the Badia as his forum for innovative public lectures on the text of *The Divine Comedy*. Curiously, Boccaccio's (and later, the Renaissance's) principal criticism of the work is that Dante chose to write about lofty, sacred things in the vulgar tongue of Tuscany.

Except for the campanile, the Badia has become a hotchpotch from too many remodellings. Inside, however, are two beautiful things from the Renaissance: the *Tomb of Count Ugo* (1481) by Mino da Fiesole and the *Madonna Appearing to St Bernard* (1485), a large painting by Filippino Lippi. Through an unmarked door to the right of the choir, you can reach the upper loggia of the **Chiostro degli Aranci**, where the Benedictines grew oranges. Built in the 1430s, it is embellished with a fine contemporary series of frescoes on the life of St Bernard, painted by an unknown artist.

*Across from the Badia looms the **Bargello**, a battlemented urban fortress, well proportioned yet of forbidding grace; for centuries it saw duty as Florence's prison. Today its only inmates are men of marble, gathered together to form Italy's finest collection of sculpture, a fitting complement to the paintings in the Uffizi (open 9–2, Sun 9–1, closed Mon; adm).*

The Bargello is 'stone Florence' squared to the sixth degree, rugged *pietra forte*, the model for the even grander Palazzo Vecchio. Even the treasures it houses are hard, definite—and almost unremittingly masculine. The Bargello offers the best insight available into Florence's golden age, and it was a man's world indeed.

Completed in 1255, the Bargello was originally intended as Florence's Palazzo del Popolo, though by 1271 it served instead as the residence of the foreign *podestà*, or chief magistrate, installed by Guelph leader Charles of Anjou. The Medici made it the headquarters of the captain of police (the *Bargello*), the city jail and torture chamber, a function it served until 1859. In the Renaissance it was the peculiar custom to paint portraits of the condemned on the exterior walls of the fortress; Andrea del Castagno was so good at it that he was nicknamed Andrea of the Hanged Men. All of these ghoulish souvenirs have long since disappeared, as have the torture instruments—burned in 1786, when the death sentence was abolished. Today the **Gothic courtyard**, former site of the gallows and chopping block, is a delightful place, owing much to an imaginative restoration in the 1860s. The encrustation of centuries of *podestà* armorial devices and plaques in a wild vocabulary of symbols, the shadowy arcades and stately stairs combine to create one of Florence's most romantic corners.

*The main ground-floor gallery is dedicated to **Michelangelo** and his century, although it must be said that the Michelangelo of the Bargello somewhat lacks the accustomed angst and ecstasy.*

His *Bacchus* (1496), a youthful work inspired by bad Roman sculpture, has all the personality of a cocktail party bore. Better to invite his noble *Brutus* (1540), even if he's just a bust—the only one the sculptor ever made, in a fit of republican fervour after the assassination of Duke Alessandro de' Medici. Also by Michelangelo is the lovely *Pitti Tondo* and the unfinished *Apollo/David*. From Michelangelo's followers there's a tippling *Bacchus* by Sansovino, and Ammannati's *Leda and the Swan* (a work inspired by a famous but lost erotic drawing by Michelangelo).

The real star of the room is Benvenuto Cellini, who was, besides many other things, an exquisite craftsman and daring innovator. His large bust of *Cosimo I* (1548), with its fabulously detailed armour, was his first work cast in bronze; the unidealized features did not curry favour with the boss that poor Cellini worked so avidly to please. Here, too, is a preliminary model of the *Perseus*, as well as four small statuettes and the relief panel from the original in the Loggia dei Lanzi.

The last great work in the room is by Medici court sculptor Giambologna, now again enjoying a measure of the fashionableness he possessed during his lifetime; art historians consider him the key Mannerist figure between Michelangelo and Bernini. Giambologna's most famous work, the bronze *Mercury* (1564), has certainly seeped into popular consciousness as the representation of the way the god should look. The stairway from the courtyard leads up to the shady **Loggia**, now converted into an aviary for Giambologna's charming bronze birds, made for the animal grotto at the Medici's Villa di Castello.

> *Upstairs the **Salone del Consiglio Generale** is dedicated to the greatest works of Donatello.*

This magnificent hall, formerly the courtroom of the *podestà*, contains the greatest masterpieces of Early Renaissance sculpture. And when Michelangelo's maudlin self-absorption and the Mannerists' empty virtuosity begin to seem tiresome, a visit to this room, to the profound clarity of the greatest of Renaissance sculptors, will prove a welcome antidote. Donatello's originality and vision are strikingly modern—and mysterious. Unlike Michelangelo, who went so far as to commission his own biography when Vasari's didn't please him, Donatello left few traces, not only of his long life, but of what may have been the sources of inspiration behind his three celebrated works displayed here. The chivalric young *St George* (1416) is from the façade of Orsanmichele; his alert watchfulness, or *prontezza*, created new possibilities in expressing movement, emotion and depth of character in stone. Note the accompanying bas-relief of the gallant saint slaying the dragon, a masterful work in perspective. Donatello's fascinatingly androgynous *David*, obviously not from the same planet as Michelangelo's David, is cool and suave, and conquers his Goliath more by his charming enigmatic smile than muscles and virile arrogance. This was the first free-standing nude figure since antiquity, and one of the most erotic, exploring depths of the Florentine psyche that the Florentines probably didn't know they had. No one knows for whom Donatello cast it, or exactly when—around 1440, give or take 10 years.

The same erotic energy and mystery surrounds the laughing, dangerous-looking, precocious boy Cupid, or *Atys Amor*; with its poppies, serpents and winged sandals, it could easily be the ancient idol people mistook it for in the 1700s. Like Botticelli's mythological paintings, Cupid is part of the artistic and intellectual undercurrents of the period, full of pagan philosophy, a possibility rooted out in the terror of the Counter-Reformation and quite forgotten soon after.

Other Donatellos in the *salone* further display the sculptor's amazing diversity. The small marble *David* (1408) was his earliest important work. In the centre of the hall, his *Marzocco*, the symbol of Florence, long stood on the Ponte Vecchio.

Although the two versions of Florence's patron saint, *John the Baptist*, are no longer attributed to Donatello, they show his influence in that they strive to express the saint's spiritual character physically rather than by merely adding his usual holy accessories. The *Dancing Putto* and two busts are Donatello's; his workshop produced the gilded bas-relief of the *Crucifixion*.

On the wall hang the two famous trial reliefs for the second set of baptistry doors, by Ghiberti and Brunelleschi, both depicting the *Sacrifice of Isaac*. Between the panels, the vigorous relief of a tumultuous *Battle Scene* is by the little-known Bertoldo di Giovanni, Donatello's pupil and Michelangelo's teacher. There are a number of other excellent reliefs and busts along the walls, by Agostino di Duccio, Desiderio da Settignano, and some of Luca della Robbia's sweet Madonnas. Currently this hall hosts celebrated busts including Verrocchio's lovely *Young Lady with a Nosegay*, with her hint of a smile and long, sensitive fingers.

*The remainder of the first floor houses fascinating collections of **decorative arts** donated to the Bargello in the last century.*

The **Sala della Torre** is devoted to Islamic art. The **Salone del Podestà** contains splendiferous Byzantine and Renaissance jewellery, watches and clocks, and a Venetian astrolabe. Off this room is the **Cappella del Podestà** with its frescoes once attributed to Giotto.

Some of the most interesting items are in the next rooms, especially the works in the **ivory collection**—Carolingian and Byzantine diptychs, an 8th-century Northumbrian whalebone coffer adorned with runes, medieval French miniatures chronicling 'The Assault on the Castle of Love', 11th-century chess pieces, and more.

A stairway from the ivory collection leads up to the **Second Floor** (*at time of writing closed for rearrangement*). It houses fine enamelled terracottas of the della Robbia family workshop, a room of portrait busts, beautiful works by Antonio Pollaiuolo and Verrocchio, including his *David*. There is also a collection of armour, and the most important collection of small Renaissance bronzes in Italy.

***Piazza San Firenze**, the strangely shaped square that both the Badia and the Bargello call home is named after the large church of **San Firenze**, an imposing ensemble, now partially used as Florence's law courts. At the corner of the square and Via Gondi,*

David del Verrocchio

*the **Palazzo Gondi** is a fine Renaissance merchants' palace built by Giuliano da Sangallo in 1489 but completed only in 1884; it's not easy to pick out the discreet 19th-century additions. Two blocks north from the square on Via Ghibellina, the **Palazzo Borghese** (no. 110) is one of the finest neoclassical buildings in the city, erected in 1822—for a party in honour of Habsburg Grand Duke Ferdinand III. The host of this famous affair was one of the wealthiest men of his day, the Roman prince Camillo Borghese, husband of Pauline Bonaparte and the man responsible for shipping many of Italy's artistic treasures off to the Louvre.*

*Still heading back northwards, Via del Proconsolo runs directly from Piazza San Firenze to the Piazza del Duomo, passing by way of the **Palazzo Pazzi-Quaratesi** (no. 10), the 15th-century headquarters of the banking family that organized the conspiracy against Lorenzo and Giuliano de' Medici. No. 12, the Palazzo Nonfinito—begun in 1593 but never completed—is now the home of the **Museo Nazionale di Antropologia ed Etnologia** (open Sat and third Sun of the month 9–1, except July, Aug and Sept).*

Founded in 1869, the first ethnological museum in Italy, this has a collection of Peruvian mummies, musical instruments collected by Galileo Chini (who decorated the Liberty-style extravaganzas at Viareggio), lovely and unusual items of Japan's Ainu and Pakistan's Kafiri, and a number of skulls from all over the world.

*Borgo degli Albizi, the fine old street passing in front of the Palazzo Nonfinito, was in ancient times the Via Cassia, linking Rome with Bologna, and it deserves a leisurely stroll for its palaces. If it, too, fails to answer to the Florence you've been seeking, take Via dell'Oriuolo (just to the left at Piazza G. Salvemini) for the **Museo di Firenze Com'Era** (Museum of Florence as It Was), located at no. 4 (open 9–2, 9–1 Sun, closed Thurs; adm).*

The jewel of this museum is right out in front, the nearly room-sized *Pianta della Catena*, most beautiful of the early views of Florence. It is a copy as the original made in 1490 by an unknown artist—that handsome fellow pictured in the lower right-hand corner—was lost during the last war in a Berlin museum. This fascinating painting captures Florence at the height of the Renaissance, a city of buildings in bright white, pink and tan; the great churches are without their façades, the Uffizi and Medici chapels have not yet appeared, and the Medici and Pitti palaces are without their later extensions.

*From Via dell'Oriuolo, Via Folco Portinari takes you to Florence's main hospital, **Santa Maria Nuova**, founded in 1286 by the father of Dante's Beatrice, Folco Portinari. Readers of Iris Origo's The Merchant of Prato will recognize it as the work-place of the good notary, Ser Lapo Mazzei. The portico of the hospital, by Buontalenti, was finished in 1612.*

Start: *Piazza Santa Trínita*
Finish: *Ognissanti*
Walking time: *one day*

IV: Piazza Santa Trínita

Palazzo Corsini

Florence has always been a city of merchants and bankers; this walk takes in what has been their fashionable high rent district since the days of the Renaissance.

Lunch/Cafés

Belle Donne, Via delle Belle Donne 16r. Popular lively place with an interior full of frescoes.

Amon, Via Pallazuolo 26–28r, ✆ 293 146. Take-away Egyptian food (closed Sun).

Coco Lezzone, Via del Parioncino 26r, ✆ 287 178. Very good traditional food, but not cheap (closed Sun and Tues eve, around L55,000).

Giacosa, Via Tornabuoni 83/r, ✆ 239 6226. Good sandwiches and ice cream and a reputation for having invented the Negroni (gin, Campari and vermouth). Popular with the Florentine aristocrats back in the 1800s, and now frequented by young trendy ones.

Il Procacci, Via Tornabuoni 64r. This is a high-quality *alimentari* —food shop— selling regional specialities as well as foreign foods and their famous *panini con tartufo* (truffle sandwiches).

---

*Three old Roman roads—Via Porta Rossa, Via delle Terme and Borgo SS. Apostoli—converge in the irregularly-shaped **Piazza Santa Trínita**. Borgo SS. Apostoli is named after one of Florence's oldest churches, the little Romanesque Santi Apostoli (11th century), which is located just off the cross roads in the sunken Piazzetta del Limbo, former cemetery of unbaptized babies.*

Piazza Santa Trínita itself boasts an exceptionally fine architectural ensemble, grouped around the 'Column of Justice' from the Roman Baths of Caracalla, given by Pius IV to Cosimo I, and later topped with a statue of Justice by Francesco del Tadda. Its pale granite is set off by the palaces of the piazza: the High Renaissance-Roman **Palazzo Bartolini-Salimbeni** by Baccio d'Agnolo (1520) on the corner of Via Porta Rossa, formerly the fashionable Hôtel du Nord where Herman Melville stayed, and now the French Consulate; the medieval **Palazzo Buondelmonti**, with a 1530 façade by Baccio d'Agnolo, once home to the reading room and favourite haunt of such literati in Florence in the 19th century as Dumas, Browning, Manzoni and Stendhal; and the magnificent curving **Palazzo Spini-Ferroni**, to the right of Borgo SS. Apostoli, built in 1289 and still retaining its original battlements. Directly across Via de' Tornabuoni, the British Consulate occupies the **Palazzo Masetti**, ironically once home to the flamboyant Countess of Albany, wife of Bonnie Prince Charlie who found happiness by leaving the Pretender for Italian dramatist Vittorio Alfieri, but insisted to the end that she was England's rightful Queen Louise.

*The church of **Santa Trínita** has stood on the west side of the piazza, in one form or another, since the 12th century; its unusual accent on the first syllable (from the Latin Trinitas) is considered to be proof of its ancient foundation.*

Piazza Santa Trínita

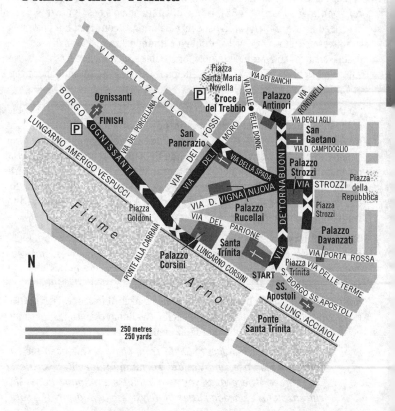

Although the pedestrian façade added by Buontalenti in 1593 isn't especially welcoming, step into its shadowy 14th-century interior for several artistic treats, beginning with the **Bartolini-Salimbeni Chapel** (fourth on the right), frescoed in 1422 by the Sienese Lorenzo Monaco; his marriage of the Virgin takes place in a Tuscan fantasy backdrop of pink towers. He also painted the chapel's graceful, ethereally coloured altarpiece of the *Annunciation*.

In the choir, the **Sassetti Chapel** is one of the masterpieces of Domenico Ghirlandaio, completed in 1495 for wealthy merchant Francesco Sassetti and dedicated to the *Life of St Francis*, but also to the life of Francesco Sassetti, the city and his Medici circle: the scene above the altar, of Francis receiving the Rule of the Order, is transferred to the Piazza della Signoria, watched by Sassetti (to the right, with the fat purse) and Lorenzo il Magnifico; on the steps stands the great Latinist Poliziano with Lorenzo's three sons. The *Death of St Francis* pays homage to Giotto's similar composition in Santa Croce. The altarpiece, the *Adoration of the Shepherds* (1485), is one of Ghirlandaio's best-known works, often described as the archetypal Renaissance painting, a contrived but charming classical treatment; the Magi arrive through a triumphal arch, a Roman sarcophagus is used as manger and a ruined temple for a stable—all matched by the sibyls on the vault; the sibyl on the outer arch is the one who supposedly announced the birth of Christ to Augustus.

Santa Trínita is a Vallombrosan church and the first chapel to the right of the altar holds the Order's holy of holies, a **painted crucifix** formerly located up in San Miniato. The story goes that on a Good Friday, a young noble named Giovanni Gualberto was on his way to Mass when he happened upon the man who had recently murdered his brother. But rather than take his revenge, Gualberto pardoned the assassin in honour of the holy day. When he arrived at church to pray, this crucifix nodded in approval of his mercy. Giovanni was so impressed that he went on to found the Vallombrosan order in the Casentino.

The Sanctuary was frescoed by Alesso Baldovinetti, though only four Old Testament figures survive. In the second chapel to the left the marble *Tomb of Bishop Benozzo Federighi* (1454) is by Luca, the first and greatest of the della Robbias, and features his trademark enamelled terracotta in a gold-ground mosaic. In the north side of the nave, in the fourth chapel, a detached fresco by Neri di Bicci portrays San Giovanni Gualberto and his fellow Vallombrosan saints; over the arch you can see him forgiving the murderer of his brother.

> The streets north of Piazza Santa Trínita have always been the choicest district of Florence, and **Via de' Tornabuoni** the city's smartest shopping street. These days you won't find many innovations—Milan's current status as headquarters of Italy's fashion industry is a sore point

Via Tornabuoni

with Florence, which used to be top dog and lost its position in the 1970s for lack of a large international airport.

In the bright and ambitious 1400s, however, when Florence was the centre of European high finance, Via de' Tornabuoni and its environs was the area the new merchant élite chose for their palaces. Today's bankers build great skyscrapers for the firm and settle for modest mansions for themselves; in Florence's heyday, things were reversed. Bankers and wool tycoons really owned their businesses. While their places of work were quite simple, their homes were imposing city palaces, all built in the same conservative style and competing with each other in size like some Millionaires' Row in 19th-century America.

*The champion among these was the **Palazzo Strozzi**, a long block up Via de' Tornabuoni from Piazza Trínita; turn right in Via Strozzi for Piazza Strozzi.*

This rusticated stone cube of fearful dimensions squats in its piazza like the inscrutable monolith in *2001: A Space Odyssey*, radiating almost visible waves of megalomania. The palazzo was begun by Benedetto da Maiano in 1489 for the extraordinarily wealthy Filippo Strozzi, head of one of Florence's greatest banking clans and adviser to Lorenzo il Magnifico. When he died in 1491, the façade facing Piazza Strozzi was almost complete; future generations had neither the money nor the interest to finish the job. And one wonders whether his son, also called Filippo, ever took much pleasure in it; though at first a Medici ally like his father and wed to Piero de' Medici's daughter, Filippo attempted to lead a band of anti-Medici exiles against Florence; captured and imprisoned in the Fortezza da Basso, he stabbed himself, while many other Strozzi went to Paris to become bankers and advisers to the king of France.

There are few architectural innovations in the Palazzo Strozzi, but here the typical Florentine palace is blown up to the level of the absurd: although three storeys like other palaces, each floor is as tall as three or four normal ones. Like Michelangelo's *David*, Florence's other beautiful monster, it emits the unpleasant sensation of what Mary McCarthy called the 'giganticism of the human ego', the will to surpass not only antiquity but nature herself. Nowadays, at least, the Strozzi palace is moderately useful as a space to hold temporary exhibitions.

> *There are two other exceptional palaces in the quarter. At the north end of Via de' Tornabuoni stands the beautiful golden **Palazzo Antinori** (1465, architect unknown), which has Florence's grandest Baroque temple, **San Gaetano** (1648, by Gherardo Silvani) as its equally golden companion. The second palace, the most celebrated example of domestic architecture in Florence, is the **Palazzo Rucellai**, in Via della Vigna Nuova.*

Its original owner, Giovanni Rucellai, was a quattrocento tycoon like Filippo Strozzi, but an intellectual as well, whose *Zibaldone*, or 'commonplace book' is one of the best sources available on the life and tastes of the educated Renaissance merchant. In 1446 Rucellai chose his favourite architect, Leon Battista Alberti, to design his palace. Actually built by Bernardo Rossellino, it follows Alberti's precepts and theories in its use of the three classical orders; instead of the usual rusticated stone, the façade has a far more delicate decoration of incised irregular blocks and a frieze, elements influential in subsequent Italian architecture— though far more noticeably in Rome than Florence itself. Originally the palace was only five bays wide, and when another two bays were added later the edge was left ragged, unfinished, a nice touch, as if the builders could return at any moment and pick up where they left off. The frieze, like that on Santa Maria Novella, portrays the devices of the Medici and Rucellai families (Giovanni's son married another daughter of Piero de' Medici), a wedding believed to have been fêted in the **Loggia dei Rucellai** across the street, also designed by Alberti.

Since 1987, the Palazzo Rucellai has housed the **Museo di Storia della Fotografia Fratelli Alinari** (*open 10–7.30, closed Wed; adm*) devoted to the history of photography. Exhibits come from the fascinating archives of the Alinari brothers, who founded the world's first photography society in 1852. Keep an eye out for posters concerning special shows.

Behind the Rucellai palace (on Via della Spada) stands the ancient church of **San Pancrazio**, with an antique-style porch by Alberti. At one point in its up-and-down career the church served as a tobacco factory. Now it's been given a new life as the **Museo Mariano Marini**, © 219432 (open 10–1, 3–6, closed Tues; 10–1, 4–7 June, July, Aug; adm), containing 180 works by Marini, one of the greatest Italian sculptors of this century (1901–80). Marini also worked as a painter and lithographer, and his portraits and favourite subjects (especially the Horse and Rider) are known for their sensuous surfaces and uncanny psychological intensity. Cross your fingers and hope that the gods ordain that the **Rucellai Chapel** behind San Pancrazio (entrance at no. 18 Via della Spada, open erratic hours) be open when you pass; a minor Renaissance gem designed in 1467 by Alberti, it houses a unique model of the Sanctuary of the Holy Sepulchre in Jerusalem. that is Giovanni Rucellai's funerary monument.

Before taking leave of old Florence's west end, head back to the Arno and **Piazza Goldoni**, which was named after the great comic playwright from Venice.

The most important building on the piazza, the **Palazzo Ricasoli**, was built in the 15th century but bears the name of one of unified Italy's first Prime Ministers, Bettino 'Iron Baron' Ricasoli. The bridge here, the **Ponte alla Carraia**, is new and nondescript, but its 1304 version played a leading role in that year's most memorable disaster: a company staging a water pageant of the *Inferno*, complete with monsters, devils and tortured souls, attracted such a large crowd that the bridge collapsed under the weight, and all were drowned. Later it was drily commented that all the Florentines who went to see Hell that day found what they were looking for.

Just to the east on Lungarno Corsini looms the enormous **Palazzo Corsini**, the city's most prominent piece of Roman Baroque extravagance, begun in 1650 and crowned with a bevy of statues.

The Corsini, the most prominent family of 17th- and 18th-century Florence, were reputedly so wealthy that they could ride from Florence to Rome entirely on their own property. The **Galleria Corsini** is considered the finest private gallery in the city (*adm by appointment only, © 283 044; enter from Via Parione*), with paintings by Giovanni Bellini, Signorelli, Filippino Lippi and Pontormo, and *Muses* from the ducal palace of Urbino, painted by Raphael's first master, Timoteo Viti.

Further east on Lungarno Corsini stood the Libreria Orioli, which published the first edition of *Lady Chatterley's Lover* in 1927.

> *To the west of Piazza Goldoni lies the old neighbourhood of the only Florentine to have a continent named after him. Amerigo Vespucci (1451–1512) was a Medici agent in Seville, and made two voyages from there to America on the heels of Columbus. His parish church,* **Ognissanti** *(All Saints), is set back from the river behind a Baroque façade, on property donated in 1256 by the Umiliati, a religious order that specialized in wool-working.*

The Vespucci family tomb is below the second altar to the right, and little Amerigo himself is said to be pictured next to the Madonna in the fresco of the Madonna della Misericordia, which is probably another Florentine tall story. Also buried in Ognissanti was the Filipepi family, one of whom was Botticelli (*open 8–12 and 4–7*).

The best art is in the **Convent**, just to the left of the church at no. 42 (open 9–12 Sat, Mon and Tues; you may have to ring). Frescoed in the refectory is the great *Last Supper*, or *Cenacolo*, painted by Domenico Ghirlandaio in 1480. It's hard to think of a more serene and elegant Last Supper, almost like a garden party with its background of fruit trees and exotic birds; a peacock sits in the window, cherries and peaches litter the lovely tablecloth. On either side of the fresco are two scholarly saints moved here from the church itself: Ghirlandaio's *St Jerome* and on the right, young Botticelli's *St Augustine*.

Start: *Santa Maria Novella*
Finish: *Palazzo Medici-Riccardi*
Walking time: *one day*

V: Santa Maria Novella

St Maria Novella

147

This walk includes two of Florence's greatest art churches and the stomping grounds of its merchant family whose members through luck, pluck and bucks hit the jackpot and became Grand Dukes.

Lunch/Cafés

Palle d'Oro, Via Sant'Antonio 43r, © 28 83 83. Sit-down or take-away good, simple food (closed Sun, around L15,000).

Trattoria Za Za, Piazza Mercato Centrale 26r, © 21 54 11. Perch on wooden stalls and eat delicious food in this good value trattoria (closed Sun, around L25,000).

Narbone, Mercato Coperto di San Lorenzo, © 21 99 49. This food counter has been going since 1872 filling the marketeers' stomachs with such hearty Florentine fare as tripe sandwiches, but for the unaccustomed there are also salads and a few tables (closed Sun, open 7am–2pm).

Cafaggi, Via Guelfa 35r, © 294 989. Family-run trattoria with three types of fixed menu: *turistico* (tourist) *leggero* (light) and *vegetariano* (vegetarian) (closed Sun eve, around L30,000).

Buca Mario, Piazza degli Ottaviani 16r, © 21 41 79. Expect to queue for quality food in underground rooms (closed Wed, Thurs lunch, around L30,000).

Italy Italy, Piazza Stazione 25r. Fast food, American style.

*As in Venice and so many other Italian cities, the two churches of the preaching orders—the Dominicans' Santa Maria Novella and the Franciscans' Santa Croce—became the largest and most prestigious in the city, where wealthy families vied to create the most beautiful chapels and tombs. In Florence, by some twitch of city planning, both of these sacred art galleries dominate broad, stale squares that do not invite you to linger; in the irregular **Piazza Santa Maria Novella** you may find yourself looking over your shoulder for the ghosts of the carriages that once raced madly around the two stout obelisks set on turtles, just as in a Roman circus, in the fashionable carriage races of the 1700s. The arcade on the south side, the **Loggia di San Paolo**, is very much like Brunelleschi's Spedale degli Innocenti, although it suffers somewhat from its use as a busy bus shelter; the lunette over the door, by Andrea della Robbia, shows the Meeting of SS. Francis and Dominic.*

Santa Maria Novella *redeems the anomie of its square with its stupendous black and white marble **façade**, the finest in Florence.*

The lower part, with its looping arcades, is Romanesque work in the typical Tuscan mode, finished before 1360. In 1456 Giovanni Rucellai commissioned Alberti to complete it, a remarkably fortunate choice. Alberti's half not only perfectly harmonizes with the original, but perfects it with geometrical harmonies to create what appears to be a kind of Renaissance sun temple. The original builders started it off by orienting the church to the south instead of west, so that at noon the sun streams through the 14th-century rose window. The only symbol Alberti put on the façade is a blazing sun; the unusual sundials, over the arches on the extreme right and left, were added by Cosimo I's court astronomer Egnazio Danti. Note how the base of the façade is also the base of an equilateral triangle, with Alberti's sun at the apex.

The beautiful frieze depicts the Rucellai emblem (a billowing sail), as on the Palazzo Rucellai. The wall of Gothic recesses to the right, enclosing the old cemetery, are *avelli*, or family tombs.

Florence Walk V:
Santa Maria Novella

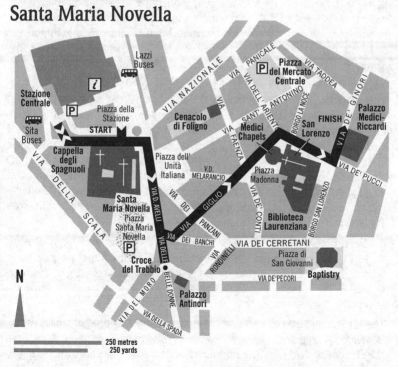

*The **interior** is vast, lofty and more 'Gothic' in feel than any other church in Florence.*

No thanks to Vasari, who was set loose to remodel the church to 16th-century taste, painting over the original frescoes, removing the rood screen and Dominicans' choir from the nave, and remodelling the altars; in the 1800s restorers did their best to de-Vasari Santa Maria with neogothic details. Neither party, however, could touch two of the interior's most distinctive features—the striking stone vaulting of the nave and the perspective created by the columns marching down the aisles, each pair placed a little closer together as they approach the altar.

Over the portal at the entrance is a fresco lunette by Botticelli that has recently been restored. One of Santa Maria Novella's best-known pictures is at the second altar on the left: Masaccio's *Trinity*, painted around 1425, and one of the revolutionary works of the Renaissance. Masaccio's use of architectural elements and perspective gives his composition both physical and intellectual depth. The flat wall becomes a deeply recessed Brunelleschian chapel, calm and classical, enclosed in a coffered barrel vault; at the foot of the fresco a bleak skeleton decays in its tomb, bearing a favourite Tuscan reminder: 'I was that which you are, you will be that which I am'. Above this morbid suggestion of physical death kneel the two donors; within the celestially rational inner sanctum the Virgin and St John stand at the foot of the Cross, humanity's link with the mystery of the Trinity. In the nearby Brunelleschi-designed pulpit Galileo was first denounced by the Inquisition for presuming to believe that the earth went around the sun.

There is little else to detain you in the aisles, but the first chapel in the left transept, the **Cappella Strozzi**, is one of the most evocative corners of 14th-century Florence, frescoed entirely by Nardo di Cione and his brother, Andrea Orcagna; on the vault pictures of *St Thomas Aquinas and the Virtues* are echoed in Andrea's lovely altarpiece of *The Redeemer Donating the Keys to St Peter and the Book of Wisdom to St Thomas Aquinas*; on the left wall there's a crowded scene of *Paradise*, with the righteous lined up in a medieval school class photograph. On the right, Nardo painted a striking view of Dante's *Inferno*, with all of a Tuscan's special attention to precise map-like detail.

In the richly decorated **Sacristy** hangs Giotto's recently restored *Crucifix* (*c.* 1300), one of the artist's first works. In the **Gondi Chapel** hangs another famous *Crucifix*, carved in wood by Brunelleschi, which, according to Vasari, so astonished his friend Donatello that he dropped the eggs he was carrying in his apron when he first saw it.

The charming fresco cycle in the **Sanctuary** (1485–90), painted by Domenico Ghirlandaio, portrays the *Lives of the Virgin, St John the Baptist and the Dominican Saints* in magnificent architectural settings; little Michelangelo

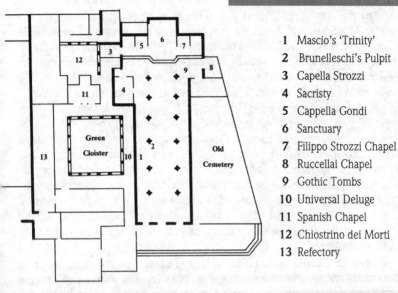

1 Mascio's 'Trinity'
2 Brunelleschi's Pulpit
3 Capella Strozzi
4 Sacristy
5 Cappella Gondi
6 Sanctuary
7 Filippo Strozzi Chapel
8 Ruccellai Chapel
9 Gothic Tombs
10 Universal Deluge
11 Spanish Chapel
12 Chiostrino dei Morti
13 Refectory

was among the students who helped him complete it. Nearly all of the bystanders are portraits of Florentine quattrocento VIPs, including the artist himself (in the red hat, in the scene of the *Expulsion of St Joachim from the Temple*), but most prominent are the ladies and gents of the Tornabuoni house. More excellent frescoes adorn the **Filippo Strozzi Chapel**, the finest work ever to come from the brush of Filippino Lippi, painted in 1502 near the end of his life; the exaggerated, dark and violent scenes portray the lives of *St Philip* (his crucifixion and his subduing of the dragon before the Temple of Mars, which creates such a stench it kills the heathen prince) and of *St John the Evangelist* (raising Drusiana from the dead and being martyred in boiling oil). The chapel's beautifully carved tomb of Filippo Strozzi is by Benedetto da Maiano. The **Rucellai Chapel** contains a marble statue of the *Madonna and Bambino* by Nino Pisano and a fine bronze tomb by Ghiberti, which makes an interesting comparison with the three Gothic tombs nearby in the right transept. One of these contains the remains of the Patriarch of Constantinople, who died in here after the failure of the Council of Florence in 1439 to reunite the Western and Eastern Churches.

> *More great frescoes await in **Santa Maria Novella's Cloisters,** all recently restored and open as a city museum (entrance just to the left of the church; open 9–2, closed Fri, weekends 8–1; adm; free Sun).*

The first cloister, the so-called **Green Cloister**, one of the masterpieces of Paolo Uccello and his assistants, is so named after the *terraverde* or green earth pigment used by the artist, which lends the scenes from *Genesis* their eerie, ghostly quality. Much damaged by time and neglect, they are nevertheless striking for their two Uccellian obsessions—perspective and animals, the latter especially on display in the scene of the *Creation*. Best known, and in better condition than the others, is Uccello's surreal *Universal Deluge*, a composition framed by the steep walls of two arks, before and after views, which have the uncanny effect of making the scene seem to come racing out of its own vanishing point, a vanishing point touched by divine wrath in a searing bolt of lightning. In between the claustrophobic walls the flood rises, tossing up a desperate ensemble of humanity, waterlogged bodies, naked men bearing clubs, crowded in a jam of flotsam and jetsam and islets rapidly receding in the dark waters. In the right foreground, amidst the panic, stands a tall robed man, seemingly a visionary, perhaps even Noah himself, looking heavenward while a flood victim seizes him by the ankles. Some of Uccello's favourite perspective studies were of headgear, especially the wooden hoops called *mazzocchi* which he puts around the necks and on the heads of his figures.

The **Spanish Chapel** opens up at the far end of the cloisters, taking its name from the Spanish court followers of Eleonora di Toledo who worshipped here; the Inquisition had earlier made the chapel its headquarters in Florence. The chapel is, again, famous for its frescoes, the masterpiece of a little-known 14th-century artist named Andrea di Buonaiuto, whose subject was the Dominican cosmology, perhaps not something we have much empathy for these days, but here beautifully portrayed so that even the *Hounds of the Lord* (a pun on the Order's name, the 'Domini canes') on the right wall seem more like pets than militant bloodhounds sniffing out unorthodox beliefs. The church behind the scene with the hounds is a fairy pink confection of what Buonaiuto imagined the duomo would look like when finished; it may well be Arnolfo di Cambio's original conception. Famous Florentines, including Giotto, Dante, Boccaccio and Petrarch, stand to the right of the dais supporting the pope, emperor and various sour-faced hierophants. Off to the right the artist has portrayed four rather urbane Vices with dancing girls, while the Dominicans lead stray sheep back to the fold. On the left wall, *St Thomas Aquinas* dominates the portrayal of the Contemplative Life, surrounded by Virtues and Doctors of the Church.

The oldest part of the monastery, the **Chiostrino dei Morti** (1270s), contains some 14th-century frescoes, while the **Great Cloister** beyond is now off limits, the property of the Carabinieri, the new men in black charged with keeping the Italians orthodox. Off the Green Cloister, the **Refectory** is a striking hall with cross vaulting and frescoes by Alessandro Allori, now serving as a museum.

*Just behind, but a world apart from Santa Maria Novella, another large, amorphous square detracts from one of Italy's finest modern buildings—Florence's **Stazione Centrale**, designed by the architect Michelucci in 1935. Adorned by only a glass block canopy at the entrance (and an early model of that great Italian invention, the digital clock), the station is nevertheless remarkable for its clean lines and impeccable practicality; form following function in a way that even Brunelleschi would have appreciated.*

*One of the medieval lanes leading south from Piazza Santa Maria Novella, Via delle Belle Donne was once known for its excellent brothels. Today it is worth a short stroll to see one of the very few cross-roads in Italy marked by a cross, a Celtic custom that never really caught on here—Italians are far more fond of corner shrines to the Madonna or some lucky saint. According to legend, **Croce del Trebbio** (from a corruption of 'trivium') marks the spot of a massacre of Patarene heretics in the 1240s, after the masses had been excited by a sermon which was given by the fire-eating Inquisitor St Peter Martyr from the pulpit of Santa Maria Novella.*

*Backtrack up Via delle Belle Donne and walk up Via Giglio to the church of **San Lorenzo**.*

The lively quarter just east of Santa Maria Novella has been associated with the Medici ever since Giovanni di Bicci de' Medici commissioned Brunelleschi to rebuild the ancient church of San Lorenzo in 1420; subsequent members of the dynasty lavished bushels of florins on its decoration and Medici pantheon, and on several projects commissioned from Michelangelo. The mixed result of all their efforts could be held up as an archetype of the Renaissance, and one which Walter Pater described as 'great rather by what it designed or aspired to do, than by what it actually achieved'. One can begin with San Lorenzo's façade of corrugated brick, the most nonfinito of all of Michelangelo's unfinished projects; commmissioned by Medici Pope Leo X in 1516, the project never got further than Michelangelo's scale model, which may be seen in the Casa Buonarroti. To complete the church's dingy aspect, the piazza in front contains a universally detested 19th-century statue of Cosimo I's dashing father, Giovanni delle Bande Nere, who died at the age of 28 of wounds received fighting against Emperor Charles V.

The **interior**, although completed after Brunelleschi's death, is true to his design, classically calm in good grey *pietra serena*. The artistic treasures it contains are few but choice, beginning with the second chapel on the right housing *The Marriage of the Virgin*, a 1523 work by the Mannerist Rosso Fiorentino. Joseph, usually portrayed as an old man, according to Rosso is a Greek god with golden curls in a flowing scene of hot reds and oranges—a powerful contrast to the chapel's haunting, hollow-eyed tomb slab of the Ray Charles of the Renaissance, Francesco Landini (died 1397), the blind organist whose madrigals were immensely popular and influential in Italian music. At the end of the right aisle, there's a lovely delicately worked tabernacle by Desiderio da Settignano.

Most riveting of all, however, are **Donatello's pulpits**, the sculptor's last works, completed by his pupils after his death in 1466. Cast in bronze, the pulpits were commissioned by Donatello's friend and patron Cosimo il Vecchio, some think to keep the sculptor busy in his old age. Little in Donatello's previous work prepares the viewer for these scenes of Christ's passion and Resurrection with their rough and impressionistic details, their unbalanced and overcrowded compositions, more reminiscent of Rodin than anything Florentine. Unfortunately they were set up on columns in the 17th century, just above eye level, like so many things in Florence, a fault somewhat redeemed by a new lighting system. Nearby, directly beneath the dome, lies buried Donatello's patron and Florence's original godfather, Cosimo il Vecchio; the grille over his grave bears the Medici arms and the simple inscription, *Pater Patriae*.

> It was the godfather's father, Giovanni di Bicci de' Medici, who in 1420 commissioned Brunelleschi to build the **Old Sacristy** off the left transept.

Often cited as one of the first and finest works of the early Renaissance, Brunelleschi designed this cube of a sacristy according to carefully calculated mathematical proportions, emphasized with a colour scheme of white walls, articulated in soft grey *pietra serena* pilasters and cornices; a dignified decoration that would become his trademark, something Florentine architects would borrow for centuries. Donatello contributed the terracotta tondi and lunettes, as well as the bronze doors, embellished with lively Apostles. The Sacristy was built to hold the sarcophagi of Giovanni di Bicci de' Medici and his wife; in 1472 Lorenzo il Magnifico and his brother Giuliano had Verrocchio design the beautiful bronze and red porphyry wall tomb for their father Piero the Gouty and their uncle Giovanni. Unfortunately Verrocchio saw fit to place this in front of Brunelleschi's original door, upsetting the careful balance.

The **chapel** across the transept from the entrance to the Old Sacristy houses a 19th-century monument to Donatello, who is buried here at his request near Cosimo il Vecchio. The lovely *Annunciation* is by Filippo Lippi; the large, colourful fresco of the *Martyrdom of St Lawrence* around the corner in the aisle is by Bronzino and has just been restored.

> *Just beyond the Bronzino a door leads into the 15th-century **Cloister**, and from there a stair leads up to Michelangelo's celebrated **Biblioteca Laurenziana** (open 9–1 Mon–Sat).*

If Brunelleschi's Old Sacristy heralded the Renaissance, Michelangelo's library is Mannerism's prototype, or Brunelleschi gone haywire, no longer serene and mathematically perfect, but complicated and restless, the architectural elements stuck on with an eye for effect rather than for any structural purpose. The vestibule barely contains the remarkable stair, flowing down from the library like a stone cascade, built by Vasari after a drawing by Michelangelo. This grand entrance leads into a collection that ranges from a very rare 5th-century Virgil and other Greek and Latin codices, beautifully illuminated manuscripts, and the original manuscript of Cellini's autobiography; ask for a look around.

> *San Lorenzo is most famous, however, for the **Medici Chapels**, which lie outside and behind the church (open 9–2, 9–1 Sun, closed Mon; adm exp).*

The entrance leads through the crypt, a dark and austere place where many of the Medici are actually buried. Their main monument, the family obsession, is just up the steps, and has long been known as the **Chapel of the Princes**, a stupefying, fabulously costly octagon of death that, as much as the Grand Dukes fussed over it, lends their memory an unpleasant aftertaste of cancerous bric-à-brac that grew and grew. Perhaps only a genuine Medici could love its insane, trashy opulence; all of Grand Duke Cosimo's descendants, down to the last, Anna Maria Ludovica, worked like beavers to finish it according to the plans left by Cosimo's illegitimate son, dilettante architect Giovanni de' Medici. Yet even today it is only partially completed, the *pietre dure* extending only part of the way up the walls. The 19th-century frescoes in the cupola are a poor substitute for the originally planned *Apotheosis of the Medici* in lapis lazuli, and the two statues in gilded bronze in the niches over the sarcophagi (each niche large enough to hold a hippopotamus) are nothing like the intended figures to be carved in semi-precious stone. The most interesting feature is the inlaid *pietra dura* arms of Tuscan towns and the large Medici arms above, with their familiar six red boluses blown up as big as beachballs. (The balls probably derive from the family's origins as pharmacists (*medici*), and opponents called them 'the pills'. Medici supporters, however, made them their battle cry in street fights: 'Balls! Balls!')

> *A passageway leads to Michelangelo's **New Sacristy**, commissioned by Leo X to occupy an unfinished room originally built to balance Brunelleschi's Old Sacristy.*

Michelangelo's first idea was to turn it into a new version of his unfinished, overly ambitious Pope Julius Tomb, an idea quickly quashed by his Medici patrons, who requested instead four wall tombs. Michelangelo only worked on two of the monuments, but managed to finish the New Sacristy itself, creating a silent and gloomy mausoleum, closed-in and grey, a chilly introspective cocoon calculated to depress even the most chatty tour groups.

Nor are the famous tombs guaranteed to cheer. Both honour nonentities: that of *Night and Day* belongs to Lorenzo il Magnifico's son, the Duke of Nemours, and symbolizes the Active Life, while the *Dawn and Dusk* is of Guiliano's nephew, Lorenzo, Duke of Urbino (and dedicatee of *The Prince*), who symbolizes the Contemplative Life (true to life in one respect—Lorenzo was a disappointment to Machiavelli and everyone else, passively obeying the dictates of his uncle Pope Leo X). Idealized statues of the two men, in Roman patrician gear, represent these states of mind, while draped on their sarcophagi are Michelangelo's four allegorical figures of the *Times of Day*, so heavy with weariness and grief they seem ready to slide off on to the floor. The most finished figure, *Night*, has always impressed the critics; she is almost a personification of despair, the mouthpiece of Michelangelo's most bitter verse:

> *Sweet to me is sleep, and even more to be like stone*
> *While wrong and shame endure;*
> *Not to see, nor to feel, is my good fortune.*
> *Therefore, do not wake me; speak softly here.*

Both statues of the dukes look towards the back wall, where a large double tomb for Lorenzo il Magnifico and his brother Giuliano was originally planned, to be decorated with river gods. The only part of this tomb ever completed is the statue of the *Madonna and Child* now in place, accompanied by the Medici patron saints, *Cosmas and Damian*.

In 1975, charcoal drawings were discovered on the walls of the little room off the altar. They were attributed to Michelangelo, who may have hidden here in 1530, when the Medici had regained Florence and apparently would only forgive the

Mercato Centrale

artist for aiding the republican defence if he would finish their tombs. But Michelangelo had had enough of their ducal pretences and went off to Rome, never to return to Florence.

What makes the neighbourhood around San Lorenzo so lively is its street market, which the Florentines run with an almost Neapolitan flamboyance every day except Sunday and Monday. Stalls selling clothes and leather extend from the square up Via dell'Ariento and vicinity (nicknamed 'Shanghai') towards the **Mercato Centrale,** *Florence's main food market, a cast-iron and glass confection of the 1870s, brimful of fresh fruit and vegetables, leering boars' heads and mounds of tripe (open 7–1.30 Mon–Sat, also 4.30–7.30 Sat).*

Beyond the market, at Via Faenza 42, is the entrance to Perugino's **Cenacolo di Foligno** *fresco, housed in the ex-convent of the Tertiary Franciscans of Foligno. This 1490s Umbrian version of the Last Supper was discovered in the 1850s and has recently been restored (visit by appointment only, © 284 272, Sun and holidays at 10.30).*

A block from San Lorenzo and the Piazza del Duomo stands the **Palazzo Medici-Riccardi** *once home to Florence's unofficial court, where ambassadors would call, kings would lodge, and important decisions would be made.*

Built in 1444 by Michelozzo for Cosimo il Vecchio, it was the principal address of the Medici for a hundred years, until Cosimo I abandoned it in favour of larger quarters in the Palazzo Vecchio and the Pitti Palace. In 1659 the Riccardi purchased the palace, added to it and did everything to keep it glittering until Napoleon and his debts drove them to bankruptcy in 1809. The palace is now used as the city's prefecture.

In its day, though, it was the largest private address in the city, where the family lived with the likes of Donatello's *David* and *Judith and Holofernes*, Uccello's *Battle of San Romano* and other masterpieces now in the Uffizi and Bargello. Frescoes are much harder to move, however, and the Palazzo Medici is worth visiting to see the most charming one in Italy, Benozzo Gozzoli's 1459 *Procession of the Magi*, located in the **Medici Chapel** upstairs (*open 9–12.30 and 3–5; Sun 9–12, closed Wed*).

Painted in a delightful, decorative manner more reminiscent of International Gothic than the awakening Renaissance style of his contemporaries, Gozzoli took a religious subject and turned it into a merry, brilliantly coloured pageant of beautifully dressed kings, knights and pages, accompanied by greyhounds and a giraffe, who travel through a springtime landscape of jewel-like trees and castles. This is a largely secular painting, representing less the original Three Kings than the annual pageant of the *Compagnia dei Magi*, Florence's richest confraternity. The scene is wrapped around three walls of the small chapel—you feel as if you had walked straight into a glowing fairytale world. Most of the faces are those of the Medici and other local celebrities (the young Lorenzo il Magnifico posed for the young king dressed in gold); Gozzoli certainly had no qualms about putting himself among the crowd of figures on the right wall, with his name written on his red cap. In the foreground, note the black man carrying a bow. Blacks, as well as Turks, Circassians, Tartars and others, were common enough in Renaissance Florence, originally brought as slaves. By the 1400s, however, contemporary writers mention them as artisans, fencing masters, soldiers and one famous archery instructor, who may be the man pictured here.

The altarpiece, an ethereal *Madonna* by Filippo Lippi (or an imitator), has been moved into the other room of the palace opened to visitors, the **Gallery**, up the second flight of stairs on the right, from the courtyard. It's hard to imagine a more striking contrast than that between Gozzoli and the Neapolitan Luca Giordano (nicknamed 'Luca fa presto' or 'Quick-draw Luke'), who painted this hilarious ceiling for the Riccardi in 1683, as a left-handed compliment to the Medici for selling them the palace. No longer mere players in a religious pageant, the Medici, or at least the overstuffed Grand Duke Cosimo III and his unspeakable heir Gian Gastone, take the leading roles, defying the laws of gravity and good taste in an apotheosis of marshmallow clouds.

Start: *San Marco*
Finish: *Opificio delle Pietre Dure*
Walking time: *one full day*

VI: San Marco

San Marco

Centred around Piazza San Marco on Florence's north side, this walk takes in two mighty opposites of the Florentine Renaissance —the gentle spiritual masterpieces of Fra Angelico and the over-weening *David* of Michelangelo in the Accademia.

Lunch/Cafés

San Zanobi, Via San Zanobi 33r, ℂ 47 52 86. Elegant, classy restaurant with finely-cooked Florentine cuisine (closed Mon, around L35,000).

Gran Caffè San Marco, Piazza San Marco. Conveniently located, typical café.

Il Micio, Via Fra Bartolomeo 52r, ℂ 573 257. As well as the full menu, the young owners also serve express single dishes at lunch— a *primo* and two veggies. or a *secondo* and two vegies. for L15,000 all in (closed Sun, around L35,000).

Birreria il Fauno, Via Cavour 89r, ℂ 471 682. American pub-bar offering snacks and drinks day and evening.

Bar Genius, Via San Gallo. Good local snack-coffee bar.

Badiani, Via dei Mille 20. Worth a detour for the fantastic ice cream, especially the *Buontalenti* with an egg-rich secret recipe.

*On the northern edge of the Renaissance city, **Piazza San Marco** is a lively square full of art students from the nearby Accademia. The north side of the square is occupied by the **Church and Dominican Convent of San Marco.***

The convent was Cosimo il Vecchio's favourite pious project; in 1437 he commissioned Michelozzo to enlarge and rebuild it, and to add to it Europe's first public library, where Florentine scholars and humanists rediscovered the ancient classics collected by Cosimo's agents (now in the Laurenziana Library). A later prior of San Marco, Savonarola, had little use for the Medici, though he owed his position to the influence of Lorenzo il Magnifico in 1491.

San Marco is best known for the works of the other-worldly Fra Angelico, in residence here between 1436 and 1447, and in charge of decorating the new convent constructed by Cosimo. His paintings and frescoes in San Marco, itself unchanged from the 1400s, offer a unique opportunity to see his works in the peaceful, contemplative environment in which they were meant to be seen (*open 9–2, Sun 9–1, closed Mon; adm*).

Every painter in the 15th century earned his living painting sacred subjects, but none painted them with the deep conviction and faith of the 'Blessed' Angelico, who communicated his Biblical visions in soft angelic pastels, bright playroom colours and an ethereal blondness, so clear and limpid that they just had to be true. 'Immured in his quiet convent', wrote Henry James, 'he apparently never received an intelligible impression of evil; and his conception of human life was a perpetual sense of sacredly loving and being loved.' Yet the gentle friar was certainly not artistically naive, and adopted many of his contemporaries' innovations, especially artificial perspective, in his technique.

> *A visit to San Marco begins with Michelozzo's harmonious **Cloister of Sant'Antonio** in which Fra Angelico painted the frescoes in the corners. Just off the cloister, the **Pilgrims' Hospice**, also by Michelozzo, has been arranged as a gallery of Fra Angelico's paintings, which have been gathered from all over Florence.*

Florence Walk VI:
San Marco

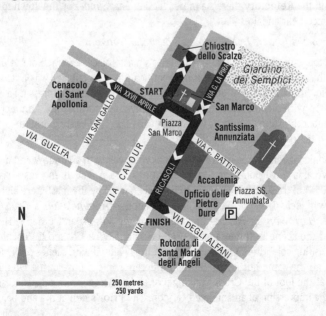

Here you'll find his great *Last Judgement* altarpiece (1430), a serenely confident work in which all the saved are well-dressed Italians holding hands, led by an angel in a celestial dance. They are allowed to keep their beautiful clothes in heaven, while the bad (mostly princes and prelates) are stripped of their garments to receive their interesting tortures.

One of the most charming works is the *Thirty-five Scenes from the Life of Christ*, acted out before strikingly bare, brown Tuscan backgrounds, painted as cupboard doors for Santissima Annunziata. Three of the scenes are by Fra Angelico's talented apprentice, Alesso Baldovinetti. The noble, gracefully lamenting figures in the magnificent *Deposition* altarpiece from Santa Trínita stand before an elegant townscape dominated by Fra Angelico's ziggurat-style concept of the Temple in Jerusalem. Other masterpieces include the **Tabernacle of the Linaioli** (the flax-workers), with a beautiful predella. The same holds true for the *Pala di San Marco*, the predella picturing SS. Cosmas and Damian, patrons of medicine and the Medici, in the act of performing history's first leg transplant.

Other rooms off the cloister contain works by Fra Bartolomeo, another resident of the convent whose portraits capture some of the most sincere spirituality of the late 15th century. The **Chapter House** contains Fra Angelico's over-restored fresco of *Crucifixion and Saints* which is a painting that lacks his accustomed grace; in the **Refectory** there's a more pleasing *Last Supper* by the down-to-earth Domenico Ghirlandaio.

Stairs lead up to Michelozzo's beautiful **Convent**.

At the top your eyes meet the Angelic Friar's masterpiece, a miraculous *Annunciation* that must have earned him his beatification. The subject was a favourite with Florentine artists, not only because it was a severe test—expressing a divine revelation with a composition of strict economy—but because the Annunciation, falling near the spring equinox, was New Year's Day for Florence until the Medici adopted the pope's calendar in the 1600s.

The monks of San Marco each had a small white cell with a window and a fresco to serve as a focal point for their meditations. Fra Angelico and his assistants painted 44 of these; those believed to have been done by the master are along the outer wall (cells 1–9, the *Noli me Tangere*, another *Annunciation*, a *Transfiguration*, a *Harrowing of Hell*, a *Coronation of the Virgin*, and others). He also painted the scene in the large cell used occasionally by Cosimo il Vecchio and other visiting celebrities. One corridor is entirely painted with scenes of the Crucifixion, all the same but for some slight difference in the pose of the Dominican monk at the foot of the Cross; walking past and glancing in the cells successively gives the impression of an animated cartoon. The **Prior's cell** at the end belonged to Savonarola; it has simple furniture of the period and a portrait of Savonarola in the guise of St Peter Martyr (with an axe in his brain) which was by his friend Fra Bartolomeo. In a nearby corridor hangs a copy of the anonymous painting in the Corsini Gallery, of Savonarola and two of his followers being burned at the stake in the Piazza della Signoria. The **Library**, entered off the corridor, is as light and airy as the cloisters below, and contains a collection of beautiful choir books. Architecturally the library was one of Michelozzo's greatest works, radiating a wonderful spirit of serenity, church-like with its vaulted nave and aisles.

The **church of San Marco** was rebuilt, along with the convent, in the 15th century, though the interior was rearranged by Giambologna and the Baroque façade added in 1780. The right aisle has an altar topped by an 8th-century mosaic from Constantinople, reminiscent of works from Ravenna. There's a painting by Fra Bartolomeo nearby of a *Madonna and Six Saints*.

> *Near San Marco, at Via G. La Pira 4, the **University of Florence** runs several small museums; nearly all the collections were begun by the indefatigable Medici.*

The **Geology and Palaeontology Museum** has one of Italy's best collections of fossils, many uncovered in Tuscany, including antiquated elephants from the Valdarno (*open 2–6 Mon; 9–1 Tues, Wed, Thurs and Sat; 9.30–12.30 first Sun of the month; closed July, Aug and Sept*). The **Mineralogy and Lithology Museum** houses strange and beautiful rocks, especially from Elba, the treasure island of minerals; there's a topaz weighing in at 151kg, meteorites, and a bright collection of Medici trinkets, worked from stones in rainbow hues (*open 9–1 weekdays, also 3–6 Wed*). The **Botanical Museum** is of less interest to the casual visitor, though it houses one of the most extensive herbariums in the world; most impressive here are the exquisite wax models of plants made in the early 1800s (*open 9–1 weekdays*). Also on Via La Pira is the entrance to the University's **Giardino dei Semplici**, the botanical garden created for Cosimo I. The garden maintains its original layout, with medicinal herbs, Tuscan plants, flowers and tropical plants in its greenhouses (*open 9–12 Mon, Wed and Fri, also Sun in April and first and second Sun in May*).

> *Backtrack to Piazza San Marco and then continue down Via XXVII Aprile to the Renaissance convent of **Sant'Apollonia** (open 9–2, 9–1 Sun, closed Mon).*

Cenacoli, or frescoes of the Last Supper, became almost *de rigueur* in monastic refectories; in several of these the Last Supper is all that remains of a convent. Until 1860, the Renaissance convent of Sant'Apollonia was the abode of cloistered nuns, and their *cenacolo* was a secret. When the convent was suppressed, and the painting discovered under the whitewash, the critics believed it to be the work of Paolo Uccello, but lately have unanimously attributed it to Andrea del Castagno, painted 1445–50. The other walls have *sinopie* of the *Crucifixion*, *Entombment* and *Resurrection* by Castagno; in the vestibule there are good works by Neri di Bicci and Paolo Schiavo

> *Not far away you can enter a radically different artistic world in the* **Chiostro dello Scalzo** *, again off Piazza S. Marco at Via Cavour 69.*

Formerly part of the Confraternity of San Giovanni Battista, all that has survived is this cloister, frescoed (1514–24) with scenes of the life of St John the Baptist by Andrea del Sarto and his pupil Franciabigio. Del Sarto, Browning's 'perfect painter', painted these in monochrome grisaille, and while the scene of the *Baptism of Christ* is a beautiful work, some of the other panels are the most unintentionally funny things in Florence—the scene of Herod's banquet is reduced to a meagre breakfast where the king and queen look up indignantly at the man bringing in the platter of the Baptist's head as if he were a waiter who had made a mistake with their order.

> *From here backtrack to Piazza San Marco where Via Ricasoli makes a beeline for the Duomo. On most days, the view is obstructed by the crowds milling around at no. 60, the* **Galleria dell'Accademia** *(open 9–2, 9–1 Sun, closed Mon; adm exp).*

In the summer the queues are as long as those at the Uffizi, everyone anxious to get a look at Michelangelo's *David*. Just over a hundred years ago Florence decided to take this precocious symbol of republican liberty out of the rain and install it, with much pomp, in a specially-built classical exedra in this gallery.

Michelangelo completed the *David* for the city in 1504, when he was 29, and it was the work that established the overwhelming reputation he had in his own time. The monstrous block of marble—5m high but unusually shallow—had been quarried 40 years earlier by the Cathedral Works and spoiled by other hands. The block was offered around to other artists, including Leonardo da Vinci, before young Michelangelo decided to take up the challenge of carving the largest statue since Roman times. And it is the dimensions of the *David* that remain the biggest surprise in these days of endless reproductions. Certainly as a political symbol of the Republic, he is excessive—the irony of a David the size of a Goliath is disconcerting—but as a symbol of the artistic and intellectual aspirations of the Renaissance he is unsurpassed.

And it's hard to deny, after gazing at this enormous nude, that these same Renaissance aspirations by the 1500s began snuggling uncomfortably close to the frontiers of kitsch. Disproportionate size is one symptom; the calculated intention to excite a strong emotional response is another. In the *David*, virtuosity eclipses vision, and commits the even deadlier kitsch sin of seeking the sterile empyrean of perfect beauty—most would argue that Michelangelo here achieves it, perhaps capturing his own feelings about the work in the *David*'s chillingly vain, self-satisfied expression. This is also one of the few statues to have actually injured someone. During a political disturbance in the Piazza della Signoria, its arm broke off and fell on a farmer's toe. In 1991 it was David's toe which fell victim when a madman chopped it off. Since then, the rest of his anatomy has been shielded by glass.

In the Galleria next to the *David* are Michelangelo's famous *nonfiniti*, the four *Prisoners* or Slaves, worked on between 1519 and 1536, sculpted for Pope Julius' tomb and left in various stages of completion, although it is endlessly argued whether this is by design or through lack of time. Whatever the case, they illustrate Michelangelo's view of sculpture as a prisoner in stone just as the soul is a prisoner of the body.

The Gallery was founded by Grand Duke Pietro Leopold in 1784 to provide students with examples of art from every period. The big busy Mannerist paintings around the *David* are by Michelangelo's contemporaries, among them Pontormo's *Venus and Cupid*, with a Michelangelesque Venus among theatre masks. Other rooms contain a good selection of quattrocento painting, including the *Madonna del Mare* by Botticelli, a damaged Baldovinetti, the *Thebaid* by a follower of Uccello, and Perugino's *Deposition*. The painted frontal of the **Adimari chest** shows a delightful wedding scene of the 1450s with the Baptistry in the background that has been reproduced in half the books ever written about the Renaissance.

The hall off to the left of the *David* was formerly the women's ward of a hospital, depicted in a greenish painting by Pontormo. Now it is used as a gallery of plaster models by 19th-century members of the Accademia, a surreal, bright white neoclassical crowd.

Around the corner from the Accademia, in Via degli Alfani 78, is the workshop of pietre dure, (inlaid 'hard stones' or semi-precious stones), the **Opificio delle Pietre Dure** *(open 9–2, closed Sun; adm). Cosimo I was the first to actively promote what was to become Florence's special craft, and it was Ferdinando I who founded the Opificio in 1588 as a centre for craftsmen.*

Still on Via degli Alfani, across Via dei Servi, stands the **Rotonda di Santa Maria degli Angeli**, an octagonal building begun by Brunelleschi in 1434, one of his last works and one of the first centralized buildings of the Renaissance.

Start: *Piazza Santissima Annunziata*

Finish: *Casa Buonarroti*

Walking time: *one full day*

VII: Piazza Santissima Annunziata

fontana di Piazza SS. Annunziata

This mightily eclectic walk runs the gauntlet from Brunelleschi's serene foundlings' hospital to an Etruscan chimera to Florence's funky flea market, with the odd forays into Tuscan Baroque in between, before ending up at Michelangelo's house.

Lunch/Cafés

La Baraonda, Via Ghibellina 67r, ✆ 234 1171. Old-fashioned style with simple regional food made with fresh, top quality ingredients (closed Sun, around L30,000).

La Mescita Fani, Via degli Alfani 70r. Low-cost wine and snack bar, popular with students.

Tavola Calda Sant'Ambrogio. Appetising snacks and meals for cheap prices (around L20,000).

La Stazione di Zima, Via Ghibellina 70r. Serves regular food and vegetarian dishes, good value, popular with university students (around L20,000).

Danny Rock, Via Pandolfini. *Crêpe* bar with loud rock music, pretty waitresses.

Cibreo, 2 Via del Verrocchio 5r, ✆ 234 5853. Here is the entrance to the poor man's Cibreo serving a limited menu at cheaper prices (around L25,000).

Caffè Latte, Via degli Alfani 39r. A good place for breakfast *cappuccino* and *brioche*; yoghurt-based cakes and coffee made with mineral water.

---

*This walk begins very near to where Walk VI ends in **Piazza Santissima Annunziata**.*

This lovely square, really the only Renaissance attempt at a unified ensemble in Florence, is surrounded on three sides by arcades. In its centre, gazing down the splendid vista of Via dei Servi towards the Duomo, stands the equestrian statue of Ferdinand I (1607) by Giambologna and his pupil Pietro Tacca, made of bronze from Turkish cannons captured during the Battle of Lepanto. More fascinating than Ferdinand is the pair of bizarre Baroque fountains, also by Tacca, that share the square. Though possessed of a nominally marine theme, they resemble tureens of bouillabaisse that any ogre would be proud to serve.

*In the 1420s Filippo Brunelleschi struck the first blow for classical calm in this piazza when he built the celebrated **Spedale degli Innocenti** and its famous portico—an architectural landmark, but also a monument to Renaissance Italy's long, hard and ultimately unsuccessful struggle towards some kind of social consciousness.*

Even in the best of times, Florence's poor were treated like dirt; although babies, at least, were treated a little better. The Spedale degli Innocenti was the first hospital for foundlings in Italy and the world, and still serves as an orphanage today, as well as the local nursery school.

Florence Walk VII:
Piazza Santissima Annunziata

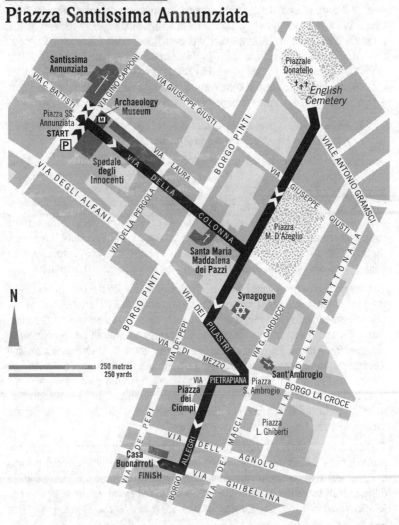

The Spedale was Brunelleschi's first completed work and demonstrates his use of geometrical proportions adapted to traditional Tuscan Romanesque architecture. His lovely portico is adorned with the famous blue and white tondi of infants in swaddling clothes by Andrea della Robbia, added as an appeal to charity in the 1480s after several children died of malnutrition. Brunelleschi also designed the two beautiful cloisters of the convent; the **Chiostro delle Donne**, reserved for the hospital's nurses, is especially fine. Upstairs, the **Museo dello Spedale** (*open 9–2, 9–1 Sun, closed Wed; adm*) contains a number of detached frescoes from Ognissanti and other churches, among them an unusual series of red and orange prophets by Alessandro Allori; other works include a *Madonna and Saints* by Piero di Cosimo, a *Madonna and Child* by Luca della Robbia, and the brilliant *Adoration of the Magi* (1488) painted by Domenico Ghirlandaio for the hospital's church, a crowded, colourful composition featuring portraits of members of the Arte della Lana, who funded the Spedale.

> The second portico on the piazza was built in 1600 in front of Florence's high society church, **Santissima Annunziata**.

Founded in 1250, the church was rebuilt by Michelozzo beginning in 1444 and funded by the Medici, who saw the need for a grander edifice to contain the pilgrims attracted by a miraculous image of the Virgin. As a shelter for the crowds, Michelozzo designed the **Chiostrino dei Voti**, an atrium in front of the church. Most of the Chiostrino's frescoes are by Andrea del Sarto and his students but the most enchanting work is Alesso Baldovinetti's *Nativity* (1462)—sadly faded, with the ghost of a transcendent landscape. Also present are two youthful works: Pontormo's *Visitation* and Rosso Fiorentino's more Mannerist *Assumption*.

The interior is the most gaudy and lush Baroque creation in the city, the only one the Florentines ever spent much money on during the Counter-Reformation. Michelozzo's design includes an unusual polygonal **Tribune** around the sanctuary, derived from antique buildings and entered by way of a triumphal arch designed by Alberti. Directly to the left as you enter is Michelozzo's marble **Tempietto**, hung with lamps and candles, built to house the miraculous *Annunciation*, painted by a monk with the help of an angel who painted the Virgin's face. Its construction was funded by the Medici, who couldn't resist adding an inscription on the floor that 'The marble alone cost 4000 florins'! The ornate canopy over the *tempietto* was added in the 17th century.

The next two chapels on the left side contain frescoes by Andrea del Castagno, painted in the 1450s but whitewashed over by the Church when it read Vasari's phoney story that Castagno murdered his fellow painter Domenico Veneziano—a difficult feat, since Veneziano outlived his supposed murderer by several years. Rediscovered in 1864, Castagno's fresco of *St Julian and the Saviour* in the first chapel has some strange Baroque bedfellows by Giambattista Foggini; the next chapel contains his highly unusual *Holy Trinity with St Jerome*. The right aisle's fifth chapel contains a fine example of an early Renaissance tomb, that of the obscure Orlando de' Medici by Bernardo Rossellino. The neighbouring chapel in the transept contains a painted crucifix by Baldovinetti, while the next one has a *Pietà*, the funerary monument of Cosimo I's court sculptor and Cellini's arch-rival Baccio Bandinelli; in this *Pietà* he put his own features on Nicodemus, as Michelangelo did in the *Pietà* in the Museo del Duomo. Bandinelli's most lasting contribution (or piece of mischief) was his establishment of the first 'Accademia' of art in 1531, which eventually did away with the old artist-pupil relationship in favour of the more impersonal approach of the art school.

Nine semicircular chapels radiate from the Tribune. The one at the rear contains the sarcophagus of Giambologna, a far more successful follower of Michelangelo; his pupil Pietro Tacca is buried with him, in this chapel designed by Giambologna before his death. The next chapel to the left contains the fine *Resurrection* by Bronzino, one of his finest religious paintings. On the left side of Alberti's triumphal arch, under a statue of St Peter, is the grave of Andrea del Sarto; next to it is the tomb of bishop Angelo Marzi Medici (1546), one of Florence's loudest Counter-Reformation blasts.

The **Chiostro dei Morti**, off the left transept, is most notable for Andrea del Sarto's highly original fresco, the *Madonna del Sacco* (1525), named after the sacks of grain on which St Joseph leans. The **Cappella di San Luca**, off the cloister (but rarely open) belongs to Florence's Academy of Design and contains the graves of Cellini, Pontormo, Franciabigio and other artists (*open 7–12.30 and 4–7*).

> *From Piazza SS. Annunziata, Via della Colonna leads to Florence's* **Museo Archeologico** *(open 9–2, Sun 9–1, closed Mon; adm), housed in the 17th-century Palazzo della Crocetta, originally built for Grand Duchess Maria Maddalena of Austria.*

Like nearly every other museum in Florence, this impressive collection was begun by the Medici, beginning with Cosimo il Vecchio and accelerating with the insatiable Cosimo I and his heirs. The Medici were especially fond of Etruscan things, while the impressive Egyptian collection was begun by Leopold II in the 1830s. At the time of writing the museum is undergoing rearrangement, but with a little luck you'll be able to find your way around.

The ground floor is devoted to Greek and Etruscan art, including the famous bronze *Chimera*, a remarkable beast with the three heads of a lion, goat and snake. This Etruscan work of the 5th century BC, dug up near Arezzo in 1555 and immediately snatched by Cosimo I, had a great influence on Mannerist artists. There is no Mannerist fancy about its origins, though; like all such composite monsters, it is a religious icon, a calendar beast symbolizing the three seasons of the ancient Mediterranean agricultural year. In the same hall stands the *Arringatore*, or Orator, a monumental bronze of the Hellenistic period, a civilized-looking gentleman, dedicated to Aulus Metellus.

Among the beautiful, often strange Etruscan urns and alabaster sarcophagi, mirrors and small bronzes, there is plenty of Greek art; Etruscan noble families were wont to buy up all they could afford. The beautiful Hellenistic horse's head once adorned the Palazzo Medici-Riccardi. The *Idolino*, a bronze of a young athlete, is believed to be a Roman copy of a 5th-century BC Greek original. There is an excellent *Kouros*, a young man in the archaic style from 6th-century BC Sicily, and some beautiful vases. An unusual, recent find, the silver *Baratti Amphora*, was made in the 4th century BC in Antioch and covered with scores of small medallions showing mythological figures. Scholars believe that the images and their arrangement may encode an entire system of belief, the secret teaching of one of the mystic-philosophical cults common in Hellenistic times, and they hope some day to decipher it.

The Egyptian collection has recently been modernized; there are some interesting small statuettes, mummies, canopic vases, and a unique wood-and-bone chariot, nearly completely preserved, found in a 14th-century BC tomb in Thebes. Out in the garden are several reconstructed Etruscan tombs (usually closed). A magnificent collection of precious stones and cameos, coins, and sculpture is kept under wraps and may only be visited by scholars with special permission.

> *East of the Archaeological Museum, Via della Colonna becomes one of Florence's typical straight, boring Renaissance streets. It's worth detouring down Borgo Pinti, to no. 58, to visit one of the city's least known but most intriguing churches,* **Santa Maria Maddalena dei Pazzi,** *a fine example of architectural syncretism (open 9–12 and 5–7).*

The church itself was founded in the 13th century, rebuilt in classically Renaissance style by Giuliano da Sangallo, then given a full dose of Baroque when the church was rededicated to the Counter-Reformation saint of the Pazzi family. Inside it's all high theatre, with a gaudy *trompe-l'oeil* ceiling, paintings by Luca Giordano, florid chapels, and a wild marble chancel. From the Sacristy a door leads down into a crypt full of mouldering ecclesiastics to the **Chapter House**, which contains a fresco of the *Crucifixion* (1496), one of Perugino's masterpieces. Despite the symmetry and quiet, contemplative grief of the five figures at the foot of the Cross and the magic stillness of the luminous Tuscan-Umbrian landscape, the fresco has a powerful impact, giving the viewer the uncanny sensation of being able to walk right into the scene.

> *Florence's Jewish community, although today only 1200 strong, has long been one of the most important in Italy, invited to Florence by the Republic in 1430, but repeatedly exiled and readmitted until Cosimo I founded Florence's Ghetto in 1551. When the Ghetto was opened up in 1848 and demolished soon after, a new* **Synagogue** *(1874–82) was built in Via L.C. Farini (turn right from Via della Colonna).*

This is a tall, charming Mozarabic Pre-Raphaelite hybrid inspired by the Hagia Sophia and the Transito Synagogue of Toledo. Although seriously damaged by the Nazis in August 1944—and later by the Arno in 1966—it has been lovingly restored. *Security is tight, but the synagogue may be toured 2–5.30 Mon, Tues and Thurs and 9.30–12.30 and 2–5.30 Sun (men must cover their heads).* There's a small **Jewish Museum** upstairs, with a documentary history of Florentine Jews as well as ritual and ceremonial items from the synagogue's treasure (*open usually May–Sept 9–6 Sun, Mon and Wed , 9–1 Tues and Thurs; in April and Oct, 9–1 Sun and Thurs. © 245 252 for information*).

> *From the synagogue it's a long two blocks north to Piazzale Donatello. Donatello's name deserves better than this traffic conundrum, a swollen artery in Florence's busy system of* viali *that take traffic around the centre. Pity Elizabeth Barrett Browning (1809–61) and the other expatriates buried in the piazza's* **English Cemetery***; they deserve better than to spend eternity in a traffic island.*

> *South of the synagogue the streets of Sant'Ambrogio are among the most dusty and piquant in the city centre, a neighbourhood where tourists seldom tread. Life revolves around* **Sant'Ambrogio** *and its neighbouring food market made of cast iron in 1873; the church (rebuilt in the 13th century, 19th-century façade) is of interest for its artwork.*

The second chapel on the right has a lovely fresco of the *Madonna Enthroned with Saints* by Orcagna (or his school) and the **Cappella del Miracolo**, just left of the high altar, contains Mino da Fiesole's celebrated marble *Tabernacle* (1481) and his own tomb. The chapel has a fresco of a procession by Cosimo Rosselli, especially interesting for its depiction of 15th-century costume and its contemporary portraits. Andrea Verrocchio is buried in the fourth chapel on the left; on the wall by the second altar, there's a *Nativity* by Baldovinetti. The fresco of an atypical *St Sebastian* on the entrance wall is by Agnolo Gaddi.

*From Sant'Ambrogio take Via Pietrapiana to the bustling **Piazza dei Ciompi,** named after the wool-workers' revolt of 1378.*

In the morning, Florence's flea market or **Mercatino** takes place here, the best place in town to buy that 1940s radio or outdated ball gown you've always wanted. One side of the square is graced with the **Loggia del Pesce**, built by Vasari in 1568 for the fishmongers of the Mercato Vecchio; when that was demolished the loggia was salvaged and re-erected here.

*From Piazza dei Ciompi walk down Borgo Allegri and turn right at Via Ghibellina for no. 70, the **Casa Buonarroti**.*

Michelangelo never lived in this house, although he purchased it in 1508. That wasn't the point, especially to an artist who had no thought for his own personal comfort, or anyone else's—he never washed, and never took off his boots, even in bed. Real estate was an obsession of his, as he struggled to restore the status of the semi-noble but impoverished Buonarroti family. His nephew Leonardo inherited the house and several works of art in 1564; later he bought the two houses next door to create a memorial to his uncle, hiring artists to paint scenes from Michelangelo's life. In the mid-19th century, the house was opened to the public as a Michelangelo museum (*open 9.30–1.30, closed Tues; adm*).

The ground floor is dedicated to mostly imaginary portraits of the artist, and works of art collected by his nephew's descendants, including an eclectic Etruscan and Roman collection and a lovely predella of the *Life of St Nicolas of Bari* by Giovanni di Francesco. The main attractions, however, are upstairs, beginning with Michelangelo's earliest known work, the beautiful bas-relief of *The Madonna of the Steps* (1490–1), the precocious work of a 16-year-old influenced by Donatello and studying in the household of Lorenzo il Magnifico; the relief of a *Battle Scene*, inspired by classical models, dates from the same period. Small models and drawings of potential projects line the walls; there's the wooden model for the façade of San Lorenzo, with designs for some of the statuary Michelangelo intended to fill in its austere blank spaces—as was often the case, his ideas were far too grand for his patron's purse and patience.

The next four rooms were painted in the 17th century to illustrate Michelangelo's life, virtues and apotheosis, depicting a polite, deferential and pleasant Michelangelo hobnobbing with popes. Those who know the artist best from *The Agony and the Ecstasy* may think they painted the wrong man by mistake. One of the best sections is a frieze of famous Florentines in the library. Other exhibits include a painted wooden *Crucifix* discovered in Santo Spirito in 1963 and believed by most scholars to be a documented one by Michelangelo, long thought to be lost; the *contrapposto* position of the slender body, and the fact that only Michelangelo would carve a nude Christ weigh in favour of the attribution.

Start: *Santa Croce*
Finish: *the Horne Museum*
Walking time: *half a day*

VIII: Santa Croce

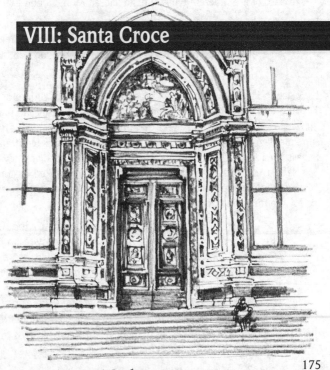

Sta Croce

175

The grand temple of Florentine contradiction, Franciscan Santa Croce is both the city's pantheon and one its greatest galleries of 14th-century frescoes.

La Maremmana, Via de' Macci 77r, © 241 226. Reasonably priced set menus, just near the Sant'Ambrogio market (closed Sun, around L25,000).

Il Francescano, Largo Bargellini, Via San Giuseppe 26. Good food, comprehensive wine list and yuppy atmosphere (closed Wed, around L50,000).

Vivoli, Via Isola delle Stinche 7r. Considered by Florentines as the best ice cream in the whole of Italy.

Acqua al Due, Via dell'Acqua 2, © 284 170. A cross between a pub atmosphere and a traditional trattoria, its winning card is the *assaggi dei primi*, samples of five different types of pasta (closed Mon, around L30,000).

Baldovino, Via San Giuseppe 22r, © 241 773. Pizzeria and osteria with a wood oven; there is a wide choice, a Friday fish-based menu and no one will bat an eye if you order just a starter (closed Tues, around L25,000).

No place in Florence so feeds the urge to dispute as the church of Santa Croce, Tuscany's 'Westminster Abbey', the largest Franciscan basilica in Italy, a must-see for every tour group. It was here that Stendhal gushed: 'I had attained to that supreme degree of sensibility where the divine intimations of art merge with the impassioned sensuality of emotion. As I emerged from the port of Santa Croce, I was seized with a fierce palpitation of the heart; I walked in constant fear of falling to the ground.' But don't be put off; most people manage to emerge from a visit without tripping over themselves.

*The contradictions begin in the **Piazza Santa Croce**, which has its interesting points—the row of medieval houses with projecting upper storeys, supported by stone brackets; the faded bloom of dancing nymphs on the **Palazzo dell'Antella**; the curious 14th-century **Palazzo Serristori-Cocchi**, opposite the church; a grim 19th-century statue of Dante (if Dante really looked like that, it's no wonder Beatrice married someone else). Because this piazza is the lowest-lying in the city, it suffered the worst in the 1966 flood, when 5.5m of oily water poured in.*

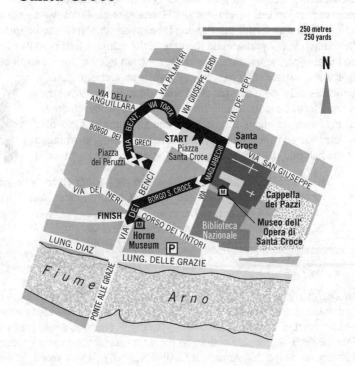

250 metres
250 yards

The eternal argument of Santa Croce heats up with rib-crunching violence every year, when the various neighbourhoods of Florence compete in a Renaissance football match.

The Calcio Storico

On 17 February 1530, the friendless republic of Florence had been besieged by the army of Charles V for three months. People were cold, hungry and miserable, but they were grimly determined to repel the emperor's troops, who could look down on Piazza Santa Croce from the surrounding hills. It was then decided to give them something worth looking at, to show

exactly what the Florentines thought of their siege: they played a rowdy, noisy game of football.

To commemorate this last great thumbing-of-the-communal-nose at the forces of reaction that would smother Florence for centuries, young bloods from the four quarters of the city don hose, baggy doublets and brightly plumed hats every year around the time of the summer solstice. After a good deal of pageantry, banner waving, gonfalon tossing, and a magnificent display of caparisoned horses, the 27 players on each side take the field—an immense rectangle of sand laid in the centre of the piazza. A cannon is fired, and the two sides charge at each other, butting heads, swinging fists, kicking, and grappling in a mix of no-holds barred rugby, football, and Roman wrestling, anything to get the ball into the adversaries' goal. The prize: a pure white calf.

> As a backdrop to all this sweat and dirt rises **Santa Croce's** neogothic façade, built in 1857–63 and financed by Sir Francis Sloane, whose Sloane Square in London has more admirers than this black and white design, derived from Orcagna's Tabernacle in Orsanmichele. Yet of all the modern façades grafted on to Italy's churches in order to atone for the chronic Renaissance inability to finish any project, this is one of the least offensive.

Santa Croce was reputedly founded by St Francis himself; during repairs after the flood, vestiges of a small early 13th-century church were discovered under the present structure. It went by the board in Florence's colossal building programme of the 1290s. The great size of the new church speaks for the immense popularity of Franciscan preaching. Arnolfo di Cambio planned it, and it was largely completed by the 1450s, but as in Santa Maria Novella, Giorgio Vasari and the blinding forces of High Renaissance mediocrity were unleashed upon the **interior**. Vasari never had much use for the art of Andrea Orcagna—he not only left him out of his influential *Lives of the Artists* but in Santa Croce he destroyed Orcagna's great fresco cycle that once covered the nave, replacing it with uninspired side altars.

For centuries it was the custom to install monuments to illustrious men in Santa Croce, and as you enter, you can see them lining the long aisles. Like many Franciscan churches, Santa Croce's large size, its architectural austerity and open timber roof resemble a barn, but at the end there's a lovely polygonal sanctuary, which shimmers with light and colour streaming through the 14th-century stained glass.

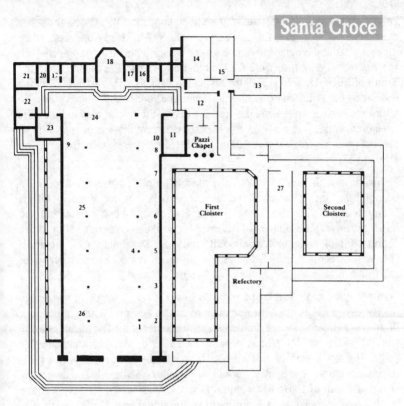

Santa Croce

1 Madonna del Latte
2 Tomb of Michelangelo
3 Monument to Dante
4 Benedetto da Maiano's Pulpit
5 Vittorio Alfieri's Tomb
6 Tomb of Machiavelli
7 Donatello's 'Annunciation'
8 Tomb of Leonardo Bruni
9 Tomb of Carlo Marsuppini
10 Tomb of Rossini
11 Castellani Chapel
12 Baroncelli Chapel
13 Medici Chapel
14 Sacristy

15 Rinuccini Chapel
16 Peruzzi Chapel
17 Bardi Chapel
18 Sanctuary
19 Bardi di Libertà Chapel
20 Bardi di Vernio Chapel
21 Niccolini Chapel
22 Bardi Chapel
23 Salviati Chapel
24 Monument to Alberti
25 Tomb of Lorenzo Ghiberti
26 Galileo's Tomb
27 Museo dell'Opera di S. Croce

Perversely, the greater the status of the person buried in Santa Croce, the uglier their memorial. A member of the Pazzi conspiracy, Francesco Nori, is buried by the first pillar in the right aisle, and is graced by one of the loveliest works of art, the *Madonna del Latte* (1478), a bas-relief by Antonio Rossellino, while the **Tomb of Michelangelo** (1570, the first in the right aisle) by Vasari is one of the least attractive. Michelangelo died in Rome in 1564, refusing for 35 years to return to Florence while alive, but agreeing to give the city his corpse. Dante has fared even worse, with an 1829 neoclassical monument that's as disappointing as the fact (to the Florentines) that Dante is buried in Ravenna, where he died in exile in 1321.

Facing the nave, Benedetto da Maiano's **marble pulpit** (1476) is one of the most beautiful that the Renaissance ever produced. Behind it, the **Vittorio Alfieri Monument** (1809) was sculpted by neoclassical master Antonio Canova and paid for by his lover, the Countess of Albany. Next is the nondescript 18th-century **Monument of Niccolò Machiavelli**, and then Donatello's **Annunciation** (1430s?), a tabernacle in gilded limestone, the angel wearing a remarkably sweet expression as he gently breaks the news to a grave, thoughtful Madonna.

Bernardo Rossellino's **Tomb of Leonardo Bruni** (1447), another masterpiece of the Renaissance, is perhaps the one monument that best fits the man it honours. Bruni was a Greek scholar, a humanist, and the author of the first major historical work of the period, *The History of Florence*, a copy of which his tranquil effigy holds. The tomb, with its Brunelleschian architectural setting, proved a great inspiration to other artists, most obviously Desiderio da Settignano and his equally beautiful **Tomb of Carlo Marsuppini** (1453) directly across the nave, and the less inspired, more imitative **Monument to Rossini** crowded in to the left. The last tomb in the aisle belongs to poet and patriot Ugo Foscolo.

Santa Croce is especially rich in trecento frescoes, which provided the unique opportunity to compare the work of Giotto with his followers. The south transept's **Castellani Chapel** has some of the later, more decorative compositions by Agnolo Gaddi (*Scenes from the Lives of Saints*, 1380s). The beautiful **Baroncelli Chapel** was painted with *Scenes from the Life of the Virgin* by Agnolo's father Taddeo, Giotto's assistant in the 1330s, and includes a bright gilded altarpiece, the *Coronation of the Virgin* by Giotto and his workshop.

The next portal gives on to a **Corridor** and the **Medici Chapel**, both designed by Michelozzo, containing one of Andrea della Robbia's finest altarpieces and a 19th-century fake Donatello, a relief of the *Madonna and Child* that fooled the experts for decades. From the corridor a door leads to the **Sacristy**, its walls frescoed by Taddeo Gaddi (*The Crucifixion*), Spinello Aretino and Niccolò di Pietro Gerini.

Behind the 14th-century grille, the **Rinuccini Chapel** was frescoed by one of Giotto's most talented followers, the Lombard Giovanni da Milano, in the 1360s.

> *The frescoes in the two chapels to the right of the sanctuary, the* **Peruzzi Chapel** *and the* **Bardi Chapel**, *were painted by the legendary Giotto in the 1330s, towards the end of his life when the artist returned from Padua and his work in the Arena chapel.*

The frescoes have not fared well during the subsequent 660 years. Firstly Giotto painted large parts of the walls *a secco* (on dry plaster) instead of *affresco* (on wet plaster), presenting the same kind of preservation problems that bedevil Leonardo's *Last Supper;* secondly, the 18th century thought so little of the frescoes that they were whitewashed over as eyesores. Rediscovered some 150 years later and finally restored in 1959, the frescoes now, even though fragmentary, may be seen more or less as Giotto painted them. The Peruzzi Chapel contains scenes from the *Lives of St John the Evangelist and the Baptist*. In the Bardi Chapel the subject is the *Life of St Francis*, which makes an interesting comparison with the frescoes in Assisi. The contrast between Giotto's frescoes and the chapel's 13th-century altarpiece, also showing scenes of the *Life of St Francis*, is a fair yardstick for measuring the breadth of the Giottesque revolution. Ruskin, in his *Mornings in Florence*, fixed his attention on St Louis, and spent breathless page upon page praising it as the perfect example of Giotto's style, never suspecting that the entire figure had been added only a few years previously by the frescoes' restorer.

Agnolo Gaddi designed the stained glass around the **Sanctuary**, as well as the fascinating series of frescoes on the *Legend of the True Cross*.

The Legend of the True Cross

This popular medieval story begins with Noah's son, Seth, as an old man, asking for the essence of mercy. The Angel Gabriel replies by giving Seth a branch, saying that 5000 years must pass before mankind may know true redemption. Seth plants the branch over Adam's grave on Mount Sinai, and it grows into a magnificent tree. King Solomon orders the tree cut, but as it is too large to move, the trunk stays where it is and is used as the main beam of a bridge. The Queen of Sheba is about to cross the bridge when she has a vision that the saviour of the world will be suspended from its wood, and that his death will mark the end of the Kingdom of the Jews. She refuses to cross the bridge, and writes of her dream to Solomon, who has the beam buried deep underground. Nevertheless, it is dug up and used to make the cross of Christ.

The cross next appears in the dream of Emperor Constantine before the Battle of Milvian Bridge, when he hears a voice saying that under this sign he will conquer. When it proves true, he sends his mother Helen to find the cross in Jerusalem. There she meets Judas Cyriacus, a pious Jew who knows where Golgotha is, but won't tell until Helen has him thrown in a well and nearly starved to death. When at last he agrees to dig, a sweet scent fills the air, and Judas Cyriacus is immediately converted. To discover which of the three crosses they find is Christ's, each is held over the coffin of a youth; the True Cross brings him back to life. After all this trouble in finding it, Helen leaves the cross in Jerusalem, where it is stolen by the Persians. Their King Chosroes thinks its power will bring him a great victory, but instead he loses the battle, and Persia, to Emperor Heraclius, who decides to return the holy relic to Jerusalem. But the gate is blocked by the Angel Gabriel, who reminds the proud Heraclius that Jesus entered the city humbly, on the back of an ass. And so, in a similar manner, the emperor returns the cross to Jerusalem.

Further to the left are two more chapels frescoed by followers of Giotto: the fourth, the **Bardi di Libertà Chapel**, by Bernardo Daddi and the last, the **Bardi di Vernio Chapel**, by Maso di Banco, one of the most innovative and mysterious artists of the trecento. The frescoes illustrate the little-known *Life of St Sylvester*—his baptism of Emperor Constantine, the resurrection of the bull, the closing of the dragon's mouth and resurrection of two sorcerers; on the other wall of the chapel are a *Dream of Constantine* and *Vision of SS. Peter and Paul*. In the corner of the transept, the richly marbled **Niccolini Chapel** offers a Mannerist-Baroque change of pace, built by Antonio Dossi in 1584 and decorated with paintings by Allori. Next, the second **Bardi Chapel** houses the famous *Crucifix* by Donatello that Brunelleschi called 'a peasant on the Cross'. The last of the funeral monuments, near the door, are those of Lorenzo Ghiberti and Galileo, the latter an 18th-century work. For running afoul of the Inquisition, Galileo was not permitted a Christian burial until 1737.

*Santa Croce's **Pazzi Chapel** carries an entrance fee, but it's well worth it (open 9–12.30, 3–5, until 6.30 in the summer, closed Wed; adm).*

Brunelleschi, who could excel on the monumental scale of the cathedral dome, saved some of his best work for small places. Without knowing the architect, and something about the austere religious tendencies of the Florentines, the Pazzi Chapel is inexplicable, a Protestant reformation in architecture unlike anything ever built before. The 'vocabulary' is essential Brunelleschi, the geometric forms emphasized by the simplicity of the decoration: *pietra serena* pilasters and rosettes on white walls, arches, 12 terracotta tondi of the Apostles by Luca della Robbia, coloured rondels of the Evangelists in the pendentives by Donatello, and a small stained-glass window by Baldovinetti. Even so, that is enough. The contemplative repetition of elements makes for an aesthetic that posed a direct challenge to the International Gothic of the time.

Leaving the Pazzi Chapel (notice Luca della Robbia's terracotta decorations on the portico), a doorway on the left of the cloister leads to another work of Brunelleschi, the **Second Cloister**, designed with the same subtlety and one of the quietest spots in Florence.

> *The old monastic buildings off the first cloister now house the* **Museo dell'Opera di Santa Croce** *(open 10–12.30 and 2.30–6.30 summer; 10–12.30 and 3–5 winter; adm).*

Here you can see Cimabue's celebrated *Crucifix*, devastated by the flood, and partly restored after one of Florence's perennial restoration controversies. The refectory wall has another fine fresco by Taddeo Gaddi, of the *Tree of the Cross* and the *Last Supper*; fragments of Orcagna's frescoes salvaged from Vasari's obliteration squads offer powerful, nightmarish vignettes of *The Triumph of Death and Hell.* Donatello's huge gilded bronze statue of *St Louis of Toulouse* (1423)—a flawed work representing a flawed character, according to Donatello—was made for the façade of Orsanmichele. The museum also contains works by Andrea della Robbia, and a painting of Mayor Bargellini with a melancholy Santa Croce submerged in the 1966 flood for a backdrop; under the colonnade there's a statue of *Florence Nightingale*, born in and named after the city in 1820.

> *The east end of Florence, which is a rambling district packed with artisans and small manufacturers, traditionally served as the artists' quarter in Renaissance times. Still one of the livelier neighbourhoods, with a few lingering artists lodged in the upper storeys, hoping to breathe inspiration from the very stones where Michelangelo walked, it is a good place to observe the workaday Florence behind the glossy façade. Just west of Piazza Santa Croce is a series of streets—***Via Bentaccordi,*** **Via Torta** *and* **Piazza dei Peruzzi***—which makes an almost complete ellipse. These mark the course of the inner arcade of the Roman amphitheatre, some stones of which can still be seen among the foundations of the old palaces.*

> *From Santa Croce, the pretty Borgo Santa Croce leads towards the Arno and the delightful* **Horne Museum,** *housed in a Renaissance palace.*

Herbert Percy Horne (1844–1916) was an English art historian, biographer of Botticelli, and Florentinophile, who bequeathed his collection to the nation (Via de' Benci 6, *open 9–1, closed Sun and holidays; adm*). A large *Deposition*, the last work of Gozzoli, sadly darkened with age, a painting by the great Sienese Pietro Lorenzetti, and a tondo by Piero di Cosimo hang on the first floor. The next room contains Horne's prize, Giotto's golden painting of young *St Stephen*, also Signorelli's *Redeemer*, a beardless, girlish youth, Beccafumi's *Decalione e Pirra*, and a saccharine *St Sebastian* by Carlo Dolci. Room 3 has a rousing quattrocento battle scene, taken from a marriage chest, good 15th-century wood inlays, and a relief of the head of *St John the Baptist* by Desiderio da Settignano. Upstairs a diptych attributed to Barna da Siena holds pride of place, together with an impressive array of Renaissance furniture and household objects.

IX: The Oltrarno

Fontana del Bacco

Start: *Santa Felicità*

Finish: *Porta San Miniato*

Walking time: *at least one full day*

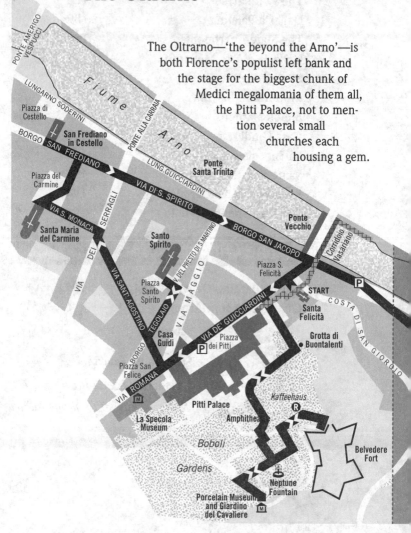

Florence Walk IX:
The Oltrarno

The Oltrarno—'the beyond the Arno'—is both Florence's populist left bank and the stage for the biggest chunk of Medici megalomania of them all, the Pitti Palace, not to mention several small churches each housing a gem.

PONTE AMERIGO VESPUCCI

Fiume Arno

LUNGARNO SODERINI

Piazza di Cestello

San Frediano in Cestello

BORGO SAN FREDIANO

PONTE ALLA CARRAIA

Ponte Santa Trìnita

LUNG. GUICCIARDINI

Piazza del Carmine

VIA DI S. SPIRITO

VIA S. MONACA

VIA DEI SERRAGLI

Santa Maria del Carmine

Santo Spirito

VIA DEL PRESTO DI S. MARTINO

BORGO SAN JACOPO

Ponte Vecchio

Corridoio Vasariano

Piazza Santo Spirito

Piazza S. Felicità

START

P

VIA MAGGIO

VIA SANT'AGOSTINO

TEGOLAIO

Casa Guidi

VIA DE' GUICCIARDINI

Santa Felicità

COSTA DI SAN GIORGIO

BORGO

Piazza San Felice

P

Piazza dei Pitti

Grotta di Buontalenti

VIA ROMANA

La Specola Museum

Pitti Palace

Amphitheatre

Kaffeehaus

R

Boboli

Gardens

Belvedere Fort

Neptune Fountain

Porcelain Museum and Giardino del Cavaliere

186

La Casalinga, Via Michelozzo 9r, just by Piazza Santo Spirito. A cheap option particularly popular with students and young tourists.

Frilli, Via San Niccolò 57. Ice cream parlour popular with the Florentines.

Beconcini, Viale Ariosto 26r. A *pasticceria* also serving *panini* with a choice of fillings and a few tables.

Il Cabiria, Piazza Santo Spirito. A pub-restaurant busy during the day and packed out at night.

Borgo Antico, Piazza Santo Spirito 6r, © 210 437. A pizzeria open day and night with tables outdoors (closed Mon).

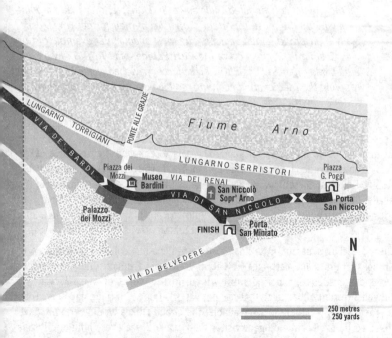

Once over the Ponte Vecchio, a different Florence reveals itself: greener, quieter, and less burdened with traffic. The Oltrarno is not a large district. A chain of hills squeezes it against the river, and their summits afford some of the best views over the city. Once across the Arno, the Medici's catwalk becomes part of the upper façade of **Santa Felicità**.

One of Florence's most ancient churches, Santa Felicità is believed to have been founded by the Syrian Greek traders who introduced Christianity to the city, and established the first Christian cemetery in the small square in front of the church. Rebuilt in the 18th century, there is one compelling reason to enter, for here, in the first chapel on the right, is the *ne plus ultra* of Mannerism: Pontormo's weirdly luminous *Deposition* (1528), painted in jarring pinks, oranges and blues that cut through the darkness of the little chapel. The composition itself is highly unconventional, with an effect that derives entirely from the use of figures in unusual, exaggerated poses; there is no sign of a cross, the only background is a single cloud. Sharing the chapel is Pontormo's *Annunciation* fresco, a less idiosyncratic work, as well as four tondi of the Evangelists in the cupola, partly the work of Pontormo's pupil and adopted son, Bronzino.

As the Medici consolidated their power in Florence, they made a point of buying up the most important properties of their former rivals, especially their proud family palaces. The most spectacular example of this was Cosimo I's acquisition of the **Pitti Palace**, *built in 1457 by a powerful banker named Luca Pitti who seems to have had vague ambitions of toppling the Medici and becoming the big boss himself. Follow the Corrodorio down Via de' Guicciardini to the palace.*

With its extensive grounds, now the Boboli Gardens, the palace was much more pleasant than the medieval Palazzo Vecchio, and in the 1540s Cosimo I and his wife Eleanor of Toledo moved in for good. The palace remained the residence of the Medici, and later the House of Lorraine, until 1868. The original building, probably designed by Brunelleschi, was only as wide as the seven central windows of the façade. Succeeding generations found it too small for their burgeoning hoards of bric-à-brac, and added several stages of symmetrical additions, resulting in a long bulky profile, resembling a rusticated Stalinist ministry on its bleak asphalt piazza.

There are eight separate museums in the Pitti, including collections dedicated to clothes, ceramics and carriages—a tribute to Medici acquisitiveness in the centuries of decadence, a period from which, in the words of Mary McCarthy, 'flowed a torrent of bad taste that has not yet dried up . . . if there had been Toby jugs and Swiss weather clocks available, the Grand Dukes would certainly have collected them'. For the diligent visitor who wants to see everything, the Pitti is pitiless; it is impossible to see all in one day.

*The Pitti museum that most people see is the **Galleria Palatina**, containing the Grand Dukes' famous collection of 16th–18th-century paintings, stacked on the walls in enormous gilt frames under the berserk opulence of frescoed ceilings celebrating planets, mythology, and of course, the Medici. The gallery is on the first floor of the right half of the palace (ticket office on the ground floor, off Ammannati's exaggerated rustic courtyard, a Mannerist masterpiece; open 9–2, 9–1 Sun, closed Mon; adm exp).*

The entrance to the Galleria is through the neoclassical **Sala Castagnoli**, with the *Tavola delle Muse* in its centre, itself an excellent introduction to the Florentine 'decorative arts'; the table, a paragon of the intricate art of *pietra dura*, was made in the 1870s. The Galleria's best paintings are in the five former reception rooms off to the left, with colourful ceilings painted in the 1640s by Pietro da Cortona, one of the most interesting Italian Baroque artists. The first is the **Sala di Venere**, with several works by Titian, including his early *Concert*, believed to have been partly painted by Giorgione and a powerful *Portrait of Pietro Aretino*, Titian's close and caustic friend, who complained to the artist that it was all too accurate and gave it to Cosimo I. There are two beautiful, optimistic landscapes by Rubens, painted at the end of his life, and an uncanny self-portrait, entitled *La Menzogna* (the Falsehood), by Neapolitan Salvator Rosa. The centrepiece statue, the *Venus Italica*, was commissioned by Napoleon from neoclassical master Antonio Canova in 1812 to replace the Venus de' Medici which he 'centralized' off to Paris—a rare case of the itchy-fingered Corsican trying to pay for something he took.

In the **Sala di Apollo** there's more Titian—his *Portrait of a Grey-eyed Gentleman*, evoking the perfect 16th-century English gentleman, a romantic character with an intense gaze, and his more sensuous than penitent *Mary Magdalene*—as well as works by Andrea del Sarto and Van Dyck.

The **Sala di Marte** has two works by Rubens, *The Four Philosophers* and the *Consequences of War*, as well as some excellent portraits by Tintoretto and Van Dyck (*Cardinal Bentivoglio*), and Titian's rather dashing *Cardinal Ippolito de' Medici* in Hungarian costume. Ippolito, despite being destined for the Church, was one of the more high-spirited Medici, and helped defend Vienna from the Ottomans before being poisoned at the age of 24.

The **Sala di Giove**, used as the Medici throne room, contains one of Raphael's best-known portraits, the lovely and serene *Donna Velata* (1516). The small painting of *The Three Ages of Man* is usually attributed to Giorgione. Salviati, Perugino, Fra Bartolomeo and Andrea del Sarto are also represented here. In the **Sala di Saturno** Raphael dominates, with several paintings from his Florence days: *Maddalena and Agnolo Doni* (1506) and the *Madonna 'del Granduca'*, influenced by the paintings of Leonardo. Some 10 years later, Raphael had found his own style, beautifully evident in his famous *Madonna della Seggiola* ('of the chair'), perhaps the most popular work he ever painted, and one that is far more complex and subtle than it appears. The rounded, intertwining figures of the Madonna and Child are seen as if through a slightly convex mirror, bulging out—one of the first examples of conscious illusionism in the Renaissance.

The last of the reception rooms, the **Sala dell'Iliade** (frescoed in the 19th century), has some fine portraits by the Medici court painter and Rubens' friend, Justus Sustermans. Two *Assumptions* by Andrea del Sarto, *Philip II* by Titian, *La Maddalena* by Artemisia Gentileschi and a Velázquez equestrian portrait of Philip IV share the room with one of the most unusual residents of the gallery, *Queen Elizabeth*, who seems uncomfortable in such company. Just off this room lies the pretty **Sala della Stufa**, frescoed with the *Four Ages of the World* by Pietro da Cortona. Caravaggio's *Sleeping Cupid* is in the next room, the **Sala dell'Educazione di Giove**. A couple of rooms down you can peek into the Empire bathroom of Elisa Baciocchi, Napoleon's sister, who ruled the Département de l'Arno between 1809 and 1814, and seemingly spent much of those years redecorating the Pitti.

Some of the more interesting paintings to ferret out in the remainder of the gallery include Filippino Lippi's *Death of Lucrezia* and Raphael's *Madonna dell' Impannata*, both in the **Sala di Ulisse**. In the adjacent **Sala di Prometeo** don't miss Filippo Lippi's lovely *Tondo of the Madonna and Child*, Rubens' *Three Graces*, and Baldassare Peruzzi's unusual *Dance of Apollo*.

> *The right half of the Pitti contains the **State Apartments** (same hours as the Galleria Palatina, though at the time of writing closed for restoration, except for the winter apartments open by appointment only, © 287 096).*

These were last redone in the 19th century by the Dukes of Lorraine, with touches by the Kings of Savoy, who occupied them during Florence's interlude as national capital. Among the garish furnishings, there is a fine series of Gobelin tapestries ordered from Paris by Elisa Baciocchi.

*On the second floor above the Galleria Palatina has been installed Florence's modern **Galleria d'Arte Moderna** with works from the late 18th and 19th centuries (tickets in the courtyard, same hours as the Galleria Palatina; adm exp).*

Though the monumental stair may leave you breathless (the Medici negotiated it with sedan chairs and strong-shouldered servants), consider a visit for some sunny painting of the Italy of your great-grandparents and some amazing, kitsch statuary, obsessed with death and beauty. The underrated 'Splatterers' or *Macchiaioli* (Tuscan Impressionists) illuminate **Room 16** and the rest of the museum, forming an excellent introduction to the works by Silvestro Lega, Giovanni Fattori, Nicolo Cannicci, Francesco Gioli, Federigo Zandomeneghi and Telemaco Signorini, with an interval dedicated to the Risorgimento battle scenes. While the canvases radiate light, the morbid statues become more frequent and stupefying: don't miss the *Pregnant Nun* and the *Suicide*, by Antonio Ciseri in **Room 19**.

*The ground floor on the left side of the Pitti was used as the Medici summer apartments and now contains the **Museo degli Argenti**, the family's remarkable collection of jewellery, vases, trinkets and pricey curiosities (open 9–2, 9–1 Sun, closed Mon; adm valid for Costume and Porcelain museums).*

The Grand Duke's guests would be received in four of the most delightfully frescoed rooms in Florence, beginning with the **Sala di Giovanni di San Giovanni**, named after the artist who painted it in the 1630s. The theme is the usual Medicean self-glorification—but nowhere does such dubious material achieve such flamboyant treatment. Here the Muses, chased from Paradise, find refuge with Lorenzo il Magnifico; Lorenzo smiles as he studies a bust of Pan by Michelangelo. His real passion, a collection of antique vases carved of semi-precious stones or crystal, is displayed in a room off to the left; the vases were dispersed with the rise of Savonarola, but Lorenzo's nephew Cardinal Giulio had no trouble in relocating them, as Lorenzo had his initials LAUR.MED. deeply incised into each. The three **Reception rooms** were painted in shadowy blue *trompe l'oeil* by two masterly Bolognese illusionists, Agostino Michele and Angelo Colonna.

The Grand Dukes' treasure hoard is up on the mezzanine. These golden toys are only a fraction of what the Medici had accumulated; despite the terms of Anna Maria's will, leaving everything to Florence, the Lorraines sold off the most valuable pieces and jewels to finance Austria's wars. Among the leftovers here, however, is a veritable apoplexy of fantastical bric-à-brac: jewelled bugs, cameos, sea monster pendants, interlaced ivory cubes, carved cherry pits, gilt nautilus shells, chalices made of ostrich eggs, enough ceramic plates to serve an army, a

Mexican mitre made of feathers, intricate paper cut-outs, cups carved from buffalo horns, and 17th-century busts and figurines made of seashells that would not shame the souvenir stand of any seaside resort.

> The **Museum of Costumes** (same hours as the Argenti) is housed in the Meridiana pavilion, the south extension of the Pitti, a dull addition added by the Lorraines; its prize exhibit is the reconstructed dress that Eleanor of Toledo was buried in—the same one that she wears in Bronzino's famous portrait. The **Porcelain Museum** (visits by appointment, © 287 096) is housed in the airy casino of Cosimo III, out in the Giardino del Cavaliere in the Boboli Gardens (follow the signs). The **Museo delle Carrozze**, with a collection of Medici and Lorraine carriages and sedan chairs, has been closed for years.

Finally, the hardest part of the Pitti to get into may be worth the trouble if you're fond of Spanish painting. Until it finds a more permanent home, the **Contini Bonacossi Collection** resides in the Meridiana pavilion.

This recent bequest includes works of Cimabue, Duccio and Giovanni Bellini, some sculpture and china, and also paintings by El Greco, Goya and Velázquez— the last represented by an exceptional work, *The Water Carrier of Seville* (open for tours at 10am, Tues, Thurs and Sat—you must make an appointment with the secretary of the Uffizi Gallery).

Stretching back invitingly from the Pitti, the shady green of the **Boboli Gardens**, Florence's largest (and only) central public garden, is an irresistible oasis in the middle of a stone-hard city (open 9am until one hour before sunset; adm).

Originally laid out by Buontalenti, the Boboli reigns as queen of all formal Tuscan gardens, the most elaborate and theatrical, a Mannerist–Baroque co-production of Nature and Artifice laid out over a steep hill, full of shady nooks and pretty walks and beautifully kept. The park is guarded by a platoon of statuary, many of them Roman works, while others are absurd Mannerist pieces like Cosimo I's court dwarf posing as a chubby Bacchus astride a turtle (near the left-hand entrance, next to Vasari's Corridor).

Just beyond this lies the remarkable **Grotta di Buontalenti** which is one of the architect's most imaginative works, anticipating Gaudì with his dripping, stalactite-like stone, from which fantastic limestone animals struggle to emerge. Casts of Michelangelo's *nonfiniti* slaves stand in the corners, replacing the originals put there by the Medici, while back in the shadowy depths stands a luscious statue of Venus coming from her bath by Giambologna. For all that, the grotto is not a favourite with the Florentines and is usually locked up.

The **Amphitheatre**, ascending in regular tiers from the palace, was designed like a small Roman circus to hold Medici court spectacles. It has a genuine obelisk, of Rameses II from Heliopolis, snatched by the ancient Romans and shipped here by the Medici branch in Rome. The granite basin, large enough to submerge an elephant, came from the Roman Baths of Caracalla. Straight up the terrace is the **Neptune Fountain**; a path leads from there to the pretty **Kaffeehaus**, a boat-like pavilion with a prow and deck offering a fine view of Florence and drinks in the summer. From here the path continues up to the **Belvedere Fort** (*see* p.200). Other signs from the Neptune Fountain point the way up to the secluded **Giardino del Cavaliere**, located on a bastion on Michelangelo's fortifications (*open same hours as the Porcelain Museum*). Cosimo III built the casino here to escape the heat in the Pitti Palace; the view over the ancient villas, vineyards and olives is pure Tuscan enchantment.

> *In the old days the neighbourhood around the Pitti was a fashionable address, but in the 19th century rents for a furnished palace were incredibly low. Shortly after their secret marriage, the Brownings found one of these, the **Casa Guidi** at Piazza San Felice 8, the perfect place to settle; during their 13 years here they wrote their most famous poetry. Now owned by the Browning Institute, you can visit it weekdays (open 3–6). Dostoevsky wrote* The Idiot *while living nearby, at no. 21 Piazza Pitti.*

> *Past the Pitti on Via Romana 17, are two of Florence's great oddball attractions, both part of the **La Specola** museum.*

The Zoological Section (*open 9–12 Mon,Thurs, Fri and 9–2.30 second Sun every month*) has a charmingly old-fashioned collection of nearly everything that walks, flies or swims, from the humble sea worm to the rare Madagascar Aye-Aye or the swordfish, with an accessory case of different blades. Some trophies bagged by the hunt-crazy House of Savoy are displayed, and near the end come small wax models of human and animal anatomy, wax eggs, a wax peeled chicken and wax skinned cat. The real horror show stuff, however, is kept hidden away in the **Museum of Waxes** (*open 2–5 Sat, 3–6 June–Sept*). Dotty, prudish old Cosimo III was a hypochondriac and morbidly obsessed with diseases, which his favourite artist, a Sicilian priest named Gaetano Zumbo, was able to portray with revolting realism. His macabre anatomical models were one of the main sights for Grand Tourists in the 18th century.

> *From La Specola walk back to Piazza San Felice, turn left briefly up Via Mazzetta then right in Borgo Tegolaio for **Santo Spirito**.*

Piazza Santo Spirito, the centre of the Oltrarno, usually has a few market stalls in the morning under the plane trees as well as a quiet café or two. In the evening it changes face and the bars fill with people, who meet and chat in the piazza and on the church steps until the early hours. On one side, a plain 18th-century façade hides Brunelleschi's last, and perhaps greatest church. He designed Santo Spirito in 1440 and lived to see only one column erected, but subsequent architects were faithful to his elegant plan for the interior. This is done in the architect's favourite pale grey and *pietra serena* articulation, a rhythmic forest of columns with semicircular chapels gracefully recessed into the transepts and the three arms of the crossing. The effect is somewhat spoiled by the ornate 17th-century *baldacchino*, which sits in this enchanted garden of architecture like a 19th-century bandstand.

The art in the chapels is meagre, as most of the good paintings were sold off over the years. The best include Filippino Lippi's beautiful *Madonna and Saints* in the right transept and Verrocchio's jewel-like *St Monica and Nuns*, an unusual composition and certainly one of the blackest paintings of the Renaissance, pervaded with a dusky, mysterious quality; Verrocchio, who taught both Leonardo and Botticelli, was a Hermetic alchemist on the side. The fine marble altarpiece and decoration in the next chapel is by Sansovino; the elaborate barrel-vaulted **Vestibule** and octagonal **Sacristy**, entered from the left aisle, are by Giuliano da Sangallo, inspired by Brunelleschi.

To the left of the church, in the refectory of the vanished 14th-century convent are the scanty remains of a *Last Supper* and a well-preserved, highly dramatic *Crucifixion* by Andrea Orcagna, in which Christ is seen alone against an enormous dark sky, with humanity ranged below and angels like white swallows swirling around in a cosmic whirlwind. The refectory also contains an interesting collection of Romanesque odds and ends, including 13th-century stone sea-lions from Naples (*open 8–12 and 3.30–6.30, closed Mon; adm*).

> *Retrace your steps down Borgo Tegolaio turning right in Via Sant'Agostino. This becomes Via S. Monaca* en route *to **Santa Maria del Carmine**.*

There is little to say about the surroundings, the piazza, the rough stone façade, or the interior of the Oltrarno's other great church, Santa Maria del Carmine, which burned in 1771 and was reconstructed shortly after. Miraculously, the Brancacci Chapel, one of the landmarks in Florentine art, survived both the flames and attempts by the authorities to replace it with something more fashionable. Three artists worked on the Brancacci's frescoes: Masolino, who began them in 1425, and who designed the cycle, his pupil Masaccio, who worked on them alone for a year before following his master to Rome, where he died at the age of 27, and Filippino Lippi, who finished them 50 years later. Filippino took care to imitate Masaccio as closely as possible, and the frescoes have an appearance of stylistic unity. Between 1981 and 1988 they were subject to one of Italy's most publicized restorations, cleansed of 550 years of dirt and overpainting, enabling us to see what so thrilled the painters of the Renaissance.

Masaccio in his day was a revolution and a revelation in his solid, convincing naturalism; his figures stand in space, without any fussy ornamentation or Gothic grace, very much inspired by Donatello's sculptures. Masaccio conveyed emotion with broad, quick brush strokes and with his use of light, most obvious in his almost Impressionistic scene of the *Expulsion of Adam and Eve*, one of the most memorable and harrowing images created in the Renaissance. In the *Tribute Money*, the young artist displays his mastery of Brunelleschian artificial perspective and light effects. The three episodes in the fresco show an official demanding tribute from the city, St Peter fetching it, on Christ's direction, from the mouth of a fish, and lastly, his handing over of the money to the official. Other works by 'Shabby Tom' include *St Peter Baptizing* on the upper register, and *St Peter Healing with his Shadow* and *St Peter Enthroned and Resurrecting the Son of the King of Antioch*, the right half of which was finished by Filippino Lippi. The more elegant and unearthly Masolino is responsible for the remainder, except for the lower register's *Release of St Peter from Prison*, *St Peter Crucified* and *St Paul Visiting St Peter in Prison*, all by Filippino Lippi, based on Masaccio's sketches (*open 7–12 and 3.30–7; adm*).

Among the detached frescoes displayed in the cloister and refectory is a good one by Filippino's dad, Fra Filippo Lippi, who was born nearby in Via dell'Ardiglione.

> *Those with the time or inclination to stroll the streets of the Oltrarno can discover one of the city's last real residential neighbourhoods, the streets lined with bakeries and barbershops instead of boutiques and restaurants. The westernmost quarter within the medieval walls, Borgo San Frediano just off Piazza del Carmine, is known for its workshops and unpretentious antique dealers. The **Porta San Frediano**, its tall tower guarding the Pisa road, has its old wooden door and locks still in place. The domed 17th-century church of **San Frediano in Cestello**, with its blank poker face, is the landmark along this stretch of the Arno.*

The neighbourhoods get trendier as you head east, especially along busy Via di Santo Spirito, its extension Borgo San Jacopo, and wide Via Maggio, leading inland from the Ponte Santa Trínita. All have fine palaces and medieval towers pruned by the Republic. Many great medieval bankers also erected their palaces in the Oltrarno. Several may still be seen along Via de' Bardi, east of the Ponte Vecchio, especially the 13th–14th-century **Palazzo dei Mozzi** in the piazza of the same name. Across the piazza is the **Museo Bardini/Galleria Corsi** (*open 9–2, 8–1 Sun, closed Wed; adm*), an eclectic collection of art and architectural fragments left to the city in 1922 by art dealer Stefano Bardini. Bardini built this rather lugubrious palace to incorporate the doorways, ceilings and stairs that he salvaged from the demolition of the Mercato Vecchio and other buildings in central Florence; he even installed a mock crypt to display his tombs and funereal altarpieces (there's an especially fine one by Andrea della Robbia). Also outstanding are Tino da Camaino's trecento *Charity*, a *Madonna* attributed to Donatello, a panel painting of *St Michael* by Antonio Pollaiuolo, and a magnificent set of Persian carpets, old musical instruments, furniture and armour. Near the museum, the nondescript postwar **Ponte alle Grazie** replaced a famous medieval bridge with seven chapels on it, home to seven nuns, who one imagines spent much of their time praying that the Arno wouldn't flood.

Further east, narrow Via di San Niccolò leads to **San Niccolò sopr'Arno**, a church rebuilt in the 14th century, with a lovely fresco in the sacristy of the *Madonna della Cintola* ('of the girdle') by Baldovinetti. The street ends with a bang at **Porta San Niccolò**, an impressively looming gate of 1340 that has recently been restored. A smaller gate just to the south, the **Porta San Miniato**, stands near the walkway up to San Miniato (*see* p.200).

Peripheral Attractions

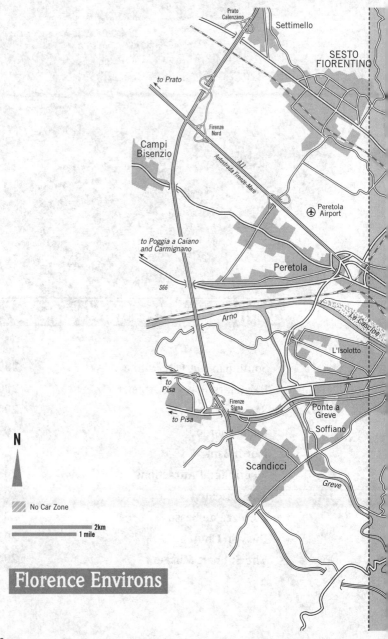

N

No Car Zone

2km
1 mile

Florence Environs

Prato
Calenzano

Settimello

SESTO
FIORENTINO

to Prato

Firenze
Nord

Campi
Bisenzio

Autostrada Firenze-Mare

A11

Peretola
Airport

to Poggia a Caiano
and Carmignano

Peretola

S66

Arno

Le Cascine

L'Isolotto

to
Pisa

Firenze
Signa

to Pisa

Ponte a
Greve

Soffiano

Scandicci

Greve

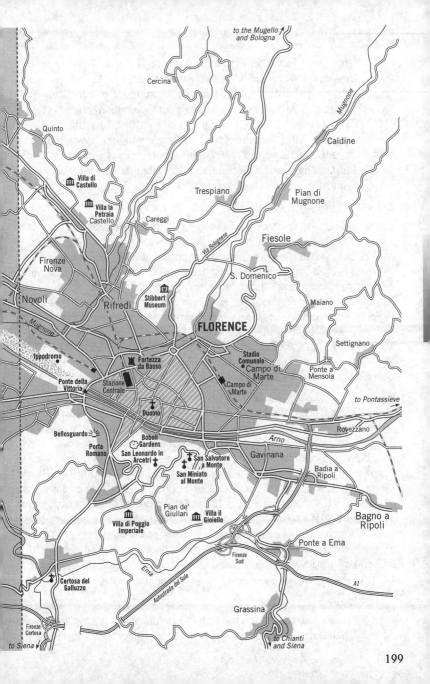

Great Aunt Florence, with her dour complexion and severe, lined face, never was much of a looker from street level, but improves with a bit of distance, either mental or from one of her hilltop balconies: the Belvedere Fort, San Miniato, Piazzale Michelangelo, Bellosguardo, Fiesole or Settignano (*see* p.209). Few cities are so endowed with stunning vistas; and when you look down upon Florence's palaces and towers, her loping bridges and red tile roofs and famous churches, Brunelleschi's incomparable dome seems even more remarkable, hovering like a benediction over the city.

Belvedere Fort and Arcetri

One of Florence's best and closest balconies is the **Belvedere Fort**, a graceful six-point star designed by Buontalenti and built 1590–5, not so much for the sake of defence but to remind any remaining Florentine republicans who was boss. Since 1958, it has been used for special exhibitions, but you can always enjoy the unforgettable views of Florence and countryside from its ramparts, daily between 8am and 8pm. It can be reached from the Boboli Gardens, or by ascending one of Florence's prettiest streets, **Costa San Giorgio**, which begins in Piazza Santa Felicità, just beyond the Ponte Vecchio. Costa San Giorgio winds up the hill, lined with old villas and walled gardens. The villa at no. 19 was, from 1610 to 1631, the home of Galileo. At the top of the street stands the arch of the **Porta San Giorgio**, guarded by a 13th-century relief of St George and the dragon.

In this part of Florence, the countryside begins right at the city wall, a rolling landscape of villas and gardens. Via San Leonardo winds its way out towards Arcetri; a 10-minute walk will take you to the 11th-century **San Leonardo in Arcetri** (*usually open Sunday mornings*). There is a wonderful 13th-century pulpit, originally built for San Pier Scheraggio, and a small rose window, made according to legend from a wheel of Fiesole's *Carroccio*, captured by Florence in 1125. A half kilometre further on, past the Viale Galileo crossroads, Via San Leonardo changes its name to Via Viviani, where it passes the **Astrophysical Observatory** and the **Torre del Gallo**, a reconstruction of a 14th-century tower by art dealer Stefano Bardini. Another kilometre further on Via Viviani reaches the settlement of Pian de' Giullari, where Galileo spent the last years of his life, in the 16th-century **Villa il Gioiello**, virtually under house arrest after his encounter with the Inquisition in 1631, and where Milton is believed to have visited him.

San Miniato

From Porta San Miniato you can walk up to San Miniato church on the stepped Via di San Salvatore al Monte, complete with the Stations of the Cross, or take the less pious bus 13 up the scenic Viale dei Colli from the station or Piazza del Duomo. High atop its monumental steps, San Miniato's distinctive and beautiful façade can be seen from almost anywhere in the city, although relatively few visitors take the time to visit one of the finest Romanesque churches in Italy.

San Miniato was built in 1015, over an even earlier church. According to legend, the head of 3rd-century martyr St Minias bounced up here when the Romans knocked it off down below in Florence. Despite its distance from the centre San Miniato has always been one of the churches dearest to the Florentines' hearts.

The remarkable geometric pattern of green, black and white marble that adorns its façade began in 1090, though funds only permitted the embellishment of the lower, simpler half of the front; the upper half was added in the 12th century, paid for by the Arte di Calimala, the medieval guild who made a fortune buying up bolts of fine wool, dyeing them a deep red or scarlet that no one else in Europe could imitate, then selling them back for twice the price; their proud gold eagle stands at the top of the roof. The glittering mosaic of Christ, the Virgin and St Minias, came slightly later.

The Calimala was also responsible for decorating the interior, an unusual design with a raised choir built over the crypt. As the Calimala became richer, so did the fittings; the delicate intarsia **marble floor** of animals and zodiac symbols dates from 1207. The lower walls were frescoed in the 14th and 15th centuries, including an enormous St Christopher. At the end of the nave stands Michelozzo's unique, free-standing **Cappella del Crocifisso**, built in 1448 to hold the crucifix that spoke to St John Gualberto (now in Santa Trínita); it is magnificently carved and adorned with terracottas by Luca della Robbia.

Off the left nave is one of Florence's Renaissance showcases, the **Chapel of the Cardinal of Portugal** (1461–6). The 25-year-old Cardinal, a member of the Portuguese royal family, happened to die in Florence at an auspicious moment, when the Medici couldn't spend enough money on publicly prominent art, and when some of the greatest artists of the quattrocento were at the height of their careers. The chapel was designed by Manetti, Brunelleschi's pupil; the ceiling exquisitely decorated with enamelled terracotta and medallions by

Luca della Robbia; the tomb of the Cardinal is beautifully carved by Antonio Rossellino; the fresco of the *Annunciation* is charmingly painted by Alesso Baldovinetti; the altarpiece of *Three Saints* is a copy of the original work by Piero Pollaiuolo.

Up the steps of the choir more treasures await. The marble transenna and pulpit were carved in 1207, with art and a touch of medieval humour. Playful geometric patterns frame the mosaic in the apse, *Christ between the Virgin and St Minias*, made in 1297 by artists imported from Ravenna, and later restored by Baldovinetti. The colourful **Sacristy** on the right was frescoed by Spinello Aretino in 1387, but made rather flat by subsequent restoration. In the **Crypt** an 11th-century altar holds the relics of St Minias; the columns are topped by ancient capitals.

The panorama of Florence from San Miniato is lovely to behold, but such thoughts were hardly foremost in Michelangelo's mind during the Siege of Florence. The hill was vulnerable, and to defend it he hastily erected the fortress (now surrounding the cemetery to the left of the church), placed cannons in the unfinished 16th-century campanile (built to replace an original which fell over), and shielded the tower from artillery with mattresses. He grew fond of the small church below San Miniato, **San Salvatore al Monte**, built by Cronaca in the late 1400s, which he called his 'pretty country lass'.

With these associations in mind, perhaps, the city named the vast, square terrace car park below, **Piazzale Michelangelo**, the most popular viewpoint only because it is the only one capable of accommodating an unlimited number of tour buses. Besides another copy of the *David* and a fun, tacky carnival atmosphere rampant with souvenirs, balloons and ice cream, the Piazzale offers views that can reach as far as Pistoia on a clear day.

Bellosguardo

Many would argue that the finest of all views over Florence is to be had from Bellosguardo, located almost straight up from Porta Romana at the end of the Boboli Gardens or Piazza Torquato Tasso. Non-mountaineers may want to take a taxi; the famous viewpoint, from where you can see every church façade in the city, is just before Piazza Bellosguardo.

North Bank Peripheral Attractions

If you are anywhere near the centre of the city it is easy to take the bus to see Florence's riverside park, its pretty Russian church or its quirkiest museum.

The Cascine

*Bus 17C which you can pick up from the station or Duomo will take you through the congestion to the **Cascine**, which is the long (3.5km), narrow public park lining this bank of the Arno. This was originally used as the Medici's dairy farm, or cascina, and later as a Grand Ducal hunting park and theatre for public spectacles.*

The newer sections of the city are irredeemably dull. Much of Florence's traffic problem is channelled through its ring of avenues, or *viali*, laid out in the 1860s by Giuseppe Poggi to replace the demolished walls. On and along them are scattered points of interest, including some of the old city gates; the distances involved and danger of carbon monoxide poisoning on the *viali* make the idea of walking insane.

A windy autumn day here in 1819 inspired Shelley to compose the 'Ode to the West Wind'. Three years later Shelley's drowned body was burnt on a pyre in Viareggio, by his friend Trelawny; curiously, a similar incineration took place in the Cascine in 1870 when the Maharaja of Kohlapur died in Florence. According to ritual his body had to be burned near the confluence of two rivers, in this case, the Arno and Mugnone at the far end of the park, on a spot now marked by the Maharaja's equestrian statue. Florentines come to the Cascine to play; it contains a riding school, race tracks, a small amusement park and zoo for the children, tennis courts, and a swimming-pool.

Fortezza da Basso

The same bus continues to the train station where just beyond cars and buses hurtle around and around the **Fortezza da Basso**, an enormous bulk built by Antonio da Sangallo on orders from Alessandro de' Medici in 1534.

It immediately became the most hated symbol of Medici tyranny. Ironically, the duke who built the Fortezza da Basso was one of very few to meet his end within its ramparts—stabbed by his relative and bosom companion Lorenzaccio' de' Medici. As a fortress, the place never saw any action which was as thrilling or vicious as the Pitti fashion shows that take place behind the walls in its 1978 aluminium exhibition hall.

Russian Church

Just east of the Fortezza, at the corner of Via Leone X and Viale Milton, there's an unexpected sight rising above the sleepy residential neighbourhood—the five graceful onion domes of the **Russian Church**, made even more exotic by the palm tree tickling its side. In the 19th century, Florence was a popular winter retreat for Russians who could afford it, among them Dostoevsky and Maxim Gorky. Completed by Russian architects in 1904, it is a pretty jewel box of brick and majolica decoration, open on the third Sunday of the month, when morning services are held in Russian.

The Stibbert Museum

From Piazza della Libertà, dull Via Vittorio Emanuele heads a kilometre north to Via Stibbert and the Stibbert Museum (alternatively, take bus 31 or 32 from the station). Those who make the journey to see the lifetime's accumulations of Frederick Stibbert (1838–1906), who fought with Garibaldi and hobnobbed with Queen Victoria, can savour Florence's most bizarre museum, and one of the city's most pleasant small parks, laid out by Stibbert with a mouldering Egyptian temple sinking in a pond (*open for tours on the hour, 9–1—when you may wander at will—9–12.30 bank holidays—closed Thurs; adm, free Sun*; and just try to obey the sign on the door: 'Comply with the Forbidden Admittances!').

Stibbert's Italian mother left him a 14th-century house, which he enlarged, joining it to another house to create a sumptuous Victorian's version of what a medieval Florentine house should have looked like—64 rooms to contain a pack-rat's treasure hoard of all things brilliant and useless, from an attributed Botticelli to snuff boxes, to what a local guide intriguingly describes as 'brass and silver basins, used daily by Stibbert'. Stibbert's serious passion, however, was armour, and he amassed a magnificent collection from all times and places. The best pieces are not arranged in dusty cases, but with a touch of Hollywood, on grim knightly mannequins ranked ready for battle.

Day Trips

The outskirts of the city have long lured the Florentines out of their streets of history into some of Tuscany's loveliest country-side. Lofty Fiesole, Florence's grandmother, and a set of Medici villas are all easily reached by public transport.

Fiesole

Florence liked to look at itself as the daughter of Rome, and in its fractious heyday explained its quarrelsome nature by the fact that its population from the beginning was of mixed race, of Romans and 'that ungrateful and malignant people who of old came down from Fiesole', according to Dante. First settled in the 2nd millennium BC, it became the most important Etruscan city in the region. Yet from the start Etruscan *Faesulae*'s relationship with Rome was rocky, especially after sheltering Catiline and his conspirators in 65 BC. Because of its lofty position, Fiesole was too difficult to capture, so the Romans built a camp below on the Arno to cut off its supplies. Eventually Fiesole was taken, and it dwindled as the Roman camp below grew into the city of Florence, growth the Romans encouraged to spite the old Etruscans on their hill. This easily defended hill, however, ensured Fiesole's survival in the Dark Ages. When times became safer, families began to move back down to the Arno to rebuild Florence. They returned to smash up most of Fiesole after defeating it in 1125; since then the little town has remained aloof, letting Florence dominate and choke in its own juices far, far below.

But ever since the days of the *Decameron*, whose storytellers retreated to its garden villas to escape the plague, Fiesole has played the role of Florence's aristo-cratic suburb; its cool breezes, beautiful landscapes and belvedere views make it the perfect refuge from the torrid Florentine summers. There's no escaping the tourists, however; we foreigners have been tramping up and down Fiesole's hill since the days of Shelley. A day trip has become an obligatory part of a stay in Florence, and although Fiesole has proudly retained its status as an independent *comune*, you can make the 20-minute trip up on Florence city bus 7 from the station or Piazza San Marco. If you have the time, walk up (or perhaps better, down) the old lanes bordered with villas and gardens to absorb some of the world's most civilized scenery.

Around Piazza Mino

The long sloping stage of Piazza Mino is Fiesole's centre, with the bus stop, the local tourist office, the cafés, and the **Palazzo Pretorio**, its loggia and façade emblazoned with coats-of-arms. The square is named after a favourite son, the quattrocento sculptor Mino da Fiesole, whom Ruskin preferred to all others. An example of his work may be seen in the **Duomo**, whose plain façade dominates the north side of the piazza. Built in 1028, it was the only building spared by the vindictive Florentines in 1125. It was subsequently enlarged and given a scouring 19th-century restoration, leaving the tall, crenellated campanile as its sole distinguishing feature. Still, the interior has an austere charm, with a raised choir over the crypt similar to San Miniato. Up the steps to the right are two beautiful works by Mino da Fiesole: the *Tomb of Bishop Leonardo Salutati* and an altar front. The main altarpiece in the choir, of the Madonna and saints, is by Lorenzo di Bicci, from 1440. Note the two saints frescoed on the columns; it was a north Italian custom to paint holy people as if they were members of the congregation. The crypt, holding the remains of Fiesole's patron, St Romulus, is supported by ancient columns bearing doves, spirals and other early Christian symbols.

Behind the Cathedral, on Via Dupré, the **Bandini Museum** contains more sacred works, including numerous della Robbia terracottas, some good trecento paintings by Lorenzo Monaco, Neri di Bicci and Taddeo Gaddi (*open 9.30–1 and 3–7 daily, exc Tues; in winter 10–1 and 3–6; adm*).

Archaeological Zone

Behind the cathedral and museum is the entrance to what remains of *Faesulae*. Because Fiesole avoided trouble in the Dark Ages, its Roman monuments have survived in much better shape than those of Florence; although hardly spectacular the ruins are charmingly set amid olive groves and cypresses. The small **Roman Theatre** has survived well enough to host plays and concerts in the summer; Fiesole would like to remind you that in the ancient times it had the theatre and plays while Florence had the amphitheatre and wild beast shows. Close by are the rather confusing remains of two superimposed temples, the baths, and an impressive stretch of Etruscan walls (best seen from Via delle Mure Etrusche, below) that proved their worth against Hannibal's siege. The **Archaeology Museum** is housed in a small 20th-century Ionic temple, displaying some very early small bronze figurines with flapper wing arms, Etruscan funerary urns and stelae, including the interesting 'stele Fiesolana' with a banquet scene (*open 9–7 summer; 10–4 winter, closed Tues; adm*).

Walking Around Fiesole

From Piazza Mino, Via S. Francesco ascends steeply (at first) to the hill that served as the Etruscan and Roman acropolis. Halfway up is a terrace with extraordinary views of Florence and the Arno sprawl, with a monument to the three *carabinieri* who gave themselves up to be shot by the Nazis in 1944 to prevent them from taking civilian reprisals. The church nearby, the **Basilica di Sant'Alessandro**, was constructed over an Etruscan/Roman temple in the 6th century, re-using its lovely *cipollino* (onion marble) columns and Ionic capitals, one still inscribed with an invocation to Venus. At the top of the hill, square on the ancient acropolis, stands the monastery of **San Francesco**, its church containing a famous early cinquecento *Annunciation* by Raffaellino del Garbo and an *Immaculate Conception* by Piero di Cosimo. A grab-bag of odds and ends collected from the four corners of the world, especially from Egypt and China, is displayed in the quaint **Franciscan Missionary Museum** in the cloister; it also has an Etruscan collection (*open 9–12 and 3–6 summer; 10–12 and 3–5 winter*).

There are much longer walks along the hill behind the Palazzo Pretorio. The panoramic Via Belvedere leads back to Via Adriano Mari, and in a couple of kilometres to the bucolic **Montecéceri**, a wooded park where Leonardo da Vinci performed his flight experiments, and where the Florentine architects once quarried their dark *pietra serena* from quarries which are now abandoned but open for exploration. In Borgunto, as this part of Fiesole is called, there are two 3rd-century BC **Etruscan tombs** on Via Bargellino; east of Borgunto scenic Via Francesco Ferrucci and Via di Vincigliata pass by Fiesole's castles, the **Castel di Poggio**, site of summer concerts, and the **Castel di Vincigliata**, dating back to 1031, while further down is American critic Bernard Berenson's famous **Villa I Tatti**, which he left, along with a distinguished collection of Florentine art, to Harvard University as the Centre of Italian Renaissance Studies. The road continues down towards Ponte a Mensola (6km from Fiesole; *see* p.209) and Settignano, with buses back to Florence.

San Domenico di Fiesole

Located between Fiesole and Florence, San Domenico is a pleasant walk down from Fiesole by way of Via Vecchia Fiesolana, the steep and narrow old road that passes, on the left, the **Villa Medici**, built by Michelozzo for Cosimo il Vecchio; in its lovely garden on the hillside, Lorenzo and his friends of the Platonic Academy would come to get away from the world; it was also the lucky Iris Origo's childhood home (*no adm*). San Domenico, at the bottom of the lane, is the church and convent where Fra Angelico first entered his monkish world. The 15th-century church of **San Domenico** contains his lovely *Madonna with Angels and Saints*, in the first chapel on the left, as well as a photograph of his *Coronation of the Virgin*, which the French snapped up in 1809 and sent to the Louvre. Across the nave there's a *Crucifixion* by the school of Botticelli, an unusual composition of verticals highlighted by the cypresses in the background. In the chapterhouse of the monastery (*ring the bell at no. 4*) Fra Angelico left a fine fresco of the *Crucifixion* before moving down to Florence and San Marco.

Badia Fiesolana

The lane in front of San Domenico leads down in five minutes to the Badia Fiesolana, the ancient cathedral of Fiesole, built in the 9th century by Fiesole's bishop, an Irishman named Donatus, with a fine view over the rolling countryside and Florence in the background. Though later enlarged, perhaps by Brunelleschi, it has preserved the elegant façade of the older church, a charming example of the geometric black and white marble inlay decoration that characterizes Tuscan Romanesque churches. The interior (*open only on Sunday mornings*) is adorned with *pietra serena* very much in the style of Brunelleschi. The convent buildings next door are now the home of the European University Institute.

Settignano

The least touristic hill above Florence sits under the village of Settignano (bus 10 from the station or from Piazza San Marco). The road passes by way of **Ponte a Mensola**, where Boccaccio spent his childhood, and where it is believed he set the first scenes of the *Decameron*, at the Villa Poggio Gherardo. A Scottish Benedictine named Andrew founded its church of **San Martino a Mensola** in the 9th century and was later canonized. Rebuilt in the 1400s, it has three good trecento works: Taddeo Gaddi's *Triptych*, his son Agnolo's panel paintings on St Andrew's casket, and on the high altar another triptych by the school of Orcagna. From the quattrocento there's a *Madonna and Saints* by Neri di Bicci and an *Annunciation* by a follower of Fra Angelico.

Settignano is one of Tuscany's great cradles of sculptors, producing Desiderio da Settignano and the brothers Antonio and Bernardo Rossellino; Michelangelo spent his childhood here as well, in the Villa Buonarroti. Strangely enough, not one of them left any work here as a reminder; the good art which is in the central church of **Santa Maria** is by Andrea della Robbia (an enamelled terracotta of the Madonna and Child) and Buontalenti (the pulpit). There are, however, more splendid views of Florence from Piazza Desiderio, and a couple of places to quaff a leisurely glass of Chianti.

Medici Villas

Like their Bourbon cousins in France, the Medici dukes liked to pass the time acquiring new palaces for themselves. In their case, however, the reason was less self-exaltation than simple property speculation; the Medici always thought several generations ahead. As a result the countryside is littered with Medici villas, most of them now privately owned, though some are partly open to the public.

Villa Careggi

Perhaps the best-known of all is Careggi (Viale Pieraccini 17, bus 14C from the station), a villa that began as a fortified farmhouse and was enlarged for Cosimo il Vecchio by Michelozzo in 1434. In the 1460s the villa at Careggi became synonymous with the birth of humanism. The greatest Latin and Greek scholars of the day, Ficino, Poliziano, Pico della Mirandola and Argyropoulos, would meet here with Lorenzo il Magnifico and hold philosophical discussions in imitation of a Platonic symposium, calling their informal society the Platonic Academy. It fizzled out when Lorenzo died. Cosimo il Vecchio and Piero had both died at Careggi, and when he felt the end was near, Lorenzo had himself carried out to the villa, with Poliziano and Pico della Mirandola to bear him company. After Lorenzo died, the villa was burned by Florentine republicans, though Cosimo I later had it rebuilt, and Francis Sloane had it restored. It is now used as a nursing home, and can only be visited by request, © 277 4329 (*ask inside at the office of the Unità Operativa Affari Generali of USL*), but you can stroll through its gardens and woods for nothing.

Villa la Petraia

Further east, amid the almost continuous conurbation of power lines and industrial landscapes that blight the Prato road, the Villa la Petraia manages to remain Arcadian on its steeply sloping hill (*very hard to reach if you're on your own; take a taxi or, if you are adventurous, bus 28 from the station, and get off after the wastelands, by Via Reginaldo Giuliano*). La Petraia was purchased by Grand Duke Ferdinando I in 1557 and rebuilt by Buontalenti, keeping the tower of the original country castle intact. Unfortunately Vittorio Emanuele II liked it as much as the Medici, and redesigned it to suit his relentlessly bad taste. Still, a tour of the villa's interior (*open 9–7; 9–4 winter, closed Mon; adm*) is worthwhile for the ornate Baroque court, frescoed with a pastel history of the Medici by 17th-century masters Volterrano and Giovanni di San Giovanni; Vittorio Emanuele II added the glass roof so that he could use the space as a ballroom. Of the remainder of the palace, you're likely to remember best the Chinese painting of Canton and the games room, with billiard tables as large as football fields and perhaps the world's first pinball machine, made of wood. A small room contains one of Giambologna's most endearing statues, *Venus Wringing Water from Her Hair*. La Petraia's beautiful garden and park which is shaded by ancient cypresses, is open throughout the afternoon.

Villa di Castello

One of Tuscany's most famous gardens is just down the hill from La Petraia, at Villa di Castello (turn right at Via di Castello and walk 450 metres). The villa was

bought
in 1477 by Lorenzo
di Pierfrancesco and Gio-
vanni de' Medici, cousins of
Lorenzo il Magnifico who were
Botticelli's best patrons, and they
hung the walls of this villa with his great mythological paintings, now in the
Uffizi. The villa was sacked in the 1530 siege, restored by Cosimo I, and today is
the headquarters of the Accademia della Crusca, founded in 1582 and dedicated
to the study of the Italian language (*no adm*). The **Garden** (*open 9–6.30 in the
summer, until 4.30 in winter, closed Mon*) was laid out for Cosimo I by Tribolo,
who also designed the fountain in the centre, with a statue of *Hercules and Ante-
naeus* by Ammannati. Directly behind the fountain is the garden's main
attraction, a fascinating example of the Medici penchant for the offbeat and excessive, an artificial cavern known as the **Grotto degli Animali**, filled by
Ammannati and Giambologna with marvellous, true-to-life statues of every
animal, fish and bird known to man (some of them are copies of Giambologna's
originals in the Bargello), and lined with mosaics of pebbles and seashells. The
shady terrace above offers the best view over the geometric patterns of the garden
below; a large statue by Ammannati of January, or *Gennaio*, emerges shivering
from a pool of water among the trees.

A 20-minute walk north from Villa di Castello to Quinto takes you to two unusual
7th-century BC Etruscan tombs. Neither has any art, but the chambers under their
8-metre artificial hills bear an odd relationship to ancient cultures elsewhere in
the Mediterranean—domed tholos tombs as in Mycenaean Greece, corbelled pas-
sages like the navetas of Majorca, and entrances that look like the sacred wells of
Sardinia. La Montagnola, Via Filli Rosselli 95 (*open 10–1 Sat and Sun, also in*

summer 10–1 Tues and Thurs and 5–7 Sat and Sun afternoons); La Mula, Via della Mula 2 *(open 10–12 Sat, also in summer 10–12 Tues and 3–6.30 Sat)*.

Sesto Fiorentino

You can change gears again by heading out a little further in the sprawl to Sesto Fiorentino, a suburb that since 1954 has been home to the famous Richard-Ginori china and porcelain firm. Founded in Doccia in 1735, the firm has opened the **Doccia Museum** on Via Pratese 31 *(signposted)* to display a neat chronology of its production of Doccia ware, including many Medici commissions (a ceramic Venus de' Medici), fine painted porcelain, and some pretty Art Nouveau works *(open 9.30–1 and 3.30–6.30 Tues, Thurs and Sat; adm)*.

Villa Demidoff at Pratolino

The village of Pratolino lies 12km north of Florence along Via Bolognese and was the site of Duke Francesco I's favourite villa in the 1570s, later demolished. Its enormous park, however, has survived and has recently been opened to the public. For its design, Francesco commissioned Buontalenti—artist, architect, and hydraulics engineer, nicknamed 'delle Girandole' for the wind-up toys he made—and he made Pratolino the marvel of its day, full of water tricks, ingenious automata and a famous menagerie. Sadly, none of Buontalenti's tricks has survived, but the largest ever example of this play between art and environment has (perhaps because it is impossible to move)—Giambologna's massive *Appennino*, a giant rising from stone, part stalactite, part fountain himself. The rest of the park is an invitingly cool refuge from a Florentine summer afternoon *(open May–Sept, 10–8 Fri, Sat and Sun; adm)*.

Poggio a Caiano

Of all the Medici villas, Poggio a Caiano, is the most evocative of the country idylls so delightfully described in the verses of Lorenzo il Magnifico; this was his favourite retreat. (*© 877 012 COPIT buses go past every half-hour, departing from the loggia in Piazza Santa Maria Novella*).

It was originally a farmhouse, purchased by Lorenzo in 1480, and he had it rebuilt by Giuliano da Sangallo in a classical style that presages Palladio. It was Lorenzo's sole architectural commission, and its classicism matched the mythological nature poems he composed here, most famously *L'Ambra*, inspired by the stream Ombrone that flows nearby.

Sangallo designed the villa according to Alberti's description of the perfect country house, and added a classical frieze on the façade, sculpted with the assistance of Andrea Sansovino (now replaced with a copy). Some of the other features—the clock, the curved stair and central loggia—were later additions. In the **interior** (*open 9–1.30, Sun 9–12.30, closed Mon; adm*) Sangallo designed an airy, two-storey **Salone**, which the two Medici popes had frescoed by 16th-century masters Pontormo, Andrea del Sarto, Franciabigio and Allori. The subject, as usual, is Medici self-glorification, and depicts family members dressed as Romans in historical scenes that parallel events in their lives. In the right lunette, around a large circular window, Pontormo painted the lovely *Vertumnus and Pomona* (1521), a languid summer scene under a willow tree, beautifully coloured. The pleasant **grounds** (*open 9–6.30, till 4.30 in winter; 9–12.30 Sun*) contain fine old trees and a 19th-century statue celebrating Lorenzo's *L'Ambra*.

Carmignano and Villa Artimino

A local bus continues 5km southwest of Poggia a Caiano to the village of **Carmignano**, which possesses, in its church of San Michele, Pontormo's uncanny painting of *The Visitation* (1530s), one of the masterpieces of Florentine Mannerism. There are no concessions to naturalism here—the four soulful, ethereal women, draped in Pontormo's accustomed startling colours, barely touch the ground, standing before a scene as substantial as a stage backdrop. The result is one of the most unforgettable images produced in the 16th century.

Also south of Poggio a Caiano, at **Comeana** (*3km, signposted*) is the well-preserved Etruscan **Tomba di Montefortini**, a 7th-century BC burial mound, 11m high and 80m in diameter, covering two burial chambers. A long hall leads down to the vestibule and rectangular tomb chamber, both carefully covered with false vaulting, the latter preserving a wide shelf, believed to have been used for gifts for the afterlife. An equally impressive tomb nearby, the **Tomba dei Boschetti**, was seriously damaged over the centuries by local farmers (*Montefortini open 9–1, closed Mon, Boschetti always open*).

The Etruscan city of Artimino, 4km west, was destroyed by the Romans and is now occupied by a small town and another Medici property, the **Villa Artimino** ('La Ferdinanda'), built as hunting lodge for Ferdinando I by Buontalenti. Buontalenti gave it a semi-fortified air with buttresses to fit its sporting purpose, but the total effect is simple and charming, the long roofline punctuated by innumerable chimneys; the graceful stair was added in the last century from a drawing by the architect in the Uffizi. An **Etruscan Archaeological Museum** has been installed in the basement, containing items found in the tombs; among them a unique censer with two basins and a boat, bronze vases, and a red figured krater painted with initiation scenes, found in a 3rd-century tomb (*villa open 9–12.30 and 3–6 Tues, winter 8.30–12 and 2–4, guided tours only by appointment, © 871 8072; museum open 9–12 Mon-Sat and 3.30–6.00 Sat, 9–12.30 Sun,* *closed Wed; adm*). There's a convenient place for lunch in the grounds. Also in Artimino is an attractive Romanesque church, **San Leonardo**, built of stones salvaged from earlier buildings.

Poggio Imperiale and the Certosa del Galluzzo

One last villa that is open for visits, the **Villa di Poggio Imperiale**, lies south of Florence, at the summit of Viale del Poggio Imperiale, which leaves Porta Romana with a stately escort of cypress sentinels. Cosimo I grabbed this huge villa from the Salviati family in 1565, and it remained a ducal property until there were no longer any dukes to duke. Its neoclassical façade was added in 1808, and the audience chamber was decorated in the 17th century by Rutilio Manetti and others. Much of the villa is now used as a girls' school (*open Wed, 10–12 by request, © 220 151*).

The **Certosa del Galluzzo** (also known as the Certosa di Firenze) lies further south, scenically located on a hill off the Siena road (*take bus 36 or 37 from the station*). Founded as a Carthusian monastery by 14th-century tycoon Niccolò Acciaiuoli, the monastery has been inhabited since 1958 by Cistercians, one of whom takes visitors around (*open 9–12 and 3–6, closed Mon*). The Certosa has a fine 16th-century courtyard and an uninteresting church, though the crypt-chapel of the lay choir contains some impressive tombs. The **Chiostro Grande**, surrounded by the monks' cells, is decorated with 66 majolica tondi of prophets and saints by Giovanni della Robbia and assistants; one cell is opened for visits, and it seems almost cosy. The Gothic **Palazzo degli Studi**, intended by the founder as a school, contains five lunettes by Pontormo, painted while he and his pupil Bronzino hid out here from the plague in 1522.

Excursions from Florence

Lovely Chianti with its wine towns and villas begins a mere 10km south of Florence; SITA buses from the station will take you to a wide selection of villages: Castellina is one of the prettiest to aim for. There are frequent trains for Prato and Pistoia, both fine art cities; Leonardo's home town of Vinci (COPIT buses from Piazza Santa Maria Novella) is a charmer set in lovely countryside and there's a museum of his inventions.

Siena

Draped on its three hills, Siena (pop. 61,400) is the most beautiful city in Tuscany, a flamboyant medieval ensemble of palaces and towers cast in warm, brown, *Siena*-coloured brick. Its soaring skyline is its pride, dominated by the blazing black and white banner of the cathedral and the taut needle of the Torre di Mangia; and yet the Campo, the very centre of Siena, is only four streets away from olive groves and orchards. The contrast is part of the city's charm; densely built-up brick urbanity, and round the corner a fine stretch of long Tuscan farmland that fills the valleys within the city's walls.

Here art went hand in hand with a fierce civic pride to make Siena a world of its own, and historians go so far as to speak of 'Sienese civilization' in summing up the achievements of this unique little city.

Ancient Rivals

Few rivalries have been more enduring than that between Florence and Siena; to understand Tuscany, take a moment to compare the two. Long ago, while Florence was off at university, busily studying her optics and geometry, Lady Siena spent her time dancing and dropping her scarf for knights at the tournament. Florence thought she had the last laugh in 1555, when Duke Cosimo and his black-hearted Spanish pals wiped out the Sienese Republic and put this proud maiden in chains. It's frustrating enough today, though, when Florence looks up in the hills and sees Siena, an unfaded beauty with a faraway smile, sitting in her tower like the Lady of Shalott.

For two towns built by bankers and wool tycoons, they could not have less in common. Siena may not possess an Uffizi or a David, but neither does it have to bear the marble antimacassars and general stuffiness of its sister on the Arno, nor her smog, traffic, tourist hordes and suburban squalor. Florence never goes over the top. Siena loves to, especially in the week around the race of the Palio, the wildest party in Tuscany, a worthy successor to the fabulous masques and carnivals, the bullfights and bloody free-for-alls of the Sienese Middle Ages. In fact, Florence has been clicking its tongue at Siena since the time of Dante, who inserted in his *Inferno* a sarcastic reference to a famous club called the *Brigata*—twelve noble Sienese youths who put up 250,000 florins for a year of nightly feasting; every night they had three sumptuously laid tables, one for eating, one for drinking, and the third to throw out the window. 'A people even more vain than the French,' sneered Dante. Another story goes that a Florentine prince was approached by the Sienese, who asked him to build a madhouse in their city. The prince replied that it was easy: all the Sienese had to do was close all their gates and they'd have the biggest madhouse of all.

But there's more to Siena than that. This is a city with its own artistic tradition; in the 1300s, Sienese painters were giving lessons to the Florentines. Always more decorative, less intellectual than Florence, Siena fell behind in the quattrocento. By then, fortunately, the greatest achievement of Sienese art was already nearing completion—Siena itself

History

Everywhere in Siena you'll see the familiar Roman symbol of the she-wolf suckling the twins. This is Siena's symbol as well; according to legend, the city was founded by the sons of Remus, Senius and Ascius. One rode a black horse, the other a white, and the simple comunal shield of black and white halves (the *balzana*) has been the other most enduring symbol of Siena over the centuries. It is most likely that somebody was living on these three hills long before this mythological pair. Excavations have found traces of Etruscan and even Celtic habitation. The almost impregnable site, dominating most of southern Tuscany, would always have been of great interest. Roman-era *Sena Julia* which was refounded by Augustus as a colony for his veterans, never achieved much importance, and we know little about the place until the early 12th century, when the emerging *comune* began keeping written records. In 1125, an increasingly independent Siena elected its first consuls. By 1169, the *comune* wrested political control away from the bishop, and some ten years later Siena developed its own written constitution.

The political development is complex, and with good reason. Twelfth-century Siena was a booming new city; control over its rich countryside, supplying some of the best wool in Italy, helped start an important cloth industry, and a small silver mine, acquired from Volterra in the 1160s, provided seed capital for what was to become one of the leading banking towns of Europe. Like so many other Italian cities, Siena was able early on to force its troublesome rural nobles to live within its walls, where they built scores of tall defence towers, fought pitched battles in the streets and usually kept the city divided into armed camps; in the narrowest part of the city, the *comune* once had to lay out new streets parallel to Via Camollia because of one particularly boisterous nobleman whose palace most Sienese were afraid to pass. Yet Siena was never completely able to bring its titled hoodlums under control. The businessmen made the money, and gradually formed their city into a sophisticated self-governing republic, but the nobles held on to many of their privileges for centuries, giving an anachronistically feudal tinge to Siena's life and art.

Like its brawling neighbours, medieval Siena enjoyed looking for trouble; in the endless wars of the 13th century they never had to look very far. Originally a Guelph town, Siena changed sides early to avoid being in the same camp with arch-rival Florence. Along with Pisa, Siena carried the Ghibelline banner through the Tuscan wars with varying fortunes. Its finest hour came in 1260, when a Florentine herald arrived with the arrogant demand that Siena demolish its walls and deliver up its large population of Ghibelline exiles from Florence. If not, the armies of Florence and the entire Guelph League—some 40,000 men—were waiting outside to raze the city to the ground. Despite the overwhelming odds, the Sienese determined to resist. They threw the keys of the city on the altar of the yet unfinished cathedral, dedicating Siena to the Virgin Mary (a custom repeated ever since when the city is endangered, most recently just before the battle for liberation in 1944). In the morning, they marched out to the **Battle of Monteaperti** and beat the Florentines so badly that they captured their *Carroccio*.

After the battle Siena had Florence entirely at her mercy and naturally was anxious to level the city and sow the ground with salt. One of the famous episodes in the *Inferno* relates how the Florentine exiles, who made up a substantial part of the Sienese forces, refused to allow it. Unfortunately for Siena, within a few years Florence and the Tuscan Guelphs had the situation back under control and Siena was never again to come so close to dominating Tuscan affairs. Nevertheless the city would be a constant headache to Florence for the next three centuries. When things were quiet at the front, the Sienese had to settle for bashing each other. The constant stream of anti-Siena propaganda in Dante isn't just Florentine bile; medieval Siena had a thoroughly earned reputation for violence and contentiousness. The impressive forms and rituals of the Sienese Republic were merely a façade concealing endless, pointless struggles between the various factions of the élite. Early on, Siena's merchants and nobles divided themselves into five *monti*, syndicates of self-interest that worked like political parties only without any pretence of principle. At one point, this Tuscan banana republic had 10 constitutions in 27 years, and more often than not its political affairs were settled in the streets. Before the Palio was invented, Siena's favourite civic sport was the *Gioco del Pugno*, a general fist-fight in the Campo with 300 on a side. Sometimes tempers flared, and the boys would bring out the axes and crossbows.

Siena's Golden Age

The historical record leaves us with a glaring paradox. For all its troubles and bad intentions, Siena often managed to run city business with disinterest and intelligence. An intangible factor of civic pride always made the Sienese do the right thing when something important was at hand, like battling with the Florentines or selecting a new artist to work on the cathedral. The Battle of Monteaperti may have proved a disappointment in terms of territorial ambitions, but it inaugurated the most brilliant period of Sienese culture, and saw the transformation of the hilltop fortress town into the beautiful city we see today. In 1287, under pressure from the Guelphs and their Angevin protectors, Siena actually allied itself with Florence and instituted a new form of government: the **'Council of the Nine'**. Excluding nobles from office, as Florence would do six years later, the rule of the Nine was to last until 1355, and it gave Siena a more stable regime than it knew at any other period.

Business was better than ever. The city's bankers came to rival Florence's, with offices in all the trading centres and capitals of Europe. A sustained peace, and increasing cultural contacts with France and Naples, brought new ideas and influences into Siena's art and architecture, just in time to embellish massive new building programmes like the **Cathedral** (begun 1186, but not substantially completed until the 1380s) and the **Palazzo Pubblico** (1295–1310). Beginning with

Duccio di Buoninsegna (1260–1319) Sienese artists took the lead in exploring new concepts in painting and sculpture and throughout the 1300s they contributed as much as or more than the Florentines in laying the foundations for the Renaissance. Contemporary records betray an obsessive concern on the part of bankers and merchants for decorating Siena and impressing outsiders. At the height of its fortunes, in the early 14th century, Siena ruled most of southern Tuscany. Its bankers were known in London, in the Baltic and in Constantinople, and its reputation for beauty and culture was matched by few cities in Europe.

The very pinnacle of civic pride and ambition came in 1339, with the fantastical plan to expand the as yet unfinished cathedral into the largest in all Christendom. The walls of that great effort, a nave that would have been longer than St Peter's in Rome, stand today as a monument to the dramatic event that snapped off Siena's career in full bloom. The **Black Death** of 1348 carried off one-third of the population—a mortality not greater than some other Italian cities, perhaps, but the plague hit Siena at a moment when its economy was particularly vulnerable, and started a slow but irreversible decline that was to continue for centuries. Economic troubles led to political instability, and in 1355 a revolt of the nobles, egged on by Emperor Charles IV, who was then in Tuscany, overthrew the Council of the Nine. Then in 1371, seven years before the Ciompi revolt in Florence, the wool-workers staged a genuine revolution. Organized in a sort of trade union, the **Compagnìa del Bruco**, they seized the Palazzo Pubblico and instituted a new government with greater popular representation.

The decades that followed saw Siena devote more and more of its diminishing resources to buying off the marauding mercenary companies that infested much of Italy at this time. By 1399 the city was in such straits that it surrendered its independence to **Giangaleazzo Visconti**, the tyrant of Milan, who was then attempting to surround and conquer Florence. After his death Siena reclaimed its freedom. Political confusion continued throughout the century, with only two periods of relative stability. One came with the pontificate (1458–63) of Pius II, the great Sienese scholar **Aeneas Silvius Piccolomini**, who exerted a dominating influence over his native city while he ruled at Rome. In 1487, a nobleman named **Pandolfo Petrucci** took over the government; as an honest broker, regulating the often murderous ambitions of the *monti*, he and his sons kept control of the republic until 1524.

The Fall of the Republic

Florence was always waiting in the wings to swallow up Siena, and finally had its chance in the 1500s. The real villain of the piece, however, was not Florence but that most imperious Emperor, **Charles V**. After the fall of the Petrucci, the factional struggles resumed immediately, with frequent assassinations and riots, and constitutions changing with the spring fashions. Charles, who had bigger prey in his sights, cared little for the fate of the perverse little republic; he feared, though, that its disorders, religious toleration, and wretched financial condition were a disease that might spread beyond its borders. In 1530, he took advantage of riots in the city to install an imperial garrison. Yet even the emperor's representatives, usually Spaniards, could not keep Siena from sliding further into anarchy and bankruptcy on several occasions, largely thanks to Charles's war taxes. Cultural life was stifled as the Spaniards introduced the Inquisition and the Index. Scholars and artists fled, while poverty and political disruptions made Siena's once proud university cease to function.

In 1550, Charles announced that he was going to build a fortress within the city's walls, and that the Sienese were going to pay for it. Realizing that even the trifling liberty still left to them would soon be extinguished, the Sienese ruling class began intrigues with Charles' great enemy, France. A French army which was led by a Piccolomini, arrived in July 1552. Inside the walls the people revolted and locked the Spanish garrison up in its own new fortress. The empire was slow to react, but inevitably, in late 1554, a huge force of imperial troops, along with those of Florence, entered Sienese territory. The siege was prosecuted with remarkable brutality by Charles's commander, the **Marquis of Marignano**, who laid waste much of the Sienese countryside (which did not entirely recover until this century), tortured prisoners and even hired agents to start fires inside the walls. After a brave resistance, led by a republican Florentine exile named **Piero Strozzi** and assisted by France, Siena was starved into surrendering in April 1555. Two years later, Charles's son Philip II sold Siena to Duke Cosimo of Florence, and the ancient republic disappeared into the new Grand Duchy of Tuscany.

If nothing else, Siena went out with a flourish. After the capture of the city, some 2000 republican bitter-enders escaped to make a last stand at Montalcino. Declaring 'Where the *Comune* is, there is the City', they established what must be the world's first republican government-in-exile. With control over much of the old Sienese territory, the **'Republic of Siena at Montalcino'** held out against the Medici for another four years.

With its independence lost and its economy irrevocably ruined, Siena withdrew into itself. For centuries there was to be no recovery, little art or scholarship, and no movements towards reform. The Sienese aristocracy, already decayed into a parasitic *rentier* class, made its peace with the Medici dukes early on; in return for their support, the Medici allowed them to keep much of their power and privileges. The once great capital of trade and finance shrank rapidly into an overbuilt farmers' market, its population dropping from a 14th-century high of 60–80,000 to around a mere 15,000 by the year 1700. This does much to explain why medieval and Renaissance Siena is so well preserved today—for better or worse, nothing at all has happened to change it.

By the 'Age of Enlightenment', with its disparaging of everything medieval, the Sienese seem to have quite forgotten their own history and art, and it is no surprise that the rest of Europe forgot them too. During the first years of the Grand Tour, no self-respecting northern European would think of visiting Siena. Few had probably ever heard of it, and the ones who stopped overnight on the way to Rome were usually dismayed at the 'inelegance' of its medieval buildings and art. It was not until the 1830s that Siena was rediscovered, with the help of literati like the Brownings, who spent several summers here, and that truly Gothic American, Henry James. The Sienese were not far behind in rediscovering it themselves. The old civic pride that had lain dormant for centuries yawned and stretched like Sleeping Beauty and went diligently back to work. Before the century was out, everything that could still be salvaged of the city's ancient glory was refurbished and restored. More than ever fascinated by its own image and eccentricities, and more than ever without any kind of an economic base, Siena was ready for its present career as a cultural attraction, a tourist town.

Highlights of Siena

The **Campo** with the Palazzo Pubblico and Fonte Gaia, the **Cathedral** complex and the **Pinacoteca** offer the culmination of Sienese civilization and art and should not be missed. But in Siena the cream is spread evenly on the top of its three hills, if not in famous monuments, in the beauty of the streets and squares, the little *contrade* fountains and private houses—even a place that sounds as dry and dusty as the state archives (in the **Palazzo Piccolomini**) is well worth a visit. Every church has at least one fine work of art; among the best are **Santa Maria dei Servi**, **Sant'Agostino**, and the **Oratorio di San Bernardino**, while the **Enoteca Nazionale** in the Fortezza Medicea contains Italy's finest works of art from the vine. If it's open, don't miss the unique frescoes in the **Ospedale Santa Maria della Scala**.

Getting Around

by car

The fastest route from Florence to Siena (68km) is the unnumbered toll-free Superstrada del Palio (1hr); the most scenic are the Chiantigiana S222 through the heart of Chianti and the Via Cassia

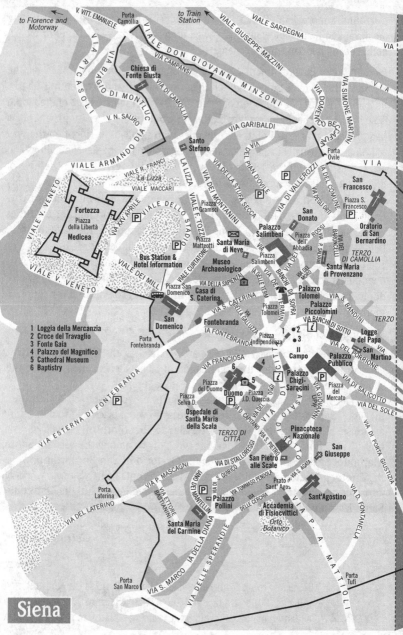

Siena

1 Loggia della Mercanzia
2 Croce del Travaglio
3 Fonte Gaia
4 Palazzo del Magnifico
5 Cathedral Museum
6 Baptistry

possible approaches from the A1: S326 by way of Sinalunga (50km) or the more scenic, winding S73 by way of Monte Sansovino (44km). Cars are forbidden to enter the centre, but there are clearly defined parking areas along all entrances to the city, especially around Piazza San Domenico, the Fortezza and along Viale del Stadio. One of the best places to hire a car is Autonoleggio A.C.I., in Via Vittorio Veneto, © 49 001.

by train

Siena's station is located below the city, 1.5km from the centre down Viale G. Mazzini and is linked to the centre by frequent buses. Siena's main line runs from Empoli (on the Florence–Pisa line) to Chiusi (Florence–Rome). There are trains roughly every hour, with frequent connections to Florence from Empoli (97km, 1hr), less frequently to Pisa from Empoli (125km, 2hrs) and to Chiusi towards Umbria and Rome (65km to Chiusi, 1hr). A secondary line runs towards Grosseto (70km, 1hr)—six a day, three continue to Orbetello. To save a trip to the station, all rail information/tickets are available at the SETI travel agency, no. 56 on the Campo.

by bus

Almost every town in southern Tuscany can be reached by bus from **Piazza San Domenico**, the big transport node on the western edge of Siena, with tourist information and hotel information booths. A board lists departure times and the location of stops; the ticket office (with a fancy, computer-operated information dispenser) is in the little building next to San Domenico church. The name of the company serving the whole of Siena province is TRA-IN, © 221 221, causing endless difficulties,

SIMONE MARTINI

DUCCIO DI BONINSEGNA

BALDASSARRE PERUZZI

DI SAN MARTINO

Santo Spirito

DI PANTANETO

V. DELL'OLIVIERA

VIA DEI SASSO

PISPINI

Porta Pispini

to Arezzo and Motorway

VIA S. MARTINO
V. DELL'ORO

VIA ROMA

Palazzo di San Galagno

VIA DEI SERVI

VIA CANTINE

VIA VAL DI MONTONE

VIA GIROLAMO GIGLI

Piazza A. Manzoni

Basilica di Santa Maria dei Servi

Porta Romana

VIA E.S. PICCOLOMINI

according to the local tourist authorities, with English tourists looking for TRA-INs in the train station. Other companies depart for other cities like Florence (SITA, about once every hour, Rome, Perugia, Pisa, etc.), but all leave from San Domenico. Within the walls, there is no public transport, though regular buses to the **train station** and everywhere else in the modern suburbs depart from **Piazza Matteotti** north of the Campo.

Tourist Information

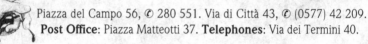

Piazza del Campo 56, © 280 551. Via di Città 43, © (0577) 42 209. **Post Office**: Piazza Matteotti 37. **Telephones**: Via dei Termini 40.

Orientation: Terzi and the Contrade

The centre of Siena and the site of the Palio is the famous piazza called simply **Il Campo**. From here, the city unfolds like a three-petalled flower along three ridges. It has been a natural division since medieval times, with the oldest quarter, the **Terzo di Città**, including the cathedral, to the southwest; the **Terzo di San Martino** to the southeast; and the **Terzo di Camollia** to the north.

Siena is tiny, barely over a square mile. The density, and the hills, make it seem much bigger. There are no short cuts across the valleys between the three *terzi*. Although there are no cars in the centre, taxis and ambulances (medieval Siena is full of medieval hospitals) will occasionally try to run you down.

Contrade

The Sienese have taken the *contrade* for granted so long that their history is almost impossible to trace. Basically, the word denotes the 17 neighbourhoods into which Siena is divided. Like the *rioni* of Rome, they were once the original wards of the ancient city—not merely geographical boundaries, but self-governing entities; the ancients often referred to them as the city's 'tribes'. In Siena, the *contrade* survived and prospered all through classical times and the Middle Ages. More than anything else, they maintained the city's traditions and sense of identity through the dark years after 1552. Incredibly enough, they're still there now, unique in Italy and perhaps all Europe. Once Siena counted over 60 *contrade*. Now there are 17, each with a sort of totem animal for its symbol:

Aquila (eagle), *Onda* (dolphin), *Tartuca* (turtle), *Pantera* (panther), *Selva* (rhinoceros) and *Chiocciola* (snail); all southwest of the Campo in Terzo di Città.

Leocorno (unicorn), *Torre* (elephant), *Nicchio* (mussel shell), *Civetta* (owl) and *Valdimontone* (ram); in Terzo di San Martino southeast of the Campo.

Oca (goose), *Drago* (dragon), *Giraffa* (giraffe), *Lupa* (wolf), *Bruco* (caterpillar) and

Istrice (porcupine); all in the north in the Terzo di Camollia.

Sienese and Italian law recognize each of these as being legally chartered communities; today a *contrada* functions as a combination social and dining club, neighbourhood improvement organization, religious confraternity and mutual assistance fund. Each elects its own officials annually in May. Each has its own chapel, museum and fountain, its own flag and colours, and its own patron saint who pulls all the strings he can in Heaven to help his beloved district win the Palio.

Sociologists, and not only in Italy, are becoming ever more intrigued with this ancient yet very useful system, with its built-in community solidarity and tacit social control. (Siena has almost no crime and no social problems, except of course for a lack of jobs.) The *contrade* probably function much as they did in Roman or medieval times, but it's surprising just what up-to-date, progressive and adaptable institutions they can be. Anyone born in a *contrada* area, for example, is automatically a member; besides their baptism into the Church, they also receive a sort of 'baptism' into the *contrada*. This ritual isn't very old, and it is conducted in the pretty new fountains which the *contrade* have constructed all over Siena in recent years as centrepieces for their neighbourhoods.

To learn more about the *contrade*, the best place to go is one of the 17 little *contrada* museums. The tourist office has a list of addresses. One of the best is that of the Goose in the Terzo di Camollia. Though the caretakers usually live close by, most of them ask visitors to contact them a day or two in advance. The tourist office also has details of the dates of the annual *contrada* festivals, and the other shows and dinners they are wont to put on; visitors are always very welcome.

The Palio

The thousands of tourists who come twice a year to see the Palio, Siena's famous horse race around the Campo, probably think the Sienese are doing it all just for them. Yet like the *contrade* which contest it, the Palio is an essential part of Sienese culture, something that means as much to the city as it did centuries ago. The oldest recorded Palio was run in 1283, though no one can say how far the custom goes back. In the Middle Ages, besides horse races there were violent street battles, bloody games of primeval rugby and even bullfights. At present, the course is three times around the periphery of the Campo, though earlier it was run on various routes through the city's main streets.

The *palio* (Latin *pallium*) is an embroidered banner, the prize offered for winning the race. Two races are held each year, on 2 July and 16 August, and the *palio* of each is decorated with an image of the Virgin Mary; after political violence the city's greatest passion was always Mariolatry. The course has room for only ten horses in each race. Some of the 17 *contrade* are chosen by lot each race to ensure that everyone has a fair chance. The horses are also selected by lot, but the *contrade* are free to select their own jockeys. Although the race itself only lasts a minute and a half, there's a good hour or two of pageantry preceding the event; the famous flag-throwers or *alfieri* of each participating *contrada* put on a dazzling show, while the medieval *carroccio*, drawn by a yoke of white oxen, is pressed into service to circle the Campo, bearing the prized *palio* itself.

The Palio is no joke; baskets of money ride on each race, not to mention the sacred honour of the district. To obtain divine favour, each *contrada* brings its horse into its chapel on race morning for a special blessing (and if a little horse manure drops during the ceremony, it's a sign of good luck). The only rule stipulates that you can't seize the reins of an opponent. There are no rules against bribing opposing jockeys, making alliances with other *contrade*, or ambushing jockeys before the race. The course around the Campo has two right angles. Anything can happen; recent Palii have featured not only jockeys but *horses* flying through the air. The Sienese say no one has ever been killed at a Palio. There's no reason to believe them. They wouldn't believe it themselves; it is an article of faith among the Sienese that fatalities are prevented by special intervention of the Virgin Mary. The post-Palio carousing, while not up to medieval standards, is still impressive; in the winning *contrada* the party might go on for days.

No event in Italy is as infectiously exhilarating as the Palio. There are two ways to see it, either from the centre of the Campo, which is packed tight and always very hot, or from an expensive (L150–300,000) seat in a viewing stand, which you must book well in advance. Several travel agencies offer special Palio tours (*see* p.6); otherwise book by April.

If you keep your eyes open while walking the back streets of Siena you'll see the city's entire history laid out for you in signs, symbols and a hundred other clues. You usually won't have trouble guessing which *contrada* you're in. Little ceramic plaques with the *contrada* symbol appear on many buildings and street corners, not to mention flags in the neighbourhood colours, bumper stickers on the cars and the fountains, each with a modern sculptural work, usually representing the *contrada's* animal.

Look for noblemen's coats-of-arms above the doorways; aristo-cratic, archaic Siena will show you more of these than almost any Italian city. In many cases they are still the homes of the original families, and often the same device is on a dozen houses on one block, a reminder of how medieval Siena was largely divided into separate compounds, each under the protection (or intimidation) of a noble family. One common symbol is formed from the letters IHS in a radiant sun. Siena's famous 15th-century preacher, San Bernardino, was always pestering the nobles to forget their con-tentiousness and enormous vanity; he proposed that they should replace their heraldic symbols with the monogram of Christ. The

Siena Walks

limited success his idealism met with can be read on the buildings of Siena today.

They don't take down old signs in Siena. One, dated 1641, informs prostitutes that the Most Serene Prince Matthias (the Florentine governor) forbids them to live on his street (Via di Salicotto). Another, a huge 19th-century marble plaque on the Banchi di Sotto, reminds us that 'In this house, before modern restorations reclaimed it from squalidness, was born Giovanni Caselli, inventor of the pantograph'. A favourite, on Via del Giglio, announces a stroke of the rope and a 16-lire fine for anyone throwing trash in the street, with proceeds to go to the accuser.

Siena Walk I:
Around the Campo

N

250 metres
250 yards

Porta Pispini

Palazzo di San Galagno

Porta Romana

VIA DEL PISPINI

VIA ROMA

VIA DI PALE DELL'OLIVIERA

VIA DEI SERVI

Piazza A. Manzoni

Basilica di Santa Maria dei Servi

Santo Spirito

VIA DEL PANTANETO

Porta Tufi

TERZO DI SAN MARTINO

VIA S. BANDINI Logge del Papa

San Martino

VIA S. MARTINO

VIA DELL'ORO

VIA DI SALICOTTO

VIA DEL SOLE

Pinacoteca Nazionale

San Giuseppe

Prato di Sant' Agostino

Sant'Agostino

VIA D. FONTANELLA

VIA DEL PORRIONE

FINISH

Palazzo Pubblico

Piazza del Mercato

Palazzo Piccolomini

VIA BANCHI

Campo START

3 2

VIA DI SOTTO

VIA GIOVANNI DUPRE

CASATO DI SOTTO

VIA P. A. MATTIOLI

Accademia di Fisiocrittici

Orto Botanico

Palazzo Chigi-Saracini

VIA DI CITTÀ

POGGIO

Piazza Indipendenza

4

VIA DEL CAPITANO

San Pietro alle Scale

VIA S. PIETRO

VIA DI STALLOREGGI

VIA DEL CORSO

VIA DELLE CERCHIA

VIA MASSIMO DELLE ROCCHE

VIA DELLE SPERANDIE

5

VIA FRANCIOSA

Duomo 6

Piazza del Duomo

Ospedale di Santa Maria della Scala

TERZO DI CITTÀ

Palazzo Pollini

PIANO DEI MANTELLINI

VIA DI S. QUIRICO

Santa Maria del Carmine

Piazza Selva D.

VIA P. MASCAGNI

VIA ETTORE BASTIANINI

VIA DELLA DIANA

VIA S. MARCO

Porta Laterina

Porta San Marco

1 Loggia della Mercanzia
2 Croce del Travaglio
3 Fonte Gaia
4 Palazzo del Magnifico

228

Start: *the Campo*
Finish: *Palazzo Piccolomini*
Walking time: *one day*

I: Around the Campo

Piazza del Campo

This walk through the Campo, Terzo di Città and Terzo Sa Martino takes in the shrines of Sienese civilization: the Palazzo Pubblico, the Cathedral and the masterpieces of Sienese art in the Pinacoteca.

Lunch/Cafés

La Torre, Via Salicotto 7–9, ℂ 28 75 48. Just behind the Campo, this good little trattoria is always jam-packed (closed Thurs, around L30,000).

Mariotti da Mugalone, Via dei Pellegrini 8/12, ℂ 283 235. Typical Sienese trattoria, around 100 (closed Thurs, around L40,000).

Enoteca Le Bollicine, Via G. Dupre 64, ℂ 42 650. Large chalices of the best Tuscan and Italian wine and plates of Italian cheeses and salamis.

Buca di San Pietro, Vicolo di San Pietro 4. Take-away or sit-down pizza and *tavola calda* (closed Wed).

Rosticeria la Mossa, Piazza del Campo 35. If you do not want to walk very far this is a fine basic take-away food place with pizza and hot ready-made dishes. Good value despite its location (closed Tues).

La Costarella, Via dei Pellegrini. Ice cream parlour.

There is no lovelier square in Tuscany than the Campo, and none more beloved by its city. The Forum of ancient *Sena Julia* was on this spot, and in the Middle Ages it evolved into its present fan shape, rather like a scallop shell or a classical theatre. The Campo was paved in brick as early as 1340; the nine sections into which the fan is divided are in honour of the Council of the Nine, rulers of the city at the time. Thousands crowd over the bricks here every year to see the Palio, run on the periphery.

> *For a worthy embellishment to their Campo, the Sienese commissioned for its curved north end the **Fonte Gaia** from Jacopo della Quercia who was their greatest sculptor, though what you see now is an uninspired copy of 1868.*

Della Quercia worked on it from 1408 to 1419, creating the broad rectangle of marble with reliefs of Adam and Eve and allegorical virtues. It was to be the opening salvo of Siena's Renaissance, an answer to the Baptistry doors of Ghiberti in Florence (for which della Quercia himself had been one of the contestants). Perhaps it was a poor choice of stone, but the years have been incredibly unkind to this fountain; the badly eroded remains of the original can be seen up on the loggia of the Palazzo Pubblico.

No one can spend much time in Siena without noticing its fountains. The Republic always made sure each part of the city had access to good water; medieval Siena created the most elaborate engineering works since ancient Rome to bring the water in. Fonte Gaia, and others such as Fontebranda, are fed by underground aqueducts that stretch for miles across the Tuscan countryside. Charles V, when he visited the city, is reported to have said that Siena is 'even more marvellous underground than it is on the surface'. The original Fonte Gaia was completed in the early 1300s; there's a story that soon after, some citizens dug up a beautiful Greek statue of Venus, signed by Praxiteles himself. The delighted Sienese carried it in procession through the city and installed it on top of their new fountain. With the devastation of the Black Death, however, the preachers were quick to blame God's wrath on the indecent pagan on the Fonte Gaia. Throughout history, the Sienese have always been ready to be shocked by their own sins; in this case, with their neighbours dropping like flies around them, they proved only too eager to make poor Venus the scapegoat. They chopped her into little bits, and a party of Sienese disguised as peasants smuggled the pieces over the border and buried them in Florentine territory to pass the bad luck on to their enemies.

*On the southeastern side of the Campo stands the **Palazzo Pubblico**.*

If the Campo is like a Roman theatre, the main attraction on stage since 1310 has been this brick and stone palace, the enduring symbol of the Sienese Republic and still the town hall today. Its façade is the face of Siena's history, with the she-wolf of Senius and Ascanius, Medici balls, the IHS of San Bernardino, and squared Guelph crenellations, all in the shadow of the tremendous **Torre di Mangia**, the graceful, needle-like tower that Henry James called 'Siena's Declaration of Independence'. At 102m, the tower was the second tallest ever raised in medieval Italy (only the campanile in Cremona beats it). At the time, the cathedral tower up on its hill completely dominated Siena's skyline; the Council of the Nine wouldn't accept that the symbol of religious authority or any of the nobility's fortress-skyscrapers should be taller than the symbol of the republic, so its Perugian architects, Muccio and Francesco di Rinaldo, made sure its height would be hard to surpass.

There was a practical side to it, too. At the top hung the *comune*'s great bell, which had to be heard in every corner of the city tolling the hours and announcing the curfew, or calling the citizens to assemble in case of war or emergency. One of the first men to hold the job of bell-ringer gave the tower its name, a fat, sleepy fellow named *Mangiaguadagni* ('eat the profits') or just Mangia for short; there is a statue of him in one of the courtyards.

*Climb the tower's endless staircase for the definitive view of Siena—on the clearest days you will also be able to see about half of the medieval republic's territory, a view that is absolutely, positively worth the slight risk of cardiac arrest (open daily 9–5.30; winter until 2.15pm; adm). At the foot of the tower, the marble **Cappella della Piazza**, with its graceful rounded arches, stands out clearly from the Gothic earnestness of the rest of the building. It was begun in 1352, in thanks for deliverance from the Black Death, but it was not finally completed until the mid-15th century.*

*Most of the Palazzo Pubblico's ground floor is still used for city offices, but the **upper floors** have been made into the **city's museum** (open daily 9.30–1.45, until 7.45 in summer; Sun 9–1; adm exp).*

Here the main attraction is the series of state rooms done in frescoes, a sampling of the best of Sienese art throughout the centuries. The first, the historical frescoes in the **Sala del Risorgimento** were done by an artist named A. G. Cassioli only in 1886: the meeting of Vittorio Emanuele II with Garibaldi, his coronation, portraits and epigrams of past patriots, and an 'allegory of Italian Liberty', all in a colourful and photographically precise style. If anything, it is a tribute to Sienese artistic conservatism; finally liberated after 300 years of Florentine rule, they immediately went back to their good old medieval habits.

Next on the same floor is the **Sala di Badia** with frescoes depicting the story of Alessandro VII and some vigorous battle scenes by the Sienese Spinello Aretino (1300s) and the *Sixteen Virtues* by Martino di Bartolomeo. The adjoining **anticamera del Concistoro** has a lovely *Madonna and Child* by Matteo di Giovanni. In the **Sala del Concistoro** (usually shut), Gobelin tapestries adorn the walls while the great Sienese Mannerist Beccafumi contributed a ceiling of frescoes in the 1530s celebrating the political virtues of antiquity; that theme is continued in the vestibule to the **Chapel**, with portraits of ancient heroes from Cicero to Judas Maccabeus, all by Taddeo di Bartolo. These portrayals, along with more portraits of the classical gods and goddesses and an interesting view of ancient Rome, show clearly just how widespread was the fascination with antiquity even in the 1300s. Intruding among the classical crew, there's also a king-sized St Christopher covering an entire wall. Before setting out on a journey it was good luck to catch a glimpse of this saint, and in Italy and Spain he is often painted extra large so you won't miss him. In a display case in the hall, some of the oldest treasures of the Sienese Republic are kept: the war helmet of the Captain of the People, and a delicate **golden rose**, a gift to the city from the Sienese Pope, Pius II.

The **Chapel** (*Cappella del Consiglio*) is surrounded by a lovely wrought-iron grille designed by Jacopo della Quercia; when it is open you can see more frescoes by Taddeo di Bartolo, an altarpiece by Il Sodoma, and some exceptional carved wood seats, by Domenico di Nicolò (*c.*1415–28). In the adjacent chamber (the **Sala del Mappamondo**), only the outline is left of Lorenzetti's cosmological fresco, a diagram of the universe including all the celestial and angelic spheres, much like the one in the Campo Santo at Pisa. Above it, there is a very famous fresco by Simone Martini (*c.*1330), showing the redoubtable condottiere **Guidoriccio da Fogliano** on his way to attack the castle of Montemassi, during a revolt against Siena. Also by Martini is an enthroned Virgin, or *Maestà*, that is believed to be his earliest work (1315) (*currently being restored*).

The Allegories of Good and Bad Government

When you enter the **Sala dei Nove** (or Sala della Pace), meeting room of the Council of the Nine, you'll understand at a glance why they ruled Siena so well. Whenever one of the councillors had the temptation to skim some cream off the top, or pass a fat contract over to his brother-in-law the paving contractor, or tighten the screws on the poor by raising the salt tax, he had only to look up at Ambrogio Lorenzetti's great frescoes to feel really like a worm. There are two complementary sets, with scenes of Siena under good government and bad, and allegorical councils of virtues or vices for each. Enthroned Justice rules the good Siena, with such counsellors as Peace, Prudence and Magnanimity; bad Siena groans under the thumb of one nasty piece of work, sneering, fanged Tyranny and his cronies: Pride, Vainglory, Avarice and Wrath among others. The good Siena is a happy place, with buildings in good repair, well-dressed folk who are dancing in the streets, and well-stocked shops where the merchants appear to be making a nice profit. Bad Siena is almost a mirror image, only the effects of the Tyrant's rule are plain to see: urban blight, crime in broad daylight, buildings crumbling and abandoned, and business bad for everybody—a landscape which for many of us modern city dwellers will seem all too familiar.

Lorenzetti finished his work around 1338, probably the most ambitious secular painting ever attempted up to that time. The work has been recently cleaned and restored; fittingly, Good Government has survived more or less intact, while Bad Government has not aged so well and many parts have been lost. In the next room is Guido da Siena's large *Madonna and Child* (mid-1200s), the earliest masterpiece of the Sienese school. If you're not up to climbing the tower, at least take the long, unmarked stairway by the Sala del Risorgimento that leads up to the **loggia**, with the second-best view over Siena and the disassembled bits and pieces of della Quercia's reliefs from the Fonte Gaia, not particularly impressive in their worn and damaged state, although *The Expulsion from Paradise* retains something of its power.

*Part of the beauty of the **Campo** lies in the element of surprise; one usually enters from narrow arcades between austere medieval palaces that give no hint of what lies on the other side. Two of Siena's three main streets form a graceful curve around the back of the Campo; where they meet the third, behind the Fonte Gaia, is the corner the Sienese call the **Croce del Travaglio** (a mysterious nickname: the 'cross of affliction').*

Here, under the eternal scaffolding of bureaucratic restoration, sleeps one of Siena's landmarks, the three-arched **Loggia della Mercanzia**, in a sense Siena's Royal Exchange, the place where the Republic's merchants made their deals and settled their differences before the city's famed commercial tribunal. The Loggia marks the transition from Sienese Gothic to the early Renaissance style—begun in 1417, it was probably influenced by Florence's Loggia dei Lanzi. The five statues of saints around the columns are the work of Antonio Federighi and Vecchietta, the leading Sienese sculptor after della Quercia.

*The three streets that meet here lead directly into the **three terzi** of Siena. All three are among the city's most beautiful streets.*

*Southwest from the Croce del Travaglio, Via di Città climbs up to the highest and oldest part of Siena, the natural fortress of the Terzo di Città. On the way it passes the grandiose **Palazzo Chigi-Saracini**.*

This is the grandiose Gothic palace with mullioned windows that follows the curve of the street and has a wretched, barely alive old tree hanging over the courtyard wall. The tower dates from the 13th century; the rest beautifully combines stone and brick, and no one minds if you enter to see the lovely courtyard with its gallery, frescoed vaulting and old well. The palace contains an internationally important music school, the Accademia Musicale Chigiana, and a large collection of instruments (Liszt's piano, Stradivarius violins, etc.) and Sienese and Florentine art, that can be seen, along with its lavish concert chamber, by appointment, ✆ 46 152. Next door is yet another reminder of the Piccolomini, the **Palazzo delle Papesse**. The family, along with the Colonna of Rome and the Correr of Venice, was one of the first really to exploit the fiscal possibilities of the papacy; Aeneas Silvius (Pius II) built this palace, designed by Rossellino, for his sister, Caterina Piccolomini.

*All approaches from Via di Città to Siena's glorious **Cathedral**, spilling over the highest point in the city, are somewhat oblique. Easiest, perhaps, is Via dei Pellegrini, which winds around the back, past the unusual crypt-baptistry tucked underneath (see p.241), up to the steps to the Piazza del Duomo, and through a portal in a huge, free-standing wall of striped marble arches, a memorial to that incredible ill-starred 1339 rebuilding plan confounded by the plague.*

Cattedrale

The cathedral the Sienese had to settle for may not be a transcendent expression of faith, and it may not be an important landmark in architecture, but it is certainly one of the most delightful, decorative ornaments in Christendom.

Begun around 1200, it was one of the first Gothic cathedrals in central Italy. It started in good Gothic tradition as a communal effort and was not really a project of the Church. There doesn't seem to have been very much voluntary labour. Even in the Middle Ages Italians were a little too blasé for that—but every citizen with a cart was expected to bring two loads of marble from the quarries each year, earning him a special indulgence from the bishop. One load must have been white and the other black, for under the influence of Pisa, the Sienese built themselves one thoroughly striped cathedral—stripes darker and bolder than Pisa's or Lucca's. The campanile, with its distinctive fenestration, narrowing in size down six levels, rises over the city like a giant ice-cream parfait. Most of the body of the church was finished by 1270, and 14 years later Giovanni Pisano was called in to create the sculpture for the lavish **façade**, with statues of Biblical prophets and pagan philosophers. The upper half was not begun until the 1390s, and the glittering mosaics in the gables are, like Orvieto's, the work of Venetian artists of the late 19th century.

*The **interior** is a treasure-box (open 7.30–1.30 and 2.30–sunset). Perhaps the cathedral is the only church in Italy that could keep a serious visitor busy for an entire day. Upon entering the main portal, the ferociously striped pilasters and the Gothic vaulting, a blue firmament* *painted with golden stars, inevitably draw the eye upwards. However, the most spectacular feature is at your very feet—the* **marble pavement**, *where the peculiar figure smiling up at you is* Hermes Trismegistus, *the legendary Egyptian father of alchemy (see* **Topics**, *p.53), depicted in elegant sgraffito work of white and coloured marble.*

In fact, the entire floor of the cathedral is covered with almost 12,000 square metres of virtuoso *sgraffito* in 56 scenes which include portraits, mystical allegories and events from the Old Testament. Like the Biccherna covers in the Palazzo Piccolomini, they are a tradition carried on over centuries. Many of Siena's best artists worked on them, beginning in 1369 and continuing into the 1600s; Giorgio Vasari claimed that Duccio di Buoninsegna himself first worked in this medium, though none of the pictures here is his.

Even in a building with so many marvels—the Piccolomini Library, Nicola Pisano's pulpit, Duccio's stained glass, works by Donatello, della Quercia, Pinturicchio, Michelangelo, Bernini and many others—this pavement perhaps takes pride of place. The greatest limitation of Sienese art was always the conservatism of its patrons, accustomed to demanding the same old images in the same old styles. Commissions from the Office of Cathedral Works, controlled by the state, were usually more liberal, allowing the artists to create such unique, and in some cases startling images, one of the greatest achievements of Renaissance Siena.

The *Hermes* on the cathedral pavement, by Giovanni di Stefano, was completed in the 1480s, a decade after Ficino's translation; it shows him together with Moses, holding a book with the inscription 'Take up thy letters and laws, O Egyptians'. On either side, all 10 prophetic *Sibyls* done by various artists at the same time decorate the aisles of the church. Nor are Hermes and the sibyls the only peculiar thing on this floor. Directly behind him begins a series of large scenes, including a *Wheel of Fortune*, with men hanging on to it for dear life, another wheel of uncertain symbolism, and emblems of Siena and other Tuscan and Latin cities. Oddest of all is a work by Pinturicchio, variously titled the *Allegory of Virtue* or the *Allegory of Fortune*; on a rocky island full of serpents, a party of well-dressed people has just disembarked, climbing to the summit where a figure of 'Socrates' accepts a pen from a seated female figure, and another, 'Crates', empties a basket of gold and jewels into the sea. Below, a naked woman with a gonfalon stands with one foot in a boat, and another on land.

Unfortunately, many of the best scenes, under the crossing and transepts, are covered most of the year to save them from wear. You'll need to come between 15 August and 15 September to see the visionary works of Alessandro Franchi— the *Triumph of Elias* and other events in that prophet's life—and Domenico Beccafumi's *Sacrifice of Elias* and the *Execution of the False Prophets of Baal*.

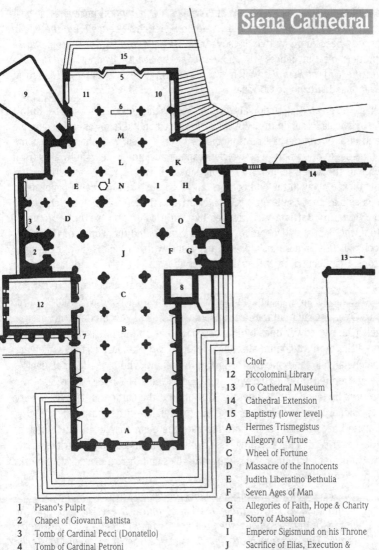

Siena Cathedral

1 Pisano's Pulpit
2 Chapel of Giovanni Battista
3 Tomb of Cardinal Pecci (Donatello)
4 Tomb of Cardinal Petroni
5 Stained Glass of Duccio
6 High Altar
7 Piccolomini Altar (della Quercia, Michelangelo)
8 Campanile
9 Sacristy
10 Cantorie
11 Choir
12 Piccolomini Library
13 To Cathedral Museum
14 Cathedral Extension
15 Baptistry (lower level)
A Hermes Trismegistus
B Allegory of Virtue
C Wheel of Fortune
D Massacre of the Innocents
E Judith Liberatino Bethulia
F Seven Ages of Man
G Allegories of Faith, Hope & Charity
H Story of Absalom
I Emperor Sigismund on his Throne
J Sacrifice of Elias, Execution &
   False Prophets
K Samson & the Philistines
L David the Psalmist
M Sacrifice of Abraham
N Moses receives the Commandments
O Story of Jephta

(Hasn't anyone in Siena ever heard of Plexiglass?) Other works uncovered all year include *The Seven Ages of Man* by Antonio Federighi, *Scenes From the Life of Moses* by Beccafumi, Matteo di Giovanni's *Massacre of the Innocents* (always a favourite subject in Sienese art), and best of all the beautifully drawn *Judith Liberating the City of Bethulia* which was a collaboration of Federighi, Matteo di Giovanni and Urbano da Cortona.

Perhaps the greatest attraction above floor level is the great Carrara marble **pulpit** done by Nicola Pisano in the 1280s. Pisano started on it directly after finishing the one in Pisa; one of the assistants he brought here to help with the work was the young Arnolfo di Cambio. The typical Pisano conception is held up by allegorical figures of the seven liberal arts—more sibyls, prophets, Christian virtues and saints tucked away in the odd corners, and vigorous, crowded relief panels from the Passion as good as the ones in Pisa. Nearby, in the left transept, the **chapel of San Giovanni Battista** has frescoes by Pinturicchio and a bronze statue of St John the Baptist by Donatello, who also contributed the **Tomb of Giovanni Pecci**, a 1400s Sienese bishop. Another tomb worth a look is that of Cardinal Petroni, an influential early Renaissance design from 1310 by Tino di Camaino.

Some of the stained glass in the cathedral is excellent, especially the earliest windows, in the apse, designed by Duccio, and the rose window with its cornucopia. Over the high altar is a bronze baldachin by Vecchietta, with bronze angels (the two lower ones by Francesco di Giorgio Martini,1499) and in the north aisle, the Piccolomini altar includes four early statues of saints which are by Michelangelo, and one by Torrigiani, the fellow who broke Michelangelo's nose and ended up in exile, working in Westminster Abbey. There is also a *Madonna* by Jacopo della Quercia. Throughout the cathedral, as everywhere else in Siena, be sure to keep an eye out for details—little things like the tiny, exquisite heads of the popes that decorate the clerestory wall. The Office of Works never settled for anything less than the best, and even such trifles as the holy water fonts, the choir stalls, the iron grilles and the candlesticks are works of genuine artistic merit.

> The **Piccolomini Library** contains the famous frescoes by Pinturicchio maintained as part of the cathedral complex. It was built to hold the library of Aeneas Silvius, the greatest member of Siena's greatest noble family. The entrance is off the left aisle, near the Piccolomini Altar (open daily 10–1 and 2.30–5; 9– 7.30 in summer; adm).

Siena's Renaissance Man

Aeneas Silvius Piccolomini (1405–64), eventually to become Pope Pius II, was the very definition of a Renaissance man. One of 18 children who were born into a branch of the mighty Piccolomini family, little Aeneas's quick intelligence soon attracted a great deal of attention, and he received the finest humanist education Siena could offer. To this he added natural charm, good looks, excellent Latin and an innate sense of diplomacy that soon earned him posts of responsibility with the leading ecclesiastics of the day.

Aeneas Silvius' interests ranged wide, and his keen observations and objective point of view on all aspects of life were invaluable to the scholarship of the day, especially in geography and topography. His *On Europe*, *On Asia* and *An Account of Bohemia* were among the most important works since ancient times; *On Asia* was closely studied by Columbus. Aeneas had enough time left over to write weighty tomes on history, on the lives of great men, on education and on antiquities; he was gifted enough in literature (he wrote poetry, a comedy and an erotic novella) to be crowned Poet Laureate. In politics, he worked fitfully to reform the Church of Rome and the constitution of Siena. He was the first to detail and describe the beauties of the Italian landscape, in which he found the greatest delight, as well as the little scenes of daily life that struck him. These, along with his thoughts and ambitions, even the unseemly, unflattering ones, went into his *Commentaries*, the most vivid and personal autobiography until Benvenuto Cellini's, and the only one ever published by a pope.

Aeneas Silvius took holy orders in 1446, marking a new serious turn in his life. Thanks to his service to popes Eugenius IV, Nicholas V and Calixtus III he became a bishop and cardinal, and was elected Pope in 1458, in a corrupt conclave that he described in frank detail. His election hardly put an end to his womanizing, although his peers, who thought they had elected a worldly humanist, were astonished at Pius II's dedicated efforts to promote the papacy and defend the faith by preaching a Crusade against the Turks who had just captured Constantinople. His chief memorial is the little Renaissance city of Pienza, southeast of Siena, which Bernardo Rossellino created out of the humble village of his birth, Corsignano. But because of the honesty of his autobiography, Pius II has never been considered a very good pope, although 15th-century historians praised his honesty, courage and consistency. The irony is that other Renaissance popes were surely just as conniving and ambitious if not worse (for one thing, Pius II was one of the first who didn't believe in magic or astrology); the difference is they never wrote down their thoughts.

In 1495, 31 years after his death, Cardinal Francesco Piccolomini, a man who would become Pope Pius III, decided his celebrated uncle's life would make a fine subject for a series of frescoes. He gave the job to Pinturicchio, his last major commission; among his assistants was the young, still impressionable Raphael—anyone who knows his *Betrothal of the Virgin* will find these paintings eerily familiar.

The 10 scenes include Aeneas Silvius' attendance at the court of James I in Scotland—a Scotland with a Tuscan fantasy landscape— where he served with an embassy. Later he is shown accepting a poet laureate's crown from his friend Emperor Frederick III, and presiding over the meeting of Frederick and his bride-to-be, Eleanor of Aragon. Another fresco depicts him canonizing St Catherine of Siena. The last, poignant one portrays a view of Ancona, and its cathedral up on Monte Guasco, where Pius II went in 1464, planning a crusade against the Turks. While waiting for the help promised by the European powers, help that never came, he fell ill and died.

Art historians and critics, following the sniping biography of the artist by Vasari, are not always kind to Pinturicchio. As with Gozzoli's frescoes for the Medici Palace in Florence, the consensus seems to be that this is a less challenging sort of art, or perhaps just a very elevated approach to interior decoration. Certainly Pinturicchio seems extremely concerned with the latest styles in court dress and coiffure. However, the incandescent colour, fairy-tale backgrounds and beautifully drawn figures prove irresistible. These are among the brightest and best-preserved of all quattrocento frescoes; the total effect is that of a serenely confident art, concerned above all with beauty for beauty's sake, even when chronicling the life of a pope. Aeneas Silvius' books have all been carted away somewhere but one of his favourite things remains, a marble statue of the *Three Graces*, a copy of the work by Praxiteles that was much studied by the artists of the 1400s.

> *Around the side of the cathedral, off the right transept, Piazza Jacopo della Quercia is the name the Sienese have given to the doomed nave of their 1330s **cathedral extension**. All around the square, the heroic pilasters and arches rise, some incorporated into the walls of later buildings. Beyond the big, blank façade, a little door on the right gives entrance to the **Museo Metropolitana**, built into what would have been one of the cathedral transepts (open daily 13 March –30 Sept 9–7.30, otherwise 9–1.30; adm).*

This is the place to go to inspect the cathedral façade at close range. Most of the statues now on the façade are modern copies, replacing the works of great sculptors like Nicola Pisano, Urbano da Cortona and Jacopo della Quercia. The originals have been moved to the museum for preservation, and you can look the cathedral's marble saints right in the eye (if you care to; many of these remarkable statues, fairly alive with early Renaissance *prontezza* (alertness), seem ready to hop off their pedestals and start declaiming if they suspect for a minute you've been skipping Sunday mass).

Besides these, there are some architectural fragments and leftover pinnacles, as well as some bits of the marble pavement that had to be replaced. On the first floor, a collection of Sienese paintings includes Duccio di Buoninsegna's master-piece, the *Maestà* that hung behind the cathedral's high altar from 1311 until 1505. Painted on both sides, the main composition is a familiar Sienese favourite, the enthroned Virgin flanked by neat rows of adoring saints—expressive faces and fancy clothes with a glittering gold background. Among the other paintings and sculptures are works by Pietro and Ambrogio Lorenzetti, Simone Martini, Beccafumi and Vecchietta.

Among the works on the top floor is the *Madonna dagli Occhi Grossi* ('of the Big Eyes') by an anonymous artist of the 1210s, a landmark in the development of Sienese painting and the original cathedral altarpiece. There's a hoard of golden croziers, reliquaries, and crucifixes from the Cathedral Treasure, including another lovely golden rose from the Vatican; this was probably a gift from Aeneas Silvius. A stairway leads up to the top of the **Facciatone**, the 'big façade' of the unfinished nave, where you can enjoy a view over the city.

*Outside the unfinished cathedral nave, a long, steep set of stairs leads down around the back of the church to Piazza San Giovanni. In this lower, but prominent setting the Office of Works architects squeezed in a **Baptistry**, perhaps the only one in Italy situated directly under a cathedral apse. Behind its unfinished 1390s Gothic façade, this baptistry contains some of the finest art in Siena. It's hard to see anything in this gloomy cellar, though; bring plenty of coins for the lighting machines.*

Frescoes by Vecchietta, restored to death in the 19th century, decorate much of the interior. The crown jewel, however, is the **baptismal font**, a king-sized work embellished with some of the finest sculpture of the quattrocento. Of the gilded reliefs around the sides, *Herod's Feast* is by Donatello, and the *Baptism of Christ* and *St John in Prison* by

Ghiberti. The first relief, with the *Annunciation of the Baptist's Birth*, is the work of Jacopo della Quercia, who also added the five statues of prophets above. Two of the statues at the corners of the font, the ones representing the virtues Hope and Charity, are also by Donatello.

Across the street from the baptistry, the Renaissance **Palazzo del Magnifico** by Cozzarelli was the family headquarters of the Petrucci, Sienese power-brokers (and perhaps would-be rulers) in the late 15th and early 16th centuries.

> *Opposite the old cathedral façade, one entire side of the piazza is occupied by the great* **Ospedale di Santa Maria della Scala**, *believed to have been founded in the 9th century and for centuries one of the largest and finest hospitals in the world.*

According to legend, the hospital had its beginnings with a pious cobbler named Sorore, who opened a hostel and infirmary for pilgrims who were on their way to Rome. (Siena was an important stop on medieval Europe's busiest pilgrimage route, the Via Francigiana.) Sorore's mother, it is said, later had a vision here—of babies ascending a ladder into heaven, and being received into the arms of the Virgin Mary—and consequently a foundling hospital was soon added. A meticulous attention to the health of its citizens was always one of the most praiseworthy features of Siena; in the 14th century it insisted on such revolutionary practices as the washing of hands by doctors and nurses, meals adapted to each patient's illness, and the use of iron beds (to prevent the spread of bed-bugs). To encourage donations, laws were passed allowing wealthy Sienese to deduct gifts from their taxes (remember, this is the 14th century) and not a few left huge sums in their wills; after the plague of 1348, the hospital was up to its ears in gold. Even in the decadence of the 1700s advances in such things as inoculations were being made here.

Since 1985 the hospital has slowly been closing down, and no longer accepts overnight patients (one of the last to die here was novelist and folktale compiler, Italo Calvino), although doctors continue to consult here while talk of turning the hospital into a museum drags on. In the meantime, pretending to be a patient may get you in to see Beccafumi's *Meeting of SS. Joachim and Anne* in the old chapel, and the **Salone dei Pellegrini**, where Domenico di Bartolo painted eleven magnificent frescoes, a realistic, almost photographic documentary of hospital practices in 1439. The adjacent 13th-century church of **Santa Maria della Scala** has a fine marble altar and handsome coffered ceiling; the bronze *Risen Christ* (1476) by Vecchietta shows the sinewy influence of Donatello.

Take Vicolo di S. Girolamo down into the ancient quarter of steep narrow streets below the hospital, all part of the **contrada** *of the Selva.*

Little Piazza della Selva in the centre has one of the most charming of the new *contrade* fountains, topped by a bronze statue of the neighbourhood's rhinoceros symbol. Here too is Selva's pretty parish church, Renaissance **San Sebastiano** *(often open Saturday afternoons)*, built in the form of a Greek cross in 1507, chock-full of interesting paintings (including an *Assumption* by Lorenzo Sabbatini), frescoes and reliquaries.

> *Leaving the cathedral in the opposite direction, go south down Via del Capitano, will lead you into the haunts of the dolphin and turtle (Onda and Tartuga). Where the street meets Via di Città, it changes its name to Via San Pietro, passing the 14th-century Palazzo Buonsignori, one of the most harmonious of the city's noble palaces, now restored as the home of the **Pinacoteca Nazionale** (open daily 8.30–7; 8.30–1 Sun; 8.30–2 in winter, closed Mon; adm).*

This is the temple of Sienese art, a representative sampling of this inimitable city's style; many of the works have been recently restored. The collection is arranged roughly chronologically, beginning on the ground floor with Guido da Siena and his school in the middle 13th century (**Room 2**), continuing through an entire room of delicate, melancholy Virgins by Duccio and his followers, reaching a climax with Duccio's luminous though damaged *Madonna dei Francescani* in **Room 4**. More Madonnas and saints fill room after room, including important works by Siena's greatest 14th-century artists. One of the most famous is Simone Martini's *Madonna and Child*; the story goes that this Madonna was a great Palio fan. When everyone had gathered in the Campo for the event, she would wander out in the empty streets and tiptoe over for a look. One day, she lingered too long in the Campo and had to run back home, losing her veil in her haste. She has yet to find it, and according to the Sienese, she weeps sweetly during the Palio, probably because she can't get through the Pinacoteca's security system. Other Madonnas that stand out are those of Pietro and Ambrogio Lorenzetti (*Madonna Enthroned* and the *Annunciation*, both in **Room 7**) and Taddeo di Bartolo (*Triptych*, in **Room 9**) stand out, with their rosy blooming faces and brilliant colour, a remarkable counterpoint to the relative austerity of contemporary painting in Florence. One element that is clearly evident in many of these paintings is Sienese civic pride; the artists take obvious delight in including the city's skyline and landmarks in the background of their works—even in nativities.

Sienese Renaissance painters are well represented, often betraying the essential conservatism of their art and resisting the new approaches of Florence: Domenico di Bartolo's 1433 *Madonna* in **Room 9**; Nerocchio and Matteo di Giovanni of the 1470s (**Room 14**); Sano di Pietro, the leading painter of the 1440s (**Rooms 16–18**). The first floor displays some of Il Sodoma's most important works, especially the great *Scourging of Christ* which is in **Room 31** (1514); in **Room 37** the *Descent into Hell* is one of the finest works by Siena's greatest Mannerist, Beccafumi.

> *Next to the Pinacoteca, the church of **San Pietro alle Scale** contains The Flight into Egypt, which is an altarpiece by Rutilio Manetti, the only significant Sienese painter of the Baroque era, a follower of Caravaggio. From here, turn right in Via Tommaso Pendola and turn left at Via di San Quirico.*

Here in the centre *contrada* of the *Chiocciola* (snail) are two works by Baldassare Peruzzi: **Palazzo Pollini** and opposite, **Santa Maria del Carmine**, a 14th-century church remodelled by Peruzzi in 1517. It houses a painting of *St Michael*, one of Beccafumi's masterpieces, and a grimly Cavaraggiesque *Last Judgement* by an anonymous 16th-century artist.

> *Via delle Cerchia will take you back towards the centre, passing by way of a path that leads to Siena's small **Botanical Gardens** (open 8–5 Mon–Fri, 8–12 Sat; book in advance for a guided tour, © 298 874). Via della Cerchia continues to the panoramic Prato Sant'Agostino and the church of **Sant'Agostino**.*

This gloomy bulk conceals a happy rococo interior of 1749 by Vanvitelli, a Dutchman born Van Wittel who was the chief architect of the kings of Naples. Most of the building dates back to the 13th century, however, and there are surviving bits of trecento frescoes and altarpieces all around. On the right, seek out Perugino's *Crucifixion*, a rare non-Sienese painting. After the war, the other works of art were gathered together in the nearby Piccolomini chapel: a fine painting of the *Epiphany* by Il Sodoma, with a background reminiscent of Leonardo da Vinci, a horrific *Massacre of the Innocents* by Matteo di Giovanni, one of his favourite subjects, and a lovely *Madonna and Saints*, frescoed in the lunette by Ambrogio Lorenzetti. In the Cappella Bichi, frescoes were uncovered in 1978, believed to be by Francesco di Giorgio Martini, an artist who went on to become more famous for his military engineering.

> *At Prato de Sant'Agostino 4 is one of Siena's Old Curiosity Shops, the **Accademia di Fisiocrittici** (usually open 3–6 Thurs, 9–1 and 3–6 Sat and holidays , but check at the tourist office).*

Founded in 1691, the academy of Fisiocritici made important contributions to the study of the natural sciences in the Enlightenment. Today it holds a delightfully dusty, old-fashioned science museum, with 2000 terracotta mushrooms, meteorites that fell near Siena in 1794, stuffed birds and a beautiful collection of minerals.

*Via Piero Andrea Mattioli continues to the city walls and the **Porta Tufi**; alternatively, head down pretty Via Sant'Agata/Via Giovanni Dupré, past **San Giuseppe**.*

This church marks Siena's uneasy compromise with the new world of the 1600s. One of the city's first Baroque churches, it was nevertheless built not in Baroque marble or travertine but in good Siena brown brick. It is in the parish of the *Onda* district; the *contrada*'s fountain is in front.

*Via Giovanni Dupré leads down to Piazza del Mercato, Siena's market square, directly under the Palazzo Pubblico; cross this to enter the populous eastern third of the city, the **Terzo San Martino**.*

The most intriguing parts of this neighbourhood are here on the hillside behind Piazza del Mercato, old streets on slopes and stairs in the *contrada* of the *Torre*—one of the 'unlucky' *contrade* that hasn't won a Palio in decades. Nevertheless they have a fine fountain with their elephant-and-tower emblem on pretty Piazzetta Franchi. If you have time, take a stroll down **Via Porta Giustizia** for a country ramble within the city walls and down into the valley that separates Terzo di San Martino from Terzo di Città.

*Alternatively, take Via di Malcontenti from Piazza del Mercato, turn right in Via di Salicotta, left at Vicolo di Coda and then right again for **Vicolo dell'Oro**, an alley of overhanging medieval houses, much like the ones in the Palazzo Pubblico's frescoes of Good and Bad Government. From here Via S. Girolamo leads around to Via dei Servi and **Santa Maria dei Servi**, its massive campanile looming over Piazza Alessandro Manzoni, the heart of the* contrada *of the* Valdimontone *(ram).*

Here, in the north transept, is one of the earliest and best Sienese nativities, the altarpiece in the second north chapel by Taddeo di Bartolo. Among the many other good paintings in this church is a *Madonna* by Coppo di Marcovaldo and the *Madonna del Popolo* by Lippo Memmi. An interesting comparison can be made between two versions of that favourite Sienese subject, the *Massacre of the Innocents*: one from the early trecento by Pietro Lorenzetti, and another from 1491 by Matteo di Giovanni.

*Just east of Piazza Alessandro Manzoni, Via Val di Montone and Via Roma descend to one of Siena's best surviving city gates, the double-fortified **Porta Romana** of 1327; in the opposite direction, it leads up to the 15th-century **Palazzo di San Galgano**, sometimes attributed to Giuliano da Maiano. At no. 71, the **Società Esecutori Pie Disposizioni***

> *(call ahead, © 220 400, open daily 9–12, closed Sun) keeps an oratory and a small but choice collection of paintings by Il Sodoma and other Sienese masters.*

> *From Via Roma turn right in Via Oliviera, then left in Vicolo del Sasso for* **Santo Spirito**.

Not many visitors make it to this little domed church with its pure Renaissance portal. It holds another set of frescoes by Il Sodoma in the Spanish chapel on the right, with a figure of *St James of Compostella* on horseback, slicing up hapless Moors with his sword and a virile *St Sebastian*.

> *Via Pispini, which passes in front of the church, is the road to Perugia, and at the end is the elegant fortified* **Porta Pispini**, *embellished by Il Sodoma with a fine Nativity, although only traces of it remain today. Via Pantanero will return you to the Croce del Travaglio by way of the* **Loggia del Papa**.

This Renaissance ornament, designed by Federighi and decorated by Francesco di Giorgio Martini, was given to Siena by Aeneas Silvius Piccolomini in 1462. Nearby, the single-naved church of **San Martino** was given a new façade in 1613 and holds a *Nativity* by Beccafumi in the left aisle, and in the right aisle, a recently restored *Circumcision* by Guido Reni.

> *Continue a short way down the graceful curve of Via Banchi di Sotto to Siena's most imposing* palazzo privato, *the* **Palazzo Piccolomini** *(open daily 9–1, Sat 9–12.30, closed Sun), done in the Florentine style by Rossellino in the 1460s.*

This palace now houses the old Sienese state archive—not a place you might consider visiting but for the presence of the famous *Tavolette della Biccherna* (the account books of the *Biccherna*, or state treasury). Beginning in the 1200s, the Republic's custom was to commission the best local artists to decorate the covers of the *tavolette*; the most interesting show such prosaic subjects as medieval citizens coming in to pay their taxes, city employees counting their pay and earnest monks trying to make the figures square—all are Cistercians from San Galgano (*see* p.377), the only people medieval Siena trusted to do the job. Among the other manuscripts and documents you'll find Boccaccio's will.

Start: *Via Banchi di Sopra*

Finish: *Porta Camollia*

Walking time: *half a day*

This walk explores medieval palaces, frescoed parish churches, city gates and delightful *contrade* fountains in Siena's third 'petal'— The Terzo di Camollia.

II: Around the Terzo di Camollia

Lunch/Cafés

Enzo, Via Camollia 49, ℭ 281 277. Mainly a fish restaurant, serving inventive and traditional dishes (closed Mon, around L60,000).

Gastronomia Morbidi, Banchi di Sopra 75, ℭ280 268. Founded in 1925, four floors of national and Sienese culinary specialities and a wine section selling all the best wines in Italy.

Il Riccio, Via Malta 44, ℭ 420 33. Large and anonymous restaurant/bar pizzeria with the bonus of two verandas and ready cut take-away pizza (closed Tues, around L15,000-30,000).

La Lizza, Piazza Gramsci 21, ℭ 289 089. Hot sandwiches, pizza and ice cream.

Gelateria Nannini, Piazza Salimbeni. Bar and ice cream parlour with a wide choice (closed Fri), also bar gelateria in Piazza Matteotti 32 .

*Leading north from the Campo, Via Banchi di Sopra, a most aristocratic thoroughfare, is lined with the palaces of the medieval Sienese élite, and forms the spine of the **Terzo di Camollia**, the largest and most populous of the terzi.*

The first important palace is also one of the oldest, that of the Tolomei family, a proud clan of noble bankers who liked to trace their ancestry back to the Greek Ptolemies of Hellenistic-era Egypt. The **Palazzo Tolomei**, begun in 1208, is the very soul of Sienese Gothic; it gave its name to Piazza Tolomei in front, the space used by the Republic for its assembly meetings before the construction of the Palazzo Pubblico. In front note Siena's she-wolf (1610); opposite, the church of **San Cristoforo** is one of the oldest in the city; two galleries of the cloister remain off to the left.

*A right turn up Via del Moro just after San Cristoforo will take you up to the 1594 proto-Baroque **Santa Maria di Provenzano**.*

Parish church of the *contrada* of the Giraffe, this is one of the last important churches erected in Siena, built by Flaminio del Turco, with the most imposing interior after the Cathedral itself; lofty pillars support a daring dome. This particular Virgin Mary, a terracotta image said to be left by St Catherine (*see* p.251), has had one of the most popular devotional cults in Siena since the 1590s; the Palio of 2 July is in her honour, and the banner is usually kept here along with a vast array of ex-votos.

*The quiet streets behind the church were Siena's red light district in Renaissance times. Walk north of Santa Maria on Via Provenzano Salvani, and turn right at Via dei Rossi, to bring you out just under one of the city's largest churches, **San Francesco**, begun in 1326.*

It's a sad tale; after a big fire in the 17th century, this great Franciscan barn was used for centuries as a warehouse and barracks. Restorations were begun in the 1880s, and the 'medieval' brick façade was completed only in 1913. The interior is still one of the most impressive in Siena, a monolithic rectangle with vivid stained glass (especially so in the late afternoon) and good transept chapels in the Florentine manner. A few bits of art have survived, including damaged frescoes by both Lorenzettis in the north transept, a *Crucifixion* by Pietro, and two fine works by Ambrogio—the strangely-coloured *Martyrdom of the Franciscans at Ceuta* and *St Louis d'Anjou at the Feet of Boniface VIII*.

Next to San Francesco is the equally simple **Oratorio di San Bernardino**, begun in the late 1400s to hold the heart of Siena's famous Franciscan preacher (1380–1444), considered the foremost and most persuasive Italian missioner of the 15th century. If Bernardino wasn't entirely successful in taming the worldly pride of Siena's nobles, his motto 'Make it clear, make it short, and keep it to the point' has earned him a difficult posthumous job as the patron saint of advertising.

The upper chapel of the oratory *(not usually open, but ring for the doorkeeper)* is one of the monuments of the Sienese Renaissance, containing fine frescoes by Beccafumi, Il Sodoma, and the almost forgotten High Renaissance master Girolamo del Pacchia, few of whose works survive.

The area west of San Francesco, traditionally a solid working-class quarter, makes up the contrada *of Bruco (the caterpillar); continue down the Via dei Rossi to see their fountain under the steps.*

Bruco's name recalls the famous Compagnìa del Bruco, the trade union that initiated the revolt of 1371 and temporarily reformed Siena's faction-ridden government. The workers paid a terrible price for it; while the revolution was under way, some young noble *provocateurs* started a fire that consumed almost the entire *contrada*. Today Bruco is the worst of the 'unlucky' neighbourhoods; it hasn't won a Palio since 1955.

Siena Walk II:
Terzo di Camollia

*Midway down Via dei Rossi, turn right for one of Siena's most delightful squares, Piazza dell'Abbadia, home to the simple little church of **San Donato**, with a delicate rose window. It enjoys a fine view over the magnificent Gothic windows of the rear façade of **Palazzo Salimbeni**; to see the front, continue down Via dei Rossi and turn right.*

This was the compound of the Tolomeis' mortal enemies, and their centuries-long vendetta dragged Sienese politics into chaos on more than a few occasions. Together with the two adjacent palaces on the square, the Salimbeni is now home of the **Monte dei Paschi di Siena**, the oldest bank in Italy, founded in 1472. This remarkable savings bank, with a medieval air, has a tremendous influence over everything that happens in southern Tuscany. Ultra-modern inside, the bank holds a good art collection, sometimes open to the public with special exhibitions.

*Continue up Via Banchi di Sopra to **Santa Maria delle Neve**.*

You may be lucky to find this suavely elegant oratory. Attributed to Francesco di Giorgio Martini (1470), open to see the altarpiece, *Our Lady of the Snows*, the masterpiece of Matteo di Giovanni.

*With Palazzo Salimbeni at your back, walk along Costa Incrociata to Via Sapienza and the **Museo Archeologico**, with an Etruscan and Roman collection (open all day summer, 9–2 winter); the **Biblioteca Communale Intronati** next door has a precious collection of manuscripts—among them, some of St Catherine's 400 letters and a copy of the* Divine comedy *with illustrations by Botticelli. From the archaeology museum, turn down Costa Sant'Antonio and turn right in Via Santa Caterina, the main street of the* contrada *of the Oca,* *which stretches down steeply to the western city walls. In contrast to poor caterpillar, the equally proletarian **Oca** (goose) seems to have always been the best-organized and most successful of the* contrade. *During the Napoleonic Wars when the Tuscan and city governments were in disarray, the* Oca's *men temporarily took charge of the city. The goose's most famous daughter, Caterina Benincasa, was born here, on Vicolo del Tiratoio, in 1347.*

St Catherine

St Catherine was the last but one of the 25 children born into the family of a wool dyer. At an early age, the visions started. By her teens she had turned her room at home into a cell, and while she never became a nun, she lived like a hermit, a solitary ascetic in her own house, sleeping with a stone for a pillow. After she received the stigmata, like St Francis, her reputation as a holy woman spread across Tuscany. But Catherine was quite a different kettle of fish. Unlike the charming, other-worldly Francis, she was tremendously political and involved in the temporal affairs of her day. The records say she never smiled. Completely illiterate, she corresponded with popes, emperors and towns that asked her to settle disputes through a secretary, and her letters are powerful masterpieces of direct, simple, righteous prose although it has been noted that her favourite words were 'fire' and 'blood'. So complete was the moral authority from her saintliness and humility that she could say: 'What I want, I order.' She wasn't always obeyed: her letter to the *condottiere* Sir John Hawkwood (of the equestrian fresco in Florence cathedral) asking him to lead a Crusade, met with a polite no, thank you.

In 1378, Florence was under a papal interdict, and the city asked Catherine to plead its case at the papal court in Avignon. She went, but with an agenda of her own—convincing Pope Gregory XI (whom in her 'holy insolence' she addressed as *Babbo mio* or 'Daddy') to move the papacy back to Rome where it belonged. As a woman, and a holy woman to boot, she was able to tell the pope to his face what a corrupt and worldly Church he was running, without ending up dangling from the palace wall.

Talking the pope (a French pope, mind you) into leaving the civilized life in Provence for turbulent, barbaric 14th-century Rome is only one of the miracles with which Catherine was credited. Political expediency probably helped more than divine intervention—much of Italy, including anathemized Florence, was in revolt against the absentee popes. She folowed them back, and died in Rome in 1380, at the age of only 33, her heart broken when she heard that an anti-pope had been enthroned in Avignon, beginning the Great Schism. Canonization came in 1460 and in our own century she has been declared co-patron of Italy (along with St Francis) and one of the Doctors of the Church. She and St Teresea of Avila are the only women to hold this honour; both of them for their inspired devotional writings are practical, incisive letters enouraging church reform.

Off Via Santa Caterina, in Vicolo di Tiratoio, St Catherine's house is preserved as a shrine, the **Santuario e Casa di Santa Caterina** *(open daily 9–12.30, 3.30–6).*

The sanctuary, behind a grand portico donated in the 1940s by the cities of Italy, occupies the whole of the Benincasa home and the dyer's workshop, each room converted into a chapel, many with ceiling frescoes by 15th- and 16th-century Sienese artists, although oddly none was inspired to paint his best. There are four oratories in the house, and relics such as St Catherine's rock-pillow. The old kitchen, now the upper oratory, has a beautiful 17th-century tile floor; another oratory now serves as the *Oca's contrada* chapel (note the goose in the detail of the façade).

> *Via Santa Caterina slopes down towards the city walls and to the* **Fontebranda,** *a simple, pointed-arched fountain of the 13th century, topped by lion gargoyles.*

It doesn't seem much now, but medieval and Renaissance travellers always remarked on it, as an important part of Siena's advanced system of fountains and aqueducts. On the hill above the Fontebranda, however, the bold Gothic lines of the apse and transepts of San Domenico give a great insight into the straightforward, strangely modern character of much of Sienese religious architecture.

> *That's the best view of* **San Domenico;** *for a closer look it's a long climb. The easiest way up is to retrace your steps to St Catherine's house and Costa Sant'Antonio, turning left in Via della Sapienza for Piazza San Domenico, which doubles as the bus depot.*

Inside, the church is as big and empty as San Francesco; among the relatively few works of art is the only portrait from the life of *St Catherine*, on the west wall, done by her friend, the artist Andrea Vanni. This church was the scene of many incidents in the saint's life—she was known to go into ecstasy in the Cappella della Volte, where many Sienese watched the Host go flying from the hand of the priest directly into her mouth. Her head is ensconced in a golden reliquary (the Romans, suspecting she would be canonized one day, cut her body into bits when she died—the Venetians, for instance, made off with a foot). The real attraction, though, is the wonderfully hysterical set of frescoes by Il Sodoma in the **Cappella Santa Caterina**, representing the girl in various states of serious exaltation. The lateral fresco on the left depicts one of the more disturbing scenes from her letters: a Sienese, Niccolo di Tuldo, was condemned to death for some misdemeanour and in rage filled his prison cell with curses. Catherine arrived to calm him down and succeeded so well in convincing him to submit to his own sacrifice that the two of them went off to the site of execution as if going to a party; Catherine undid his collar for him, and let his head drop on her own lap after the chop. The saint wrote: 'When the cadaver was taken away, my soul rested in such delicious peace and I rejoiced so in the perfume of that blood that I did not wish them to take away that thing that lay upon my clothes.'

> *The open, relatively modern quarter around San Domenico offers a welcome change from the dark and treeless streets of this brick city. From Piazza San Domenico, walk down Via dei Mille and turn right at Via XXV Aprile for the shady park of* **La Lizza,** *and down Via C. Maccari for the* **Fortezza Medicea.**

Though the site is the same, this is not the hated fortress Charles V compelled the Sienese to build in 1552; as soon as the Sienese chased the imperial troops out, they razed it to the ground. Cosimo I forced its rebuilding after annexing Siena, but to make the bitter pill easier to swallow he employed a Sienese architect, Baldassare Lanci, and let him create what must be the most elegant and civilized, least threatening fortress in Italy. The Fortezza, a long, low rectangle of Siena brick profusely decorated with Medici balls, seems more like a setting for garden parties or summer opera than anything designed to intimidate a sullen populace. The Sienese weren't completely won over; right after Italian reunification they renamed the central space of the fortress **Piazza della Libertà**. The grounds are now a city park, and the vaults of the munition cellars have become the **Enoteca Nazionale**, the 'Permanent Exhibition of Italian Wines'. Almost every variety of wine Italy produces can be bought here—by the glass or by the bottle; the Enoteca's purpose is to promote Italian wines, and it ships thousands of bottles overseas each year (*open 3pm–midnight daily*).

> *From the Fortezza walk up Viale Franci, and then turn left, passing Santo Stefano and turn left in Via di Camollia for the charming little Renaissance church of* **Fonte Giusta**, *in Vicolo Fontegiusta.*

Designed in 1482 by Urbano da Cortona, Fonte Giusta has a square plan, divided into three short naves. There is an elaborate marble altar, and a lovely painting of *The Sybil Announcing to Augustus the Coming of Christ* by architect and stage designer Baldassare Peruzzi (1481–1536), a native of Siena who spent most of his career in Rome—where he built the Villa Farnesina for Sienese banker Agostino Chigi, a building generally considered the finest secular building of the High Renaissance. He later worked as architect of St Peter's after the death of Raphael in 1520. His architectural style was more delicate and graceful than any other of his age, and his services were always in demand, but according to Vasari he never made any money because he was too good natured to demand any from his wealthy patrons.

> *From here it is a short walk along the Via di Camollia to the* **Porta Camollia** *in the northernmost corner of Siena, which underwent the Baroque treatment in the 1600s.*

Here you will see the famous inscription 'Wider than her gates Siena opens her heart to you'. Old Siena was never that sentimental. The whole thing was added in 1604—undoubtedly under the orders of the Florentine governor—to mark the visit of Grand Duke Francesco I, who wasn't really welcome at all.

Peripheral Attractions

From Porta Camollia, Viale Vittorio Emanuele leads through some of the modern quarters outside the walls. Soon after the Camollia gate it passes a pretty stone column, commemorating the meeting of Emperor Frederick III and his bride-to-be Eleanor of Aragon in 1451—the event captured in one of the Pinturicchio frescoes in the Piccolomini Library. Next looms a great brick defence tower, the **Antiporto**, erected just before the Siege of Siena, and rebuilt in 1675. Further down, the **Palazzo dei Diavoli**, built in 1460, was the headquarters of the Marquis of Marignano during that siege.

There isn't much to see on the outskirts of the city—thanks largely to Marignano, who laid waste lovely and productive lands for miles around. Some 2km east of the city (take Via Simone Martini from the Porta Ovile), in the hills above the railway station, the basilica and monastery of **L'Osservanza** has been carefully restored after serious damage in the last war. Begun in 1422, a foundation of San Bernardino, the monastery retains much of its collection of 13th-and 14th-century Sienese art.

To the west of the city, the road to Massa Marittima passes through the hills of the Montagnola Sienese which is an important centre of monasticism in the Middle Ages (*see* San Galgano, p.377). Near the village of Montecchio (6km), the hermitage of **Lecceto**, one of the oldest in Tuscany, has been much changed over the centuries but retains some Renaissance frescoes in the church and a 12th-century cloister; nearby, the hermitage of **San Leonardo al Lago** is mostly in ruins; the 14th-century church survives, with masterly frescoes (*c.* 1360) by Pietro Lorenzetti's star pupil, Lippo Vanni. Just outside the village of Sovicille (13km), there is a Romanesque church of the 12th century, the **Pieve di Ponte alla Spina**. The village of Rosia (17km) has another Romanesque church, and just to the south the Vallombrosan **Abbey of Torri** has much to show from its original foundation in the 1200s; there is a rare three-storey cloister, with three different types of columns.

Excursions from Siena

TRA-IN buses from Piazza San Domenico will take you to two of Tuscany's most distinctive hill towns, Etruscan **Volterra** and **San Gimignano** with its medieval skyscrapers intact; both have enough sights to occupy a full day. You need a car, however, for the great monastery of **Monte Oliveto Maggiore** with its delightful frescoes by Il Sodoma. **Chianti** begins just north of Siena: TRA-IN buses will take you to most of the villages.

Baptistery

Pisa

Pisa (pop. 104,000) is at once the best-known and the most mysterious of Tuscan cities. Its most celebrated attraction has become, along with the Colosseum, gondolas and spaghetti a symbol for the entire Italian republic; even the least informed recognize the 'Leaning Tower of Pizza' even if they've never heard of Florence or Siena. Tour buses disgorge thousands every day into the Field of Miracles, who spend a couple of hours and leave again for places more tangible, like Florence, Elba or Rome. At night even the Pisani make a mass exodus into the suburbs, as if they sense that the city is too big for them, not physically, but in terms of unfulfilled ambitions, of past greatness nipped in the bud.

Yet go back to about 1100, when according to the chroniclers, precocious Pisa was 'the city of marvels', the 'city of ten thousand towers', with a population of 300,000—or so it seemed to the awed writers of that century, who, at least outside Venice, had never before seen such an enormous, cosmopolitan and exotic city in Christian Europe since the fall of Rome. Pisan merchants made themselves at home all over the Mediterranean, bringing back new ideas and new styles in art in addition to their fat bags of profit; Pisa contributed as much to the rebirth of Western culture as any city. Pisan Romanesque, with its stripes and blind arcades, which had such a wide influence in Tuscany, was inspired by the great Moorish architecture of Andalucía; Nicola Pisano, first of a long line of great sculptors, is as important to the renaissance of sculpture as Giotto is to painting.

Like a Middle Eastern city, Pisa has put all its efforts into one fabulous spiritual monument, while the rest of the city wears a decidedly undemonstrative, almost anonymous face, a little run down. It is a subtle place, a little sad perhaps, but strangely seductive if you give it a chance. After all, one can't create a Field of Miracles in a void.

History

In the Middle Ages, Pisa liked to claim that it began as a Greek city, founded by colonists from Elis. Most historians, however, won't give them credit for anything earlier than 100 BC or so, when a Roman veterans' colony was settled there. Records of what followed are scarce, but Pisa, like Amalfi and Venice, must have had an early start in building a navy and establishing trade connections. By the

11th century, the effort had blossomed into opulence; Pisa built itself a small empire, including Corsica, Sardinia, and for a while the Balearics. Around 1060, work was begun on the great cathedral complex, inaugurating the Pisan Romanesque. The city was a wonder to all who saw it: the great traveller Benjamin Tudela wrote that it had 10,000 towers. No wonder they made one or two lean, just to stand out.

In 1135 Pisa captured and sacked its greatest rival in the Western Mediterranean, Amalfi. The First Crusade, when Pisa's archbishop led the entire fleet in support of the Christian knights, turned out to be an economic windfall for the city. Unlike Amalfi, from the start Pisa had adopted a course of combat with the states of the Moslem world, less from religious bigotry than a clear eye on the main chance. When the Pisans weren't battling with the Moslems of Spain and Africa, they were learning from them. A steady exchange of ideas brought much of medieval Arab science, philosophy and architecture into Europe through Pisa's port. Pisa's architecture, the highest development of the Romanesque in Italy, saw its influence spread from Sardinia to Apulia in southern Italy; when Gothic arrived in Italy Pisa was one of the few cities to take it seriously, and the city's accomplishments in that style rank with Siena's. In science, Pisa contributed a great though shadowy figure, that most excellent mathematician Leonardo Fibonacci, who either rediscovered the principle of the Golden Section or learned it from the Arabs, and also introduced Arabic numerals to Europe. Pisa's scholarly traditions over the centuries would be crowned in the 1600s by its most famous son, Galileo Galilei.

Pisa was always a Ghibelline city, the greatest ally of the emperors in Tuscany if only for expediency's sake. When a real threat came, however, it was not from Florence or any of the other Tuscan cities, but from the rising mercantile port of Genoa. After years of constant warfare, the Genoese devastated the Pisan navy at the Battle of Meloria (an islet off Livorno) in 1284. It signalled the end of Pisan supremacy, but all chance of recovery was quashed by an even more implacable enemy: the Arno. Pisa's port was gradually silting up, and when the cost of dredging became greater than the traffic could bear, the city's fate was sealed. The Visconti of Milan seized the economically enfeebled city in 1396, and nine years later Florence snatched it from them. Excepting the period 1494–1505, when the city rebelled and kept the Florentines out despite an almost constant siege of 15 years, Pisa's history was ended. The Medici dukes did the city one big favour, supporting the university and even removing Florence's own university to Pisa. In the last 500 years of Pisa's long, pleasant twilight, this institution has helped the city stay alive and vital, and in touch with the modern world; one of its students was the nuclear physicist Enrico Fermi.

Getting Around

by train

The airport is linked to Pisa by train or city bus no. 5, departing from Piazza Stazione, in front of the main station, which lies south of the Arno, © 28 546. Many trains (Florence–Pisa or Genoa–Rome lines) also stop at Stazione San Rossore; if you're making Pisa a day trip you may want to get off there, as it's only a few blocks from the cathedral and Leaning Tower—or else bus no. 1 will take you there from the central station.

by bus

All intercity buses depart from near Piazza Vittorio Emanuele II, the big roundabout just north of the central station: APT buses for Volterra, Livorno and the coastal resorts (to the left on Via Nino Bixio, © 501 038) and LAZZI buses to Florence, Lucca, La Spezia (on Via d'Azeglio, © 42 688). Many of these buses also stop at Piazza D. Manin, just outside the walls of the cathedral. The Natural Park Migliarino San Rossore Massaciuccoli may be reached by city bus no. 11 from Lungarno Gambacorti. Pisa lends itself well to **bicycles**; you can hire one at Via Nino Bixio, near the station.

Tourist Information

Piazza Duomo, near the Leaning Tower, © (050) 560 464, or Via Benedetto Croce 26, © 40 903. Just outside the central station, there's an accommodation/information office, © 42 291.

Highlights of Pisa

There's a lot more to Pisa besides the **Leaning Tower**, beginning with the extraordinary set of monuments and museums just near the big tipster on and around the emerald lawn of the **Campo dei Miracoli**, all covered in Walk I.

Most tourists get no further; the rest of Pisa seems remarkably calm compared to Florence and Siena, and makes for delightful walking. Don't miss the fine art and sculpture collection in the **Museo Nazionale di San Matteo**, the monuments around **Piazza Cavalieri** and the churches of **San Nicola**, **San Francesco**, **Santa Maria della Spina** and **Santa Caterina**, nor the attractive **medieval market core** around Borgo Stretto, Via dei Sette Volte and Piazza Vettovaglie.

Walk I: The Field of Miracles

Start: *The Field of Miracles*

Finish: *Palazzo Arcivescovale*

Walking time: *a morning or afternoon*

Truly one might as well try to describe the face of one's angel as those holy places of Pisa.

Edward Hutton

259

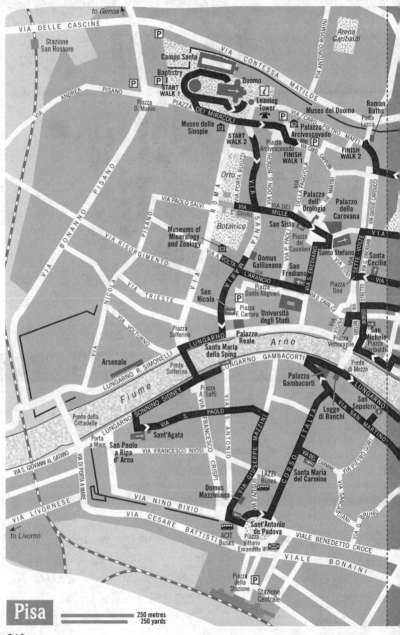

to Genoa

VIA DELLE CASCINE

Stazione
San Rossore

VIA CONTESSA MATILDE

Arena
Garibaldi

VIA ANTONIO ROSMINI

Campo Santo

Baptistry
START
WALK 1

Duomo

Leaning
Tower

Museo del Duomo

Roman
Baths

Porta
Lucca

VIA ANDREA PISANO

Piazza
D. Manin

PIAZZA DEI MIRACOLI

VIA CARD. PIETRO MAFFEI

Museo delle
Sinopie

START
WALK 2

Piazza
Arcivescovado

Palazzo
Arcivescovado

FINISH
WALK 2

VIA S. MARIA

VIA CARD. CAPPINI

Orto

FINISH WALK 1

VIA PAOLO SALVI

VIA ROMA

VIA SANTA

Palazzo
dell'
Orologio

Palazzo
della
Carovana

VIA GIOSUE CARDUCCI

Botanico

VIA DEI
MILLE

VIA DON G. BOSCHI

VIA P. PAOLI

Museums of
Mineralogy
and Zoology

VIA VOLTA

San Sisto

Piazza
dei
Cavalieri

Santo Stefano

Santa
Cecilia

VIA BONANNO PISANO

VIA RISORGIMENTO

Domus
Galilaeana

San Frediano

VIA S. FREDIANO

VIA DINI

SETTE VOLTE

VIA OBERDAN

VIA NICOLA PISANO

VIA TRIESTE

VIA VOLTURNO

VIA S. MARIA

VIA L'ARANCIO

San Nicola

Piazza
Dante Alighieri

Piazza
Dini

VIA D. CAVALCA

BORGO STRETTO

San
Michele

Piazza
Garibaldi

Piazza
F. Carrara

Università
degli Studi

Piazza
Solferino

Arno

VIA VIGNA

Ponte
di Mezzo

Arsenale

LUNGARNO R. SIMONELLI

Palazzo
Reale

Santa Maria
della Spina

Piazza
Vettovaglie

LUNGARNO MEDICEO

Ponte
Solferino

Fiume

LUNGARNO GAMBACORTI

Palazzo
Gambacorti

LUNGARNO GALILEO

San
Sepolcro

VIA SAN MARTINO

Ponte della
Cittadella

LUNGARNO SONNINO SIDNEY

Piazza
A. Saffi

VIA S. PAOLO

VIA S. FRANCESCO

VIA S. ANTONIO

Logge
di Banchi

CORSO ITALIA

Porta
a Mare

Sant'Agata

VIA S. FRANCESCO

VIA DEL CARMINE

VIA PIETRO GORI

VIA S. GIOVANNI AL GATANO

San Paolo
a Ripa
d' Arno

VIA FRANCESCO NIOSÌ

CRISPI

Santa Maria
del Carmine

VIA SANGALLO CIANI

VIA DI PORTA A MARE

Domus
Mazziniana

LAZZI
Buses

VIA D'AZEGLIO

VIA GIUSEPPE MAZZINI

VIA G. BRUNO

VIA LIVORNESE

to Livorno

VIA NINO BIXIO

VIA CESARE BATTISTI

ACIT
Buses

Sant'Antonio
de Padova

Piazza
Vittorio
Emanuele II

VIALE BENEDETTO CROCE

VIALE BONAINI

Piazza
della
Stazione

Stazione
Centrale

Pisa

250 metres
250 yards

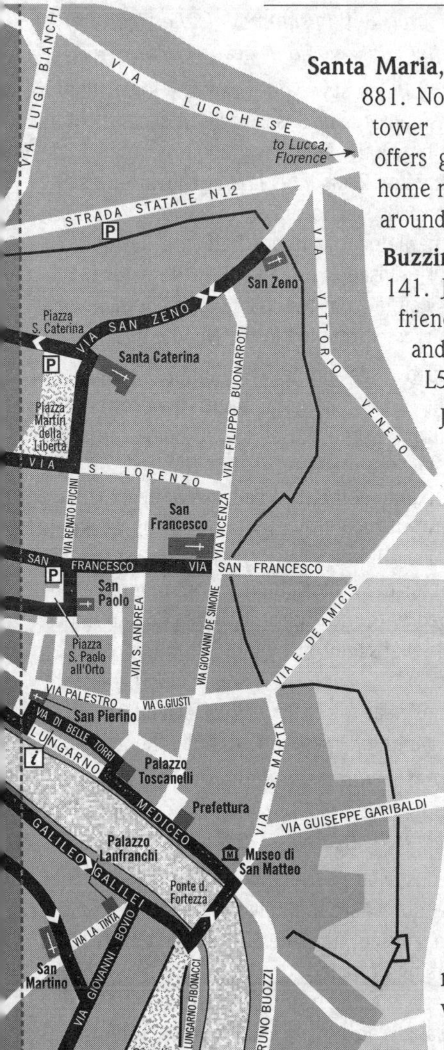

Santa Maria, Via Santa Maria, ✆ 561 881. Not far from the leaning tower this typical trattoria offers good mixed roasts and home made *tiramisù* (closed Wed, around L35,000).

Buzzino, Via Carlo Cammeo 44, ✆ 562 141. Just outside the walls a family-run friendly place serving good quality food and fresh seafood (closed Wed, around L50,000).

Just outside the walls are two handy, run-of-the-mill, *tavola calda* food counters: **Asmara**, Via C. Cammeo 27 (closed Fri); **Giardino**, Piazza Manin 1 (closed Mon).

Almost from the time of its conception, the Field of Miracles was the nickname given to medieval Italy's most ambitious building programme. As with Florence's cathedral, too many changes were made over two centuries of work to tell exactly what the original intentions were. But of all the unique things about this complex, the location strikes one first—a broad expanse of green lawn at the northern edge of town, just inside the walls. The cathedral was begun in 1063, the famous Leaning Tower and the baptistry in the middle 1100s, at the height of Pisa's fortunes, and the Campo Santo in 1278. (For the museums and monuments on the Field of Miracles, you can save by getting the joint ticket, for L12,000).

Map labels: VIA LUIGI BIANCHI, VIA LUCCHESE, to Lucca, Florence, STRADA STATALE N12, San Zeno, VIA SAN ZENO, VIA VITTORIO VENETO, VIA FILIPPO BUONARROTI, Piazza S. Caterina, Santa Caterina, Piazza Martiri della Libertà, VIA REMÌGIO FUCINI, S. LORENZO, San Francesco, VIA VICENZA, VIA SAN FRANCESCO, SAN FRANCESCO, San Paolo, Piazza S. Paolo all'Orto, VIA S. ANDREA, VIA GIOVANNI DE SIMONE, VIA G.GIUSTI, VIA E. DE AMICIS, VIA PALESTRO, San Pierino, VIA DI BELLE TORRI, LUNGARNO, Palazzo Toscanelli, MEDICEO, VIA S. MARTA, VIA GUISEPPE GARIBALDI, Prefettura, Palazzo Lanfranchi, GALILEO GALILEI, Museo di San Matteo, Ponte d. Fortezza, VIA LA TINTA, San Martino, VIA GIOVANNI BOVIO, LUNGARNO FIBONACCI, LUNGARNO BRUNO BUOZZI, Giardino Scotto, Piazza A. Toniolo, Bastione S. Gallo, Piazza Guerrazzi, Piazza Don Minzoni, Ponte D. Vittoria, VIA G.MATTEOTTI

*The **Baptistry** (open 9–5 in winter; 8–9 in summer) is the biggest of its kind in Italy; those of many other cities would fit neatly inside.*

The original architect, Master Diotisalvi ('God save you'), saw the lower half of the building done in the typical stripes-and-arcades Pisan style. A second colonnade was intended to go over the first, but as the Genoese gradually muscled Pisa out of trade routes, funds ran short. In the 1260s, Nicola and Giovanni Pisano, members of that remarkable family of artists who did so much to re-establish sculpture in Italy, redesigned and completed the upper half in a harmonious Gothic crown of gables and pinnacles. The Pisanos also added the dome over Diotisalvi's original prismatic dome, still visible from the inside. Both domes were impressive achievements, among the largest attempted in the Middle Ages.

Inside, the austerity of the simple, striped walls and heavy columns of grey Elban granite is broken by two superb works of art. The great **baptismal font** is the work of Guido Bigarelli, the 13th-century Como sculptor who made the crazy pulpit in Barga. There is little figurative sculpture on it, but the 16 exquisite marble panels are finely carved in floral and geometrical patterns of inlaid stones, a northern, almost monochrome variant on the Cosmati work of medieval Rome and Campania. Nicola Pisano's **pulpit** (1260) was one of the first of that family's masterpieces, and established the form for their later pulpits, the columns resting on fierce lions, the relief panels crowded with intricately carved figures in impassioned New Testament episodes, a style that seems to owe much to the reliefs on old Roman triumphal arches and columns. The baptistry is famous for its uncanny acoustics; try singing a few notes from as near to centre as they will allow you. If there's a crowd the guards will be just waiting for someone to bribe them to do it.

*One of the first and finest works of the Pisan Romanesque, the **cathedral façade**, with four levels of colonnades, turned out to be a little more ornate than Buscheto, the architect, had planned back in 1063.*

These columns, with similar colonnades around the apse and the Gothic frills later added around the unique elliptical dome, are the only showy features on the calm, restrained exterior. On the south transept, the late 12th-century **Porte San Ranieri** has a fine pair of bronze doors by Bonanno, one of the architects of the Leaning Tower. The Biblical scenes are enacted among real palms and acacia trees; naturally, the well-travelled Pisans would have known what such things looked like.

*Of the **interior**, little of the original art survived a fire in 1595 (open 7.45–12.45 and till sunset in summer, on Sundays, in the summer; the cathedral is often closed to tourists for most of the day).*

The roof went, as well as the Cosmati pavement, of which only a few patches still remain. A coffered Baroque ceiling and lots of bad painting were contributed during the reconstruction, but some fine work survives. The triumphal arch still has its fresco of the *Madonna and Child* by the Maestro di San Torpè (St Tropez) and the great mosaic of Christ Pantocrator in the apse by Cimabue, and there are portraits of the saints by Andrea del Sarto framed on the entrance pier (the charming *St Agnes*), in the choir and his *Madonna della Grazia* in the right nave. Giambologna's bronze angels stand at the entrance to the choir, and in the right transept note the sarcophagus carved by Tino di Camaino for Emperor Henry VII, who enjoyed his election for less than a year when he died near Siena in 1313.

The **pulpit** (*c.* 1300), by Giovanni Pisano, is the acknowledged masterpiece of the family. The men of 1595 used the fire as an opportunity to get rid of this nasty old medieval relic, and the greatest achievement of Pisan sculpture sat disassembled in crates, quite forgotten until this century. Works of genuine inspiration often prove profoundly disturbing to ages of certainty and good taste. Pisano's pulpit is startling, mixing classical and Christian elements with a fluency never seen before his time. St Michael, as a telamon, shares the honour of supporting the pulpit with Hercules and the Fates, while prophets, saints and sibyls look on from their appointed places. The relief panels, jammed with expressive faces, diffuse an electric immediacy equal to the best work of the Renaissance. Notice particularly the *Nativity*, the *Massacre of the Innocents*, the *Flight into Egypt*, and the *Last Judgement*. Next to the pulpit is a 16th-century bronze lamp known as the **Lamp of Galileo**, which Galileo observed when it was newly hung on its long rope. It swung for a long time, and Galileo noticed that although the swings shortened, they didn't seem to go any slower or faster; it formed the basis for his calculations on oscillations and his discovery of the principle of the pendulum.

> *The stories claiming the tilt of the **Leaning Tower** was accidental were most likely pure fabrications, desperate tales woven to account for what, before mass tourism, must have seemed a great civic embarrassment. The argument isn't very convincing. It seems hard to believe that the tower would start to lean when only 10m tall; half the weight would still be in the foundations. The argument then insists that the Pisans doggedly kept building it after the lean commenced. The architects who measured the stones in the last century to get to the bottom of the mystery concluded that the tower's odd state was absolutely intentional from the day it was begun in 1173. Mention this to a Pisan, and he will be as offended as if you had suggested lunacy is a problem in his family.*

The leaning campanile is hardly the only strange thing in the Field of Miracles. The more time you spend here, the more you will notice: little monster-griffins, dragons and such, peeking out of every corner of the oldest sculptural work, skilfully hidden where you have to look twice to see them, or the big bronze griffin sitting on a column atop the cathedral apse (a copy) and a rhinoceros by the door, Moslem arabesques in the Campo Santo, perfectly classical Corinthian capitals in the cathedral nave and pagan images on the pulpit. The elliptical cathedral dome, in its time the only one in Europe, shows that the Pisans had not only the audacity but the mathematical skills to back it up. You may have noticed that the baptistry too is leaning—about 1.5m, in the opposite direction. And the cathedral façade leans outwards about 40cm, disconcerting from the right angle. This could hardly be accidental. So much in the Field of Miracles gives evidence of a sophisticated, strangely modern taste for the outlandish. Perhaps the medieval master masons simply thought that perpendicular buildings were becoming a litle trite.

Whatever, the campanile is beautiful and something unique in the world—also an expensive bit of whimsy, with its 190 marble and granite columns. At the moment, it's also proving expensive to the local and national governments as they try to decide how best to shore up the tower. In the past few decades, the tilt has been increasing by a millimetre a year (some experts blame the construction of the enceinte in 1838, which seriously altered the water table, and say the 1934 injection of a hundred tons of cement in the footing of the wall has only made matters worse). In 1989, the sudden of the medieval (and perpendicular) Torre Civica in Pavia decided the diligent doctors of the campanile that it had become too precarious to withstand the traffic and it was closed indefinitely.

A flood of screwball proposals to stabilize the 15,000-ton tower poured into Pisa; among them, tying it to a blimp, planting sequoias all around it, propping it up with the world's largest bottle of Coke. Many engineers would simply lighten the tower by knocking off the upper bell chamber, added in the 1300s. What has actually happened so far seems modest in comparison: in 1992 the tower was girdled with steel cables, and encased in a Teflon coating that matches the colour of the stone in the hopes that this will prevent the marble from moving, cracking and breaking into bits, while hundreds of tons of concrete have been poured in to reinforce the base in an attempt to freeze the tilt. Whether or not the tower ever reopens depends on the success of these interventions—some 90 cameras installed throughout the tower wait to record the slightest budge.

> *If one more marvel in the Campo dei Miracoli is not excessive, there is the* **Campo Santo,** *a remarkable cloister as unique in its way as the Leaning Tower (open 9–5 Oct–Mar; 8–8 April–Sept; adm). Basically, the cemetery is a rectangle of gleaming white marble, unadorned save for the blind arcading around the façade and the beautiful Gothic tabernacle of the enthroned Virgin Mary over the entrance. With its uncluttered, simple lines, the Campo Santo seems more like a work of our own century than the 1300s.*

The cemetery began, according to legend, when the battling Archbishop Lanfranchi, who led the Pisan fleet into the Crusades, came back with boatloads of soil from the Holy Land for extra-blessed burials. Over the centuries an exceptional hoard of frescoes and sculpture accumulated here. Much of it went up in flames on a terrible night in July 1944, when an Allied incendiary bomb hit the roof and set it on fire. Many priceless works of art were destroyed and others, including most of the frescoes, damaged beyond hope of ever being perfectly restored. The biggest loss, perhaps, was the set of frescoes by Benozzo Gozzoli— the *Tower of Babylon, Solomon and Sheba, Life of Moses* and the *Grape Harvest* and others; in their original state they must have been as fresh and colourful as his famous frescoes in Florence's Medici Palace. Even better known, and better preserved, are two 14th-century frescoes of the *Triumph of Death* and the *Last Judgement* by an unknown artist (perhaps Andrea Orcagna of Florence) whose failure to sign the work unfortunately passed him down to posterity as the 'Master of the Triumph of Death'. In this memento of the century of plagues and trouble, Death (in Italian, feminine: *La Morte*) swoops down on frolicking nobles, while in the *Last Judgement* (which has very little heaven, but plenty of hell) the damned are variously cooked, wrapped up in snakes, poked, disembowelled, banged up and chewed on; still, they are some of the best paintings of the trecento, and somehow seem less gruesome and paranoid than similar works of centuries to come (though good enough to have inspired that pop classic, Lizst's *Totentanz*).

For another curiosity, there's the *Theological Cosmography* of Piero di Puccio, a vertiginous diagram of 22 spheres of the planets and stars, angels, archangels, thrones and dominations, cherubim and seraphim, etc; in the centre, the small circle trisected by a T-shape was a common medieval map pattern for the known earth. The three sides represent Asia, Europe and Africa, and the three lines the Mediterranean, the Black Sea and the Nile. Among the sculpture in the Campo Santo, there are sarcophagi and Roman bath tubs, and in the gallery of prewar photographs of the lost frescoes, a famous Hellenistic marble vase with bas-reliefs.

> *There are two museums surrounding the Campo dei Miracoli: opposite the cathedral, the **Museo delle Sinopie** (open 9.30–12.40 and 3–6.40, later in summer; adm).*

Housed in the 13th-century Ospedale Nuovo di Misericordia, this contains the pre-painted sketches on plaster of the frescoes lost in the Campo Santo fire. The name *sinopia* comes from Sinope, a Turkish port on the Black Sea, from where the reddish pigment originally derived; once the *sinopia* was drawn, the artist would cover the area he meant to cover in one day with wet plaster (*grasello*). When a fresco is detached from the wall, it is often possible to save the sinopia. During the restoration of the Campo Santo, these works of art in their own right were brought here—*The Triumph of Death* and the *Last Judgement* and others that were lost in the bombing.

> *The second museum,* **Museo del Duomo,** *housed in a former convent near the Leaning Tower in Piazza Arcivescovado (open 9–1 and 3–5; summer 9.30–1 and 3–7.30; adm exp), has been newly arranged in the old Chapter House, with descriptions in English available for each room.*

The first rooms contain the oldest works—beautiful fragments from the cathedral façade and altar; two Islamic works, the very strange, original **Griffin** from the top of the cathedral, believed to have come from Egypt in the 11th century, and a 12th-century bronze basin with an intricate decoration. Statues by the Pisanos from the baptistry were brought in from the elements too late; worn and bleached, they resemble a convention of mummies. Other sculptures in the next room survived better: Giovanni Pisano's grotesque faces, his gaunt but noble *St John the Baptist* and the lovely *Madonna del Colloquio*, who speaks to her child with her eyes; and in the next room are fine works by Tino di Camaino, including the tomb of San Ranieri and his sculptures from the tomb of Emperor Henry VII, sitting among his court like some exotic oriental potentate. In **Room 9** are works by Nino Pisano and in **Rooms 10–11**, the Cathedral Treasure, Giovanni Pisano's lovely ivory *Madonna and Child* steals the show, curving to the shape of the elephant's tusk; there's an ivory coffer and the cross that led the Pisans on the First Crusade. Upstairs are some extremely big angels used as candlesticks, intarsia and two rare illuminated 12th- and 13th-century scrolls (called exultet rolls), perhaps the original visual aids; the deacon would unroll them from the pulpit as he read so the congregation could follow the story with the pictures. The remaining rooms have some Etruscan and Roman odds and ends (including a good bust of Caesar) and prints and engravings of the original Campo Santo frescoes made in the 19th century. The courtyard has a unique view of the Leaning Tower, which seems to be bending over to spy inside.

> *One last building to look at in Piazza Arcivescovado is the* **Palazzo Arcivescovale.**

Although now the university faculty of Theology, you can pop in to see the disarmingly lovely 15th-century courtyard, a classic Tuscan arrangement of arcades and statues in traditional Tuscan colours.

Sta Maria della Spina

Walk II: North/South of the Arno

Start: *Via Santa Maria*
Finish: *Roman Baths*
Walking time: *a morning*
or afternoon

With or without a map you can get lost in a jiffy. The cathedral on the very edge of town, Pisa has no real centre. Still, the Pisans are very conscious of the division made by the Arno; every year in June the north and south sides fight it out on the Ponte di Mezzo in the *Gioco del Ponte*, a sort of medieval tug-of-war where the opponents try to push a big decorated cart over each other.

Lunch/Cafés

Tavola Calda, Via San Lorenzo, east of Piazza dei Cavalieri. If you just want a snack, try the offerings here.

Gastronomia Gratin, Via Crispi 66. A smart general food store with a good selection of salami, ham, oil and wine. Ask for a *pannino* to be prepared or choose one of the ready-made local treats such as Pisan soup, ravioli or lasagna to take away.

Casa della Panna, Via dei Mille 16. A coffee shop popular for its *caffè* served with a topping of whipped cream.

Ditta Federico Salza, Via del Borgo Stretto 44/46. This *pasticceria* is almost 100 years old and sells some of the best pastries in town. From 12.30 to 2.30 exquisite lunchtime dishes are served in an adjacent room.

Trattoria Stellio, Piazza Dante. Good for cheap meals and popular with students (around L20,000).

Antico Caffè dell'Ussero, Lungarno Pacinotti 27. Pisa's oldest coffee house.

Gelateria Sergio, Lungarno Pacinotti 1. Run by the same people as the restaurant next door and considered by many to be the best ice cream parlour in Pisa. Don't miss their delicious *perfetto al croccantino* made with cream and crunchy biscuit.

For centuries the main artery between the Campo dei Miracoli and the Arno has been the gracefully curving Via Santa Maria, lined with elegant palaces.

This is the only street in Pisa where you'll see many tourists, but few ever pause to poke their heads in the doors for a look at the secret gardens and courtyards, or the curiosities of the façades. At Via L. Ghini, you can turn right for the 16th-century **Orto Botanico**, the botanical gardens created by Cosimo de Medici for the university; the institute in the gardens has a façade, entirely covered with shells and mother-of-pearl *(open Mon–Fri 8–1 and 2–5.30; Sat 8–1)*.

Turn left at Via dei Mille, which broadens into a square at the foot of
San Sisto, *a simple 11th-century church in brick, containing a handful
of good Romanesque columns and a pretty 13th-century Madonna. Just
behind it opens* **Piazza dei Cavalieri**, *encircled by beautiful palaces .*

Duke Cosimo I started what was probably the last crusading order of knights, the
Cavalieri di Santo Stefano, in 1562. The crusading urge had ended long before,
but the duke found the knights a useful tool for placating the anachronistic fan-
tasies of the Tuscan nobility—most of them newly titled bankers—and for
licensing out freebooting expeditions against the Turks. Cosimo had Vasari build
the **Palazzo della Carovana** for the order, conveniently demolishing the old
Palazzo del Popolo, the symbol of Pisa's lost independence. Vasari gave the
palace an outlandishly ornate *sgrafitto* façade (*covered for restoration at the
time of writing*); the building now holds the prestigious Scuola Normale
Superiore, which was founded by Napoleon in 1810. In front of it stands a statue
of Cosimo I by Francavilla.

Santo Stefano

Next to the palace is the order's church, **Santo Stefano**,
built by Vasari in 1565, although the façade was
designed by a young Medici dilettante. The history of the order is told on the lavish coffered
ceiling, and its pirate trophies
are on display—eight
gilded leather lanterns
and long, fantastical pen-
nants snatched by the
order's pirates from defeated
Turkish and North African
galleys; one is claimed to have
been captured from the flag-
ship of Ali Pasha in the
Battle of Lepanto. On the
left hangs a *Nativity* by Bronzino and by a *Holy Family*
by Orazio Gentileschi.

Also on the Piazza, the **Palazzo dell'Orologio** was built around the 'Hunger
Tower' (left of the big clock—see plaque), famous in Dante's story of Count
Ugolino della Gherardesca, the Pisan podestà who was walled in here with his
sons and grandsons after his fickle city began to suspect intrigues with the
Genoese after Pisa's defeat at Meloria in 1284. If the intent was to kill off the
family and its progeny, the cruel punishment failed: the Gherardesca ruled as
signori from 1316 to 1341, and in 1330 founded Pisa's university.

*Via San Frediano leads to the church of **San Frediano**, with a typical Pisan façade and some of the most elaborate marble confessionals in Italy, as well as an Adoration of the Magi by Orazio Gentileschi. To the left, Piazza Dante Alighieri is the site of **Università degli Studi**, founded c. 1330 by the Gheradesca, and revived in 1472 by Lorenzo de' Medici.*

*From here, take Via L'Arancio back to Via Santa Maria, where no. 26 is the **Domus Galilaeana**, Galileo's house (open 9–12 and 3–6), with only a few dusty bits and bobs to recall Pisa's genius (see **Topics**, 53). Continue across to Via Volta, appropriately the site of Pisa's two science museums, although zoology and mineralogy were the two fields Galileo never much cared for. Then walk down Via Santa Maria towards the Arno, to the large 12th-century church of **San Nicola**.*

Take a good look at the octagonal belltower. Designed by Nicolò Pisano, it has exactly the same kind of tilt as the Leaning Tower itself, built to lean forward before curving back again towards perpendicular. Ask the sacristan to show you the famous spiral stair inside, which Vasari claimed inspired Bramante's Belvedere stair in the Vatican. The church itself, patched together here and there over the centuries, shelters a fine painting of the *Madonna* by Traini, a sculpture of the same by Nino Pisano, and a painting of *St Nicholas of Tolentino* shielding Pisa from the plague.

*Beyond the neighbouring **Palazzo Reale**, grafted on top of an old tower, lies the **Arno**, the river that first made the city great before forsaking it in silt.*

After the Campo dei Miracoli, the thing that has most impressed Pisa's visitors is its languidly curving river front, an exercise in Tuscan gravity. Two mirror image lines of blank-faced yellow and ochre buildings, all the same height, with no remarkable bridges (they were all blown up in the last war, but never were very showy), with none of the picturesque quality of Florence. 'The lung'Arno is so beautiful a sight, so wide and magnificent, so gay and smiling, that one falls in love with it,' wrote the poet Leopardi in the last century, while Norman Douglas on a winter's evening found that 'In Pisa, at such an hour, the Arno is the emblem of Despair...So may Lethe look or Styx: the nightmare of a flood'.

*The uncanny monotony is broken by only one landmark, but it is something special. Cross the Ponte Solferino and turn left for **Santa Maria della Spina**, sitting on the south bank like a precious jewel-box.*

A reliquary for one of the thorns from Christ's crown of thorns brought back from the Crusades, Santa Maria della Spina is one of the few outstanding achievements of Italian Gothic. Originally it wasn't Gothic at all, but when partially rebuilt in 1323, the new architect—perhaps, one of the Pisanos—turned it into an extravaganza of pointed gables and blooming pinnacles. All the sculptural works are first class, especially the figures of Christ and the Apostles in the 13 niches facing the streets. Although its placement on the Lungarno Gambacorti is perfect, it was not originally here at all, but located at the mouth of the Arno, where it suffered so many floods that it was at the point of vanishing in 1871, when the city decided to dismantle and rebuild it on this new site.

> *Continue downriver along Lungarno Sonnino Sidney, passing the ex-Convento San Benedetto, decorated with terracotta tiles. Ahead you can see remains of the old **Citadel**, built by the Florentines in the 15th century, and the **Arsenal** (1588), marking the site of the famous 'Golden Gate'—medieval Pisa's door to the sea. Just before the Ponte della Cittadella is **San Paolo a Ripa del Arno**.*

San Paolo stands in a small park, and interestingly is believed to have been built over the site of Pisa's oldest church and original cathedral; perhaps building cathedrals in open fields was an old custom. It has a ravishing 11th-century (but not tilting) façade believed to have been the prototype for the Duomo itself. Behind it, don't miss the little octagonal brick chapel of **Sant'Agata**, crowned with a prismatic roof like an Ottoman tomb.

> *Via San Paolo leads back towards the centre; turn right at Via Mazzini where at no. 29 you can pay your respects to the original romantic revolutionary at the **Domus Mazziniana** (open 8–2, Sat 8–12, closed Sun).*

Mazzini

Giuseppe Mazzini was born in Genoa in 1805, the son of a doctor enamoured of the French Revolution and a mother who, even more than the typical Italian mamma, thought her son was the Messiah. At age 16, the young Giuseppe witnessed a tide of refugees passing through Genoa hoping to escape to Spain after the failed Piedmont revolution of 1821. The sight of people suffering so much for political ideals moved him deeply. He started wearing black, as if in mourning for freedom; he continued to dress in mournful monochrome for the rest of his life.

His career as an active revolutionary began in 1827 when he joined the Carbonari, a strict, hierarchical secret society which plotted armed revolution in Italy. He was not one, however, to obey orders blindly , and in 1830 he was betrayed to the police by his own local leader and sent to prison for three months. During that time, Mazzini developed a political philosophy that never wavered: a belief in the unity and perfect equality of humanity (including even women and workers) and in humanity's ability to progress thanks to education. Not only did every individual have equal rights, but duties and obligations to the public good. He believed in God, but a God incarnate in the will of the people: his religion was democracy.

To make all this possible, Mazzini thought that the first goal of revolution should be an independent, unified Italy. From exile in Switzerland, he founded his own semi-secret society called *La Giovine Italia*, 'Young Italy', with the goal of instilling a sense of national identity in the Italian people and helping them to lead the revolution that would make Italy a democratic republic. Italy, Mazzini reasoned, could then lead a great democratic revolution across Europe. The society was called 'Young Italy' because one of its initial concerns was avoiding what Mazzini called 'middle-aged scepticism'; at first no one over age 40 was allowed to join, although Mazzini realized he was cutting out too many essential people. One of the first recruits was a sailor named Garibaldi.

Mazzini's sense of mission meant he spent most of his life writing and plotting in exile, under the threat of the death penalty back home in Genoa. His first insurrection in 1834 was a fiasco after his commander, entrusted with Young Italy's funds, lost all the money gambling in Paris. It led, however, to over a decade of exile for Mazzini in London, where he kept the flame of revolt alive by making contacts and writing, earning a pitiful income from journalism. Accounts of Mazzini in London (where the only thing he loved was the fog) tell of him giving most of his money to beggars, who soon learned that the affable Italian in black would never say no. He lived in a cramped book-filled room, where canaries flew about everywhere because he could not bear to confine them in cages. He founded a free evening school in the city in order to teach poor Italian immigrant children to read and write.

Mazzini next returned to Italy in 1849 when the Roman Republic was declared. Thanks to his reputation and integrity, he was acclaimed its natural leader, and gave the city the most tolerant, enlightened government it ever had—while working for no pay and dining every day in a workers' canteen. The experiment, however, lasted only three months before the French troops summoned by Pius IX arrived and defeated the heroic defence of the people of Rome, led by the dashing Garibaldi.

Hopelessly romantic republican insurrections supported by Mazzini in 1853 and 1857 went down to tragic defeat in Milan and Naples; ironically, it was an equally hopelessly romantic insurrection in 1860, in which Mazzini had no direct part, that finally succeeded when Garibaldi led his Thousand to Sicily. But Mazzini declared that the resulting kingdom of Italy of Vittorio Emanuele II was not the real Italy, not the tolerant democracy of his dreams and he refused to live in it.

Although Mazzini helped in the organization of the First International in London, his beliefs in private property and his insistence on a social as well as political revolution saw his influence quickly lose out to Marx, especially when he failed to support the Paris commune in 1871 (because French republicans had crushed the Republic of Rome, he simply could not trust them). In 1872, he returned clandestinely to Italy under the alias of John Brown, the firey American abolitionist, only to die in this house in Pisa. His other chief memorial in Italy is the nice big tomb they gave him in Genoa, with an epitaph by poet Giosuè Carducci, which ends: 'The man/who sacrified everything/who loved much/and forgave much and never hated/GIUSEPPE MAZZINI/after forty years of exile/today passes freely on Italian soil/now that he is dead/O Italy/such glory and such baseness/and such a debt for the future.'

*From Mazzini's last address, continue south past **Sant'Antonio de Padova** (note the finely cut tombstones in front), then cut across the vast oval of Piazza Vittorio Emanuele to Pisa's main shopping street, pedestrian-only Corso Italia. Here too are some palaces of note, especially no. 46, with a remarkable coffered 'beehive' ceiling that the owners often illuminate after dark. Midway along the Corso a piazza opens to the right with **Santa Maria del Carmine**, housing a pretty 17th-century organ and an Ascension by Alessandro Allori. At the end the handsome 14th-century **Palazzo Gambacorti** now contains the offices of the mayor, facing the arcades of the 17th-century wool and silk market, the **Logge di Banchi**. It overlooks the **Ponte di Mezzo**, scene of the annual Gioco del Ponte which is enacted in 16th-century costumes with all the swish medieval pageantry that the Tuscans in particular do so well.*

*Upstream from the Logge di Banchi, along the Lungarno Galileo Galilei stands the octagonal domed church of **San Sepolcro**.*

Built in 1150 by Diotisalvi for the Knights Templars, who were fond of such geometric shapes, it contains the tomb of Maria Mancini, one of the few women to have a brand of cigars named after her. The niece of Cardinal Mazarin and wife of powerful Prince Colonna, the beautiful Maria was the great love of the young Louis XIV—so great that Mazarin thought she was driving his charge to distraction and sent her back to Italy.

*From the left side of San Sepolcro runs Via San Martino, an attractive street with tiny alleys running into it from all sides. At no. 7 a Roman relief was incorporated into the building, known since the Middle Ages as Chinsica, a maiden who saved Pisa when the Saracens sailed up to the Golden Gate. Continue east to **San Martino**.*

Built over and around a 14th-century church, San Martino has a white marble façade that seems austere by Pisan ice-cream parfait standards, although adorned with an excellent relief by Andrea Pisano of *St Martin and the Beggar* (actually a copy—the original is inside).

*Continue along the Via San Martino to Piazza Toniolo, where the remains of the city wall, the **Bastione Sangallo**, now shelters a small but shady park.*

Just to the north are the gardens of the Palazzo Scotto, where P.B. Shelley lived from 1820–2 and wrote *Adonais, Epipsychidion* and about Pisa and the Arno:

> *Within the surface of the fleeting river*
> *The wrinkled image of the city lay,*
> *Immovably unquiet, and forever*
> *It trembles, but it never fades away.*

'Evening: Ponte al Mare, Pisa"

*From the garden, walk up to the river by way of Via Giovanni Bovio, passing the **Palazzo Lanfranchi**, where exhibitions often take place. Cross over the Ponte di Fortezza, reconstructed in 1958; just to the left is the church of **San Matteo**.*

Built in the 11th century, San Matteo was lavishly Baroqued with fake marbles and gold in the 17th century. The ceiling over the single nave is one huge *trompe l'oeil* painting on *The Glory of God* and the holy-water stoups, covered with angels and *putti*, are good enough to eat.

*The old convent attached to the church later served as prison for many years; now it immures much of the best of Pisa art from the Middle Ages and Renaissance in the **Museo di San Matteo** (open 9–7, 9–1 Sun, closed Mon; adm).*

It has works by Giunta Pisano, believed to be the first artist ever to sign his work (early 1200s), and an excellent and well-arranged collection of 1300s paintings by Pisans and other schools gathered from the city's churches; a polyptych by Simone Martini, paintings by Francesco Traini, Taddeo di Bartolo, Agnolo Gaddi, Antonio Veneziano and Turino Vanni; some sculptures by the Pisanos (especially the *Madonna del Latte* by Andrea and Nino); medieval ceramics from the Middle

East, brought home by old Pisan sea dogs. In **Room 7**, after all the trecento works, the Early Renaissance comes as a startling revelation, as it must have been for the people of the 15th century: here is Neri di Bicci's wonderfully festive *Coronation of the Virgin*, bright with ribbons, a *Madonna* from the decorative Gentile da Fabriano, a sorrowful *St Paul* by Masaccio, whose features and draperies are softly moulded, an anonymous *Madonna with Angel Musicians*, and a beautifully coloured *Crucifixion* by Gozzoli that looks more like a party than an execution. The last great work is Donatello's gilded bronze reliquary bust of *San Lussorio*, who could pass for Don Quixote. Some day the museum's collection of Mannerists and other later artists will be arranged downstairs.

*Next to the museum on the Lungarno is the **Prefettura**, housed in the lovely 13th-century stone brick and marble Palazzo Medici, decorated with slender twin and triple columns; it was a favoured residence of the magnificent Lorenzo. Continue up the Lungarno Mediceo to the corner of Via delle Belle Torri, where Byron lived from 1821–2 in the 16th-century **Palazzo Toscanelli** —just a short swim up the Arno from his friend Shelley. From here, turn up Via delle Belle Torri, lined with houses from the 12th and 13th centuries. At Via Cavour and the 11th-century **San Pierino**, turn back to Lungarno Mediceo to lively Piazza Garibaldi, located between the Ponte di Mezzo and a casbah of little market streets; Via Donzelle will take you into Pisa's arcaded market square, **Piazza Vettovaglie** ('victuals square') where every morning except Sunday the city's ancient mercantile traditions are renewed over stands of olives and cheese.*

*Leave Piazza Vettovaglie by way of Via Sant'Orsola, then turn left in old arcaded Borgo Stretto, site of **San Michele en Borgo**, built in 990— just as Pisa was beginning to feel its oats as a maritime republic. If it happens to be open, pop in to see some fine Romanesque chapels. Continuing along the Borgo Stretto, turn right at Via Mercanti for the striking 12th-century façade of **San Paolo all'Orto**. From here walk north along Via Fucini to Via San Francesco and turn right for **San Francesco**.*

Built in three separate stages between the 13th and 17th centuries, San Francesco is essentially Gothic behind its plain marble façade. The vast interior (as always a testimony to the extraordinary religious revival inspired by the preaching orders) contains some fine art: a marble 15th-century high altarpiece by Tomaso Pisano and frescoes from 1342 in the vault by Taddeo Gaddi. Flanking the altar, the second chapel on the right is shared by a beautiful 14th-century Florentine polyptych and the tomb of the unfortunate Count Ugolino, his sons and grandsons. Opposite, in the last chapel on the left, look up to see the *sinopie*, also by Taddeo

Gaddi. The sacristy was frescoed with *Scenes from the Life of the Virgin* by Taddeo di Bartolo in 1397; in the Chapterhouse there are more frescoes, this time by Niccolò di Pietro Gerini.

> *Backtrack along Via San Francesco, passing the 12th-century* **Santa Cecilia***, whose façade and campanile are decorated with majolica tiles. At the end, cross the Borgo for a look at one of Pisa's most charming little squares, Piazza Ulisse Dini; just up Via Ulisse Dini, the bank, the Cassa di Risparmio di Pisa, occupies one of the prettiest medieval buildings in the city. Backtrack to Piazza Dini and turn up narrow* **Via delle Sette Volte***, lined with medieval buildings, covered with vaults and utterly romantic after dark. At the top of the lane, turn right down Via San Lorenzo for Piazza Martiri della Libertà, where the plane trees create a shady oasis in the summer. Cut across this for the church of* **Santa Caterina***.*

Pisa's Dominican headquarters, Santa Caterina has a beautiful, typically Pisan marble façade of 1330. The equally attractive interior has a sculptural group of the *Annunciation* on its high altar and the tomb of Archbishop Saltarelli on the left, all the work of Nino Pisano. On the left wall note the large painting from the 1340s attributed to Francesco Traini of the *Apotheosis of Saint Thomas Aquinas*, with Plato and Aristotle in attendance and the defeated infidel philospher Averroes below.

> *From Santa Caterina, turn right in Via San Zeno for* **San Zeno***, a deconsecrated Romanesque chapel, in parts as old as the 5th century; a left turn in the same street will bring you back to the vestiges of Pisa's* **Roman baths** *from the 2nd century AD, near the medieval* **Porta di Lucca***. From here, Via Cardinale Pietro Maffi leads west back to the Campo dei Miracoli.*

Peripheral Attractions

A couple of kilometres up river to the east stands 'Pisa's second leaning tower', the campanile of the Romanesque **San Michele dei Scalzi**. **Calci**, under the slopes of Monte Pisano, has a good 11th-century church and an eroded giant of a campanile; 11km from Calci, in a prominent site overlooking the Arno, is the ornate **Certosa di Pisa**, founded in 1366, but completely Baroqued in the 18th century, in a kind of 1920s Spanish-California exhibition style with three fine cloisters (*open 9–4, 9–6 in the summer*). There are lavish pastel frescoes by Florentine Baroque artist Bernardo Poccetti and his school, and a giraffe skeleton, stuffed penguins, Tuscan minerals, wax intestines—all part of the university's **Natural History Collections**, founded by the Medici, housed in the Certosa

m Piero a Grado

since 1981 (*guided visits, 9-7 May-Oct, 9-4 Nov-April, closed Mon; adm; for the natural history collections, by appointment © 937 092*).

Towards the coast, 6km from Pisa, is the beautifully isolated basilica of **San Piero a Grado**. According to tradition it was founded in the first century by St Peter himself, and in the Middle Ages was a popular pilgrimage destination. Although first documented in the 8th century, the current buildings are 11th-century, embellished with blind arcades and ceramic *tondi*. Like many early churches and basilicas, it has an apse on either end, though in different sizes; the columns were brought in from a variety of ancient buildings. The altar stone, which was believed to have been set there by Peter himself, was found in recent excavations that also uncovered the remains of several previous churches. Frescoes which were in the nave by a 14th-century Lucchese, Deodato Orlandi, tell the *Story of St Peter* with effigies of the popes up to the millennium (John XVIII) and a view of heaven.

In 1822, a strange ceremony took place on the wide, sandy beach of **Gombo**, near the mouth of the Arno, described in morbid detail by Edward Trelawny: 'the brains literally seethed, bubbled, and boiled as in a cauldron, for a very long time. Byron could not face this scene, he withdrew to the beach and swam off to the *Bolivar*.' Such was Shelley's fiery end, after he drowned sailing from Livorno. Gombo, and Pisa's other beaches, the **Marina di Pisa** and **Tirrenia** are often plagued by pollution, although Marina di Pisa makes a pretty place to stroll, with its Liberty-style homes and pine forests.

Excursions from Pisa

From Pisa you can catch a morning train down to Piombino and sail in an hour to **Elba**, with its lovely beaches. APT buses north of the Stazione Centrale will take you south to the haunting hilltown of **Volterra** or north to Puccini's old haunts around **Torre del Lago**; **Viareggio**, just to the north, may have lost some of its fashionable cachet but still has a good beach and some wonderful Liberty villas.

Lucca Walls

Lucca

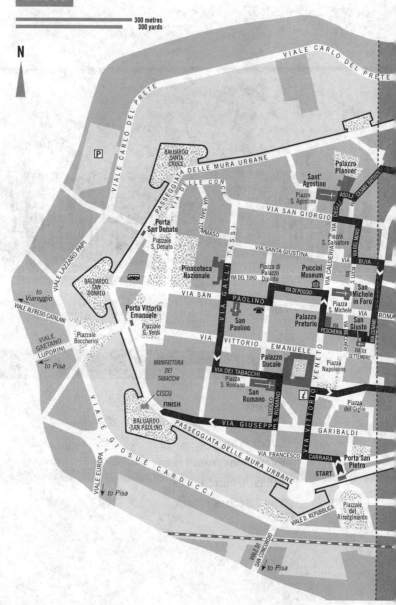

Lucca

300 metres
300 yards

N

VIALE CARLO DEL PRETE

VIALE CARLO DEL PRETE

P

BALUARDO
SANTA
CROCE

PASSEGGIATA DELLE MURA URBANE

VIA DELLE CONCE

Palazzo
Pfanner

Sant'
Agostino

Piazza
S. Agostino

VIA DEGLI ASILI

VIA CESARE BATTISTI

VIA SAN GIORGIO

VIALE CARLO DEL PRETE

VIA SAN TOMMASO

Porta
San Donato

Piazzale
S. Donato

VIALE LAZZARO PAPI

Pinacoteca
Nazionale

VIA GALLI TASSI

Piazza di
Palazzo
Dipinto

VIA DEL TORO

VIA SANTA GIUSTINA

Piazza
S. Salvatore

VIA CALDERIA

VIA DEL MORO

VIA BUIA

VIA S. LUCIA

Puccini
Museum

San
Michele
in Foro

BALUARDO
SAN
DONATO

to
Viareggio

VIALE ALFREDO CATALANI

Porta Vittoria
Emanuele

VIA SAN PAOLINO

VIA DI POGGIO

Piazza
S. Michele

San
Giusto

VIA CENAMI

ROMA

VIALE GAETANO LUPORINI

to Pisa

Piazzale
Boccherini

Piazzale
G. Verdi

San
Paolino

VIA
VITTORIO

Palazzo
Pretorio

VIA PESCHERIA

VIA BECCHERIA

EMANUELE

VIA VENETO

VIA XX
SETTEMBRE

MANIFATTURA
DEI
TABACCHI

VIA DEI TABACCHI

Palazzo
Ducale

Piazza
Napoleone

CISCU

FINISH

Piazza
S. Romano

San
Romano

VICOLO S. ROMANO

VIALE GIOSUE CARDUCCI

BALUARDO
SAN PAOLINO

PASSEGGIATA DELLE MURA URBANE

VIA GIUSEPPE

VIA VITTORIO VENETO

GARIBALDI

Piazza
del Giglio

VIALE EUROPA

VIA FRANCESCO

CARRARA

START

Porta San
Pietro

to Pisa

VIALE D. REPUBBLICA

Piazzale
del
Risorgimento

VIALE DI SAN CONCORDIO

to Pisa

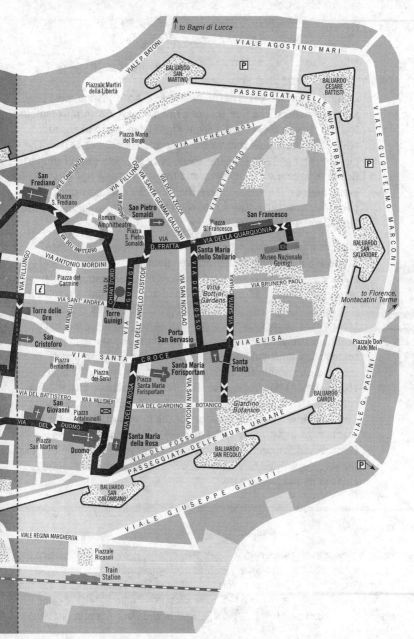

to Bagni di Lucca

VIALE AGOSTINO MARI

VIALE P. BATONI

BALUARDO SAN MARTINO

Piazzale Martiri della Libertà

BALUARDO CESARE BATTISTI

PASSEGGIATA DELLE MURA URBANE

VIALE GUGLIELMO MARCONI

Piazza Maria del Borgo

VIA MICHELE ROSI

VIA DEL FOSSO

VIA D. CAVALLERIZZA

San Frediano

Piazza S. Frediano

VIA FILLUNGO

VIA SANTA GEMMA GALGANI

VIA DELLA ZECCA

VIA BUSDRAGHI

San Pietro Somaldi

Roman Amphitheatre

Piazza S. Pietro Somaldi

San Francesco

Piazza S. Francesco

VIA DELLA QUARQUONIA

BALUARDO SAN SALVATORE

VIA DELL'ANFITEATRO

VIA ANTONIO MORDINI

VIA D. FRATTA

Santa Maria dello Stellario

Museo Nazionale Guinigi

to Florence, Montecatini Terme

VIA DI CHIAVI D'ORO

VIA GUINIGI

Piazza del Carmine

VIA SANT' ANDREA

Villa Bottini Gardens

VIA BRUNERO PAOLI

VIA SAN NICOLAO

VIA DEL FOSSO

VIA SANTA CHIARA

VIA FILLUNGO

i

VIA FATINELLI

Torre delle Ore

Torre Guinigi

VIA DELL'ANGELO CUSTODE

San Cristoforo

Porta San Gervasio

VIA ELISA

Piazzale Don Aldo Mei

VIA SANTA CROCE

Piazza Bernardini

Piazza dei Servi

Santa Maria Forisportam

Santa Trinità

BALUARDO CAIROLI

VIALE G. PACINI

VIA DEL BATTISTERO

VIA A. VALLISNERI

Piazza Santa Maria Forisportam

San Giovanni

Piazza Antelminelli

VIA DELLA ROSA

VIA DEL GIARDINO

VIA SAN NICOLAO

BOTANICO

Giardino Botanico

VIA DEL DUOMO

Piazza San Martino

Duomo

Santa Maria della Rosa

PASSEGGIATA DELLE MURA URBANE

BALUARDO SAN REGOLO

P

BALUARDO SAN COLOMBANO

VIALE GIUSEPPE GIUSTI

VIALE REGINA MARGHERITA

Piazzale Ricasoli

Train Station

P

281

Nowhere in Lucca
will you see the face of a Philistine.

Travels in Lucca, Heine

Of all Tuscany's great cities, Lucca (pop. 92,500) is the most cosy, sane and domestic, a tidy gem of a town encased within its famous walls. Yet even these hardly seem formidable, more like garden walls than something that would keep the Florentines at bay. The old ramparts and surrounding areas, once the outworks of the fortifications, are now full of lawns and trees, forming a miniature green belt; on the walls, where the little city's soldiers once patrolled, now the citizens ride their bicycles and walk their dogs, and often stop to admire the view.

Like paradise, Lucca is entered by way of St Peter's Gate. Once inside you'll find tidy, well-preserved Romanesque churches and medieval towers that destroyed Ruskin's romantic notion that a medieval building had to be half ruined to be beautiful, a revelation that initiated his study of architecture. Nor do Lucca's numerous Liberty-style shop signs show any sign of rust; even the mandatory, peeling ochre paint and green shutters of the houses seem part of some great municipal housekeeping plan. Bicycles have largely replaced cars within the walls. At first glance it seems too bijou, a good burgher's daydream. But after its long and brave history it has certainly earned the right to a little quiet. The annual hordes of Tuscan tourists leave Lucca alone for the most part, though there seems to be a small number of discreet visitors, many of them German and Swedish, who come back every year. They don't spread the word, apparently trying to keep one of Italy's most beautiful cities to themselves.

History

Lucca's rigid grid of streets betrays its Roman origins; it was founded as a colony in 180 BC as *Luca*, and in 56 BC entered the annals of history when Caesar, Pompey and Crassus met here to form the ill-fated First Triumvirate. It was converted to Christianity early on by St Peter's disciple Paulinus, who became first bishop of Lucca. The city did especially well in the Dark Ages; in late Roman times it was the administrative capital of Tuscany, and under the Goths managed to repulse the murderous Lombards; its extensive archives were begun in the 8th century, and many of its churches were founded shortly after. By the 11th and 12th centuries Lucca emerged as one of the leading trading towns of Tuscany, specializing in the production of silk, sold by colonies of merchants in the East and West, who earned enough to make sizeable loans to Mediterranean potentates. A Lucchese school of painting developed, such as it is, and beautiful Romanesque churches were erected, influenced by nearby Pisa. Ghibellines and Guelphs, and then Black and White Guelphs made nuisances of themselves as they did everywhere else, and Lucca often found itself pressed to maintain its independence from Pisa and Florence.

In 1314, at the height of the city's wealth and power, the Pisans and Ghibellines finally managed to seize Lucca. But Lucca had a trump card up a secret sleeve: a remarkable adventurer named Castruccio Castracani. Castracani, an ambitious noble who for years had lived in exile—part of it in England—heard the bad news and at once set forth to rescue his hometown. Within a year he had chased the Pisans out and seized power for himself, leading Lucca into its most heroic age, capturing most of Western Tuscany to form a little Luccan empire, subjugating even big fish like Pisa and Pistoia. After routing the Florentines at Altopascio in 1325, Castracani was planning to snatch Florence too, but died of malaria just before the siege was to begin—another example of Florence's famous good luck. Internal bickering between the powerful families soon put an end to Lucca's glory days, though in 1369 the city managed to convince Emperor Charles IV to grant it independence as a republic, albeit a republic ruled by oligarchs like Paolo Guinigi, the sole big boss between 1400 and 1430.

But Lucca continued somehow to escape being gobbled up by its voracious neighbours, functioning with enough tact and tenacity to survive even after the arrival of the Spaniards—a fact one can attribute not so much to its great walls as to its relative insignificance. Amazingly enough, after the Treaty of Câteau-Cambrésis, Lucca found itself standing together with Venice as the only truly independent states in Italy. And like Venice, the city was an island of relative tolerance and enlightenment during the Counter-Reformation, its garden walls in this case proving stout enough to deflect the viperous Inquisition. In 1805 Lucca's independence ended when Napoleon gave the republic to his sister Elisa Baciocchi, who ruled as its princess; it was given later to Marie Louise, Napoleon's widow, who governed well enough to become Lucca's favourite ruler and earn a statue in the main Piazza Napoleone. Her son sold it to Leopold II of Tuscany in 1847, just in time for it to join the Kingdom of Italy.

Getting Around

The railway station is just south of the walls on Piazza Ricasoli, with lots of trains on the Viareggio-Pisa-Florence line, © 47 013. Buses leave from Piazzale Verdi, just inside the walls on the western end: LAZZI buses to Florence, Pistoia, Pisa, Prato, Abetone, Bagni di Lucca, Montecatini and Viareggio, © 584 876, and CLAP (that's right, CLAP) buses to towns in Lucca province, including Collodi, Marlia, and Segromigno, and the Serchio valley, © 587 897. Get around Lucca itself like a Lucchese by hiring a bicycle from the tourist office in Piazzale Verdi or from **Barbetti** Via Anfiteatro 23, © 954 444.

Tourist Information

Vecchia Porta San Donato, Piazzale Verdi, © (0583) 419 689, and Piazza Guidiccioni 2, © (0583) 491 205.

Lunch/Cafés

Gelateria Veneta, Via Veneto 7 and Chaisso Barletti 23. The best ice cream in Lucca, this family-run establishment has over 150 years of experience and they use only fresh ingredients without any additives (closed Tues).

Antico Caffè della Mura, Piazzale Vittorio Emanuele 2, © 47 962. This café/restaurant is the only place situated right on the town walls. There are tables outdoors and a bar open until 1am in the summer (closed Tues, around L50–60,000).

Bar Torrefazione Triestina, Via Buia 36. Good classic coffee bar (closed Sun).

The two best take-away pizzerias are **La Sbragia** in Via Fillungo, so popular that it has a ticket number system, or else **Da Felice** round the corner in Via Buia.

Highlights of Lucca

Although Lucca has two museums of paintings, its finest art, sculpture and architecture are concentrated in the **Cathedral**, **San Michele in Foro** and **San Frediano**. Don't miss atmospheric **Piazza dell'Anfiteatro**, a climb up to the top of the **Torre Guinigi** and a stroll down delightful **Via del Fosso**, the main street, **Via Fillungo** and up to the **Walls**.

Start: *Porta San Pietro*
Finish: *Baluardo San Paolino*
Walking time: *one day*

Lucca Walk

The charming little universe of Lucca that time has mostly forgotten and the decades could never improve is made on a scale for pedestrians; it doesn't even have the hills that can make Siena a sweat in the summer. Few cars penetrate its *cordon sanitaire* of walls—you're more likely to be knocked over by a bicycle. Lucca is to be savoured; make this walk a whole day. A stroll around the walls themselves makes a delicious second helping.

*Lucca's lovely bastions evoke images of the walled rose gardens of chivalric romance, enclosing a smaller, more perfect cosmos. They owe their considerable charm to Renaissance advances in military technology. Prompted by the beginning of the Wars of Italy, Lucca began to construct the **walls** in 1500.*

The councillors wanted up-to-date fortifications to counter new advances in artillery, and their (unknown) architects gave them the state of the art, a model for the new style of fortification that would soon be transforming the cities of Europe. Being Renaissance Tuscans, the architects also gave them a little more elegance than was strictly necessary. The walls were never severely tested.

Today, with the outer ravelins, fosses and salients cleared away (such earthworks usually took up as much space as the city itself), Lucca's walls are just for decoration; under the peace-loving Duchess Marie Louise they were planted with a double row of plane trees to create a splendid elevated garden boulevard that extends around the city for nearly 4km, offering a continuous bird's-eye view over Lucca. They are among the best preserved in Italy. Of the gates, the most elaborate and flowery is the **Porta San Pietro** (1566) near the station, its portcullis still intact, with Lucca's proud motto of independence, LIBERTAS, inscribed over the top.

Just inside the gate, turn left at Via di Porta San Pietro, and then right at Via Francesco Carrara for Piazza Napoleone and Piazza Giglio.

These shady twin squares are Lucca's civic centre and the focus of its evening *passeggiata*. The yellow hodgepodge of a palace in Piazza Napoleone, formerly the seat of the lords of Lucca and the republican council, has been known as the **Palazzo Ducale** ever since it was used by Lucca's queens for a day, Elisa Bonaparte and Duchess Maria Louisa; now it contains local government offices. The most important architect to have a crack at it was Ammannati in the 16th century, and signs of his Mannerist handiwork survive in the courtyard.

*From Piazza del Giglio, Via del Duomo leads past the church of **San Giovanni**.*

The pious Lucchesi once required 70 churches to minister to their spiritual needs. Fewer are necessary today, and even fewer stay open during the day, but their fine medieval façades constitute some of Lucca's chief ornaments. One of these is San Giovanni, Lucca's first cathedral with an 1187 portal and lions on its capitals. It has recently been reopened, along with its 14th-century baptistry and excavations of constructions dating back to Roman times, including an immersion font.

*Facing San Giovanni are another pair of squares, Piazzas San Martino and Antelminelli; the former sees an **Antiques Market** every third*

> Saturday and Sunday of each month, watched over by Lucca's **Cathe-dral of San Martino**, begun by Pope Alexander II in 1070 and not completed until the 15th century.

This is perhaps the most outstanding work of the Pisan style outside Pisa, begun in the 11th century and completed only in the 15th. Above the singular **porch**, with three different sized arches, are stacked three levels of colonnades, with pillars arranged like candy sticks, while behind and on the arches are exquisite 12th- and 13th-century reliefs and sculpture—the best work Lucca has to offer. See especially the *Adoration of the Magi* by Nicola Pisano, the column carved with the Tree of Life, with Adam and Eve crouched at the bottom and Christ on top, and a host of fantastical animals and hunting scenes, the Months and their occupations, dancing dragons and a man embracing a bear, the circular Labyrinth of Theseus on one of the columns, even *Roland at Roncevalles*, all by unknown masters. Walk round the back, where the splendidly ornate apse and transepts are set off by the green lawn. The **Campanile**, crenellated like a battle tower, dates from 1060 and 1261.

> The dark **interior** offers an excellent introduction to the works of Lucca's one and only great artist, **Matteo Civitali** *(1435–1501)*, who worked as a barber until his mid-30s, when he decided he'd much rather be a sculptor. He deserves to be better known— but may never be since everything he made is still in Lucca.

His most famous work is the octagonal **Tempietto** (1484), a marble tabernacle in the middle of the left aisle, containing Lucca's most precious holy relic, the world-weary *Volto Santo* ('Holy Image'), a cedar-wood crucifix said to be a true portrait of Jesus, sculpted by Nicodemus, an eyewitness to the crucifixion. Saved from the iconoclasts, it was set adrift in an empty boat and floated to Luni, where the bishop was instructed by an angel to place it in a cart drawn by two white oxen, and where the oxen should halt, there too should the image remain. They made a lumbering beeline for Lucca, where the *Volto Santo* has remained ever since. Its likeness appeared on the republic's coins, and there was a devoted cult of the image in medieval England; Lucca's merchant colony in London cared for a replica of the *Volto Santo* in old St Thomas's, and according to William of Malmesbury, King William Rufus always swore by it, '*per sanctum vultum de Lucca*'. Long an object of pilgrimage, the image goes out for a night on the town in a candlelight procession each 13 September.

Further up the left aisle a chapel contains Fra Bartolomeo's *Virgin and Child Enthroned*, and in the transept, the remarkable **Tomb of Ilaria del Carretto** (*c.* 1406), the first known and one of the most beautiful works of Sienese sculptor Jacopo della Quercia, decorated with typical Renaissance doodahs like *putti* and swags, but topped with a transcendently graceful, tender and tranquil effigy of the young bride of boss Paolo Guinigi, complete with the family dog, waiting for his mistress to awaken. Here, too, is an altar by Giambologna, of *Christ with Saints Peter and Paul*. Civitali carved the cathedral's high altar, and also two expressive tombs in the south transept. A door from the right aisle leads to the sacristy, with a good *Madonna Enthroned with Saints* by Domenico Ghirlandaio; a side altar near here has a typically strange composition from the Venetian Tintoretto, a *Last Supper* with a nursing mother in the foreground and cherubs floating around Christ. In the centre, unfortunately often covered up, is a particularly fine section of the inlaid marble floor; on the entrance wall, a 13th-century sculpture of St Martin has been brought in from the façade.

> An **Antiques Market** takes place in the cathedral's Piazza di San Martino the third Saturday and Sunday of each month. Next to the cathedral is the newly opened **Museo della Cattedrale** (open 10–6 daily exc Mon; winter 10–1, 3–6, closed Mon).

This displays more of the cathedral's treasures, including the ornaments (the crown and garments) of the **Volto Santo**, della Quercia's *St John the Baptist* and tapestries and paintings from San Giovanni.

> Walk along the flank and behind the Duomo towards the walls, then turn left up Via della Rosa, passing the sweet little oratory of **Santa Maria della Rosa**, built in 1309 in the Pisan Gothic style. Via della Rosa follows the outer line of the old Roman enceinte (if Santa Maria della Rosa breaks its rule of always being closed, you can see parts of the ancient wall inside). In the early 12th century, when the first church was built outside the gates it took the name **Santa Maria Forisportam** ('outside the gates'); it's just ahead, to your right, set in a charming square with a column, once used as a turning post in Lucca's medieval palio.

A pretty church with blind arcades in the Pisan style, it was Santa Maria Forisportam that converted Ruskin (and through Ruskin, millions of others) to medieval architecture: 'Here in Lucca I found myself suddenly in the presence of twelfth-century buildings, originally set in such balance of masonry that they could all stand without mortar; and in material so incorruptible, that after six hundred years of sunshine and rain, a lancet could not now be put between their joins. Absolutely for the first time I now saw what medieval builders were and what they meant. I took the simplest of façades for analysis, that of Santa Maria Foris-Portam, and thereon literally *began* the study of architecture.' Inside, it not only looks old but smells terribly old: the font is made from a Palaeo-Christian sarcophagus and there are two paintings by Guercino, by the fourth altar on the right and in the left transept; near the latter is a remarkable 14-century painting on wood on the *Dormition and Assumption of the Virgin*.

*From Piazza Santa Maria Forisportam, turn right in Via Santa Croce, where **Porta San Gervasio** is the best preserved gate from Lucca's second set of walls, built in 1260; it gives onto the former moat, now a picturesque little canal running alongside Via del Fosso. Just over this, beyond the gate, is **Santa Trinità**, home of Civitali's **Madonna della Tosse** (Our Lady of the Cough), a bit too syrupy sweet, but perhaps that helped the cure (if closed, ask for the key in the convent next door). If you need to have a break at this point, continue briefly along Via Elisa; the next lane to the right after Santa Trinità will take you into the **Botanical Gardens**, and a left into the gardens of the **Villa Bottini** (open 9–1.30), the only two oases of green inside the city walls.*

*Otherwise, backtrack a few paces and turn right (north) up Via del Fosso, with its fine perspective of the 17th-century column of **Santa Maria dello Stellario**. At the column turn right in Via della Quarquonia, where a long piazza opens up on your left, named after its 13th-century church, **San Francesco**.*

Adorned with a marble font and rose window, San Francesco is a typical church of the preaching order, with the tombs of Castruccio Castricani (d. 1328) and the Lucchese composer of the famous minuet, Luigi Boccherini (1743–1805). To the right of the high altar are fine, detached 15th-century frescoes of the Florentine school. There are more frescoes in the cloister, and a good 13th-century tomb.

*From San Francesco, continue down Via Quarquonia for the palatial brick Villa Guinigi, built in 1418 by the big boss Paolo Guinigi in his glory days. It now houses the **Museo Nazionale Guinigi** (open 9–2, closed Mon; adm).*

Its ground floor houses an interesting collection of Romanesque reliefs, capitals and transennas, some of which are charmingly primitive—St Michael slaying the dragon, Samson killing the lion, a 9th-century transenna with birds and beasts, spirals and daggers. **Room IV** has a lovely *Annunciation* by Civitali, and beyond, a set of neoclassical reliefs from the Palazzo Ducale of the *Triumphs of Duchess Maria Luisa*. The painting gallery upstairs contains intarsia panels from the cathedral, each with scenes of Lucca as seen from town windows, some trecento works by the Lucca school and a charming quattrocento *Madonna and Child* by the 'Maestro della Vita di Maria'. Other rooms contain a miasma of oversize 16th-century canvases, some by Vasari.

*Backtrack down Via della Quarquonia and Via D. Fratta to **San Pietro Somaldi**, a 12th-century church with a grey and white striped façade; the relief over the door is by Guido da Como and dated 1203. From here turn south briefly down the street of the Guardian Angel (Via dell'Angelo*

Custode) to Via Guinigi, into a neighbourhood of Lucca that has scarcely changed in the past 500 years, Here the medieval ancestors of the Guinigi had their stronghold in a block of 14th-century houses and the **Torre Guinigi** *(open 9–7.30 April–Sept; 10–4.30 Oct–Mar, adm).*

This is one of Lucca's landmarks; like the walls, it has trees sprouting out of the top—the best example of this quaint Italian fancy that you'll see here and there throughout the country. One of the most elaborate of medieval family fortresses, the tower has recently been restored, and it's worth the slight risk of cardiac arrest to climb the 230 steps for the view over the city and the marbly Apuan Alps.

From the tower, follow Via Sant'Andrea to Via di Chiavi d'Oro (golden key street). This leads directly to Via dell'Anfiteatro and into the most remarkable relic of Roman Luca, the **Piazza dell'Anfiteatro**—*the Roman amphitheatre.*

Like a fossil, only outlines of its arches are still traceable in the outer walls, while within the inner ring only the form remains—the marble was probably carted off to build San Michele and the cathedral—but Lucca is a city that changes so gradually and organically that the outline has been perfectly preserved. The foundations of the grandstands now support a perfect ellipse of medieval houses. Duchess Marie Louise cleared out the old buildings in the former arena, and now, where gladiators once slugged it out, there is a wonderfully atmospheric piazza, where the boys play football and the less active sit musing in sleepy cafés.

Walk directly across the amphitheatre for Piazza San Frediano and the tall church and even taller campanile of **San Frediano***, built in the early 1100s and shimmering with the colours of the large 13th-century mosaic on its upper façade, showing Christ and the Apostles in an elegant flowing style, often attributed to Berlinghiero Berlinghieri.*

The 11th-century bronze Arabian falcon at the top is a copy—the original is so valuable that it's locked away. The palatial **interior** houses Tuscany's most remarkable baptismal font, the 12th-century *Fontana lustrale*, covered with reliefs; behind is an equally beautiful terracotta lunette of the *Annunciation* by Andrea della Robbia. The chapels are richly decorated—the fourth on the left has an altarpiece in the form of a Gothic polyptych by Jacopo della Quercia, who also sculpted the two tombstones. Near the altar is a chapel frescoed by Amico Aspertini in 1508 (*currently under restoration*).

The bedecked mummy is of St Zita, patroness of domestic servants; born in 1218, she entered the service of a family in Lucca at the age of 12 and remained with them until her death. She would not only give her clothes and food to the poor, but that of her masters, which at first caused her to be maltreated. Ever since her canonization in 1696 she has been greatly venerated, not only in Italy, but in England, where maids belong to the Guild of St Zita. The Lucchesi are very fond of her, and on 26 April they bring her uncorrupted body out to caress.

> Follow the church along to Via Cesare Battista and turn left in Via degli Asili for the **Palazzo Pfanner**.

An 18th-century palace with a delicious, statue-filled garden (for a look into it and at San Frediano's handsome apse, climb up the city wall beyond), it has a famous grand stairway of white marble, and is used to display a collection of silks made in Lucca, and 17th–19th-century costumes (*closed for works at the time of writing*). Just behind Palazzo Pfanner is **Sant'Agostino** (1300s), with a campanile sitting on the ruins of the Roman theatre.

> South of Sant'Agostino, turn left in Via San Giorgio, and right in **Via del Moro**, lined with medieval houses. Turn left again in Via Buia, and right in Lucca's main street, medieval **Via Fillungo**.

Via Fillungo and its surrounding lanes make up the busy shopping district, a tidy nest of straight and narrow alleys where the contented cheerfulness that distinguishes Lucca from many of its neighbours seems somehow magnified. A number of shopfronts have remained unchanged for over a century—one of the most charming is the jeweller's at no. 104. Even older are the loggias of the 14th-century palaces, now bricked in, and the ancient **Torre dell' Ore**, which since 1471 has striven to keep the Lucchesi on time, and perhaps now suggests that it's time for a coffee in Lucca's historic **Caffè di Simo** at no. 58. There's of course a church to be seen, 13th-century **San Cristoforo**, now used for exhibitions. It is also Lucca's war memorial, with the names of the dead all along the walls. Opposite in Via Roma a plaque marks **Boccherini's house**.

> Where Via Fillungo becomes Via Cenami, turn right in Via Pescheria for the **Palazzo Pretorio**, built in 1492 by Matteo Civitali, whose statue stands in the portico. Beyond the palazzo turn right in Via Vittorio Emanuele for handsome Piazza San Michele, Lucca's Roman forum and site of **San Michele in Foro**, a masterpiece of Pisan Gothic and a church so grand that many people mistake it for the cathedral.

The ambitious façade rises high above the level of the roof, to make the building look even grander (the Italians call the style 'wind-breaker'). Every column in the five levels of Pisan arcading is different: some doubled, some twisted like corkscrews, inlaid with mosaic Cosmati work or carved with monsters, while in between are friezes richly carved with animals. The whole is crowned by a giant statue of the Archangel, and on the corner of the façade is a *Madonna* by Civitali, paid for by the city in gratitude for deliverance from a plague in 1480; the graceful, rectangular campanile is Lucca's tallest and loveliest.

The interior is more austere, but there's a glazed terracotta *Madonna and Child* attributed to Luca della Robbia, a striking 13th-century *Crucifixion* hanging over the high altar, and a painting of plague saints by Filippino Lippi. Giacomo Puccini began his musical career here as a choirboy (his father and grandfather had been organists in the cathedral).

> *Young Puccini didn't have far to walk; he lived in narrow Via di Poggio 30, just opposite San Michele's façade. His house is now a little **Puccini Museum** (entrance in Corte San Lorenzo 9, open summer 10–1 and 3–6; winter 11–1 and 2–4, closed Mon).*

The museum has a few odds and ends left by Puccini (1858–1924), including manuscripts, letters, mementoes, his overcoat and other bits and pieces, as well as his piano. Once his operas had made him famous, he bought a villa at Torre del Lago, just south of Viareggio, where he said, 'I can practise my second favourite instrument, my rifle' on the coots and ducks in Lake Massaciuccoli; he was famous for terrorizing the local peasants by tearing around like a demon in his motorcar. His villa is also a museum, rather more extensive than the one here, and the maestro is buried in the adjacent chapel—he died just after having run through his last opera, *Turandot,* with Toscanini. In August, Torre del Lago hosts an opera festival in Puccini's honour.

> *At the end of Via di Poggio, turn left in Piazza del Palazzo Dipinto for Via San Paolino (the Roman decumanus major, or main east-west street) and the church of **San Paolino** (1539) where little Puccini played the organ to earn his pin-money.*

Dedicated to the native of Antioch who converted Lucca and made it the first Christian city of Tuscany around the year 65, San Paolino contains two beautiful works: a 13th-century French *Virgin and Child* carved in stone brought back by Lucchese silk merchants from Paris, and an anonymous quattrocento Florentine *Coronation of the Virgin*, with Mary hovering over a city of pink towers; she is crowned by God the Father instead of Christ, who usually does the honours.

> *Walk past the church and turn right in Via Galli Tassi. A few steps off Via Galli Tassi stands the 17th-century Palazzo Mansi, home of the Pinacoteca Nazionale (open 9–2, closed Mon, adm).*

Most of the art, as well as the rich furnishings in several of the rooms, dates from the 17th century; the few paintings which might be interesting, portraits by Pontormo and Bronzino, are all indefinitely at the restorer's. In the study hangs a dark and damaged Veronese, and Tintoretto's *Miracle of St Mark Freeing the Slave*, showing, with typical Tintorettian flamboyance, Venice's patron saint dive-bombing from heaven to save the day. The 1600s frescoes are more fun than the paintings, especially the *Judgement of Paris*, which Venus wins by showing a little leg. And one can't help but wonder what Rococo dreams tickled the fancy of the sleeping occupants of the amazing bedroom.

> From the picture gallery, turn left down Via Galli Tassi towards the big state tobacco company, which perfumes the whole quarter with a fine aroma that disguises the fact that it produces Toscanelli cigars, one of the world's vilest smokes. Turn left in Via dei Tabacchi for **San Romano**, a rarely-opened Dominican church that preserves the Tomb of San Romano (1490), one of Civitali's finest works.

> Turn right in Vicolo San Romano, and right at Via Guiseppe Garibaldi, where you can climb up to the city walls and to **Baluardo San Paolino**.

And so this walk through Lucca ends where it begins, at the walls—where another walk can easily begin. Baluardo San Paolino is the site of the headquarters of the 'International Institute for the Study of City Walls' (CISCU), © 46 257 which will get you in for a tour of the bastion's interior (*open 10–12.30 and 3.30–6*).

Excursions from Lucca

Villas around Lucca

In 16th-century Lucca, as elsewhere in Italy, trade began to flounder, and once-plucky, daring merchants, or at least those sufficiently well-upholstered, turned to the more certain joys of real estate, where they could genteelly decline in a little country palace and garden. For the Lucchesi, the favourite area to construct such pleasure domes was in the soft, rolling countryside to the north and northeast of the city. Three of these villas or their grounds are open for visits. In Segromigno, 10km from Lucca in the direction of Pescia, there's the charming, mid-16th-century but often modified **Villa Mansi**, embellished with a lovely half-Italian (i.e. geometric) and half-English (i.e. not geometric) garden laid out by the great Sicilian architect Juvarra (*open 10–12.30 and 2.30–5, in summer 3.30–8; adm*). Nearby in Camigliano, the even more elaborate **Villa Torrigiani**, also begun in the 16th century, was long celebrated for its fabulous parties and entertainments. Set in a lush park of pools and trees, it is furnished with 16th–18th-century furnishings (*villa open 9.30–11 and 2.30–5 April–Oct; 3–7.30 winter; park open same hours all year; adm exp*). Elisa Bonaparte Baciocchi combined a villa and a summer palace to make her country retreat, now called the **Villa Pecci-Blunt ex-Villa Reale** in Marlia. Only the park and the Giardino Orsetti are open, but they are lovely, and used as the site of Lucca's **summer music festival**, which not surprisingly features more than a pinch of Puccini (*guided tours by appointment, © 30 108, Oct–June 10, 11, 3, 4, 5 and 6 daily exc Mon; in July, Aug and Sept 10, 11, 4, 5 and 6 Tues–Thurs and Sun; adm*).

The Lucchese Plain

East and west of Lucca, what was swampland in the Middle Ages has been reclaimed to form a rich agricultural plain. One of its features are its 'courts'—farm hamlets not constructed around a central piazza, but with houses in neat rows. At one time there were 1100 such 'courts' on the plain. Among the highlights of the area is curious **Castello di Nozzano** just to the west, built by Matilda of Tuscany on a hill, its pretty tower now incongruously topped by a large clock. To the east, one of the first villages, **Capannori**, is the head town of several 'courts' and has a couple of interesting Romanesque churches, especially the 13th-century **Pieve San Paolo**, around which a small village incorporated itself, using the campanile for defence. The most imposing monument near Capannori is the 19th-century **Acquedotto del Nottolini**, which is also visible from the autostrada. Just south is the pretty hilltop village of **Castelvecchio**, its tall houses forming an effective circular wall. **Altopàscio**, on the Lucca–Empoli road, was built around an 11th-century hospice run by an obscure chivalric order called the Hospitaller Knights of the Order of Altopàscio, who originally occupied themselves with rescuing travellers from the swamps. Only the campanile of their church remains in the village today. **Montecarlo** gives its name to a very good dry white wine produced in the immediate area.

Further east of Lucca you can take the waters at **Montecatini Terme** (LAZZI buses), one of Italy's biggest and most elegant spas; or to the north, visit the charming, older spa of **Bagni di Lucca** on the Serchio river, popular in the early 19th century. CLAP buses go to **Collodi**, where there's a Pinocchio park for the kids and the magnificent 17th-century Castello Garzoni with its superb Italian gardens for the adults; **Barga**, further north, is a hilltown overlooking the marble mountains of Carrara, with a great cathedral begun in the year 1000. Lucca is also convenient for **Viareggio**, Puccini's **Torre del Lago**, and the coastal resorts (LAZZI buses).

Food and Drink

In Italy, the three Ms (the Madonna, Mamma and *Mangiare*) are still a force to be reckoned with, and in a country where millions of otherwise sane people spend much of their waking hours worrying about their digestion, standards both at home and in the restaurants are understandably high. Everybody is a gourmet, or at least they think they are, and food is not only something to eat, but a subject approaching the heights of philosophy—two Umbrian businessmen were once overheard on a train heatedly discussing mushrooms for over four hours. Although ready-made pasta, tinned minestrone and frozen pizza in the *supermercato* tempt the virtue of the Italian cook, few give in (although many a working mother wishes she could at times).

Regional traditions are strong in Italy, not only in dialect but in the kitchen. Tuscany is no exception and firmly maintains its distinctive cuisine, although it does not rank among the great culinary regions of Italy; it offers good, honest, traditional dishes, often humble, rarely elaborate. The Medici may have put on some magnificent feeds, but the modern Tuscan is known by his fellow Italians as a *mangiafagioli*, or bean-eater. Some observers hold it as part of the austere Tuscan character, others as another sign of their famous alleged miserliness.

The truth is that, although beans and tripe often appear on the menu, most people when dining out want to try something different, from other regions, perhaps, or the recent concoctions of Italian *nouvelle cuisine*, or *cucina nuova*, or perhaps a recipe from the Middle Ages or Renaissance. Some of the country's finest restaurants are in Tuscany; and, in practice, the diversity of dishes, from traditional to bizarre, is almost endless. First, though, a few general comments on eating out.

Eating Out

In Italy the various types of restaurants—*ristorante, trattoria* or *osteria*—have been confused. A *trattoria* or *osteria* can be just as elaborate as a restaurant, though rarely is a *ristorante* as informal as a traditional *trattoria*. Unfortunately the old habit of posting menus and prices in the windows has fallen from fashion, so it's often difficult to judge variety or prices. Invariably the least expensive restaurant-type place is the increasingly rare *vino e cucina*, a simple place serving simple cuisine for simple everyday prices. It is essential to remember that the fancier the fittings, the fancier the bill, though neither of these points has anything at all to do with the quality of the food. If you're uncertain, do as you would at home—look for lots of locals.

Prices

When you eat out, mentally add to the bill (*conto*) the bread and cover charge (*pane e coperto*, between L1500–3000) and a 10 per cent service charge. This is often included in the bill (*servizio compreso*); if not, it will say *servizio non compreso*, and you'll have to do your own arithmetic. Additional tipping is at your discretion, but never do it in family-owned and -run places. Prices quoted for meals in this book are for an average complete meal Italian-style, with wine, for one person. We have divided restaurants into the following price categories.

very expensive	over L80,000
expensive	L50,000—80,000
moderate	L30,000—50,000
inexpensive	below L30,000

People who haven't visited Italy for years and have fond memories of eating full meals for under a pound will be amazed at how much prices have risen; though in some respects eating out in Italy is still a bargain, especially when you figure out how much all that wine would have cost you at home. In many places you'll often find restaurants offering a *menu turistico*—full, set meals of usually meagre inspiration for L20–25,000. Good, imaginative chefs often offer a *menu degustazione*—a set-price gourmet meal that allows you to taste their daily specialities and seasonal dishes. Both of these are cheaper than if you had ordered the same food à la carte. When you leave a restaurant you will be given a receipt (*ricevuto fiscale*) which according to Italian law you must take with you out of the door and carry for at least 300m. If you aren't given one, it means the restaurant is probably fudging on its taxes and thus offering you lower prices. There is a slim chance the tax police may have their eye on you and the restaurant, and if you don't have a receipt they could slap you with a heavy fine.

Eating on the Hoof

There are several alternatives to sit-down meals. The 'hot table' (*tavola calda*) is a buffet which sells hot and cold foods, where you can choose a simple prepared dish or a whole meal, depending on your appetite. The food in these can be truly impressive, though many offer only a few hot dishes, pizza and sandwiches. Little shops that sell pizza by the slice are common in city centres; some, called *gastronomie*, offer other take-out delicacies as well. At any delicatessen (*pizzicheria*), or grocer's (*alimentari*) or market (*mercato*) you can buy the materials for picnics. For really elegant picnics, have a *tavola calda* pack up something nice for you. And if everywhere else is closed, there are always the railway station bars—these will at least have sandwiches and drinks, and perhaps some surprisingly good snacks you've never heard of before. Common snacks you'll encounter include *panini* of prosciutto, cheese and tomatoes, or other meats; *tramezzini*, little sandwiches on plain, square white bread that are always much better than they look; pizza, of course, or the traditional sandwich of Tuscany, a hard roll filled with warm *porchetta* (roast whole pig stuffed with fennel and garlic).

The Meals

Breakfast (*prima colazione*) in Italy is no lingering affair, but an early morning wake-up shot to the brain: a *cappuccino*, a *caffè latte* (white coffee), or a *caffè lungo* (a generous portion of espresso), accompanied by a croissant-type roll, called a *cornetto* or *briosce*. This can be consumed in nearly any bar, and repeated during the morning as often as necessary, which is why breakfast in most Italian hotels is no big deal and seldom worth the price charged.

Lunch or *pranzo*, generally served around 1pm, is the most important meal of the day for the Italians, with a minimum of a first course (*primo*—any kind of pasta dish, broth or soup, or rice dish or pizza), a second course (*secondo*—a meat or fish dish, accompanied by a *contorno* or side dish—a vegetable, salad or potatoes usually), followed by fruit or dessert and coffee. You can, however, begin with a platter of *antipasti*—the appetizers Italians do so brilliantly, ranging from warm seafood delicacies, to raw ham (*prosciutto crudo*), salami in a hundred varieties, lovely vegetables, savoury toasts, olives, pâté, and many, many more. There are restaurants that specialize in *antipasti*, and they usually don't take it amiss if you decide to forget the pasta and meat and just nibble on these scrumptious *hors d'oeuvres* (though in the end it will probably cost as much as a full meal). Most Italians accompany their meal with wine and mineral water (*acqua minerale*, with or without bubbles, *con* or *senza gas*, which supposedly aids digestion), concluding their meals with a *digestivo* (liqueur).

The evening meal, *cena, is* usually eaten at around 8pm. This is much the same as *pranzo* although lighter, without the pasta: a pizza and beer, eggs, or a fish dish. In restaurants, however, Italians often order all the courses, so if you have only a sandwich for lunch you can have a full meal in the evening.

Some Regional Specialities

The Tuscans will tell you that the basic simplicity of their cooking is calculated to bring out the glories of their wine, which may well be true, as it tends to be the perfect complement to a glass of Chianti or Vino Nobile. Nearly all their specialities are born of thrift, like *bruschetta*, a Tuscan and Umbrian favourite that takes sliced stale bread, roasted over the fire, covered with olive oil and rubbed with garlic. *Acqua cotta*, popular in southern Tuscany, is *bruschetta* with an egg; another version adds mashed tomatoes. The other traditional Tusco-Umbrian *antipasto* is *crostini*, thin slices of toast with a piquant pâté spread of chicken livers, anchovies, capers and lemons, or other variations.

For *primo*, the traditional Tuscan relies mostly on soups. Perhaps most traditional is *ribollita* ('reboiled'), a hearty mushy vegetable soup with beans, cabbage, carrots and chunks of boiled bread. Another is *pappa col pomodoro*, which is basically *ribollita* with fresh tomatoes. *Panzanella*, or Tuscan *gazpacho* (a cold soup of tomatoes, cucumbers, onions, basil, olive oil and bread) can be a godsend on a hot summer's day. Other first courses you'll find are *fagioli al fiasco* (beans with oil and black pepper simmered in an earthenware pot) or *fagioli all'uccelletto* (beans with garlic and tomatoes). The most Tuscan of pasta dishes is *pappardelle alla lepre* (wide noodles with a sauce of stewed hare); others are the simple but delicious *spaghetti con briciolata* (with olive oil, breadcrumbs and parsley); *nastri alla Borracina* (ribbons of pasta served with a 'moss' of freshly chopped spinach and marjoram, basil, rosemary, mint and sage); and, most splendid of all, *turtui cu la cua* (*tortellini* with tails), filled with mascarpone, ricotta and spinach, with a butter and basil sauce.

Tuscany does not offer exceptional *secondi*. There is the famous steak, *bistecca alla fiorentina* (cooked over coals, charred on the outside and pink in the middle, and seasoned with salt and pepper); otherwise Tuscans are content with grilled chops—lamb, pork or veal. *Fritto misto* is an interesting alternative, where lamb chops, liver, sweetbreads, artichokes and courgettes (*zucchini*) are dipped in batter and deep fried. Otherwise, look for *arista di maiale* (pork loin with rosemary and garlic), *francesina* (meat, onion and tomato stew in Vernaccia di San Gimignano wine), *anatra* (duck), *piccione* (stuffed wild pigeon), *cinghiale* (boar), either roasted or in sausages or *stufato* (stewed). Tuscans are rather too fond of their *girarrosto*, a great spit of tiny birds and pork livers. It's fairly easy to find seafood as far inland as Florence—one traditional dish is *seppie in zimino*, or cuttlefish simmered with beets. Hardy souls in Florence can try *cibreo* (cockscombs with chicken livers, beans and egg yolks).

Tuscany's tastiest cheese is tangy *pecorino* made from ewe's milk; the best is made around Pienza. When it's aged it becomes quite sharp and is grated over pasta dishes. Typical desserts, to be washed down with a glass of Vinsanto, include Siena's *panforte* (a rich, spicy dense cake full of nuts and candied fruit), *cenci,* a carnival sweet (deep-fried strips of dough), *castagnaccio* (chestnut cake, with pine nuts, raisins and rosemary), Florentine *zuccotto* (a cake of chocolate, nuts and candied fruits) and *crostate* (fruit tarts).

Tuscan Wines

Quaffing glass after glass of Chianti inspired Elizabeth Barrett Browning to write her best poetry, and the wines of Tuscany may bring out the best in you as well. The first really to celebrate Tuscan wines was a naturalist by the name of Francesco Redi in the 1600s, who, like many of us today, made a wine tour of the region, then composed a dithyrambic eulogy called 'Bacchus in Tuscany'. Modern Bacchuses in Tuscany will find quite a few treats, some famous and some less well known, and plenty of cellars and *enoteche* (wine bars) where you can do your own survey—there's a famous one in Siena with every wine produced in Tuscany, and the rest of Italy as well.

Most Italian wines are named after the grape and the district they come from. If the label says DOC (*Denominazione di Origine Controllata*) it means that the wine comes from a specially defined area and was produced according to a certain traditional method; DOCG (the G stands for *Garantita*) means that a high quality is also guaranteed, a badge worn only by the noblest wines. *Classico* means that a wine comes from the oldest part of the zone of production; *Riserva*, or *Superiore*, means a wine has been aged longer. Most Tuscan farmers also make a cask of *Vinsanto*, a dessert wine that can be sweet or almost dry, and which according to tradition is holy only because priests are so fond of it.

Tuscany produces 19 DOC and DOCG wines, including some of Italy's noblest reds: the dry, ruby red **Brunello di Montalcino** and the garnet **Vino Nobile di Montepulciano**, deep red with the fragrance of violets. Chianti may be drunk young or as a *Riserva*, especially the higher octane Chianti Classico. There are seven other DOC Chianti wines (Montalbano, Rufina, Colli Fiorentini, Colli Senesi, Colli Aretini, Colline Pisa and simple Chianti). Sangiovese is the chief grape of all Chianti as well as all the classified red wines of Tuscany. Lesser known DOC reds include dry, bright red **Rosso delle Colline Lucchesi**, from the hills north of Lucca; hearty **Pomino Rosso**, from a small area east of Rufina in the Mugello; **Carmignano**, a consistently fine ruby red that can take considerable ageing, produced just west of Florence; and **Morellino di Scansano**, from the hills south of Grosseto, a dry red to be drunk young or old. The three other DOC reds from the coast are **Parrina Rosso**, from Parrina which is near Orbetello; **Montescudaio Rosso**; and **Elba Rosso**, a happy island wine, little of which makes it to the mainland. All three have good white versions as well.

Of the Tuscan whites, the most notable is **Vernaccia di San Gimignano** (also a *Riserva*), dry and golden in colour, the perfect complement to seafood; delicious, but more difficult to find, are dry, straw-coloured **Montecarlo** from the hills east of Lucca and **Candia dei Colli Apuani**, a light wine from mountains of marble near Carrara. From the coast comes **Bolgheri**, white or rosé, both fairly dry. Cortona and its valley produce **Bianco Vergine Valdichiana**, a fresh and lively wine; from the hills around Montecatini comes the golden, dry **Bianco della Valdinievole**. **Bianco di Pitigliano**, of a yellow straw colour, is a celebrated accompaniment to lobster.

Eating Out in Florence   *(055–)*

Florence in its loftier moods likes to call itself the 'birthplace of international haute cuisine', a claim that has very much to do with Catherine de' Medici, a renowned trencherwoman, who brought a brigade of Florentine chefs with her to Paris and taught the Frenchies how to eat artichokes, but has little to do with the city's contribution to the Italian kitchen. Florentine food is on the whole extremely simple, with the emphasis on the individual flavours and fresh ingredients. A typical primo could be pappardelle, a type of wide tagliatelle egg-pasta, served usually with a meat sauce, or game such as wild boar, rabbit and duck. Soups are also popular: try the minestrone toscano with a base of cauliflower, borlotti beans and potatoes. The most famous main course in Florence is the bistecca alla fiorentina, a large steak on the bone, two inches thick, cut from loin of beef and cooked on charcoal simply seasoned with salt and pepper. As for the vegetables, you could try piselli alla fiorentina, peas cooked with oil, parsley and diced bacon, or tortino di carciofi, a delicious omelette with fried artichokes. Florentine desserts tend to be sweet and fattening: bomboloni alla crema are vanilla-filled doughnuts and le fritelle di San Giuseppe are bits of deep-fried batter covered in sugar. If you prefer cheese, try the sturdy pecorino toscano. For better or worse, the real Florentine specialities rarely turn up on many restaurant menus, and you'll probably never learn what a Florentine cook can do with cockscombs, calves' feet and tripe.

Like any sophisticated city with lots of visitors, Florence has plenty of fine restaurants; even in the cheaper places standards are high, and if you don't care for anything fancier, there will be lots of good red Chianti to wash down your meal. Please note that many of the best places are likely to close for all of August; you would also be wise to call ahead and reserve, even a day or two in advance.

very expensive

The Bristol, Via dei Pescioni 2, ℂ 287 814. For top-quality cooking and elegant surroundings where you can eat well-prepared Italian food, as well as local specialities.

La Capannina di Sante, Piazza Ravenna, ℂ 688 345. Considered to be the best fish restaurant in town (closed Sun).

Enoteca Pinchiorri, Via Ghibellina 87, near the Casa Buonarroti, ℂ 242 777. One of the finest gourmet restaurants in Italy; the owners inherited the building, a wine shop, some 10 years ago, and have converted it into a beautifully appointed restaurant, with meals served in a garden court in the summer; they've also increased what was already in the cellars to an astonishing collection of some 80,000 bottles of the best Italy and France have to offer. The cooking, a mixture of *nouvelle cuisine* and traditional Tuscan recipes, wins prizes every year. You may leave behind as much as L150,000 here—much more if you order a prestigious wine or champagne (closed Sun and Mon lunch, and Aug).

Relais le Jardin, Piazza d'Azeglio 5, ℂ 245 247. This restaurant in the Regency Umbria Hotel is rapidly establishing itself as one of Florence's best; the setting is lovely and refined, and dishes like delicate *crêpes* filled with *zucchini* blossoms, artichoke hearts, or asparagus and medallions of veal with rhubarb bring Florentines and visitors back for more (closed Sun).

expensive

Buca Lapi, Via del Trebbio 1/r, ℂ 213 768. Another traditional Florentine restaurant, located since 1800 in the old wine cellar of the lovely Palazzo Antinori. Experiment with *pappardelle al cinghiale* (wide pasta with boar), which tastes better than it sounds; the *bistecca fiorentina con fagioli* here is hard to beat, downed with many different Tuscan wines.

Cibreo, Via dei Macci 118/r, ℂ 234 1100. One of the most Florentine of Florentine restaurants overlooking the market of Sant'Ambrogio. The decor is simple—food is the main concern, and all of it is market-fresh. You can go native and order tripe *antipasto*, pumpkin soup, and cockscombs and kidneys, or play it safe with *prosciutto* from the Casentino, a fragrant soup (no pasta here) of tomatoes, mussels and bellpepper, leg of lamb stuffed with artichokes or duck with sultanas and pine nuts. Top it off with a delicious lemon *crostata* or cheese-cake; accompany it with an excellent choice of Italian or French wines, or a prized bottle of Armagnac (closed Sun and Mon, Easter, mid-July–mid-Sept).

Le Fonticine, Via Nazionale 79, © 282 106. Surrounded by the tourist madness near the railway station, this restaurant has not let its considerable success ruin it. Try fine homemade pasta cooked in the style of Italy's culinary capital, Bologna, the thickest *bistecca* in Florence, and lots of truffles, served in a cosy atmosphere with beamed ceiling and walls covered with Tuscan paintings (closed Sun and Mon, Aug).

Pierot, Piazza Taddeo Gaddi, near Ponte Vittoria in the Oltrarno, © 702 100. An old-style place with good food, wine and prices. Try the fresh salmon with red pepper (closed Sun).

Quattro Amici, Via degli Orti Oricellari 29, © 21 54 13. An all-fish menu which has well-cooked fresh dishes (closed Wed).

Sabatini, Via Panzani 9a, behind S. Maria Novella, © 282 802. The only Florentine restaurant with a branch in Tokyo, Sabatini has been a favourite with tourists and locals for decades. It's a little old-fashioned, but you may find the sober elegance the perfect setting for enjoying their big Florentine steaks, the flamboyant *spaghetti alla lampada* and *pappardelle con lepre*, herb-strewn leg of lamb, and a decadent *semifreddo al croccantino* with hot chocolate sauce (closed Mon and first two weeks July).

Taverna del Bronzino, Via delle Route 25r, © 495 220. Pleasant, spacious atmosphere and good place to try the *osso buco alla fiorentina* (closed Sun).

La Vie en Rose, Borgo Allegri 68r, near the Piazza dei Ciompi, © 245 860. A popular place serving delights like fresh green pasta with clams and saffron, and duck with prunes (closed Tues).

moderate

Angiolino, Via Santo Spirito 57r, © 239 8976. Perhaps the most characteristic place on the south side of the river, with a stove in the centre of the room and the kitchen in full view; the food is typical and of good quality—their vegetable *antipasti* are especially tasty (closed Sun evening and Mon).

Caffè Concerto, Lungarno C. Colombo 7, © 677 377. If *cucina nuova fiorentina* sounds intriguing, try the fare served on a fine veranda overlooking the Arno; unlike most restaurants it remains open late for light midnight suppers (closed Sun and three weeks in Aug).

Cammillo, Borgo San Jacopo 57r, © 212 427. You will find good food here and a lively bustling atmosphere.

Il Cantinone, Via S. Spirito 5, © 218 898. Housed in a subterranean wine cellar, it specializes in Chianti Classico and country cooking—*pappa al* *pomodoro* (thick tomato soup), polenta with boar, beans and sausage. One room is devoted to wine tasting and *antipasti*.

Don Chisciotte, Via Cosimo Ridolfi 4r, © 475 430. You should book ahead for this restaurant serving good inventive fish and meat dishes (closed Sun and Mon lunch).

La Frasca, Via Faentina 70r, © 571 244. There is a limited, but excellent, choice with dishes such as *carpaccio* with artichoke hearts, or a spicy soup with onions and fresh *pecorino* cheese (closed Tues and lunch).

Ristorante Alfredo Sull'Arno, Via dei Bardi 46, © 28 38 88. Magnificent position overlooking the Ponte Vecchio.

Sostanza, Via della Porcellana 25r. The place to come for *bistecca alla fiorientina*, known as *La Troia* (the prostitute) by Florentines. Great atmosphere and food.

inexpensive

Borgo Antico, Piaza San Spirito 6, © 51 04 37. Very busy with tables in the piazza. Good pizzas, fantastic salads, large portions, jugs of wine at 15,000 per litre.

Benvenuto, Via dei Neri, situated just behind the Uffizi. A good place for a sit-down snack or full meal.

Burde-Via Pistoiese, Via Pistoiese 6r, © 317 206. One of the last remaining authentic Tuscan *trattorie* with genuine Tuscan prices (open for lunch).

La Casalinga, Via Michelozzo 9r, just by Piazza Santo Spirito. A cheap option which is particularly popular with students and young tourists.

Il Cuscussù, Via Farini 2a, © 241 890. Eat here for a change of pace; imaginative meals—couscous, goulash and Near Eastern favourites, served with Chianti or Israeli wines.

Garga, Via del Moro 48r, © 239 898. A charming if slightly cramped place run by a Florentine and his Canadian wife, serving mouthwatering homemade pasta, and delicately prepared meat and fish dishes (closed Mon).

Il Latini, Via dei Palchetti 6r, near Santa Maria Novella, © 210 916. Noisy, chaotic and great fun—huge hams hang from the ceiling and you share the long tables with fellow eaters; the food is good local fare and the prices are modest. You cannot book so come early to avoid the queues.

Pane e Vino, Via San Nicolò 60–70r, © 242 221. Simple and spartan with service to match.

Ristorante Dino, Via Ghibellina 51, © 241 452. The place for excellent seasonal dishes and a famous *filettino di maiale al cartoccio* (pork fillets baked in paper) and a wide selection of wines (closed Sun evening and Mon).

Ruggero, Via Sienese 82r, ℂ 220 542. Good value typical *trattoria* (closed Tues).

Sant'Ambrogio Market Lunch Counter. The cheapest meal in Florence: no tables, no courtesies, and plenty of butchers and grocers to rub elbows with, but two courses of home cooking for L15,000.

Central Florence, by popular demand, is full of *tavole calde*, pizzerias, cafeterias and snack bars, where you can grab a sandwich or a salad instead of a full sit-down meal (one of the best pizza-by-the-slice places is just across from the Medici Chapels). This may change. Lately the city has been trying to banish 'fast food' from the centre, in a bizarre attempt to upscale its tourism—they would prefer that we bought fewer hamburgers and more jewellery.

vegetarian

Centro Vegetariano Fiorentino, Via delle Ruote 30r, ℂ 475 030. One-year membership (L2,000) is required for entrance to the centre which has excellent fresh food (closed Mon and Sun lunch).

Gaugin, Via degli Alfani 24r, ℂ 234 0616. Serves delicate international and Mediterranean cooking, good wine and not a hint of meat for around L40,000 (closed Sun and Mon lunch).

restaurants around Florence

Biagio Pignatta, near the Medici villa in Artimino, ℂ 871 8080. Go here for excellent *ribollita*, *crêpes alla Catherine de' Medici* and more (moderate).

Cave di Maiano, Via delle Cave 16, Maiano, ℂ 59 133. In Fiesole there are plenty of mediocre overpriced restaurants but this one has excellent food. On its beautiful garden terrace are served delights like green *tortellini* filled with veal and chicken, or an excellent risotto; roast pigeon, *involtini* of veal and mushrooms, followed by excellent desserts (moderate, closed Mon evening and Tues).

Da Delfina, Via della Chiesa, Artimino, near Carmignano, ℂ 871 8074. Worth the drive out for its enchanting surroundings, lovely views, the charming atmosphere and sublime cooking—homemade *tagliatelle* with a sauce made from greens, risotto with garden vegetables, wild asparagus, succulent kid and lamb dishes—at equally lovely prices (moderate).

Osteria alla Piazza, La Piazza, near Santi Donato e Sicelle, ℂ (0577) 733580. If you're on, or heading to or from the Florence–Siena *superstrada*, this is a convenient lunch stop where you will be treated to Tuscan classics in refined rustic surroundings (moderate).

Il Trebbiolo, Fiesole, ℂ 830 0098. This also has a picturesque terrace with views over the valley, the food is good and the atmosphere is relaxed. After the meal you can retire into the *soggiorno* to sip a liqueur and coffee (closed Sat evening and Mon).

Cabiria Café, Piazza Santo Spirito. One of Florence's most recherché
terraces for a campari.

Caffè Doney, Piazza Strozzi. Traditional style Florentine café.

Dolce Vita, Piazza del Carmine. The place where fashionable young
Florentines strut their latest togs—a favourite pastime since the 14th century (closed Sun and two weeks in Aug).

Dolci e Dolcezze, Piazza Cesare Beccaria 8r, at the top of Ponte San Niccolò,
℃ 234 5438. The most delicious cakes, pastries and marmelades in the
city—the *crostate, torte* and *bavarese* are expensive but worth every lira.

Fiaschettieria Vecchio Casentino, Via dei Neri 5. A welcoming little wine
bar, serving Tuscan vintages and *charcuterie* (closed Mon and Aug).

Giacosa, Via Tornabuoni 83. Has a certain sparkle, good sandwiches and ice
cream, and a reputation for having invented the Negroni (gin, Campari
and vermouth).

Gilli, Piazza della Repubblica 13–14r. Dates back to 1733, when the Mercato
Vecchio still occupied this area; its two panelled back rooms are especially
pleasant in the winter.

Giubbe Rosse, Piazza della Repubblica. Another famous café, rendezvous of
Florence's literati at the turn of the century; the chandelier-lit interior has
changed little since.

Maneresi, Via de' Lamberti 16r. Considered by many to serve the best coffee in
Florence.

Rivoire, Piazza della Signoria 5r. Florence's most elegant and classy watering
hole is, with a marble detailed interior, as lovely as the piazza itself.

Gelaterie

Festival del Gelato, Via del Corso 75r. Over 100 variations of ice cream.

Il Granduca, Via dei Calzaiuoli 57r. Creamy concoctions that challenge those of
nearby rival Perché No? (closed Wed).

Dei Neri, Via dei Neri 20/22r, near Santa Croce. Tasty cones, but no seats
(closed Wed).

L'Oasi, 5 Via dell'Oriuolo, near the Duomo. A sophisticated flavour and a choice
of cakes.

Perché No, Via Tavolini 194, near Via Calzaiuoli. Another challenger for the
gelato throne with wonderful ice cream in 1940s surroundings.

Ricci, Piazza Santo Spirito. A huge choice and a scrumptious *tiramisú* (closed Sun
and first half of August).

Il Triangulo delle Bermude, Via Nazionale 61r. Has a superb choice.

Vivoli, Via Isola delle Stinche 7r (between the Bargello and S. Croce). Florence's claim to being the ice-cream capital of the world owes much to the decadently delicious confections and rich *semifreddi* served here (closed Mon).

Eating Out in Siena (0577–)

Sitting between three of Italy's greatest wine-producing areas, the Chianti, the Brunello of Montalcino and the Vino Nobile of Montepulciano, there is always something distinguished to wash down the simple dishes of the Sienese table. This city's real speciality is sweets, and quite a few visitors to Siena find they have no room for lunch or dinner after repeated visits to the pastry shops for slices of *panforte* (an alarmingly heavy but indecently tasty cake laced with fruits, nuts, orange peel and secret Sienese ingredients), or *panpepato* (similar but with pepper in it). They are all artists—shop windows flaunt gargantuan creations of cakes and crystallized fruit, metres high, and as colourful as a Lorenzetti fresco, set out for all to admire before they are carted off to some wedding party. The **Enoteca** inside the Medici fortress (*see* p.253) is another distraction; sometimes they organize special wine tastings, concentrating on one particular region of Italy. Siena being a university town, snacks and fast food of all kinds are common; a *cioccina* is Siena's special variation on pizza; *pici* (thick south Tuscan spaghetti) with a sauce prepared from ground fresh pork, *pancetta*, sausages and chicken breasts, added to tomatoes cooked with Brunello wine, is the city's favourite pasta dish.

Siena's Salami

Buristo is a cooked salami made from the blood and fatty leftovers of sausages and heavily spiced; *finocchiona* is peppered sausage meat seasoned with fennel seeds and stuffed into the sausage skin; *soppressata* is a boiled salami made from a mixture of rind and gristle; the alternative version, *soppressata in cuffia*, is made in the same way and stuffed into a boned pig's head. The *salsiccioli secchi* are perhaps the most appetising salami of all, made from the leanest cuts of pork or wild boar, enhanced with garlic and black or red pepper.

Restaurants

very expensive

Certosa di Maggiano, Via di Certosa 82, © 28 81 80.

Al Marsili, Via del Castoro 3, just off the Piazza del Duomo, © 47 154. Another of Siena's best, in a singularly elegant setting—not very traditional, with dishes like *gnocchi* in duck sauce, but it's hard to complain (closed Mon).

Il Campo, Piazza del Campo 50, © 28 07 25. In a fantastic location, this has a wonderful choice, but be prepared to pay for it (closed Thurs in winter).

moderate

L'Angolo, Via Garibaldi 15, © 289 295. A large traditional trattoria where *osso buco* and green *gnocchi* are the specialities (closed Sat).

Antica Botteganova, Strada Chiantigiana 29, just outside Siena on the road to Gaiole (S408), © 284 230. Offers earthy Sienese cooking, such as veal cooked in Chianti Classico (closed Sun).

Cane e Gatto, Via Paglairesi 6, off Via San Martino, © 220 751. Booking is essential here; the cuisine is modern-style Tuscan (closed Thurs).

Osteria dell'Artista, Via Stalloreggi 11, © 280 306. Typical Sienese food—a small and quiet place not usually inundated with tourists (closed Thurs).

Osteria Le Logge, Via del Porrione 33, just off the Campo, © 48 013. If you've survived the wine and the pastry shops, you'll appreciate the succulent risottos and pasta dishes here with exotic second courses like stuffed guinea-fowl (*faraona*) and a fine wine list (closed Sun, booking ahead).

Taverna di Cecco, Via Cecco Angioleri 19, near the Campo, © 288 518. Specializes in pasta dishes, meats and nearly everything else done up with either truffles or *porcini* mushrooms (closed Wed).

Tullio ai Tre Cristi, Vicolo Provenzano, © 280 608. On this site since about 1830, this is perhaps the most authentic of Sienese restaurants; its menu includes things like *ribollita*, tripe with sausages and roast boar from the Maremma. The *pici* are home made. There are tables outside in the summer (closed Mon).

inexpensive

Less expensive places—and there are many good ones—are usually found a little further away from the Campo.

Il Cavallino Bianco, Via di Città 20, © 44 258. Serves regional food and pizza, but its main bonus is that it is open until late (closed Wed).

Da Marino, Via Salicotto 137, © 42 249. It is always busy here, with home cooking on the menu.

Pizzeria Carlo e Franca, Via Pantaneto 138, © 220 485. Pizza and pasta dishes at reasonable prices (closed Wed).

La Torre, Via Salicotto 17. The restaurant here is a fun, lively place, popular with students.

La Vecchia Taverna di Baccho, Via Beccheria 9–11, © 49 33 1. Just off the Campo.

Trattoria da Dino, Casato di Sopra 71, © 289 036. Makes a good *spiedini alle Senese* (closed Fri).

Gelaterie

Siena isn't as obsessed with ice cream as Florence is, but there are a couple of central places to cool off with a cone. Both have a wide choice of luscious home-made flavours.

Gelateria Artisanale Costarella Arnoldo, at the angle of Via di Città and Via Costarella di Barbieri.

Gelateria Fonte Gaiai, Piazza del Campo 21.

Eating Out in Pisa   (050–)

In Pisa you will find eating out difficult on a Sunday night. At other times, walks on the wild side of the Tuscan kitchen seem more common than in other towns—eels and squid, *baccalà*, tripe, wild mushrooms, 'twice-boiled soup' and dishes that waiters cannot satisfactorily explain. Don't be intimidated; there's always more common fare on the menu, and occasionally the more outlandish items turn into surprising treats.

Restaurants

very expensive

Ristorante Sergio, Lungarno Pacinotti. near the Royal Victoria, © 48 245. A highly regarded temple of Pisan cuisine in a medieval setting. The menu changes according to what's available and fresh, and although the quality of the food can vary, the chances are you are in for a truly superb meal. There's a *menu degustazione* for L90,000, where you can sample the best dishes of the day; *à la carte* may be considerably cheaper (closed Sun).

Ristoro dei Vecchi Macelli, Via Volturno 49, on the north bank of the Arno, near Ponte Solferino, © 20 424. A cheaper gourmet stronghold with highly imaginative dishes based on coastal Tuscan traditions (closed Wed and Sun lunch).

moderate

Pisa is well endowed with unpretentious *trattorie*, many of them near the centre around the university.

Da Bruno, Via Luigi Bianchi, © 560 818. Outside the walls a few blocks east of the Campo dei Miracoli, this is another place to see how well you like simple Pisan cooking—things like polenta with mushrooms and *baccalà* (dried cod).

La Mescita, Via Cavalca 2, © 544 292. Has varied, good quality food for reasonable prices (closed Sat lunch and Sun).

Il Nuraghe, Via Mazzini 58, © 443 68. A traditional *trattoria* which has specialities such as ricotta ravioli and snails (closed Mon).

Osteria dei Cavalieri, Via San Frediano 16, © 49 008. There are good game dishes here such as rabbit with thyme (closed Sat lunch and Sun).

Da Poldino, Via Cascine Vecchie 13, © 531 763. This restaurant is in a panoramic position; the rustic specialities include *pernice* (partridge) baked in foil with *porcini* mushrooms (closed Tues).

Lo Schiaccianoci, Via Vespucci 104, east of the station, © 21 024. Those eels from Lake Massaciuccoli and other fresh seafood delicacies hold pride of place.

Sergio a Villa di Corliano, 8km out of Pisa in Loc. Rigoli (direction Lucca), © 818 858. Under the same ownership as Sergio in town, with the same top-quality food, in the stunning setting of a 16th-century villa (closed Wed).

Tavern Kostas, Via del Borghetto 39, © 571 467. Italian dishes with a sophisticated Greek bias can be had here; try the duck or rabbit.

inexpensive

Il Cavallino, Via San Lorenzo 66, © 432 290. A cheap and dreary *trattoria* frequented by locals and students (closed Mon).

Da Gino, Piazza Vittorio Emanuele 19, © 23 437. Cheap prices and simple 'tratt' decor.

Redipuglia, Via Aurelia Sud 7, Loc. Mortellini, ✆ 960 157. Try this for food fresh from the farm; there's a wide selection and comprehensive wine list (closed Mon, Tues and lunch times).

Salza, Via di Borgo Stretto 44, ✆ 580 144. Popular *pizzeria* especially in the evening (closed Mon).

San Francisco, Via dei Tinti 26, ✆ 580 240. Busy *pizzeria* (closed Mon).

Cafés and Gelaterie

Al Banco della Berlina, Piazza della Berlina 9 (between Piazza Garibaldi and Piazza Mazzini). As warm and welcoming as an Italian café can get in a charming little piazza. Serves tasty cocktails.

Bar Moderno Gelateria, Via Corsica 10, near the Piazza dei Cavalieri. For stylish post-modern ice cream.

Bottega del Gelato, Piazza Garibaldi 11. For a delicious cone, even late at night, with a wide choice and heavenly frozen yoghurts.

Pasticceria Federico Salza, Borgo Stretto 46 (off Piazza Garibaldi). The best cakes in Pisa await, and a lovely large terrace for lingering (closed Mon).

Pick a Flower, Via Serafini 14. A popular student bar located in a handsome old palazzo (closed Sun).

Eating Out in Lucca   *(0583–)*

expensive

Hotel Universo, Piazza del Giglio, Il Giglio, ✆ 494 058. Lucca's best seafood place—river trout is a speciality as well.

Ristorante Enoteca Donati, Via per Santo Stefano 957, ✆ 34 22 77. Booking is essential in this family-run restaurant; fresh fish dishes and a good list of wines (closed Mon).

moderate

Antica Locanda dell'Angelo, Via Pescheria 21, ✆ 47 711. A traditional *trattoria.* (closed Sun evening and Mon).

Il Buca di Sant'Antonio, Via della Cervia 1, ✆ 55 881. This has been an inn within the walls since 1782, offering old recipes like smoked herring and kid on a spit, and newer dishes like ravioli with ricotta and sage.

Il Campo Bar da Cesare, Loc. Pieve S. Stefano, ✆ 59 245. You can eat, drink and listen to music in the open air until dawn; all in the presence of a beautiful Tuscan panorama (summer only, closed Mon and lunch).

Canuleia, Via Canuleia, ✆ 47 470. Situated near the amphitheatre in a medieval workshop, this serves local food with some surprises and usually a choice of vegetarian dishes (closed Sat and Sun).

inexpensive

Barsotti da Guido, Via C. Battisti, ✆ 28 47219. You can get a three-course meal here for L16,000 (closed Sun).

Da Giulio in Pelleria, Via Conce, ✆ 55 948. In the northwest corner within the walls, here you can enjoy some surprising dishes at rock-bottom prices. Popular enough to warrant reservations, with top-quality 'peasant' fare, (closed Sun and Mon).

K2, Via del Anfiteatro 107, ✆ 47 170. A restaurant and *pizzeria* with a set meal for L16,000, or pizza meal for around L13,000, and tables outdoors (closed Wed).

Da Leo, Via Tegrimi 1, ✆ 492 236. Serves typical Lucchese dishes with a few tables outdoors (closed Sun).

around Lucca

Lucca does especially well at table if you have the horsepower to reach its immediate surroundings.

Forassiepi, Porta Belvedere, Montecarlo, ✆ 22 005. Located in a former oil press. Try a bottle of local wine as an excellent accompaniment to dishes like truffle *crêpes*; from the terrace you can see as far as Collodi and the Valdinievole (moderate to expensive).

La Mora, Via Sesto di Moriano 104, Ponte a Moriano, ✆ 406 402. A good choice north of town, located in an old posthouse with four cosy rooms inside and dining under the pergola in summer, serving, according to season, delicious ravioli with asparagus or truffles, or gourmet roast lamb (expensive).

Solferino, Via delle Gavine 50, ✆ 59 118, situated 6km west of Lucca in San Macario in Piano on the Viareggio road. Run by the same family for four generations and famous throughout Tuscany for almost as long. Duck with truffles, wild boar and grilled seafood are a few of the treats on the extensive menu. Simple Tuscan country specialities are also in evidence but this is one place where you may want to splurge (expensive).

Vipore, Pieve Santo Stefano, ✆ 59 245. In a 200-year-old farmhouse which has views over the fertile plain of Lucca. Top-quality ingredients go into fresh pasta and meat dishes (expensive).

Where to Stay

Hotels

Florence, Siena, Pisa and Lucca are endowed with hotels (*alberghi*) of every description, from the spectacular to the humble. These are rated by the government's tourism bureaucracy, from five stars at the luxurious top end to one star at the bottom. The ratings take into account such things as a restaurant on the premises, plumbing, air-conditioning, et cetera, but not character, style or charm. Use the stars, which we include in this book, as a quick reference for prices and general amenities only. Another thing to remember about government ratings is that a hotel can stay at a lower rating than it has earned, so you may find a hotel with three stars as comfortable one with four.

Breakfast is optional only in some hotels, and in pensions it is mandatory. And you may as well expect to face half-board (breakfast and lunch or dinner) or full-board requirements in the hotels that can get away with it—seaside, lake or mountain resorts in season, spas and country villa hotels. Otherwise, meal arrangements are optional. Although eating in the hotel restaurant can be a genuine gourmet experience, in the majority of cases hotel food is bland, just as it is anywhere else.

Prices

There's no inflation in Italy, if you believe the government; the prices just go up by themselves. With the holiday business booming, this curious paradox is well expressed in hotel prices; every year costs rise by 6–8 per cent across the board, and are often more expensive than hotels in northern Europe. The prices listed in this book are for double rooms only. For a single room, count on paying two-thirds of a double; to add an extra bed in a double will add 35 per cent to the bill. (A *camera matrimoniale* is a room with a double bed, a *camera doppia* has twin beds, a *camera singola* is a single.) Taxes and service charges are included in the given rate. Some establishments charge L10–25,000 for air-conditioning. Also note that if rooms are listed without bath, it simply means the shower and lavatory are in the corridor. Prices are by law listed on the door of each room and will be printed in the hotel lists available from the local tourist office; any discrepancies should be reported to the tourist office. Most rooms have two or three different rates, depending on the season. Costs are sometimes a third less if you travel in the district's low season. Some hotels close down altogether for several months of the year.

Throughout this book, prices listed are for a double room in high season; and, unless otherwise stated, including a private bath. Here is the range of prices you are likely to encounter for hotels in the various classifications in

1994–5; for rooms without bath, subtract 20–30 per cent. Many resort hotels in particular offer discounts for children and children's meals.

Category	Double with Bath
***** *luxury*	L450–800,000
**** *very expensive*, Class I	250–450,000
*** *expensive*, Class II	L160–250,000
** *moderate*, Class III	L85–160,000
* *inexpensive*, Class IV	up to 85,000

Hotel Chains and Useful Organizations

There are several hotel chains in Italy. **CIGA** (*Compagnia Grandi Alberghi*) has many of the most luxurious, many of them grand turn-of-the-century establishments that have been exquisitely restored. Another plush chain, **Châteaux et Relais** specializes in equally comfortable, but more intimate accommodation, often in historical buildings. Both chains pride themselves on their gourmet restaurants. Even the once fairly standard **Jolly Hotels**, Italy's oldest chain, are quickly up-grading. The petrol company **AGIP** operates most of the motels along the major motorways, and usually makes a decent effort to give them good restaurants. The National Tourist Office has a complete list of these and booking information for both motels and five- and four-star hotels and chains. If you want to stay in a different kind of accommodation, you'll have to book ahead on your own. Outside the high season this is generally unnecessary; otherwise, and especially if you have a certain place in mind, it is essential to book several months in advance or even earlier if possible, considering the sorry state of the Italian post. (While you're at it, remember to request a room with a view, in places where that is the hotel's chief attraction.) If your Italian is non-existent, the *National Tourist Office's Travellers' Handbook* has a sample letter and list of useful terms. Under Italian law, a booking is valid once a deposit has been paid. If you have to cancel your reservation, the hotel will keep the deposit unless another agreement has been reached. If you're coming in the summer without reservations, start calling around for a place in the morning.

One Italian institution, the **Albergo Diurno** (Day Hotel), may prove handy, though there seem to be fewer of them all the time. Located in the centre of the largest cities and at the railway stations, these are places where you can take a shower, a shave, have your hair done, et cetera. They are open 6am–midnight.

Inexpensive Accommodation

Bargains are few and far between in Italy. The cheapest kind of hotel is an inn, or *locanda*; some provinces treat these as one-star hotels or list them separately (or not at all). The majority of inexpensive places will always be around the railway station, though in the large cities you'll often find it worth your while to seek out some more pleasant location in the historic centre. You're likely to find anything in a one-star Italian hotel. Often they will be practically perfect, sometimes almost luxurious; memorably bad experiences will be few, and largely limited to the major cities. In rural areas and islands that see some tourists, ask around for rooms in private homes.

Besides the youth hostels (*see* below), there are several city-run hostels, with dormitory-style rooms open to all. In Florence religious institutions often rent out extra rooms. Monasteries and convents in the country sometimes take guests as well; if you seek that kind of quiet experience, bring a letter of introduction from your local priest or pastor.

youth and student hostels

You'll find youth hostels in Florence and Lucca. The head organization in Italy is **Associazione Alberghi per la Gioventù**, Via Cavour 44 (terzo piano), Roma, © (06) 487 1152. They can send you a list and map of all the hostels in Italy, which officially require an IYHF card. There are no age limits, and senior citizens are often given added discounts. Many youth hostels sell cards or you can pick up one in advance from the offices listed below.

UK: Youth Hostels Association, 14 Southampton St, London WC2E 7HY, © (071) 836 8452.

USA: American Youth Hostels, PO Box 37613, Washington, DC 200013, © (202) 783 6161.

Canada: Canadian Hostelling Association, 1600 James Naismith Drive, Suite 608, Gloucester, Ontario, K1B 5N4, © (613) 748 5638.

Accommodation—a bunk bed in single-sex room and breakfast—costs around L16,000 per day. There is often a curfew, and you usually can't check in before 5 or 6pm. You can book in advance by sending your arrival and departure dates along with the number of guests (mention their sex) to the individual hostel, including international postal coupons for the return reply. The worst time to use the hostels is the spring, when noisy Italian school groups use them for field trips.

Another organization helps students find lodgings in Italy—Centro Turistico Studentesco e Giovanile (CTS), which has offices in every Italian city of any size (and one in London, *see* above) and can book cheap accommodation for you, in their own town or at your next stop.

Self-catering Holidays: Villas, Farmhouses and Flats

Renting a villa or flat has always been the best way to visit Tuscany. If you're travelling with a family it is the most economic alternative—there are simple, inexpensive cottages as well as the fabulous Renaissance villas furnished with antiques, gourmet meals and swimming-pools. One place to look for holiday villas is in the Sunday paper; or, if you have your heart set on a particular area, write to its tourist office for a list of local rental agencies. These ought to provide photos of the accommodation to give you an idea of what to expect, and make sure all pertinent details are written down in your rental agreement to avoid misunderstandings later. In general minimum lets are for two weeks; rental prices usually include insurance, water and electricity, and sometimes linen and maid service. Don't be surprised if upon arrival the owner 'denounces' (*denunziare*) you to the police; according to Italian law, all visitors must be registered upon arrival. Many of the companies listed below offer in addition to homes, savings on charter flights, ferry crossings or fly-drive schemes to sweeten the deal. Try to book as far in advance as possible for the summer season.

Holiday Rental Companies
in the UK

International Chapters, 102 St John's Wood Terrace, London NW8 6PR, ℗ (071) 722 9560 has the listings and handles bookings for the major Italian holiday home companies, the largest of which is **Cuendet** which publishes an extensive illustrated catalogue of holiday villas, flats and farmhouses. Their headquarters are at Il Cerreto, 53030 Strove, Siena; they also have the listings of **Tuscan Enterprises**, a company with headquarters in Castellina in Chianti, and their own listings called **Italian Chapters**. Other firms include:

Citalia, Marco Polo House 3–5, Lansdowne Road, Croydon CR9 9EQ, ℗ (081) 686 5533.

Continental Villas, 3 Paxton Walk, Phoenix St, London WC2H 8PW, ℗ (071) 497 0444.

Hoseasons Holidays Abroad Ltd, Sunway House, Lowestoft, Suffolk NR32 3LT, ℗ (0502) 500 555.

Interhome, 383 Richmond Rd, Twickenham TW1 2EF, ℗ (081) 891 1294.

Magic of Italy, 227 Shepherds Bush Rd, London W6 7AS, ℗ (081) 748 7575.

David Newman's European Collection, PO Box 733, 40 Upperton Rd, Eastbourne, ℗ (0323) 410 347.

Perrymead Properties Overseas, 55 Perrymead Street, London SW6, ℰ (081) 878 5788.

Sovereign, Astral Towers, Betts Way, Crawley, West Sussex, RH10 2GX, ℰ 0293 599 988.

Vacanze in Italia, Bignor, Pulborough, West Sussex RH20 IQD; call for brochure ℰ (07987) 421.

in the USA

At Home Abroad, 405 East 56th St, New York, NY 10022, ℰ (212) 421 9165.

CUENDET: Posarelli Vacations, Suzanne T. Pidduck, 1742 Calle Corva, Camarillo, CA93010, ℰ (805) 987 5278.

Hideaways International, PO Box 4433, Portsmouth, New Hampshire 03801, ℰ (603) 430 4433.

Homeowners International, 1133 Broadway, New York, NY 10010, ℰ (212) 691 2361 or (800) 367 4668.

Italian Villa Rentals, 550 Kirkland Way, Suite 100, Kirkland, Washington 98033, ℰ (206) 827 3694.

Overseas Connection, 70 West 71st St, Suite 1C, New York, NY 10023, ℰ (212) 769 1170.

RAVE (Rent-a-Vacation-Everywhere), 383 Park Ave, Rochester, NY 14607, ℰ (716) 256 0760.

Rent in Italy, Elaine Muoio, 3801 Ingomar St N.W., Washington, DC 20015, ℰ (202) 244 5345, fax (202) 362 0520. Specialist in Italian villa rentals.

in Italy

The Best in Italy, Via Ugo Foscolo 72, Firenze, ℰ (055) 223 064, which specializes in posh villas with domestic staff.

Casaclub, Via Termini 83, Siena, ℰ (0577) 44 041 (villas in Chianti).

Toscana Vacanze, Via XX Settembre 6, 52047 Marciano della Chiana, ℰ (0575) 845 348 (villas in Chianti and environs).

Toscanamare Villas, Via W della Gheradesca 5, Castagneto Carducci (LI), ℰ (0565) 744 012, fax 744 339 (villas on the Versilia coast).

Tuscan Enterprises, for houses in Chianti; write to Podere Casamonti, Castellina in Chianti, 53011 Siena, ℰ (0577) 740 623.

Vela, Via Colombo 16, Castiglione della Pescaia, ✆ (0564) 933 495 (villas and flats on the seaside and panoramic locations).

Italian Chapters (have apartments and villas in all four cities), 102 St Johns Wood Terrace, London NW8 9PL, ✆ (071) 722 9560, fax (071) 722 9140.

Camping

Florence

Camping de Fiesole, on top of the hill. Lovely, but packed and expensive in the summer.

Camping Internazionale, Via S. Cristofano 2, south of the city in Bottai Tavarnuzze, ✆ 202 0445, near the A1 exit Autostrada Firenze–Certosa; convenient for motorists (open end of March to mid-Oct).

Camping Muncipale Olivades, Viale Michelangelo 80, ✆ 653 1089. Has fine views over the city and free hot showers; arrive early to get a spot. On the other hand, there's no shade and a disco until 1am. Bus 13 will take you there from the station.

Mugello Verde Internaional Camping, 25km north of Florence on the road to Bologna, at Via Masso Rondinaio 2, in San Piero a Sieve, ✆ 848 511. Very pleasant setting among hills and forests, and frequent buses down to Florence.

Siena

Camping Colleverde, Strada di Scacciapensieri 37, ✆ 280 044. 3km north of the city, bus 8 from Piazza Gramsci (open April–Oct).

Camping Luxor, 8km north on the SS2. Well kept and set in the woods, free pool.

Pisa

Camping Internazionale, Via Litoreana. 15km away near the beach at Marina de Pisa, ✆ 36 553, (open mid-April to mid-Oct).

Camping San Mikael, Via Bigattiera, Marina di Pisa, ✆ 33 103. Nice and shady, open June–mid Sept.

Campeggio Torre Pendente, Via delle Cascine 86, ✆ 560 665 or 561 704. 1km from the Leaning Tower (bus 5 from the station); the closest, if not amazingly atmospheric (open 15 March–15 Oct).

Florence has some exceptionally lovely hotels, and not all of them at Grand Ducal prices, although base rates here are the highest in Tuscany. In this town historic old palace-hotels are the rule rather than the exception; those listed below are some of the more atmospheric and charming, but to be honest few are secrets, so reserve as far in advance as possible. There are almost 400 hotels in Florence, but not enough for anyone who arrives in July and August without a reservation. Don't despair: there are several hotel consortia that can help you find a room in nearly any price range for a small commission. If you're arriving by car or train, the most useful will be ITA.

ITA: in Santa Maria Novella station, © 282 893, open 9–8.30; in the AGIP service station at Peretola, to the west of Florence on A11, © 421 1800. Between March and November there's an office in the Chianti-Est service plaza on the A1, and another in the Fortezza da Basso, © 471 960. No bookings can be made over the telephone.

Florence Promhotels: Viale A. Volta 72, © 570 481.

Toscana Hotels 80: Viale Gramsci 9, © 247 8543. These last two take bookings by phone or mail.

Nearly every hotel in Florence with a restaurant will require half-board, and many will lay down a heavy breakfast charge as well that is supposed to be optional.

luxury

★★★★★ **Excelsior**, Piazza Ognissanti 3, © 264 201, the luxury leader, is the former Florentine address of Napoleon's sister Caroline. Lots of marble, neoclassically plush, lush and green with plants, immaculately staffed, with a smart roof garden with views down the Arno, and decadently luxurious bedrooms; not even Gian Gastone de' Medici had heated towel rails. The bar and restaurant are added amenities.

★★★★★ **Regency**, Piazza d'Azeglio 3, © 245 247, charming and intimate with only 29 air-conditioned rooms; between the two wings there's an elegant town garden. The public rooms are beautifully panelled, and the fare in the dining room superb; there's a private garage for your car.

very expensive

★★★★ **Anglo-American**, near the Cascine on Via Garibaldi 9, © 282 114. A large but attractive hotel in an older palace, decorated in a light, airy garden style that makes a pleasant retreat after pounding the pavements; the rooms are air-conditioned and there's parking nearby.

★★★★ **Atlantic Palace**, Via Nazionale 12, © 294 234, one of the most attractive hotels near the train station with large, striking bedrooms built in the framework of a 17th-century convent, luxuriously furnished and air-conditioned.

★★★★ **Mona Lisa**, Borgo Pinti 27, © 247 9751. A Renaissance palace now owned by the descendants of sculptor Giovanni Dupre, this is one of the most charming small hotels in Florence, hiding behind its stern façade. The palazzo is well preserved, the furnishings are family heirlooms, as are the many works of art. Try to reserve one of the tranquil rooms that overlook the garden; all are air-conditioned and have frigo-bars. The Mona Lisa has no restaurant, though breakfast is available; it has private parking.

★★★★ **Principe**, Lungarno Vespucci 34, © 284 848. Among the many hotels along the Arno, this is one of the most pleasant—a small, comfortable hotel, centrally air-conditioned and sound-proofed, with a little garden at the back; the nicer rooms have terraces over the Arno.

★★★★ **Rivoli**, Via della Scala 33, © 50123 28 28 53, fax 29 40 41, is an elegant and refined 15th-century building with air-conditioning and TV in all rooms.

★★★★ **Villa Carlotta**, Via Michele di Lando 3, © 220 501. This Tuscan-Edwardian hotel is in a quiet residential district in the upper Oltrarno, close to the Porta Romana. The 26 sophisticated rooms have recently been tastefully refurnished and have every luxury. There's a garden and glassed-in veranda, where the large breakfasts are served; a private garage offers safe parking.

expensive

★★★ **Annalena**, Via Romana 34, © 222 402. A grand and famous old *pensione* in a 15th-century palace in the Oltrarno with high ceilings, antiques and art; large, comfortable rooms, all with private baths, and a friendly atmosphere. The large garden at the back is a boon.

★★★ **Beacci Tornabuoni**, Via Tornabuoni 3, © 212 645. Another excellent small hotel, which puts you in the centre of fashionable Florence, on the top three floors of an elegant Renaissance palace. The rooms are comfortable, air-conditioned and equipped with mini-bars, though it's more fun to sit over your drink on the panoramic roof terrace.

★★★ **Hotel Quisisana e Pontevecchio**, Lungarno Archibusieri 4, ✆ 21 66 92, fax 268 303. The beautiful hotel where *A Room with a View* was filmed. It has exceptional views of the Ponte Vecchio and a lovely loggia.

★★★ **Loggiato dei Serviti**, Piazza SS. Annunziata 3, ✆ 289 592. The most delightful choice in this category was designed for the Servite fathers by Antonio da Sangallo the Elder, who added a loggia to match Brunelleschi's Spedale degli Innocenti across the square. The interior has since been redone with the best of Florentine taste and refinement, with Italian and English antiques; all rooms have mini-bars, and air-conditioning and colour TVs are available as well; parking is possible in a nearby garage. The lovely garden is a blessing in the middle of Florence.

★★★ **Morandi alla Crocetta**, Via Laura 50, ✆ 234 4747, fax 248 0954. This converted Renaissance convent, run by an English woman, has only 9 rooms, all with air-conditioning and TV.

★★★ **Villa Liberty**, Viale Michelangelo 40, ✆ 68 38 19, fax 681 25 95. On the southeastern side of town, this small hotel has 16 rooms all done in Liberty style; very good value for money.

moderate

★★★ **Aprile**, Via della Scala 6, ✆ 216 237, fax 28 09 47. Near the station but miles away in atmosphere. Housed in a 15th-century Medici palace, it is still decorated with frescoes and paintings, and there's a small courtyard for sitting outside.

★ **Bandini**, Piazza S. Spirito 9, ✆ 215 308. Located on a busy, noisy square in the Oltrarno, far from tourist Florence. Recently endowed with a lift. Guests are rewarded with a beautiful Tuscan loggia; it was one of the first buildings to have this delightful architectural feature. However, the rooms themselves are uncomfortable and expensive.

★★★ **Hermitage**, very near the Ponte Vecchio in Vicolo Marzio 1, ✆ 287 216. One of the best places to stay in the heart of Florence; reserve well in advance to get one of its 14 cosy old rooms, even further in advance to get one overlooking the Arno; the views from the roof garden while sipping your morning coffee make it worth the trouble.

★★★ **Hotel Calzaiuoli**, Via Calzaiuoli 6, ✆ 212 456, fax 268 310, is a peaceful hotel on this central traffic-free street. All rooms are well decorated and comfortable, and there are great views from those on the top floor.

★★★ **Hotel Pensione Pendini**, Via Strozzi 2, © 210 712, fax 210 156. There are 42 large comfortable rooms in this old hotel which is bang in the centre of town.

★★★ **Hotel Silla**, Via dei Renai 5, © 234 28, fax 234 1437, is a 16th-century building with a garden overlooking the Arno.

★★★ **Porta Rossa** at Via Porta Rossa 19, © 287 551. Right in the middle of Florence, on a narrow lane off Piazza della Signoria, there's this noisy, ageing, dimly-lit hotel. It isn't for everyone, but there are plenty of visitors to Florence who swear they wouldn't stay anywhere else. The Porta Rossa, which traces its origins back to the Middle Ages, has character, with its frayed 19th-century grandeur and a difficult, classically Florentine staff, who have plenty of tales to tell from the hotel's long history.

★★★ **La Residenza**, on top of a Renaissance palace at Via Tornabuoni 8, © 284 197, has the overgrown Palazzo Strozzi for a neighbour, and you can gaze down Florence's version of Fifth Avenue from the roof garden. The decor is pretty and welcoming, the elevator a well-maintained antique.

★★★ **Select Hotel**, Via G. Galliano 24, © 681 0581, fax 351 506, is out in the northern suburbs though it is easy to get into the centre. There are 36 comfortable, decent-sized rooms, 10 of which are singles, it's good for parking and there are facilities for the disabled.

★★ **La Scaletta**, Via Guicciardini 13, © 283 028. A good choice if you want to stay over in the less frenetic Oltarno—near the Ponte Vecchio, offering good rooms and a great roof terrace.

inexpensive

The obvious place to look is the seedy, crowded, tourist-student inferno that surrounds the central station, especially in Via Nazionale, Via Fiume, Via Guelfa and Via Faenza down to Piazza Indipendenza. Many of the cheapest places post minions in the station to snatch up weary back-packers. Although convenient if you arrive by train, few of these hotels will brighten your stay in Florence; grouchy owners who lock the door at midnight seem to be the rule.

★★ **Desireé**, Via Fiume 20, © 238 2382.

★★ **Splendor**, Via San Gallo 30 (off Via Guelfa), © 483 427, is on the fringe of the zone, near Piazza S. Marco and is a noteworthy exception to the general run; its old frescoes and antiques hint of past splendour, and some of the bedrooms are palatial; others aren't, but there's an attractive terrace.

★ **Ausonia e Rimini**, Via Nazionale 24, ✆ 496 547, is another basic hotel in this area.

★ **Casa Cristina**, Via B. Lupi 14, a small inexpensive hotel which is not far from San Marco.

★ **La Mia Casa**, Piazza S. Maria Novella 20, ✆ 213 061, near S. Maria Novella, and within spitting distance of the station. Simple rooms, inexpensive breakfasts, free showers and a free film in English every night.

★ **Tony's Inn**, Via Faenza 77, ✆ 217 975. Another solid recommendation in the area, Tony's is run by a friendly Italian-Canadian couple; rooms are pleasant, most have private baths.

The Old Town

The old town has a number of inexpensive hotels which are less touristic than those by the station.

★ **Bavaria**, Borgo Albizi 26, ✆ 234 0313, has only eight rooms in a 16th-century palace (L55,000 without bath, L65,000 with).

★ **Brunori,** Via del Proconsolo 5, ✆ 289 648. A small, friendly place.

★ **Firenze**, Piazza dei Donati, ✆ 214 203, right in the centre near the Duomo, the classiest inexpensive hotel in Florence; ask for one of the newer rooms and book in advance.

★ **Maxim**, Via de' Medici 4, ✆ 217 474, just off Via Calzaiuoli, has nice, quiet rooms.

★ **Orchidea**, Borgo degli Albizi 11, ✆ 248 0346. You can sleep in this charming old palace of Dante's in-laws, but there are no private baths or breakfast.

Rooms to Let

Besides hotels, a number of institutions and private homes let rooms—there's a complete list in the back of the annual provincial hotel book. Many take women only, and fill up with students in the spring when Italian schools make their annual field trips.

There are two youth hostels to choose from in Florence: Ostello Europa Villa Camerata, Viale A. Righe 2/4 (bus 17B from the station), ℃ 601 451, has 500 beds for people with IYHF cards. Located in an old palazzo with gardens, it is a popular place, and you'd be wise to show up at 2pm to get a spot in the summer; maximum stay three days. Ostello Santa Monaca, Via Santa Monaca 6, ℃ 268 338, has 111 beds near the Carmine church; sign up for a place in the morning. Istituto Gould, Via dei Serragli 44, is so popular that you must book well in advance, ℃ 212 576.

In Fiesole

Many frequent visitors to Florence wouldn't stay anywhere else: it's cooler, quieter, and at night the city far below twinkles as if made of fairy lights. If money is no object, the superb choice is:

★★★★★ **Villa San Michele**, Via Doccia 4, ℃ 59 451. In a breathtaking location just below Fiesole with a façade and loggia reputedly designed by Michelangelo himself. Originally a monastery in the 14th century, it has been carefully reconstructed after bomb damage in the Second World War to create one of the most beautiful hotels in Italy, set in a lovely Tuscan garden, complete with a pool. Each of its 29 rooms is richly and elegantly furnished and air-conditioned; the more plush suites have jacuzzis. The food is delicious, and the reasons to go down to Florence begin to seem insignificant; a stay here is complete in itself. Paradise, however, comes at a price (L450–750,000 per person on half-board terms, closed mid-Nov–mid-March).

★★★★ **Villa Aurora**, Piazza Mino, right in the centre of Fiesole, ℃ 59 100, has air-conditioned rooms in a totally modernized, very elegant 19th-century building .

★★★ **Pensione Bencista**, Via B. da Maiano 4, in S. Domenico di Fiesole, ℃ 59 163. Even if you aren't driving, you can get here by bus 7. The *pensione* is located in a sprawling villa dating back to the 14th century, added to over the centuries. Many of the rooms are furnished with antiques and there's a garden and view. The hotel has recently been revamped to push it up a category (moderate to expensive).

If you're driving, you may be inspired to lodge outside central Florence, where you can park without hassles or paying a fortune for the privilege.

luxury

★★★★★ **Grand Hotel Villa Cora**, Viale Machiavelli 18–20, ✆ 229 8451. A luxurious choice near Piazzale Michelangelo, the opulent 19th-century mansion is set in a beautiful formal garden overlooking the Oltrarno. Built by the Baron Oppenheim, it later served as the residence of the wife of Napoleon III, Empress Eugénie. Its conversion to a hotel has dimmed little of its splendour; some of the bedrooms have frescoed ceilings and lavish 19th-century furnishings—all are air-conditioned and have frigobars, and there's a pretty pool. In the summer meals are served in the garden, and there's a fine view of Florence from the roof terrace.

very expensive

★★★★★ **Villa La Massa**, Via La Massa 6, ✆ 633 035. Another lovely choice, located up the Arno some 6km from Florence at Candeli. The former 15th-century villa of Count Giraldi, the hotel retains the old dungeon (now one of two restaurants), the family chapel (now a bar), and other early-Renaissance amenities, combined with 20th-century features like tennis courts, a pool and air-conditioning. The furnishings are fit for a Renaissance princeling, there's dining and dancing by the Arno in the summer, a shady garden, and a hotel bus to whizz you into the city.

★★★★ **Torre di Bellosguardo**, Via Roti Michelozzi 2, ✆ 229 8145. In the 12th century a tower was built at Bellosguardo, enjoying one of the most breathtaking views over the city. It was later purchased by the Cavalcanti, friends of Dante, and a villa was added below the tower; Cosimo I confiscated it; the Michelozzi purchased it from the Medici; Elizabeth Barrett Browning wrote about it. In 1988 it opened its doors as a small hotel. Frescoes by Baroque master Poccetti adorn the entrance hall, fine antiques adorn the rooms, each unique and fitted out with modern bath. The large and beautiful terraced garden has a pool. For a splurge, reserve the two-level tower suite, with fabulous views in four directions.

★★★★ **Villa Villoresi**, Via Ciampi 2, Colonnata di Sesto Fiorentino, ✆ 443 692. A lovely oasis on a hill above one of Florence's more unbecoming tentacles. One of its charms is that it hasn't been too pristinely restored, and has kept much of its slightly faded appeal as well as its frescoed ceilings, antiques, chandeliers and hospitable *contessa*. There's a garden and pool—a great place to bring the children.

★★★★ Paggeria Medicea, Viale Papa Giovanni XXIII 3, Artimino, near Carmignano, © 871 8081. You can play the Medici in the refurbished outbuildings of Grand Duke Ferdinand's villa. It has some unusual amenities—a hunting reserve and a lake stocked with fish, also a pool and tennis court, and pleasant modern rooms, many with balconies, all air-conditioned.

★★★ Villa le Rondini, Via Bolognese Vecchia 224, © 400 081, north of the centre, has a number of separate villas in a large park, a heated pool and tennis.

★★★ Villa Liberty, Viale Michelangelo 40, © 681 0581. A 14-room charmer, with a garden and air-conditioned rooms.

moderate

★★★ Hermitage, Via Gineparia 112, Bonistallo, © 877 040. Further afield, near Poggio a Caiano, this is a fine affordable choice for families; there's a pool in the grounds, air-conditioned rooms, not to mention gallons of fresh air and quiet (moderate).

★★ Villa Natalia, Via Bolognese 106, © 490 773, has a garden and quiet rooms.

Where to Stay in Siena   *(0577–)*

Many of Siena's finest and most interesting hotels are outside the walls—out in the lovely countryside, or near the city gates, as close to the centre as cars can logically penetrate. What's left, in the centre, is simple but comfortable enough. In the summer, rooms are in short supply and it would be a good idea to book ahead. If you come without a reservation, your first stop should be the **Hotel Information Centre** run by the city's innkeepers, © 288 084. It's conveniently located in Piazza San Domenico, the terminus of all intercity bus routes (*open 9–7 Mon–Sat*). If you arrive by train, take the city bus up from the station to Piazza Matteotti, and walk a block down Via Curtatone. Even at the worst of times, they should be able to find you something—except during the Palio, of course, when you should make your bookings several months in advance.

If you have a car, a number of hotels outside the walls have a rural Tuscan charm and views of the city that more than make up for the slight inconvenience.

★★★★ La Certosa di Maggiano, near the Porta Romana, ✆ 288 180. About 1km southeast of the city, this is one of the most remarkable establishments in Italy, a restored 14th-century Carthusian monastery. There are only 14 rooms, and the luxuries include a heated pool, air-conditioning that works, a quiet chapel and cloister, a salon for backgammon and chess, tennis courts, an excellent restaurant, and a library that would be an antiquarian's dream. Of course, all this doesn't come cheap.

very expensive

★★★★ Park Hotel, Via Marciano 18, ✆ 448 03, fax 490 20. Situated on the hill that dominates Siena with stunning views of the Tuscan landscape, the 16th-century building designed by Peruzzi offers 69 rooms with all the comforts of a class 1 hotel.

★★★★ Villa Patrizia, Via Fiorentina 58, ✆ 504 31, fax 504 31, is a large old villa north of the town with air-conditioning, tennis, parking and a pool.

expensive

★★★★ Villa Scacciapensieri, Strada Scacciapensieri 10, 3km north of the city, ✆ 41 441. There are sunset views over Siena from this quiet country house divided into 29 spacious rooms; besides the view, it features a pool and a good restaurant with an outdoor terrace.

★★★ Santa Caterina, Via Enea Silvio Piccolomini 7, ✆ 22 11 05, fax 27 10 87. An 18th-century house not far from Porta Romana, with 19 attractive rooms which are double glazed and air-conditioned.

moderate–expensive

Many of Siena's two- and three-star hotels cluster around the entrances to the city.

★★★ Garden, Via Custoza 2, ✆ 47 056, has a swimmimg pool.

★★★ Palazzo Ravizza, Pian dei Mantellini, near the Porta Laterina, just inside the walls, ✆ 280 462. Its 30 rooms occupy an old town house, the restaurant isn't anything special, but the rooms are cosy and there is a pretty terrace.

moderate

★★★ Chiusarelli, Via Curtatone 15, ✆ 280 562, fax 271 177. An attractive villa in a pretty garden, with the bonus of a car park. Conveniently near the bus station.

★★★ **Continentale**, Via Banchi di Sopra 85, © 41 451. A very central location in a 16th-century palace complete with faded frescoes and grand stairway.

★★★ **Duomo**, Via Stalloreggi 34, south of the Duomo, © 289 088. A comfortably old-fashioned choice close to the centre.

★★★ **Minerva**, Via Garibaldi 72, © 284 474, fax 284 474. Situated on a busy road but all the rooms are ranged round an inner courtyard; there is a also a lift and facilities for the disabled.

★★★ **Moderno**, Via B. Peruzzi 19, © 270 596, fax 270 596. A large hotel in a central location with a garden and parking.

★★ **Lea**, Viale XXIV Maggio 10, © 28 3207. Centrally located at the end of the pedestrian zone.

inexpensive–moderate

★★ **Canon d'Oro**, Via Montanini 28, near the bus station, © 44 321, is a well-run establishment and a good bargain.

★★ **Centrale**, Via Cecco Angolieri 26, © 280 379.

★★ **Piccolo Hotel Il Palio**, Piazza del Sale 19, © 281 131. A little way from the centre, but it has the advantages of a quiet location and a friendly, English-speaking proprietress.

★ **Tre Donzelle**, Via delle Donzelle, © 280 358, is quite genteel.

inexpensive

Inexpensive places are a little hard to find—especially before term when they're full of university students looking for a permanent place.

★★ **Il Giardino**, Via Baldassare Peruzzi 43, © 220 090, highly recommended in readers' letters, is situated near the Porta Pispini, with good views and a swimming pool.

★ **La Perla**, Via delle Terme, © 288 088.

Youth Hostel

The city of Siena runs its own youth hostel, the **Ostello della Gioventù Guidoriccio**, Via Fiorentina 17, © 52 212, in Lo Stellino, 2km from the city (bus no. 15 from Piazza Gramsci). No cards are required, but in 1993 good modern doubles and dorm rooms with breakfast were going for L18,000 a head; arrive early in July and August.

Capital of day trippers, Pisa isn't known for fine hotels, but there's usually enough room for the relatively few visitors who elect to stay overnight.

expensive–luxury

★★★★ **Grand Hotel Duomo**, Via S. Maria 94, © 561 894. The best, very close to the Campo dei Miracoli, a modern though richly appointed luxury hotel with a roof garden and a garage; all the rooms are air-conditioned.

★★★ **Royal Victoria**, Lungarno Pacinotti, © 502 130. A tasteful and modern establishment, its best features are rooms overlooking the Arno and its own garage; parking can be a problem in Pisa (L70,000 without bath, L115,000 with).

moderate

★★★ **California Park Hotel**, San Giuliano Terme, just outside the city on S1 (Via Aurelia), © 890 726. A good place to stay if you're driving—a large hotel with a park and a pool (open March–Oct).

★★★ **Resthouse Primavera**, Via Aurelia 342, 75 Loc. Migliarino, © 803 310, fax 80 33 15. A modern hotel with air and noise conditioning, well located for the Florence–Coast motorway.

★★★ **Terminus e Plaza**, Via Colombo 45, © 500 303. Like many middle-range hotels south of the Arno, near the train station (L58–115,000 depending on the plumbing).

★★★ **Villa Corliano**, Loc. Rigoli, © 818 193. A stunning 15th-century villa halfway between Lucca and Pisa with Baroque frescoes and antique furniture, set in beautiful grounds .

★★★ **Villa Kinzica**, Piazza Arcivescovado 2, © 560 419, fax 551 204. In a marvellous location, with air-conditioning.

inexpensive

Inexpensive places are spread throughout town, and most of them are often full of students; it's always best to call first.

★★ **Amalfitana**, Via Roma 44, © 290 00, is small and cheap, but on a busy road.

★★ **Il Campaldino**, Via Tagliamento 24, © 562 373 has a central location and reasonable prices.

★★	**Leon Bianco**, Piazza Pozzetto 6, ✆ 543 673, has doubles.
★	**Albergo Giardino**, in Piazza Manin, just outside the walls, ✆ 563 101.
★	**Di Stefano** at Via Sant'Apollonia 35, ✆ 553 559.
★	**Gronchi**, Piazza Arcivesovado 1, ✆ 561 823.
★	**Helvetia**, Via Don Boschi 31, ✆ 553 084.

Where to Stay in Lucca   *(0583–)*

Lucca can be less than charm city if you arrive without booking ahead; there simply aren't enough rooms (especially inexpensive ones) to meet demand, and the Lucchesi aren't in any hurry to do anything about it.

very expensive–luxury

★★★★★**Principessa Elisa**, outside the city, at Massa Pisana on Via SS del Brennero 1616, ✆ 379 737. Here you can bed down in Castruccio Castracani's own palace, built for the great Lucchese warlord in 1321. Often rebuilt since, it currently wears the façade of a stately Rococo mansion, and is surrounded by acres of 18th-century gardens and a pool. Thoroughly modern inside, amenities include air-conditioning, TVs and minibars in the rooms (Mar–Nov).

moderate

★★★ **La Luna**, Corte Compagni 12, ✆ 493 634. In a quiet part of the centre, this is a cosy place, with a private garage.

★★★ **Piccolo Hotel Puccini**, Via di Poggio 9, ✆ 55 421, fax 534 87. A small and comfortable hotel right in the heart of things, with 14 rooms.

★★★ **Rex**, Piazza Ricasoli 19, ✆ 955 443, fax 954 348. A good hotel with 25 rooms, all but one with a bathroom.

★★★ **Universo**, Piazza Puccini, ✆ 493 678. Inside the walls you cannot do better than this slightly frayed, green-shuttered and thoroughly delightful place, although some rooms are nicer than others; Ruskin and nearly everyone else who followed him to Lucca slept here.

★★★ **Villa Rinascimento**, Santa Maria del Giudice, 9km along the S12 from Lucca to Pisa, ✆ 378 292, fax 378 292. Large, clean and simply decorated rooms in a 15th-century villa, with the added attractions of a rustic dining room and swimming pool.

★★ **Ilaria**, Via del Fosso 20, ✆ 47 558, offers 14 quaint rooms on Lucca's baby canal.

★★ **Diana**, Via del Molinetto 11, near the cathedral, ✆ 490 368. Friendly and well-run with some of the nicest inexpensive rooms in Tuscany, some with bath.

★★ **Moderno**, Via V. Civitalli 38, ✆ 55 840, has a central location. Modern, comfortable and rarely crowded.

★★ **Villa Casanova**, Via Casanova, Balbano, just outside the city (city bus 5 and then a 1½-mile up-hill walk, or take a taxi), ✆ 548 429, has simple rooms but a pleasant garden, tennis and a swimming-pool to lounge by.

★ **Cinzia**, Via della Dogana 9, ✆ 491 323. Is one of the cheapest inside the walls.

Youth Hostel

The youth hostel is 2km north of town on Via del Brennero, in Salicchi (bus 7 from the station), ✆ 341 811 (open 10 Mar–10 Oct).

Nightlife with Great Aunt Florence is still awaiting its Renaissance; according to the Florentines she's conservative, somewhat deaf and retires early—1am is very, very late in this city. However, there are plenty of people who wish it weren't so, and slowly, slowly, Florence by night is beginning to mean more than the old *passeggiata* over the Ponte Vecchio and an ice cream, and perhaps a late trip up to Fiesole to contemplate the lights.

Look for listings of concerts and events in Florence's daily, *La Nazione*; the tourist office's free *Florence Today* contains bilingual monthly information and calendar, as does a booklet called *Florence Concierge Information*, available in hotels and tourist offices; the monthly *Firenze Spettacolo*, sold in news-stands, is published only in Italian but fills you in on ecology and trekking

Entertainment and Nightlife

activities, film societies, bar music and the latest New Age mumbo jumbo to rock Florence. The annual guide *Guida locali di Firenze* also gives listings. For a listing of all current films being shown in Florence (Italian and dubbed in Italian), call © 198.

In Siena, Pisa and Lucca classical music lovers are the most likely to be rewarded. Take note of the cities festivals which can be great fun, listed on p.19.

Irish Pub, Piazza Santa Maria Nuova, live music and an ex-pat atmosphere.
Robin Hood Pub, Via dell'Oriuolo, same as above.

meeting places

The evening in Florence will usually begin by meeting up in a piazza. For typical crowds, head to **Piazza Michelangelo**, where local lads and lasses perch on their scooters eating ice cream. Or stroll along to the central **Piazza della Repubblica** then down **Via Calzaiuoli** to the **Ponte Vecchio** and back again.

For the more alternative and trendy crowd, head for **Piazza Santo Spirito**, especially in the summer months when the piazza and the church steps are packed with young people served by the surrounding pubs and bars. Or you could meet in **Piazza del Carmine** in front of La Dolce Vita and Il Cabiria disco bars. Other meeting places include Parteere and Le Cascine.

performance arts

The opera and concert season runs from November to April at the **Teatro Comunale**. Big-name jazz performers, classical artists and others are brought to Florence by **Musicus Concentus**, Piazza del Carmine 14, © 287 347; rock and jazz tours happen in the big **Palasport**, Campo di Marte, Viale Paoli.

Live Music

Classical Concerts

Concerts are held in the churches of Santo Stefano al Ponte Vecchio and Santa Croce, and Teatro Comunale, Corso Italia 16, © 27 9236 and Teatro della Pergola, Via della Pergola 18. The following **orchestras** perform frequently: ORT Orchestra della Toscana, Via dei Benci 20, © 242 767; Amici della Musica, Via G Sirtori 49, © 608 420; Orchestra da Camera Fiorentina, Via E. Poggi 6, © 787 7322.

Rock and Jazz Concert Venues

Teatro Puccini, Via delle Cascine 41; Auditorium Flo, Via M. Mercati 24b, © 490 437; Teatro Verdi, Via Ghibellina 101, © 212 320. Concerts are arranged by **Toscana Music Pool** © 243 280. Box Office, Via Faenza 139r, © 210 804.

cinemas

Films in English are shown daily at the **Cinema Astro**, Piazza San Simone near Santa Croce (no tel; closed Mon and July). **Spazio Uno in Via del Sole**, 10 occasionally has films in their original language.

Check out each club's offerings as many places have themed evenings. Or head to one of the squares listed below and ask around to find out what is going on.

Amadeus, Via Alfani 26r, for jazz and rock music.

Caffè Caruso, Via Lambertesca 16r, for live music and dancing.

Caffedecò, Piazza della Libertà 45–46r. If you want to join Florence's swells, put on the dog and head out to this elegant place done up in tasteful art deco, with live jazz (closed Mon).

Caffé Latino, Via Faenza 27, for live music and dancing .

Caffè Voltaire, Via della Scala 9r (Piazza S. Maria Novella), frequented for the past 10 years by alternative-minded Florentines and where on any given evening you may find a poetry reading, salsa, reggae, jazz, samba, blues, or *cucina nuova*; if you're going to live in Florence for a while, consider becoming a member of its club (closed Sun).

Central Park, Via Fosso Macinante 3. Summer club with live music, three dance floors, shows and snacks

Dolce Vita, Piazza del Carmine, is one of the most popular places in the Oltrarno, a bar to see and be seen in.

Drunk's Ladder, Piazza IV Novembre, Sesto Fiorentino. Italian craziness and banana splits are on tap here, a video-pub with the occasional live band.

Du Monde, Via San Niccolò 103r, a cocktail bar offering food, drink and music for the elegant Florentine which stays open to 5 in the morning.

Flog Concerti, Via Michele Mercati 24b. Dance music and live concerts (especially the more alternative Italian 'ragamuffin' bands such as 99 Posse and Mano Negra). (Every Thurs–Sun, summer only).

KGB, Borgo degli Albizi 9. Underground music, acid jazz depending on the night.

Mago Merlino, Via dei Pilastri 31r. A relaxed tea-room/bar with live music, theatre, shows and games.

Maracanà, Via Faenza 4, for live samba, mambo and bossanova.

Parterre, Piazza della Libertà, outdoors—two bars, concerts and video screens.

Puerto Rico, Viale Redi 29b, has Caribbean music and exotic cocktails on offer.

Il Rex, Via Fiesolana 23r. Currently number one hotspot, popular in winter.

Riflessi d'Epoca, Via dei Renai 13r, frequently has live jazz in a smoky ambience. It stays open later than the average club (i.e. after 1am).

Rifrullo, Via S. Niccolò 55r, is an older pub/wine bar, probably the most popular of all and one of the first to attract people to the Oltrarno. There's no word for 'cosy' in Italian, but the Rifrullo does the best it can.

Stonehenge, Via dell'Amorino 16r, near S. Lorenzo, with rock and cocktails from 10pm until after 1am.

gay clubs

There are two **gay clubs** in Florence; the best is **Flamingo**, Via Pandolfi 26.

discos

Andromeda, Via dei Climatori 13, is particularly popular with young foreigners.

Jackie 'O, Via Erta Canina 24. An old favourite, early 30 age group.

Rock Caffè, Borgo degli Albizi 66r, is the current hotspot with a theme every night.

Tenax, out near the airport in Via Pratese 47, is always busy.

Space Electronic Disco, Via Palazzuolo 37, is a high-tech noise box and, with Yab (below) an old standby.

Yab, Via dei Sassetti 5, shows a preference for acid jazz.

055, Via Verdi 57r, is open only on weekends and organizes themed evenings.

Meccanó, Viale degli Olmi 1, is where the younger crowd get their kicks—a different music policy each night.

Happyland, where the music pounds and the atmosphere is feverish (open only at weekends).

Siena

One of the loveliest things to do on a summer evening is to attend a free concert given by the students and teachers at the **Accademia Musicale Chigiana**, Via de la Città 85, © 46152; the tourist office has the programme as well. From the end of April until early Sept, the *contrade* hold their annual festivals: the Dragon, Turtle, Giraffe, Owl, Unicorn, Snail and Dolphin in June; the Caterpillar, Elephant, Mussel Shell, Rhinoceros, Porcupine and Panther in July–August.

Pisa

Associazione di Cultura Cinematografica, Vicolo Scaramucci 4, © 502 640, on the south bank near Piazza San Martino, shows an excellent selection of films from around the world. Concerts take place at **Teatro Comunale Verdi** in Via Palestro, more off-beat shows at a former church at the end of Via San Zeno.

Lucca

On the third weekend of every month there is an enormous **antiques market** in and around Piazza San Martino. The summer **Festival de Malia** (at the Villa Neale 8km towards Pistoia) and September's Settembre Lucchese (in the city's Teatro Comunale) centre around classical music and ballet.

Shopping

'Made in Italy' has long been a byword for style and quality, especially in fashion and leather, but also in home design, ceramics, kitchenware, jewellery, lace and linens, glassware and crystal, chocolates, hats, straw-work, art books, engravings, handmade stationery, gold and silverware, a hundred kinds of liqueurs, wine, aperitifs, coffee machines, gastronomic specialities, antique reproductions, as well as the antiques themselves. If you are looking for the latter and are spending a lot of money, be sure to demand a certificate of authenticity—reproductions can be very, very good. To get your antique or modern art purchases home, you will have to apply to the Export Department of the Italian Ministry of Education—a possible hassle. You will have to pay an export tax as well; your seller should know the details.

Florence, which increasingly resembles a glittering medieval shopping mall, has the best variety of goods in the region. There are major monthly antique fairs in Arezzo (first Sunday), Gubbio and Pistoia (second Sunday), Lucca (third Sunday), and Florence (last Sunday). Ceramics are an old tradition in Montelupo, Gubbio and Deruta; porcelain in Sesto Fiorentino; glassware in Empoli. Volterra is famous for its alabaster and alabaster art, Castelfidardo for its accordions; in Elba you can buy semi-precious stones and minerals, in the Mugello and Casentino wrought iron and copperware, straw goods in the lower Valdarno, and marble in Carrara, though taking it home may pose a bit of a problem. Wine and olive oil, bags of *porcini* mushrooms, jars of truffles and other gastronomic specialities are available everywhere.

Italians don't like department stores, but there are a few chains—COIN stores often have good buys on almost the latest fashions. Standa and UPIM are more like Woolworth's; they have a reasonable selection of clothes, houseware, etc., and often supermarkets in their basements. Most stay open throughout the day, but some take the same break as other Italian shops—from 1pm to 3 or 4pm. Non-EC nationals should make sure to save their receipts for Customs on the way home. Shipping goods is a risky business unless you do it through a very reputable shop. Note well that the attraction of shopping in Italy is strictly limited to luxury items; for less expensive clothes and household items you'll always, always do better in Britain or America. Prices for clothes, even in street markets, are often ridiculously high. Bargains of any kind are rare, and the cheaper goods are often very poor quality.

Italian clothes are lovely, but if you have a large-boned Anglo-American build, you may find it hard to get a good fit, especially on trousers or skirts (Italians are a long-waisted, slim-hipped bunch). Shoes are often narrower than the sizes at home.

sizes

Women's Shirts/Dresses

UK	10	12	14	16	18
US	8	10	12	14	16
Italy	40	42	44	46	48

Sweaters

10	12	14	16		
8	10	12	14		
46	48	50	52		

Women's Shoes

3	4	5	6	7	8
4	5	6	7	8	9
36	37	38	39	40	41

Men's Shirts

UK/US	14	14½	15	15½	16	16½	17	17½
Italy	36	37	38	39	40	41	42	43

Men's Suits

UK/US	36	38	40	42	44	46
Italy	46	48	50	52	54	56

Men's Shoes

UK	2	3	4	5	6	7	8	9	10	11	12
US	5	6	7	7½	8	9	10	10½	11	12	13
Italy	34	36	37	38	39	40	41	42	43	44	45

weights and measures

1 kilogramme (1000 g)—2.2 lb

1 etto (100 g)— 1/4 lb (approx)
1 litre—1.76 pints

1 lb—0.45 kg

1 pint—0.568 litres

1 quart—1.136 litres

1 Imperial gallon—4.546 litres

1 US gallon—3.785 litres

1 metre—39.37 inches
1 kilometre—0.621 miles

1 foot—0.3048 metres
1 mile—1.61 kilometres

Antiques and Art Galleries

Borgo Ognissanti and the various Lungarni are the places to look for antiques and art galleries.

Antica Maraviglia, Borgo San Jacopo 6r, © 238 1489. Antique toys and games, objects and porcelain.

Atelier Alice, Via Faenza 12, and **I Mascheroni Atelier**, Via dei Tavolini 13r, both sell Italian carnival masks.

P. Bazzanti e Figli, Lungarno Corsini 44, where you can pick up an exact replica of the bronze pig in the Mercato Nuovo.

La Bottega di Marino, Via Santo Spirito 8r, © 213 184. Family restorers and antiques merchants.

Casa dei Tessuti, Via de' Pecori 20–24r, keeps Florence's ancient cloth trade alive with lovely linens, silks and woollens.

Auction Houses

Serious collectors may want to check Florence's busy auction houses.

Casa d'Aste Pandolfini, Borgo degli Albizi 26, © 234 0888.

Casa d'Aste Pitti, Via Maggio 15, © 239 6382.

Palazzo Internazionale delle Aste ed Esposizioni, Via Maggio 11, © 282 905.

Sotheby's Italia, Via G. Capponi 26, © 247 9021.

Books

Bookworms do better in Florence than most Italian cities, although the prices of books in English will make you weep.

After Dark, Via Del Moro 86r, new and second-hand English books.

BM Bookshop, Borgo Ognissanti 4r, has books in English and an excellent selection of art books.

Feltrinelli, Via Cavour 12–20r. The English department is on the first floor and there is also a good selection of art books.

Franco Maria Ricci, Via delle Belle Donne 41r, a fabulous collection of art books.

For the widest selections in English, with many books about Florence:

The Paperback Exchange, Via Fiesolana 31r.

Seeber, Via Tornabuoni 70r.

Caponi, Borgo Ognissanti 12r, has a fairytale selection of dresses if you happen to have or know the kind of little girl who can wear white.

Città del Sole, Borgo Ognissanti, near Piazza Goldoni, is the best toy shop in Florence.

Department Stores

COIN, Via dei Calzaiuoli 56r.

UPIM, Piazza della Repubblica.

Fashion

Although central Florence sometimes seems like one solid boutique, the city is no longer the queen of Italian fashion—the lack of an airport, more than anything else, has sent most of the big designers to Milan. Many of the big names of the 1960s and 70s, the international chain stores of the 1980s and 90s, are represented in smart Via Tornabuoni and in the streets around the Duomo. Clothes shops generally are to be found in Via Roma and Via Calzaiuoli.

designer wear

Giorgio Armani, Via della Vigna Nuova 51r.

Enrico Coveri, Via Tornabuoni 81r.

Oliver, Via Vacchereccia 15r. Fashionable casual men's wear.

Principe, Via degli Strozzi 21–19r. Classical men's and women's wear.

Valentino, Via della Vigna Nuova 47r.

hats

Borsellino Hat, Via dei Cimatori 22r, classic hat makers.

shoes

Beltrami, Via Tornabuoni.

Ferragamo, Via de'Tornabuoni 14r. Best boots in town.

Food and Wine

food

There are a number of speciality food shops around the Mercato Centrale, or you can try the following:

> **Allrientar Gastronomia**, in Borgo SS. Apostoli, where you can pick up items like truffle creams.

Biagini, Via dei Banchi 57, off Piazza S. Maria Novella, good for wines and spirits.

La Bottega del Brunello, Via Ricasoli 81r. Shop divided in two parts—for display and for tasting the wine and specialities on sale.

De Rhan International, Via del Campofiore 112, has a wide range of Tuscan and Italian wines and olive oil products.

Old English Stores, Via Vecchietti 28r, for that pot of Marmite or Worcester sauce.

Il Procacci, Via Tornabuoni 64r. This is a high quality *alimentari* (food shop) selling regional specialities as well as foreign foods.

La Porta del Tartufo, Borgo Ognissanti 133r. Virtually only sells different types of truffles or 'truffled' foods ranging from *grappa* to salmon paste. Also good wines and other typical products.

wine

Laudemio, Via dei Serragli 133, © 233 7134.

Marchesi de' Frescobaldi, Via di S Spirito 11, one of the largest wine suppliers in Italy; visit their ancient cellars.

Jewellery

Florence is famous for its jewellery, and the shops on and around the Ponte Vecchio are forced by the nature of their location into wide-open competition, and good prices for Florentine brushed gold (although much of it is made in Arezzo these days) and antique jewellery are more common than you may think.

Cibola, Via XXVII Aprile 47r, © 499 113. Halfway between a shop and an art gallery—interesting artistic jewellery.

Pietro Agnoletti, Via de'Pepi 18, © 240 810. Handmade gold jewellery, but you must book for an appointment.

Kitchen ware

Il Tegame, Piazza Gaetano Salvemini 7.

Leather

Florence is still known for its leather, and you'll see plenty of it in the centre, around Via della Vigna Nuova and Via del Parione, and less expensively at an unusual institution called the **Leather School**, which occupies part of Santa Croce's cloister (entrance at Piazza Santa Croce 16 or Via S. Giuseppe 5r).

Giulio Giannini e Figlio, Piazza Pitti 37, ⓒ 212 621; originally book binders, now they also produce leather albums and leather desk-top objects as well as handmade paper following a 17th-century technique.

Gucci, Via Tornabuoni 73–75.

Some of the cheapest places for leather jackets are the stalls and shops around San Lorenzo market, but be prepared to bargain.

Linen

Ghezzi, Via Calzaiuoli 110r, has fashionable towels and bed linens.

Marbled Paper

Florence is one of the few places in the world to make marbled paper, an art brought over from the Orient by Venice in the 12th century. Each sheet is hand-dipped in a bath of colours to create a delicate, lightly coloured clouded design—no two sheets are alike. Marbled-paper-covered stationery items or just sheets of marbled paper are available at:

La Bottega, Artigiana del Libro, Lungarno Corsini 40r.

Giulio Giannini e Figlio, Piazza Pitti 37r.

Il Papiro, the oldest manufacturer, has three shops at Via Cavour 55r, Piazza del Duomo 24r, and Lungarno Acciaiuoli 42r.

Il Torchio, Via dei Bardi 17, ⓒ 234 2862, sells all types of coloured paper. The workbench is in the shop so you can see the artisans in action.

These shops (and many others) also carry Florentine paper with its colourful Gothic patterns.

Medieval Cures

Farmaceutica di Santa Maria Novella, Via della Scala 16n, hasn't changed much since 1612 and still sells medieval cures and Dominican remedies.

Silver, Crystal, Mosaics and Porcelain

Ceramiche Gambone, Via della Robbia 82. Ceramics, crystal, glass and bronze.

Paci, Viuzzo delle Case Nuove 1, ⓒ 732 2624. A father and son make and restore hard stone mosaic objects. Ronald Reagan shopped here!

A. Poggi, Via Calzaiuoli 105r and 116r, has one of the city's widest selections of silver, crystal and porcelain (including Florence's own Richard-Ginori).

Florence's lively street markets offer good bargains, fake designer clothing and even some authentic labels. The huge **San Lorenzo market** is the largest and most boisterous, where many Florentines buy their clothes; **Sant'Ambrogio** is a bustling food market; the **Mercato Nuovo** or Straw Market is the most touristic, but not flagrantly so. On the last Sunday of the month there's a bric-à-brac and food market in **Piazza Santo Spirito**. There's an extensive clothes and shoes market every Tuesday morning in the Cascine, but perhaps the most fun is the **Mercato delle Pulci** (Flea Market) on Sundays in Piazza dei Ciompi, offering all kinds of desirable junk.

Shopping in Siena

Siena, with its population of only 60,000, is blissfully short of designer boutiques and such. Even the usual tourist trinkets seem lacking—illuminated plastic models of the cathedral are harder to find every year! Nevertheless, a thorough search of the back streets will turn up plenty of unpretentious artisan workshops—almost all of them so unconcerned with tourism they don't even bother hanging out a sign.

Vetrate Artistiche Toscane, Via della Gallozza 5, glass workers and restorers, also selling small objects and mirrors, lampshades etc.

Via di Città 94 sells interesting ceramic pieces.

Via Galuzza 5, just off Piazza Independenza, where an artist with a distinctive modern style creates works in stained glass (most of them portable).

Via San Girolamo 15, brass and pewter shields of the *contrade*, and other paraphernalia of Siena's great obsession, can be had here.

Books

Libreria Senese, Via di Città 64, is Siena's best bookshop.

Food

Antica Drogheria Manganelli, Via di Città 71–73, with one hundred-year-old original wooden shelving and a beautiful display of delicious regional foods and wines.

Forno dei Galli, Via dei Termini 45, historic Sienese bakers selling bread, fresh pasta and *pasticceria*.

Gastronomia Morbidi, Banchi di Sopra 75, ℰ 280 268. Founded in 1925, this
wonderful shop has four floors of national and Sienese culinary specialities
and a wine section selling all the best wines in Italy.

Pasticceria Nannini, Via F. Tozzi 2, typical Sienese sweets and pastries.

Shoes

Pasqui, Via di Città 9, ℰ 282 151. Expensive and elegant shoe shop.

Shopping in Pisa

Pisa is the best place in Tuscany to purchase bizarre and tacky **souvenirs**, and the
best selection is crowded around the Campo dei Miracoli. Light-up Leaning
Towers in pink and yellow come in all sizes and are an amazingly good buy; some
have pen and pencil set attached for the scholar, or grinning plastic kittens for the
kids' room, or naked ladies for your favourite uncle. The other specialities are
medieval weapons—crossbows, cudgels, maces, whips—and plastic skulls, rep-
tiles and insects. If you'd prefer a **book** in English to these delights, try Feltrinelli
at Corso Italia 117. I.u8y

Clothes

If it is the boutiques you're after, head down Via Oberdan and Corso Italia. Borgo
Stretto is good for boutiques and smart clothes shops, for example:

Casa del Guanto, Via di Borgo Stretto 48, selling all types of gloves.

Nazareno Gabrielli, Via di Borgo Stretto 25.Sells clothes, leather wear and
accessories.

Food

L'altra Roba, Piazza delle Vettovaglie 3, sells dried fruit,vegetables preserved in
oil as well as conserves, oil and wine.

Enogastronomia F.lli Simi, Via San Martino 6, pasta, cheeses, wines, olive oil
and homemade cakes are what the Simi family have been selling for over
100 years.

Gastronomia Gratin, Via Crispi 66. A smart general food store with a good
selection of salami, ham, oil and wine

Piazza delle Vettovaglie, food market in pretty medieval square.

La Badiola, Via del Parco 10, località San Pancrazio. Produces and sells good quality reasonably priced wines in a beautiful setting, an old villa in a large park.

La Botteghina del Vipore, loc. Pieve Santo Stefano. All the most delicious Tuscan products are on sale here including some exclusively made for the Botteghina such as butter made from pure buffalo milk.

Pasticceria Taddeucci, Piazza San Michele 34, pastries both savoury and sweet, as well as homemade ricotta tart and other local specialities.

Sports and Activities

Boats and Sailing: The sailing is beautiful among the coves of the Tuscan archipelago and around the Argentario; if you want to learn how, there's a good sailing school in Torre del Lago Puccini, © (0584) 342 084.

Golf: The nearest golf course to Florence is the 18-hole **Golf Club Ugolino**, in Gràssina, 7km southeast of the city, on the Chiantigiana-Impruneta, © 230 1096; a lovely course laid out among olives and cypresses.

Medieval Sports: Some ancient sports like the annual horse races, or palios (two in Siena) are still popular, and not entirely as a tourist attraction: the rivalries between neighbourhoods and cities are intense. The Florentines play three games of Renaissance football a year (calcio in costume); in Lucca crossbow archers compete from different city quarters. Pistoia has an annual joust; in Pisa it's medieval tug-of-war.

Racing and Riding: Horse riding is increasingly popular, and **Agriturist** has a number of villa and riding holidays on offer in Tuscany. **The National Association of Equestrian Tourism** (ANTE) is probably more active here than anywhere in Italy. The Cascine has **Florence's** race course (Ippodromo Le Cascine, © 360 598) and trotting course (Ippodromo della Mulina, © 411 107). The nearest place to go riding in the **Tuscan hills** is the Country Riding Club, Via di Grioli, at Badia a Settimo in Scandicci, 6km southwest of Florence, © 790 277. In **Pisa** you can go riding at the Cooperativa Agrituristica in Via Tre Colli in Calci. For more information, write directly to the local Agriturist office:

> Via della Sapienza 39, 53100 **Siena**, © (0577) 46 194
> Via B. Croce 62, 56100 **Pisa**, © (050) 26 221
> Viale Barsanti e Matteucci, 55100 **Lucca**, © (0583) 332 044.

Rowing: There is an annual rowing race between the four old maritime republics of Venice, Amalfi, Genoa and Pisa, which alternates between the cities. If there's enough water in the Arno, you can try rowing or **canoeing**; contact the Società Canottieri Comunali, Lungarno Ferrucci 6, © 681 2151, or the Società Canottieri Firenze, Lungarno dei Medici 8, © 282 130 (membership only).

Swimming: The one activity many summertime visitors begin to crave after tramping through the sights is a dip in a pool. The prettiest one in **Florence** is the Piscina le Pavoniere, in the Cascine, open June–Sept 10–6.30; others are Bellariva, up the Arno at Lungarno Colombo 2, open June–Sept 11–5. There are two covered, year-round pools: Amici del Nuoto, Via del Romito 38, © 483 951, and Costoli, Via Paoli, near Campo di Marte, © 669 744. In **Pisa** you can swim in the pool in Via Andrea Pisano.

Tennis: Tennis-courts are nearly everywhere. In Florence try the Circolo Tennis alle Cascine, © 356 651.

The fathers of modern Italian were Dante, Manzoni, and television. Each did their part in creating a national language from an infinity of regional and local dialects; the Florentine Dante, the first 'immortal' to write in the vernacular, did much to put the Tuscan dialect in the foreground of Italian literature. Manzoni's revolutionary novel, *I Promessi Sposi* (The Betrothed), heightened national consciousness by using an everyday language all could understand in the 19th century. Television in the last few decades is performing an even more spectacular linguistic unification; although the majority of Italians still speak a dialect at home, school, and work, their TV idols insist on proper Italian.

Perhaps because they are so busy learning their own beautiful but grammatically complex language, Italians are not especially apt at learning others. English lessons, however, have been the rage for years, and at most hotels and restaurants there will be someone who speaks some English. In small towns and out of the way places, finding an Anglophone may prove more difficult. The words and phrases below should help you out in most situations, but the ideal way to come to Italy is with some Italian under your belt; your visit will be richer, and you're much more likely to make some Italian friends.

Pronunciation

Italian words are pronounced phonetically. Every vowel and consonant (except *h*) is sounded. Consonants are the same as in English, except the *c* which, when followed by an 'e' or 'i', is pronounced like the English 'ch' (*cinque* thus becomes cheenquay). Italian *g* is also soft before 'i' or 'e' as in *gira*, pronounced jee-ra. *H* is never sounded; *z* is pronounced like 'ts'. The consonants *sc* before the vowels 'i' or 'e' become like the English 'sh' as in *sci*, pronounced shee; *ch* is pronounced like a 'k' as in *Chianti*, kee-an-tee; *gn* as 'ny' in English (*bagno*, pronounced banyo; while *gli* is pronounced like the middle of the word million (*Castiglione*, pronounced Ca-steely-oh-nay).

Vowel pronunciation is: *a* as in English father; *e* when unstressed is pronounced like 'a' in fate, as in *mele*, when stressed can be the same or like the 'e' in pet (*bello*); *i* is like the 'i' in machine; *o*, like *e*, has two sounds: 'o' as in hope when

Language

unstressed (*tacchino*), and usually 'o' as in rock when stressed (*morte*); *u* is pronounced like the 'u' in June.

The accent usually (but not always!) falls on the penultimate syllable. Also note that in the big northern cities, the informal way of addressing someone as you, *tu*, is widely used; the more formal *lei* or *voi* is commonly used in provincial districts.

Useful Words and Phrases

yes/no/maybe	*sì/ no/ forse*
I don't know	*Non lo so*
I don't understand (Italian)	*Non capisco (italiano)*
Does someone here	*C'è qualcuno qui*
speak English?	*che parla inglese?*
Speak slowly	*Parla lentamente*
Could you assist me?	*Potrebbe aiutarmi?*
Help!	*Aiuto!*
Please	*per favore*
Thank you (very much)	*(Molte) grazie*
You're welcome	*Prego*
It doesn't matter	*Non importa*
All right	*Va bene*
Excuse me	*Mi scusi*
Be careful!	*Attenzione!*
Nothing	*Niente*
It is urgent!	*È urgente!*
How are you?	*Come sta?*
Well, and you?	*Bene, e Lei?*
What is your name?	*Come si chiama?*
Hello	*Salve* or *ciao* (both informal)
Good morning	*Buongiorno* (formal hello)
Good afternoon, evening	*Buonasera* (also formal hello)
Good night	*Buona notte*
Goodbye	*ArrivederLa* (formal), *arrivederci*, *ciao* (informal)
What do you call this in Italian?	*Come si chiama questo in italiano?*
What?	*Che?*
Who?	*Chi?*
Where?	*Dove?*
When?	*Quando?*
Why?	*Perché?*
How?	*Come?*
How much?	*Quanto?*
I am lost	*Mi sono smarrito*
I am hungry	*Ho fame*
I am thirsty	*Ho sete*
I am sorry	*Mi dispiace*
I am tired	*Sono stanco*

I am sleepy	*Ho sonno*
I am ill	*Mi sento male*
Leave me alone	*Lasciami in pace*
good	*buono/ bravo*
bad	*male/ cattivo*
slow	*lento*
fast	*rapido*
big	*grande*
small	*piccolo*
hot	*caldo*
cold	*freddo*
up	*su*
down	*giù*
here	*qui*
there	*lì*

Shopping, Service, Sightseeing

I would like...	*Vorrei...*
Where is/are...	*Dov'è/ Dove sono...*
How much is it?	*Quanto viene questo?/ Quant'è/ Quanto costa questo?*
open	*aperto*
closed	*chiuso*
cheap/expensive	*a buon prezzo/ caro*
bank	*banca*
beach	*spiaggia*
bed	*letto*
church	*chiesa*
entrance	*entrata*
exit	*uscita*
hospital	*ospedale*
money	*soldi*
museum	*museo*
newspaper (foreign)	*giornale (straniero)*
pharmacy	*farmacia*
police station	*commissariato*
policeman	*poliziotto*
post office	*ufficio postale*
sea	*mare*
shop	*negozio*
room	*camera*
telephone	*telefono*
tobacco shop	*tabaccaio*
WC	*toilette/ bagno*
men	*Signori/ Uomini*
women	*Signore/ Donne*

Time

What time is it?	*Che ore sono?*
month	*mese*
week	*settimana*
day	*giorno*
morning	*mattina*
afternoon	*pomeriggio*
evening	*sera*
today	*oggi*
yesterday	*ieri*
tomorrow	*domani*
soon	*fra poco*
later	*dopo/ più tardi*
It is too early	*È troppo presto*
It is too late	*È troppo tardi*

Days

Monday	*lunedì*
Tuesday	*martedì*
Wednesday	*mercoledì*
Thursday	*giovedì*
Friday	*venerdì*
Saturday	*sabato*
Sunday	*domenica*

Numbers

one	*uno/ una*
two	*due*
three	*tre*
four	*quattro*
five	*cinque*
six	*sei*
seven	*sette*
eight	*otto*
nine	*nove*
ten	*dieci*
eleven	*undici*
twelve	*dodici*
thirteen	*tredici*
fourteen	*quattordici*
fifteen	*quindici*
sixteen	*sedici*
seventeen	*diciassette*
eighteen	*diciotto*
nineteen	*diciannove*
twenty	*venti*

twenty-one	*ventuno*
twenty-two	*ventidue*
thirty	*trenta*
thirty-one	*trentuno*
forty	*quaranta*
fifty	*cinquanta*
sixty	*sessanta*
seventy	*settanta*
eighty	*ottanta*
ninety	*novanta*
hundred	*cento*
one hundred and one	*cent' uno*
two hundred	*duecento*
one thousand	*mille*
two thousand	*duemila*
million	*milione*
a thousand million	*miliardo*

Transport

airport	*aeroporto*
bus stop	*fermata*
bus/coach	*autobus/pullman*
railway station	*stazione ferroviaria*
train	*treno*
platform	*binario*
port	*porto*
port station	*stazione marittima*
ship	*nave*
automobile	*macchina*
taxi	*tassì*
ticket	*biglietto*
customs	*dogana*
seat (reserved)	*posto (prenotato)*

Travel Directions

I want to go to...	*Desidero andare a...*
How can I get to...?	*Come posso andare a...?*
Do you stop at...?	*Ferma a...?*
Where is...?	*Dov' è...?*
How far is it to...?	*Quanto siamo lontani da...?*
What is the name of this station?	*Come si chiama questa stazione?*
When does the next ... leave?	*Quando parte il prossimo...?*
From where does it leave?	*Da dove parte?*
How long does the trip take...?	*Quanto tempo dura il viaggio?*
How much is the fare?	*Quant' è il biglietto?*

Have a good trip	*Buon viaggio!*
near	*vicino*
far	*lontano*
left	*sinistra*
right	*destra*
straight ahead	*sempre diritto*
forward	*avanti*
backwards	*indietro*
north	*nord*
south	*sud*
east	*est/ oriente*
west	*ovest/ occidente*
round the corner	*dietro l'angolo*
crossroads	*bivio*
street/road	*strada*
square	*piazza*

Driving

car hire	*noleggio macchina*
motorbike/scooter	*motocicletta/ Vespa*
bicycle	*bicicletta*
petrol/diesel	*benzina/ gasolio*
garage	*garage*
This doesn't work	*Questo non funziona*
mechanic	*meccanico*
map/town plan	*carta/ pianta*
Where is the road to...?	*Dov'è la strada per...?*
breakdown	*guasto* or *panna*
driving licence	*patente di guida*
driver	*guidatore*
speed	*velocità*
danger	*pericolo*
parking	*parcheggio*
no parking	*sosta vietata*
narrow	*stretto*
bridge	*ponte*
toll	*pedaggio*
slow down	*rallentare*

Italian Menu Vocabulary

Antipasti

These before-meal treats can include almost anything; among the most common are:

| *Antipasto misto* | mixed antipasto |
| *Bruschetta* | garlic toast (sometimes with tomatoes) |

Carciofi (*sott' olio*)	artichokes (in oil)
Crostini	liver pâté on toast
Frutti di mare	seafood
Funghi (*trifolati*)	mushrooms (with anchovies, garlic, and lemon)
Gamberi ai fagioli	prawns (shrimps) with white beans
Mozzarella (*in carrozza*)	cow or buffalo cheese (fried with bread in batter)
Olive	olives
Prosciutto (*con melone*)	raw ham (with melon)
Salami	cured pork
Salsicce	sausages

Minestre (Soups) and Pasta

These dishes are the principal typical first courses (*primi*) served throughout Italy.

Agnolotti	ravioli with meat
Cacciucco	spiced fish soup
Cannelloni	meat and cheese rolled in pasta tubes
Cappelletti	small ravioli, often in broth
Crespelle	crêpes
Fettuccine	long strips of pasta
Frittata	omelette
Gnocchi	potato dumplings
Lasagne	sheets of pasta baked with meat and cheese sauce
Minestra di verdura	thick vegetable soup
Minestrone	soup with meat, vegetables, and pasta
Orecchiette	ear-shaped pasta, often served with turnip greens
Panzerotti	ravioli filled with mozzarella, anchovies, and egg
Pappardelle alla lepre	pasta with hare sauce
Pasta e fagioli	soup with beans, bacon, and tomatoes
Pastina in brodo	tiny pasta in broth
Penne all'arrabbiata	quill-shaped pasta with tomatoes and hot peppers
Polenta	cake or pudding of corn semolina
Risotto (*alla Milanese*)	Italian rice (with stock, saffron and wine)
Spaghetti all' Amatriciana	with spicy sauce of salt pork, tomatoes, onions, and chili pepper
Spaghetti alla Bolognese	with ground meat, ham, mushrooms, etc.

Spaghetti alla carbonara	with bacon, eggs, and black pepper
Spaghetti al pomodoro	with tomato sauce
Spaghetti al sugo/ ragù	with meat sauce
Spaghetti alle vongole	with clam sauce
Stracciatella	broth with eggs and cheese
Tagliatelle	flat egg noodles
Tortellini al pomodoro/ panna/ in brodo	pasta caps filled with meat and cheese, served with tomato sauce/with cream/in broth
Vermicelli	very thin spaghetti

Carne (Meat)

Abbacchio	milk-fed lamb
Agnello	lamb
Animelle	sweetbreads
Anatra	duck
Arista	pork loin
Arrosto misto	mixed roast meats
Bistecca alla fiorentina	Florentine beef steak
Bocconcini	veal mixed with ham and cheese and fried
Bollito misto	stew of boiled meats
Braciola	chop
Brasato di manzo	braised beef with vegetables
Bresaola	dried raw meat similar to ham
Capretto	kid
Capriolo	roe-buck
Carne di castrato/ suino	mutton/pork
Carpaccio	thin slices of raw beef served with a piquant sauce
Cassoeula	winter stew with pork and cabbage
Cervello (al burro nero)	brains (in black butter sauce)
Cervo	venison
Cinghiale	boar
Coniglio	rabbit
Cotoletta (alla Milanese/ alla Bolognese)	veal cutlet (fried in bread crumbs/with ham and cheese)
Fagiano	pheasant
Faraona (alla creta)	guinea fowl (in earthenware pot)
Fegato alla veneziana	liver (usually of veal) with filling
Lepre (in salmì)	hare (marinated in wine)
Lombo di maiale	pork loin
Lumache	snails
Maiale (al latte)	pork (cooked in milk)

Manzo	beef
Osso buco	braised veal knuckle with herbs
Pancetta	rolled pork
Pernice	partridge
Petto di pollo (*alla fiorentina/ bolognese/ sorpresa*)	boned chicken breast (fried in butter/with ham and cheese/stuffed and deep fried)
Piccione	pigeon
Pizzaiola	beef steak with tomato and oregano sauce
Pollo (*alla cacciatora/ alla diavola/ alla Marengo*)	chicken (with tomatoes and mushrooms cooked in wine/grilled/fried with tomatoes, garlic and wine)
Polpette	meatballs
Quaglie	quails
Rane	frogs
Rognoni	kidneys
Saltimbocca	veal scallop with *prosciutto* and sage, cooked in wine and butter
Scaloppine	thin slices of veal sautéed in butter
Spezzatino	pieces of beef or veal, usually stewed
Spiedino	meat on a skewer or stick
Stufato	beef braised in white wine with vegetables
Tacchino	turkey
Trippa	tripe
Uccelletti	small birds on a skewer
Vitello	veal

Pesce (Fish)

Acciughe or *Alici*	anchovies
Anguilla	eel
Aragosta	lobster
Aringa	herring
Baccalà	dried salt cod
Bonito	small tuna
Branzino	sea bass
Calamari	squid
Cappe sante	scallops
Cefalo	grey mullet
Coda di rospo	angler fish
Cozze	mussels
Datteri di mare	razor (or date) mussels

Dentice	dentex (perch-like fish)
Dorato	gilt head
Fritto misto	mixed fried delicacies, usually fish
Gamberetto	shrimp
Gamberi (di fiume)	prawns (crayfish)
Granchio	crab
Insalata di mare	seafood salad
Lampreda	lamprey
Merluzzo	cod
Nasello	hake
Orata	bream
Ostriche	oysters
Pesce spada	swordfish
Polipi/ polpi	octopus
Pesce azzurro	various types of small fish
Pesce di San Pietro	John Dory
Rombo	turbot
Sarde	sardines
Seppie	cuttlefish
Sgombro	mackerel
Sogliola	sole
Squadro	monkfish
Stoccafisso	wind-dried cod
Tonno	tuna
Triglia	red mullet (rouget)
Trota	trout
Trota salmonata	salmon trout
Vongole	small clams
Zuppa di pesce	mixed fish in sauce or stew

Contorni (Side Dishes, Vegetables)

Asparagi (alla fiorentina)	asparagus (with fried eggs)
Broccoli (calabrese, romana)	broccoli (green, spiral)
Carciofi (alla giudia)	artichokes (deep fried)
Cardi	cardoons, thistles
Carote	carrots
Cavolfiore	cauliflower
Cavolo	cabbage
Ceci	chickpeas
Cetriolo	cucumber
Cipolla	onion
Fagioli	white beans
Fagiolini	French (green) beans
Fave	broad beans
Finocchio	fennel

Funghi (*porcini*)	mushrooms (boletus)
Insalata (*mista, verde*)	salad (mixed, green)
Lattuga	lettuce
Lenticchie	lentils
Melanzane (*al forno*)	aubergine/eggplant (filled and baked)
Patate (*fritte*)	potatoes (fried)
Peperoni	sweet peppers
Peperonata	stewed peppers, onions, etc. similar to ratatouille
Piselli (*al prosciutto*)	peas (with ham)
Pomodoro(*i*)	tomato(es)
Porri	leeks
Radicchio	red chicory
Radice	radish
Rapa	turnip
Sedano	celery
Spinaci	spinach
Verdure	greens
Zucca	pumpkin
Zucchini	courgettes

Formaggio (Cheese)

Bel Paese	a soft white cow's cheese
Cacio/ Caciocavallo	pale yellow, often sharp cheese
Fontina	rich cow's milk cheese
Groviera	mild cheese (gruyère)
Gorgonzola	soft blue cheese
Parmigiano	Parmesan cheese
Pecorino	sharp sheep's cheese
Provolone	sharp, tangy cheese; *dolce* is less strong
Stracchino	soft white cheese

Frutta (Fruit, Nuts)

Albicocche	apricots
Ananas	pineapple
Arance	oranges
Banane	bananas
Cachi	persimmon
Ciliege	cherries
Cocomero	watermelon
Composta di frutta	stewed fruit
Datteri	dates
Fichi	figs
Fragole (*con panna*)	strawberries (with cream)

Frutta di stagione	fruit in season
Lamponi	raspberries
Macedonia di frutta	fruit salad
Mandarino	tangerine
Mandorle	almonds
Melagrana	pomegranate
Mele	apples
Melone	melon
Mirtilli	bilberries
More	blackberries
Nespola	medlar fruit
Nocciole	hazelnuts
Noci	walnuts
Pera	pear
Pesca	peach
Pesca noce	nectarine
Pignoli/ pinoli	pine nuts
Pompelmo	grapefruit
Prugna/ susina	prune/plum
Uva	grapes

Dolci (Desserts)

Amaretti	macaroons
Cannoli	crisp pastry tubes filled with ricotta, cream, chocolate or fruit
Coppa gelato	assorted ice cream
Crema caramella	caramel-topped custard
Crostata	fruit flan
Gelato (produzione propria)	ice-cream (homemade)
Granita	flavoured ice, usually lemon or coffee
Monte Bianco	chestnut pudding with whipped cream
Panettone	sponge cake with candied fruit and raisins
Panforte	dense cake of chocolate, almonds, and preserved fruit
Saint Honoré	meringue cake
Semifreddo	refrigerated cake
Sorbetto	sorbet/sherbet
Spumone	a soft ice cream
Tiramisù	layers of sponge fingers and Mascarpone, coffee and chocolate
Torrone	nougat
Torta	cake, tart
Torta millefoglie	layered pastry with custard cream

Zabaglione	whipped eggs and Marsala wine, served hot
Zuppa inglese	trifle

Bevande (Beverages)

Acqua minerale con/ senza gas	mineral water with/without fizz
Aranciata	orange soda
Birra (alla spina)	beer (draught)
Caffè (freddo)	coffee (iced)
Cioccolata (con panna)	chocolate (with cream)
Gassosa	lemon-flavoured soda
Latte	milk
Limonata	lemon soda
Succo di frutta	fruit juice
Tè	tea
Vino (rosso, bianco, rosato)	wine (red, white, rosé)

Cooking Terms, Miscellaneous

Aceto (balsamico)	vinegar (balsamic)
Affumicato	smoked
Aglio	garlic
Alla brace	on embers
Bicchiere	glass
Burro	butter
Cacciagione	game
Conto	bill
Costoletta/ Cotoletta	chop
Coltello	knife
Cucchiaio	spoon
Filetto	fillet
Forchetta	fork
Forno	oven
Fritto	fried
Ghiaccio	ice
Griglia	grill
In bianco	without tomato
Limone	lemon
Magro	lean meat/or pasta without meat
Marmellata	jam
Menta	mint
Miele	honey
Mostarda	candied mustard sauce, eaten with boiled meats
Olio	oil
Pane (tostato)	bread (toasted)
Panini	sandwiches

Panna	cream
Pepe	pepper
Peperoncini	hot chili peppers
Piatto	plate
Prezzemolo	parsley
Ripieno	stuffed
Rosmarino	rosemary
Sale	salt
Salmi	wine marinade
Salsa	sauce
Salvia	sage
Senape	mustard
Tartufi	truffles
Tazza	cup
Tavola	table
Tovagliolo	napkin
Tramezzini	finger sandwiches
Umido	cooked in sauce
Uovo	egg
Zucchero	sugar

Useful Hotel Vocabulary

Vorrei una camera doppia, per favore	I'd like a double room, please
Vorrei una camera singola, per favore	I'd like a single room, please
con bagno, senza bagno	with bath, without bath
per due notti	for two nights
Partiamo domani mattina	We are leaving tomorrow morning
C'è una camera con balcone?	Is there a room with a balcony?
Mancano acqua calda, sapone, luce, carta igienica,	There isn't (aren't) any hot water, soap, light,
asciugamani, coperte, cuscini, gruccie	toilet paper, towels, blankets, pillows, coathangers
Posso pagare con carta di credito?	May I pay by credit card?
Per favore, potrei vedere un'altra camera?	May I see another room, please?
Si, va bene, grazie	Yes, that's fine, thank you
E compresa la prima colazione?	Is breakfast included?
Come posso raggiungere il centro città?	How do I get to the town centre?

Note: page numbers in *italics* indicate maps or plans. **Bold** entries indicate main references.

Index

Answers to 'A Florentine Puzzle' (pp.56–7)

1   Façade, San Miniato.
2   Baptistry, interior apse.
3   Windows at the rear of San Iacopo sopr'Arno, visible from Santa Trínita.
4   Windows, Orsanmichele.
5   Façade, Santa Croce (inspired by Orcagna's tabernacle in Orsanichele)
6   Baptistry doors (Pisano's and Ghiberti's first set); Portico of the Bigallo, interior apse, Santa Croce.
7   Loggia dei Lanzi.
8   Rucellai Chapel, San Pancrazio.